Published by
Whittles Publishing,
Dunbeath,
Caithness KW6 6EY,
Scotland, UK
www.whittlespublishing.com

© 2007 H. Brown

ISBN 978-1870325-29-5

Typeset by Mark Mechan

Printed by Athenaeum Press Ltd.

Dedication

For the Companions of the way
      and Mustapha who goes nowhere.

I could make a necklace of names
and hang it on the Atlas years.
But that is playing God, determining;
whereas my part has been to watch
awhile. So let me hand this book
reverently, into the crippled hands
of a brave child who knows the pains
of dreaming, and dying.

(Alas, the twisted hands
no longer clasp the weight
of days. Mustapha now rides a star
beyond sad sunsets and laughs,
I like to think, at the little
bloom he grew on earth.)

THE ATLAS RANGES

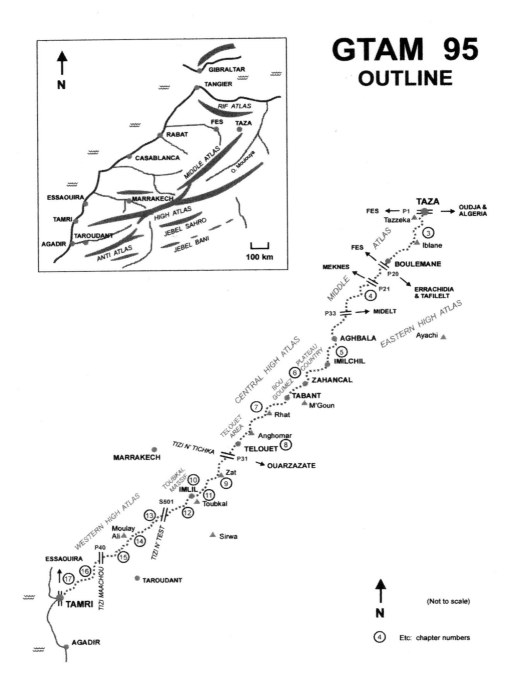

GTAM 95
OUTLINE

N

GIBRALTAR
TANGIER
RIF ATLAS
FES TAZA
RABAT
CASABLANCA
MIDDLE ATLAS
O. Moulouya
ESSAOUIRA
MARRAKECH
TAMRI
HIGH ATLAS
JEBEL SAHRO
AGADIR
TAROUDANT
ANTI ATLAS
JEBEL BANI

100 km

TAZA
FES ← P1 → OUDJA & ALGERIA
Tazzeka
③ Iblane
FES
MEKNES
BOULEMANE
P20
P21 ERRACHIDIA & TAFILELT
④ MIDELT
P33 MIDELT
ATLAS
MIDDLE
AGHBALA Ayachi
EASTERN HIGH ATLAS
⑤ IMILCHIL
⑥ ZAHANCAL
BOU GOUMEZ PLATEAU COUNTRY
CENTRAL HIGH ATLAS
⑦ TABANT M'Goun
Rhat
Anghomar
TELOUET ⑧
TELOUET AREA
P31
MARRAKECH → OUARZAZATE
TIZI N' TICHKA
Zat
⑩ ⑨
TOUBKAL MASSIF
IMLIL ⑪ Toubkal
S501 ⑫
⑬
Moulay Ali Sirwa
⑭
WESTERN HIGH ATLAS
P40
ESSAOUIRA ⑮
⑯ TIZI N' TEST
⑰ TAROUDANT
TIZI MAACHOU
TAMRI

AGADIR

N (Not to scale)

④ Etc: chapter numbers

Contents

MAP 1:
TAZA TO COL DU ZAD

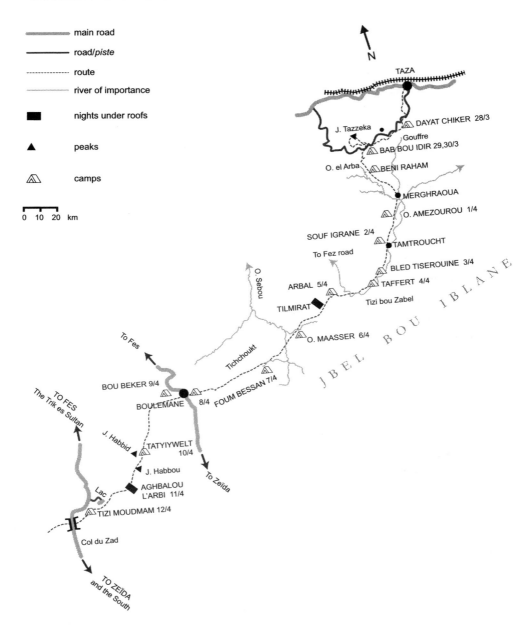

main road	
road/*piste*	
route	
river of importance	
■	nights under roofs
▲	peaks
⌂	camps

0 10 20 km

N

TAZA

DAYAT CHIKER 28/3

J. Tazzeka

Gouffre

BAB BOU IDIR 29,30/3

O. el Arba

BENI RAHAM

MERGHRAOUA

O. AMEZOUROU 1/4

SOUF IGRANE 2/4

TAMTROUCHT

To Fez road

BLED TISEROUINE 3/4

ARBAL 5/4

TAFFERT 4/4

TILMIRAT

Tizi bou Zabel

O. Sebou

O. MAASSER 6/4

To Fes

Tichchoukt

BOU BEKER 9/4

FOUM BESSAN 7/4

TO FES
The Trik es Sultan

BOULEMANE

8/4

J. Habbid

TATYIYWELT
10/4

To Zeïda

J. Habbou

Lac.

AGHBALOU
L'ARBI 11/4

TIZI MOUDMAM 12/4

Col du Zad

TO ZEÏDA
and the South

J B E L   B O U   I B L A N E

Prologue

Three people crowded into a two-man tent in a jet stream wind on top of the highest mountain in North Africa sounds as attractive as an undeserved parking ticket but truth to tell, I would not have been anywhere else. I was hugely happy to be there and was as warm, cosy and well fed as long experience and good gear allowed. Outside the tent was a different world.

I was already dressed in thermal layers and outer clothing but still pulled on constricting overtrousers, big Berghaus jacket, wrapped my *shen* around my face so only eyes showed, tightened the hood over this cocooning, donned boots, added head torch and thick mitts and only then unzipped the outer tent to crawl out into the maelstrom. Jbel Toubkal, 4167 metres high, lords it over the High Atlas Mountains of Morocco. As I'd been exploring the Atlas for thirty years and have climbed from the Andes to Arctic and home hills to Himalaya our predicament was hardly one of innocents abroad. If only, if only, one did not need to pee.

The sky was a lurid purply-black, touched with dirty yellows and reds. The last time I'd seen colours like that was in a hospital ward on a body bruised in a car accident. The sky was in serious confrontation with massed clouds. Occasionally the moon tried to mediate, changed its mind and vanished for long spells in the darkness. The winner was the wind, a screaming brutal monster that tried to blow me bodily away. Wind can be exhilarating to near madness but that was evil with the severest wind-chill I've ever known. Crawling to the lee of some rocks, I knelt, back to the blast, and tried to shove my trousers down to reach the zip of my fly. This was impossible in clumsy mitts and the few seconds with bare hands meant they had a less than happy hour thereafter warming up again inside my sleeping bag.

"What's it like out there?" Graeme asked.

"A bit breezy."

Ali giggled.

Before crawling back inside the tent I had stood, leaning like the Tower of Pisa, supported at a gravity-defying angle by the wind. A gusty wind sometimes catches one out, with childish glee, shuts off in an instant, and the supported sprawls on the ground. Not this wind: it was a constant. Familiar mountains surrounded our high perch but I'd not surveyed them from black night before. Looking south, far away and down, down, lay a spray of lights which had to be Ouarzazate, the town beyond the Atlas that introduces the desert to the sown. Looking north—nearer, bigger and brighter but equally down—lay a great spread of glow worm dots which could only be Marrakech, the eagle's head for the spread wings of Atlas, the hub for its sweeping rim of unlikely snows. I'd chosen this book's title for romantic associations so laughed aloud to see the conceit made reality. And why not? I had put feet to my dream and this book is the story of that dream, the end-to-end trek of the Atlas Mountains, a 900 mile walk in 96 days, which I want to share before everything recedes like a tide into the flat waters of memory.

I have come to love the Berber peoples of the Atlas, I admire their proud history and rich culture and this story is about them as much as about us. In some ways I find it difficult to describe this other world as, for me, Marrakech and the mountains are like the familiar, comfy garment, slipped on for a spell, whereas to the newcomer the cultural kaleidoscope of Morocco can be startling. But if familiarity has bred content the journey was no less hard graft. I have a certain pride in what we achieved and owe the team and helpers this record of our undertaking.

Above all, the journey was one of enjoyment, and that at nearly every turn and not just in retrospect (even in the wind on top of Toubkal) so I apologise to the sensation seekers: we had no fatalities, nobody was mugged, we ran into no revolution, the flight out was not hijacked. As Ali put it everything went "roughly smoothly". We were not superstars doing super feats, just a couple of greying codgers happily defying the slippery slope of years for a bit longer. Justifiably then, 'I speak of Africa and golden joys' (Shakespeare) and beg, in the Arab saying, 'May Allah show mercy on the tongues of travellers'.

MAP 2:
COL DU ZAD TO ZAOUIA AHANCAL

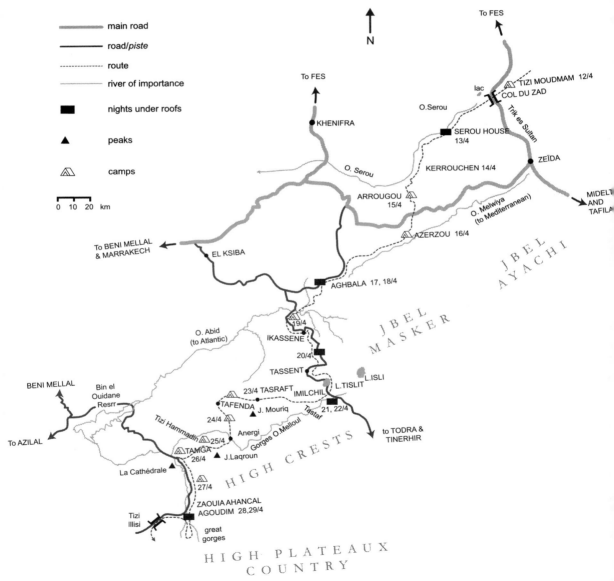

Acknowledgements

A first note of thanks has to go to Charles, Ali and Hosain, without whom there would have been no GTAM. Aït Idir Mohamed who looked after things in Marrakech also was a vital part of the team. Ilham Berrada, Farouk and all the staff at the Hotel Ali in Marrakech can never be praised enough. Mohammed Achari (Bou Guemez) and Elyazid Mohammed (Anmiter) were both hospitable and gave practical help. Friends who joined for various sections are named in the text so I won't embarrass them further here; they certainly made the journey more interesting. The Hotel Bahia in Agadir and the Hotel Central in Rabat are remembered gratefully as is Ahmed's hospitality at the Telouet auberge.

The biggest debt in producing the book is to Sheila Gallimore who typed the full text at least twice and put up with all the many changes along the way. John Gallimore created the Outline map, for which thanks. The National Library of Scotland provided helpful sources and I'm also indebted to Margaret Ecclestone for days spent in the Alpine Club's Library. John Mitchell and John Needham shared some of the chapter headings with me, for which thanks. Sir David Attenborough kindly provided information about the Tiout fossils. Charles Aitchison kept me correct on flower names.

We had much essential equipment supplied and are especially indebted to our big three of *Berghaus, Brasher* and *Vango*, and also to *Scottish Mountain Gear* and *Reebok*.

Special thanks go to Michael Peyron whose two volumes were invaluable and often the only notes on many areas. I would also like to thank John Willison's father, Graham Willison, for permission to quote extensively from John's journal.

Quotations acknowledged with thanks include Colin Smythe and Terry Pratchett for one of the latter's inimical Disc World descriptions from *Equal Rites*, Richard Gilbert for the quote about scorpions from his *Young Explorers*, Jim Crumley for the chapter heading quoted from his *Waters of the Wild Swan*, Adam Nicolson for permission to use a quotation from Harold Nicolson's *Diaries*, Dervla Murphy for her books and insights and a valuable quote from *Full Tilt*, and Nick Crane for the entertaining lines from his classic *Clear Waters Rising*. I have tried to contact all likely copyright holders but, as an inveterate quotation user, my apologies if anyone has gone unacknowledged.

Lastly, a thank you to Keith Whittles, who took on the book and saw it through to publication, and the editor Elaine Rowan who did the donkey work needed to control this word wanderer.

MAP 3:

ZAOUIA AHANCAL TO TELOUET

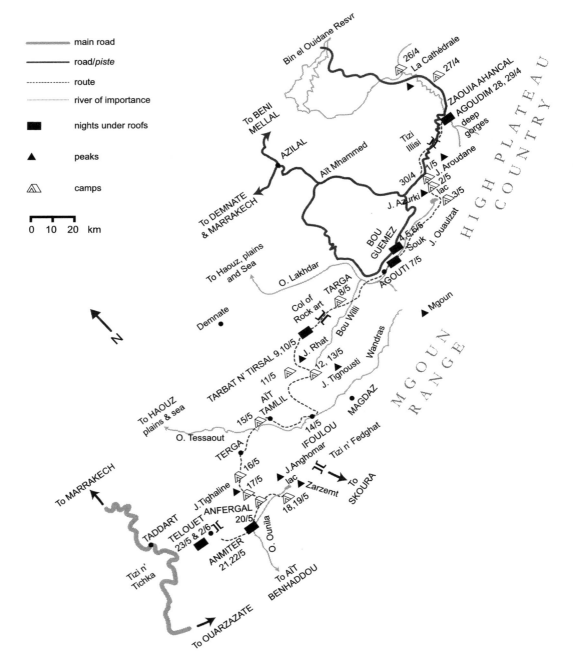

main road

road/piste

route

river of importance

nights under roofs

peaks

camps

0 10 20 km

N

Bin el Ouidane Resvr

26/4
La Cathédrale
27/4

ZAOUIA AHANCAL
AGOUDIM 28, 29/4
deep
gorges

To BENI
MELLAL

AZILAL

Tizi
Illisi

To DEMNATE
& MARRAKECH

Aït Mhammed

1/5
J. Aroudane

30/4
2/5

J. Azurki
3/5
J. Oualzat

To Haouz, plains
and Sea

BOU
GUEMEZ
Souk
4,5,6/5
AGOUTI 7/5

O. Lakhdar

Demnate

Col of
Rock art
TARGA
8/5
Bou Willi

Mgoun

TARBAT N' TIRSAL 9,10/5
J. Rhat
12, 13/5
J. Tignousti

Wandras

M G O U N
R A N G E

To HAOUZ
plains & sea

11/5

AÏT
TAMLIL
15/5

14/5
IFOULOU

MAGDAZ

O. Tessaout

TERGA

16/5

J.Tighaline
17/5

J.Anghomar
lac
Zarzemt

Tizi n' Fedghat

To
SKOURA

To MARRAKECH

TADDART

TELOUET
23/5 & 2/6
ANFERGAL
20/5

18,19/5

O. Ounila

ANMITER
21,22/5

To AÏT
BENHADDOU

Tizi n'
Tichka

To OUARZAZATE

HIGH PLATEAU
COUNTRY

MAP 4:

TELOUET TO IJOUKAK (TOUBKAL MASSIF)

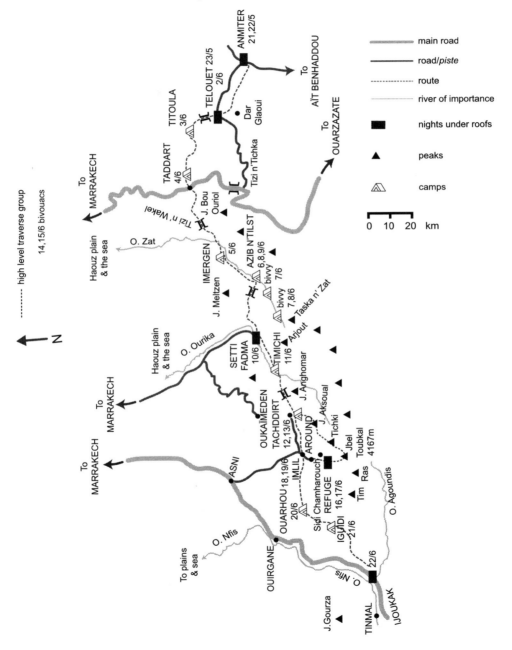

main road

road/*piste*

route

river of importance

nights under roofs

peaks

camps

0   10   20   km

MAP 5:
IMLIL TO TAMRI

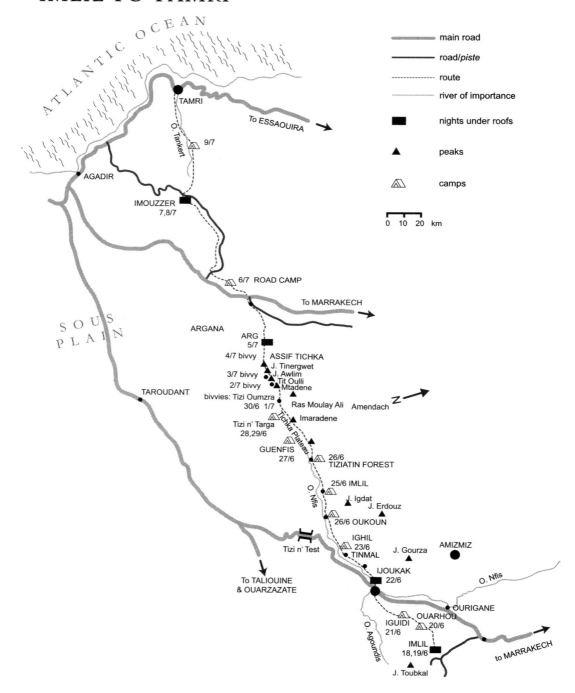

main road

road/*piste*

route

river of importance

nights under roofs

peaks

camps

0 10 20 km

ATLANTIC OCEAN

TAMRI

To ESSAOUIRA

O. Tankert

9/7

AGADIR

IMOUZZER
7,8/7

6/7 ROAD CAMP

To MARRAKECH

SOUS
PLAIN

ARGANA

ARG
5/7

4/7 bivvy   ASSIF TICHKA
              J. Tinergwet
3/7 bivvy   J. Awlim
2/7 bivvy   Tit Oulli
              Mtadene
bivvies: Tizi Oumzra
30/6   1/7   Ras Moulay Ali   Amendach

TAROUDANT

Imaradene

Tizi n' Targa   Tichka Plateau
28,29/6

GUENFIS
27/6   26/6
              TIZIATIN FOREST

25/6 IMLIL
       J. Igdat
       J. Erdouz

26/6 OUKOUN

O. Nfis

IGHIL
23/6   J. Gourza   AMIZMIZ
Tizi n' Test   TINMAL

To TALIOUINE
& OUARZAZATE

IJOUKAK
22/6

O. Nfis

OURIGANE

OUARHOU
IGUIDI   20/6
21/6

O. Agoundis

IMLIL
18,19/6

to MARRAKECH

J. Toubkal

xiv

CHAPTER 1

The Learning Curve

A traveller without knowledge is like a bird without wings.
Mushariff-Ud-Din (d. 1291)

When I give my standard slide show on Morocco I start by suggesting most people have an idea
the country is all camels and *kasbahs*. I then show half a dozen pictures to confound the image:
one of the world's most attractive waterfalls; plains carpet-bright to the horizon with flowers;
tiered terraces of vivid green crops edged with purple iris; towering mountains draped with snow
and the face of a young Berber girl, beautiful beyond the telling. These pictures show all that is
Morocco and hint at the lure which finally led me to dream of walking the Atlas end-to-end.

In the 60s I was employed in Fife in pioneering what would become Outdoor Education and,
to balance my heavy responsibilities (alone in the field with gangs of kids was a 24/7 job!) I was
granted a winter term sabbatical. A dream of sunshine and good mountains fuelled the search
for somewhere to go and Morocco was high on the list being near, not too costly and virtually
unknown in winter. Reports, such as there were, tended to be a bit grim but two people I knew
showed an unalloyed enthusiasm for the Atlas: Tom Weir, the Scottish climber and author who
had filmed in the Atlas, and Gavin Maxwell, who was researching his fascinating historical tome
The Lords of the Atlas.

We constituted ourselves an 'expedition': The British Atlas Mountains Winter Expedition
(the acronym BAWE soon pronounced BARMY). I've never really liked the word 'expedition'
which has something of an imperial ring to it. ('Trip' may sound a bit flippant, but that was
what we called our Atlas traverse.) We made a ridiculous overkill on the matter of food, sending
tea chests of European junk food to a country where everyday food is superior. (As someone

would later declare: "We ate the eggs we heard the hens laying".) Food is an important matter, contributing to health and therefore success, especially in the greater ranges.

In that first season in Morocco (1965) we learned the ropes of Atlas procedures. Morocco can be quite a culture shock, but with a background of world wanderings I found the country fascinatingly different, not overwhelming. Everything proved up to expectations: magical Marrakech, the grand scenery, the climbing and trekking, the people, the climate, the food. We were befriended by one Berber family and Mohammed, then the boy of the house, would thirty years on be our base manager for GTAM 95, the story of which is told here.

The following winter term was also spent in the Atlas, the school then closed and eventually I walked out of a bureaucratic job to have mountains first. By then I was hooked on the Atlas. For a number of years however there seemed to be a 'Toubkal trap', all our doings based on that *massif* whether climbing, trekking or skiing, but the emphasis steadily grew on trekking, exploring afoot, from which came the richest rewards. Of course there was a dearth of information about other areas and finding Roger Mailly's *Villes et Montagnes Maroccaines* was something of a revelation and simply increased the itch to explore. Morocco was more than just Toubkal.

Mailly was one of the leading post war pioneers of Atlas mountaineering. Briefly, the French Protectorate was only established a couple of years before World War One so it was the late 20s and 30s before the country was completely pacified and climbers began to explore the Atlas systematically. World War Two put an end to this, however, and no sooner was activity picking up again than the troubles leading to Independence meant another pause. A good pre-war Toubkal guide (reprinted later) kept the spotlight on that area alone. Fortunate people like Mailly, Fougerolles and Peyron stayed on, living and working in independent Morocco. They were the discoverers of the true scope of the Atlas ranges. (Heavens, the South Pole was reached twelve years before Toubkal was climbed by Europeans!) Peyron, who lived and taught most of his life in Morocco used his unrivalled knowledge to eventually shape guidebooks around the theme and title *La grand traversée de l'Atlas Marocain,* hence the acronym GTAM.

Various people have used this information to make multi-day treks through extensive reaches of the Atlas but there had been no complete traverse over the maximum possible route entirely on foot. Priority does have a certain appeal! I felt such a trek was within my capabilities; after all my wanderings in the Scottish Highlands had included many coast-to-coast treks, I'd tramped a mountain route from John O'Groats to Land's End, across Ireland, and had been the first to climb the Munros (Scotland's 3000-foot hills) in a continuous walk—quite apart from all the Atlas seasons. As with all of those there had to be fixed points on which to hang the variables and, like the Munro trip, GTAM was backed by extensive past experience—perhaps the biggest factor in the success of mountain challenges.

There are striking similarities between life in the remote Atlas and the crofting Highlands I knew as a boy—or with life in Nepal or the Andes (wherever deserts or harsh landscapes rear up into snowy heights). All these places face the same stern, pared world, free of the accumulations of the affluent superfluous, yet rich in culture and stable family life; a lot of singing and laughter is heard in Atlas villages. That is my yardstick for judging the ripeness of civilisation. In the end it is the people, not the mountains or our antics on them, that yield the deepest pleasure. They have taught me to love and laugh again, and what I have of patience and courage has come from them. I have dedicated my simple tale to Mohammed's boy Mustapha. He will never read the words, but I am moved that I meant something to him. Symbolically, he was all of Morocco to me: young, loving, brave. *Hamadullah* (Allah be praised).

A GTAM 'Route Book' was compiled over the two years between concept and beginning. Into the lever arch file went A4 colour copies of the maps required (mostly 1:100,000, some 1:50,000) and copies of any text relating to the route. For many areas there was nothing in print and, for some areas which we all knew well, there were no need of descriptions. Peyron had pinned down one main GTAM line but this had not really influenced us; I simply worked from what we knew and, in some places, wanted to explore. Peyron still remained our chief reference guide and nobody even now will wander off the honeypot areas without carrying Peyron. The already out-of-date 1:100,000 maps were often barely adequate for such vertical, rugged country but we'd already learnt to accept that inadequate maps make for more entertaining travel! Preparation like that paid off, and always does. An hour of research at home can save a day or a week or a whole expedition in the field. I'm afraid I now give rather short shrift to those who phone me wanting help or maps a week before their departure date. (There's an Arab saying: 'First dig your well, then build your house'.) One ridiculous example occurred just a few weeks before starting GTAM and initially gave me heart failure. "I'm off soon to do a traverse of the Atlas", the conversation began. It proved to be from a student, three weeks off his summer vacation, asking what I thought about his idea of trekking the Atlas end-to-end in five weeks. Where could he buy maps? Could he keep to the crest all the way? Were the natives hostile? What about food? No, he had never been abroad before. Injections? What for?

Our timing was determined by my old climbing partner Charles either being made redundant or retiring. Passing sixty calls for a gesture. Being dromomanic helps of course. I baited him with an entry in Harold Nicolson's Diaries: 'What is sad about becoming sixty is that one loses all sense of adventure'. The response was brief Anglo Saxon.

We were a team of four, with the addition of two mules Taza and Tamri (who would become marked personalities in their own right). Charles had been with me on dozens of previous Atlas ploys, often to the remotest areas, and Ali was our most regular Berber associate, from the Western Atlas, from where he enrolled the crofter Hosain as muleteer.

Ali was the most vital member of the team. Charles and I had a pact that if either of us broke a leg or fell out for any reason, the other could and would continue, for the trip was all laid out in the Route Book. Ali, on the other hand, was indispensable: fluent in English, Arabic and Berber tongues, brilliant hill-man, skilled cook (and baker), fine animal handler and gifted at making friends wherever he went, a paragon indeed. Most guides are just content to do their minimum and take the pay—the same the world over. I remember how disillusioned I was in the Alps when the one guide I knew turned down the chance of a good climb together because that year he was under contract to do the Hörnli ridge of the Matterhorn every day. Something the same happens with the Toubkal Trail and the Imlil guides. They know their stuff, yes, but stuffing isn't the flesh of the bird. Ali has wings and flies. However, bureaucracy denies him a guide's certificate because he had inadequate schooling. Ironically, he spends years training city lads who know nothing of the mountains. An example of his practical enthusiasm is when years ago I noted that the highest point of the Anti-Atlas was not the Jbel Kest range near Tafraoute as everyone seemed to think but a peak Jbel Aklim to the southest of Taroudant. Naturally this went on my list of desirable ploys and Ali hurried off to explore the area during the winter in order to help our spring visit.

The Atlas, while being something of a boundary and barrier, is also a range with a surprisingly large indigenous population which means long-standing routes connect villages and markets as well as criss-crossing the mountains. GTAM, quite knowingly, linked such tracks, some which must go back many centuries, while all exploration has depended upon them.

Finding the scant early published material was relatively easy in 1965, now nothing turns up at all. My magpie habit of collecting everything relevant over thirty years proved very useful. Maps of the less-known Atlas areas are impossible to obtain, which was one reason for photocopying the A4s we needed. The originals were too precious to risk on a trek.

In the autumn of 1994 Charles and I went out to Morocco, taking enormous loads with GTAM in mind and also finalised plans with Ali. Ali and I travelled to Taza to survey the practicalities of buying mules and Ali went to Anmiter to sort out our complicated mid-term plans there.

In creating the original brief outline and the ultimately comprehensive Route Book I could *visualise* the stages. "How far?" (so often asked) was meaningless; the practical reality meant a pass had to be crossed, a peak climbed, a *souk* (market) reached, or a water source assured. Our mileage is probably an underestimate (Cumont, going from Midelt to the Marrakech-Agadir road, gave a similar distance for his trip) and the total ascent we didn't even try to record, being both unimportant and no doubt frightful. The joy was the journeying, not its statistics and relishing the 'endless successions of changing beauty' (De Quincey) made even keeping a daily logbook tedious. For recalling our doings I lean heavily on my logbooks of the time so this is very much my story and Charles and Ali, my two main companions, would no doubt write a different version.

For the first month, mostly in the Middle Atlas, we four were together but, thereafter, we were regularly accompanied by small groups of friends usually for two-week sessions. These groups rendezvous'd by Land Rover and used local mules hired for their length of stay. Only our mules Taza and Tamri (bought at the start) went all the way. We had the friendly Hotel Ali in Marrakech as base and store, and our regular Imlil guide and friend, Aït Idir Mohammed, looked after Marrakech and the transport practicalities. People joining us meant we had definite fixed points (and dates) which drove us on but between these we had some freedom and leeway when, as early on, the heavy snowfalls changed the route and we suffered some abominably wet weather.

In retrospect the campsites were one of the greatest delights and when I marked the 'extra good' sites on the summary I found I'd marked nearly all of them! We earned our respites after all, and mornings and evenings were the *alpha* and *omega* of our days. The only regret was that we only had one night in most places, however magical. We *had* to push on: Land Rovers were booked and the temporary trekkers who joined us had flights to catch. Nobody missed a flight home, whatever the temptation. They were all making breaks from their normal routines and broke from such with varying success, some diving into refreshing pools of novelty, others unable to free themselves from the clutter of home affairs. Charles and I found GTAM became the routine (the shock was returning to the UK). We also had the motivation, dedicated for three months to the trek alone, whereas at home one is always a mere tadpole in unquiet waters.

The changing membership of the party (both Brits and Berbers) also ensured that Charles and I didn't become too bored with each other. We only slanged each other a couple of times that I can recall. In some ways we'd done too much together. We'd both heard each other's patter before and, while I can enjoy a companionable silence, Charles needs to share his thoughts. (This perhaps the antithesis of Sir Hugh Munro and the Rev A E Robertson who seldom went out together as each claimed they could never get a word in because of the other's non-stop talking.) I must add that the various Berber combinations were a great success. Their simple social graciousness forever showed up the cluttered clumsiness of our western ways. That all systems worked, that little needed practical changing, was due both to our past experience as a team and to the unfailing good humour and hard work of the muleteers, with Ali the vital hub of all. Voltaire's *Candide* was to note 'It seems that Europeans only have milk in their veins but it's fire that flows through the inhabitants of Mount Atlas'.

A day-to-day diary of our doings would be tedious and the vital statistics are summarised in Appendix I. A detailed account of the trip was made, almost like a report for shareholders (in A4 form, with comb binding), to thank those involved, reward Moroccan helpers and have a record which might help anyone else contemplating something similar. This *Atlas Traverse; Afoot from Taza to Tamri* was deposited in the various national libraries and libraries of the Alpine Club, Royal Geographical Society, Royal Scottish Geographical Society, and Scottish Mountaineering Club. The present work was based on this but has been given a more romantic title, a play on Byron, whose mountains looked on Marathon. (A pat on the back for those who spotted the conceit.)

One reason I'm sure the Atlas Mountains are not better known is the difficulty of the names. Nobody gets much credit down the pub when he can't hold forth about his most recent ego trip. I do not joke; what do you make of Igui Wanjegjyoun or Jbel Ouaouansaout or Isk Igouramene Wirezzalene? (Don't ever complain about Gaelic again!) When T E Lawrence was questioned on the inconsistency of spelling proper names he replied that

'Arabic names won't go into English, exactly, for their consonants are not the same as ours, and their vowels, like ours, vary from district to district. There are some 'scientific systems' of transliteration, helpful to people who know enough Arabic not to need helping, but a wash-out for the world. I spell my names anyhow, to show what rot the systems are.'

I've tried to be consistent but when Bled el Makhzen has nine variant spellings, for example, this is not easy. The names are only milestones and they, or the asides, can be skipped.

There are also certain words, in Arabic, Berber dialects or French, which are used regularly by all travellers in the Atlas (there is a glossary included as Appendix IV). There's a peculiarly British laziness that wants everything translated into English. I cringe every time I see 'Mount Toubkal' for instance. What is wrong with Jbel Toubkal? What is right with Mont Nevis or Aiguille de Napes?

I've tried to keep to names as best known (on maps) rather than seek scholarly correctness as Peyron does. For instance he gives Meghrawa for the map's Merhraoua, which is closer to the actual punctuation. And in that name too is probably the most vital clue to name pronunciation: *ou* comes over as a *w/wa* sound - which at once makes Ouarzazate or Essaouira intelligible (Warzazat, Essaweera). Note the dropping of the final *e*; Mizzane is Missan (not Mizzaine), Ouazzane is Wassan.

The geographical setting of GTAM within Morocco and an outline of the route are given with an indication of the appropriate chapters covering each area. There are also five larger scale sketch maps to help follow the route. These may have different scales—always shown—and north is always indicated however practicalities align the maps. While minimalist, at least they will allow those difficult-looking names to be set in place.

Over the years both Charles and I had wandered quite extensively in the Atlas so its historical geography was almost taken for granted, not that we ever failed to respect the vast scale and its vigorous demands. The ranges sweep from the Atlantic seaboard in a scimitar curve to the northeast, the point in the sea and the handle at Taza. Several ranges overlap in reality so the rivers have cut deep gorges to escape onto the plains and wend to the sea or, in the south, simply vanish into the desert. The Middle Atlas is cut off by the Oued Moulouya (Melwiya) which heads, alone, for the Mediterranean coast. South of the main High Atlas, where there are hundreds of summits over 3000 m, lie lesser ranges: the Anti-Atlas west of the Oued Drâa and the Jbel Sarhro east of the Drâa. South of them a last line, the Jbel Bani, edges the vastness of the desert landscape. The Rif, in the north of the country, is the result of Africa colliding with Europe.

The mountain regions and the south ('old Morocco') is Berber speaking with several differing languages rather than dialects. None of these have any connection with Arabic—it arrived many millennia after the Berbers were established. Trekking, the language problem seldom proves a barrier; in most places someone will speak some French, probably at a friendly level of mutual incompetence, and the visitor soon learns vital words like bread, water, mule, etc. In my early years ex-legionnaires would often appear and thoroughly enjoyed being sociable and re-living their world wanderings. We can still create misunderstandings. We had one amusing incident where one of our party chatted up a hotel chef to indicate her preference for rabbit. The girl finished by putting her hands to her forehead and waggling them like ears while making Bugs Bunny mouthings. What arrived was not rabbit *tagine* (stew) but a salver of beef. Ali ensured we had no problem on GTAM and Hosain, with no English or French and minimal Arabic seemed to communicate with remarkable facility.

Charles and I between us took over 2000 slides during the traverse. Photography is not always easy; in remote places the camera can be regarded as the evil eye or with superstitious dread so people will hide their faces or flee—or even throw stones. We had our temporary groups bring in film and take out and post the used collection. Because changing lenses is often too slow to capture the desired picture I carry two cameras to cover from telephoto to wide angle. 'Simple and fast' was the motto. The results have been satisfactory.

We had some occasions where we were known enough to be allowed to photograph more intimate family scenes. It helps to know how to behave and we are often shocked (looking at TV especially) to see so many brash social mistakes. One example: the gesture for 'Come here' with us is a sweeping of the hand towards the body, palm up; in Morocco it is palm down - and the former could be taken for something rather impolite. The Berbers fortunately have a great sense of humour.

Sometimes, giving slide shows, I'm asked if I am not helping to spoil the very thing I love. This is a somewhat elitist question, as if we had some right to manipulate or fossilise other people for our own entertainment. Of course there are elements of progress I dislike. There are cafés in Marrakech I no longer visit because the air is thick with the pollution from vehicle exhausts. Should everyone walk because of this? Forty years ago almost everyone wore eye-catching kaftans and *djellabas* (garments with long hoods and long sleeves), now ordinary western clothes predominate. However, exactly the same has happened in my own country where the kilt is now relegated to weddings, dinners and folklore occasions. The world is shrinking and the special, 'different' places are disappearing. I have been lucky to see the autumn flowering of the Berber culture and way of life in the High Atlas. But do not ask me to deny Mohammed's children their chance of schooling by *not* telling about their father's tourist business.

I cannot remember exactly where or when the idea of GTAM was pinned down but the real commitment was perhaps made, if not on the back of an envelope, at least on a few lines in a notebook no larger. I wrote down a brief outline of the sections of a potential GTAM and how long they would take. And that was what we did, the apparently casual estimate became the reality a couple of years later. About that stage I decided I really should ask Charles if he would join Ali and me.

He answered the phone. "Knowles here."

"Hello Charles. Hamish. How's things?" and, quickly, before this renowned talker could answer (and land me with a forty minute bill) I asked, "Would you like to join Ali and me in traversing the Atlas end-to-end?"

"Yes."

Heavens! Charles, an insurance surveyor and meticulous over the small print of life, never answered in one word.

"Oh well, yes, good..." I gabbled.

Bloody hell, we'd have to go and do it then.

CHAPTER 2

Journey to Taza

The world is big and I mean to have a look at it before it gets dark.
John Muir

I was certainly glad to leave Scotland in mid-March for the start of GTAM. I travelled to Sheffield for a couple of nights with Charles, gaining some amusement from his frantic last-minute preparations as mine had passed in discreet privacy. We took a bus from Sheffield to Heathrow direct and flew via Tangier to change at Casablanca and on to Agadir. *Pas de problème* but oh, such interminable boredom. We took a *grand taxi* and could almost feel the driver deflating as he realised we'd been many times before so he couldn't go over the recognised rate, which is stiff enough. (What airport doesn't pile it on?) Within cities the *petit taxis* are a fast and easy way of moving about, the cost being no more than a bus at home. There may be a meter, there may not. Negotiate, as ever. Though I'm often rude about them, tour companies can serve a useful purpose in giving an easy first introduction to a new country and its differing practicalities. Morocco is tough for the innocent traveller. The friendly welcome from the El Bahia Hotel pushed the air journey into oblivion.

This is a small hotel near the top end of the town, handy for buses and with nearby good but cheap eating options, and I've seen us there for odd days without ever seeing the sea or the tourist parts of Agadir. Agadir, while partly a sprawling holiday trap, is also a busy 'county town', and one can make what one will of the place. We were only in Agadir overnight, breakfasting on the square and dozing the miles away in a bus to Taroudant, fifty miles to the east.

Before the bus departed, an endless succession of touts and beggars fought their way up the narrow passage: boys selling chewing gum or cakes, a water-seller, a blind man who chanted *surahs* from the Koran endlessly, another who gave a pathetic spiel and then lifted his garb to display a colostomy, and a youth who sold several plastic propellers on the end of sticks. Two beamy women jammed between the seats in the narrow passage and entertained with their verbal and physical wrestling. A carrier bag wedged in the inadequate storage shelf escaped, showering down on mother and child their supply of sick bags, *Sidi Ali*, *Yopla*, oranges and bread. A bus journey beats TV any day. Many of the posh buses have videos but most, mercifully, have stopped working. Everyone muttered "Bismilah" ("In the name of God") as they settled into their cramped seats. There were quite a few tourists on the bus and they gave us some odd looks as, when we stepped out, we were hugged and ceremoniously greeted by several people. These included Ali and the deaf and dumb shoeshine boy. We were also greeted by Aziz, still effectively Ali's boss. More about him later.

The boss of the Hotel Roudani then embraced us as did Moussa, the cheery waiter whom we have known for years. We had our usual rooms on the terrace, looking down on the square with its solitary palm and, from the rooftop, a view northwards to the white fangs of Awlim and Tinergwet—the last big GTAM peaks of the Atlas which we hoped to traverse eventually. The Roudani is not a classified hotel but is cheap and friendly and has that prime position. The shower is heated with a boiler which looks like something out of a 19th century children's encyclopedia. A fluffy cat with her suckling kittens lay in a wooden box—when not trying to drag her offspring into Charles' bed. We made a rendezvous with Ali for 1700 and went off to the other square for one of our traditions, a cake lunch in the *patisserie* by the *souk* entrance. We bought oranges and *Sidi Harazem*, bottled water from a pilgrim spring near Fes (*Sidi Ali* and the fizzy *Oulmès* come from a Middle Atlas hill station). We went over our schedule again, with copies for everyone, but had to scamper 'home' to beat a thunder plump that turned the streets into rivers.

The only drawback of the Roudani is that it faces five daily loud-speaking, pre-recorded calls to prayer and, for good measure, the *Fejr* (dawn) call comes at 0500 and adds half an hour of Koranic reading. (The other calls come less violently: *Dhuhr*, noon; *'Asr*, between zenith and sunset; *Maghrib*, sunset; and *'Acha*, about the time of the evening meal.)

Most of the day was spent on logistics and we met Hosain who would complete our basic quartet. We liked him at once: a tough, cheery character which was a relief as we'd received a posed studio photograph that made him look like a real Mr Glum. Charles visited the *hammam* (public steam baths) while I went to tea with the family whose house we often used up in Tagmout. The children were named Mustapha, Nadia, Rachid and Fatima, and their old father had died leaving them in difficulties. The two youngest had been sad and withdrawn and used to sit for hours with me in the house, or followed like puppies outside. I came to love them dearly. My welcome was boisterous. Mustapha, at seventeen, was handsome, spoilt and feckless. He was tried out as a potential muleteer and discarded (but then with Ali as standard, who could match up?) and Nadia was into high heels and western make-up—the typical teenager. They had to rent their house to the Tagmout schoolteachers and move down to Taroudant, where their widowed mother works and keeps the home going.

Charles and I met up again to eat at the Roudani, Moussa bringing us each an *orange pressé* on the house. Moussa (Moses) is a real character. He used to work at another café and when he moved to the Roudani most of his regular customers moved too. With *panache* and humour he keeps everyone happy. At the end of a meal some first-timer will be presented with a bill about ten times the true price while Moussa creates consternation; those of us in the know find it difficult to hold in our laughter. On one occasion, I observed a middle-aged American couple being unnecessarily objectionable and, at the end, Moussa quoted them a quite outrageous sum. They handed this and more over with the dismissive gesture of the spoilt rich and for a moment Moussa hesitated, before walking stiffly away. He gave me the briefest wink as he passed.

I'm convinced Moroccans can read visitors quicker than a TV commercial. They spend so much time in personal contact that they acquire, without even knowing, great facility at people watching. Moussa, in the course of serving the meal, will have unerringly chosen the one most likely to panic when selected for his regular game. He had tremendous authority too. When two kids started a fight in front of the Roudani he simply pulled them apart and held each by the collar while delivering a lecture before sending them on their way. There's a scary homeless youth who roams round the city, foaming at the mouth and sometimes roaring like a lion. This raving figure appearing among the tables can be startling, to put it mildly, but Moussa will put his arms round the mad character and lead him away without fuss: practical 'care in the community'. There's also a snotty young Down's syndrome boy who is allowed to sit in the café. On his arrival he will go round to be given a hug or a kiss by all the regulars. Not a few beggars will depart with food at the end of day, quite a normal way for restaurateurs to fulfil their religious obligations. How stiff and self-centred our public life is in comparison.

Taroudant is very old, older than Marrakech for instance, as it was captured by the Almoravid dynasty in 1030. Marrakech was founded in 1062, before William became The Conqueror. Taroudant was later the Merinid dynasty's capital in the south and the Saadians spent twenty years gaining strength there before conquering north of the Atlas. The city still nestles within strong ramparts and the feel of the place can't have changed much in centuries. Taroudant is a mini Marrakech, without the hassles.

The dawn call to prayer found us waiting for the bus office to open. Ali saw all the baggage aboard, fetched Hosain and we still had time for a coffee. We had a double seat each so snoozed most of the way along the Sous plains by Oulad Berhil and Tafinegoult but roused for the road up to the Tizi n' Test, the argan trees petering out as we gained height, the mountains rising above in a seemingly impossible barrier. The road makes huge sweeps back and forth, in one place cut into the cliff like an open-sided tunnel, the tortuous ascent ending at a casual col marked by a small café, 2092 m, having climbed from near sea level in a single haul. Those with serious vertigo travel with their eyes shut. The road was crisp with new snow, the air bracing.

The road wound along on a high in-and-out traverse which opened out views to the northern peaks above the Nfis river: Igdat and Oumzra which, *Insh 'Allah* (God willing), we'd climb, weeks, months ahead. They were enhanced by the new whitewashing of snow and, from the zigzags of the onward descent of the bus, the whole Toubkal massif glittered silver, a surprisingly small area when seen from this angle, small but tough and demanding, with the highest Atlas peaks.

At Talat n' Yacoub the bus stopped at a blacksmith's and he welded a rattling luggage rack while we stretched our legs and looked down to the old Goundafa *kasbah* (castle) by the Oued Nfis. We would pass it too, *Insh 'Allah*, the phrase slipping out as readily as from any local.

There was the usual tea stop at Ijoukak where our GTAM route would cross the Test road so both memories and expectations were accumulating. We off-loaded at Asni and 'Mohammed the taxi' (*le grand noir*) chanced to be there so stowed our rucksacks etc. in his car while we went off for a *tagine* in our favourite café before he ran us up to Imlil. This Mohammed was called *le grand noir* to differentiate him from all the other Mohammeds but he was now old and grey and shrunken compared to thirty years previous. He'd nursed only two vehicles up and down the tough Imlil *piste* (dirt track) in that time, but retired after that year. In both of his taxis his head had completely worn through the lining and much of the metal of the roof. He was big. He took us to near the school and I reckon we did well to make it in one trip up to Mohammed's house with our baggage. Our host was in Marrakech but we were family enough to be looked after by his wives. They brought our permanent Atlas gear out of the store and we had the biggest ever sorting out and packing. Ali and Hosain were kitted out with the gear supplied by Berghaus and Brasher, which sometimes made us look like a stage show of identikit comics. They were impressed both by the gear and our insistence on all of us being equally equipped.

The following day saw everything done so we had time to sit in the Café Soleil with Mohammed that night, drinking excellent coffee. It was a wolf-cold night with the moon just trimmed from full. We had our gear taken down to the square by mules and then waited for a tourist minibus to arrive, disgorge, and then take Charles, me and all the luggage direct to the Hotel Ali in Marrakech while Mohammed took Ali and Hosain in his car. For most of the day our hotel room looked a shambles while we had a complex repacking: leaving one bag each which we'd want for a half-way break, a bag of gear for some friends to bring in May, a big case to act as a store in the hotel (from which groups would add and subtract to order) and then the array that would go with us to the start: a rucksack and a small bag each besides the communal gear.

We had lunch in the Bahja, where the *haj* owner (one who has made his pilgrimage to Mecca) had recently been on a cookery programme on British TV. This was followed by coffee in the Iceberg, which serves beer and the best coffee in the *medina* (old town). Ali went to the bus station and we two to the railway station to sort out travel tickets. I rang the Hotel des Remparts in Essaouira as we'd be ending there in high season (they placed me with "*Ah, le vieux Ecossais avec la barbe grise*"), and luckily met a homeward-bound tourist who agreed to post letters to those who'd be joining us along the way. A last coffee in the Argana with life on the Fna square fading as the moon strengthened was traditional too, as was tramping out some laundry in the bath which would dry on the roof overnight.

At 0500 we carried down some gear. The garden opposite was already noisy with bulbuls. We called a *petit taxi* and saw Ali and Hosain depart for a 0600 CTM bus to Taza. They both had a large rucksack and something in each hand. Apart from local fresh food purchasing in Taza we were now at maximum loading. All we had to do was shift everything to Taza. Ali and Hosain were off a week before us in order to search, find and purchase two mules and their accoutrements. I'm sure Ali had never had so much money in his pocket before. At dawn we went up onto the rooftop to make sure nobody had stolen the Atlas overnight. Swifts screamed overhead like children in the sheer joy of motion. We took a No. 1 bus along to the Gueliz (new town). I don't think the signs on the bus made much sense to the crush of passengers: '*Niet roken, Verbandtrommel*', or '*Voor de streep geen staanplaatsen*'. The heady scent of orange blossom filled Avenue Mohammed V. We went in to the covered market to top up our range of spice jars and shop for a few special items. We eyed a Jaques Majorelle painting in a gallery: the price was more than the cost of our entire trip. We resisted the temptation to buy any books. In the evening we saw Farouk, the hospitable *patron* of the Hotel Ali and left more mail for the UK. There was a note from Mohammed Achari in the Bou Guemez so we confirmed our dates via the driver who'd brought the note. I'm always astonished how communications and arrangements work so effectively.

In bed that night the idea of a story for a book came to me and I lay awake for a long time developing the idea and even wrote down the first sentence. As I couldn't carry dozens of books to read I determined to write one.

Charles and I then went to Rabat for five days, just marking time but with people to visit and plenty to see and do, the days passed quickly. We even winkled some maps out of the authorities. We spent time in the Oudaïas quarter and over the river in historic Salé, we visited the potteries and carpet *souk*, bookshops and favourite eating-places. Rabat is always very pleasant.

Having said that, I've a vivid picture of two kids dressed in tatters, cringing against a sea wall, blotto from solvent sniffing. Hidden away in the hills backing the capital, the mountains of dumped city garbage are covered with a vast *bidonville* (shanty town); in the fifty countries I've seen this is the most nauseous habitation I've ever encountered. If this book paints a somewhat idyllic picture I'm not unaware of the wretchedness too—whose origin is partly in the very prosperity of the hills. The picture is one that hangs in my own Scottish history gallery too.

In the Highlands enforced peace and assured crops led to a population explosion after Culloden and Waterloo. The surplus headed for the cities or overseas. Morocco does not have a diaspora option and the problem is colossal as is seen in the huge expansion of building in every town. High unemployment and a large young adult population does not help. In my lifetime, however, the overall prosperity of the country has grown prodigiously. What other African country can match Morocco?

Back in February 1965 during our first-ever visit, when I'd only been a few weeks in Morocco, I wrote in my log "This is a country to come to for months at a time and, even when older, it will attract me as much". Time has certainly borne out that speculative statement. It would be easy to spend weeks in Rabat and Salé, exploring the coast or the other Imperial Cities of Meknes and Fes. Over the years I have. Fes, especially, is endlessly fascinating and such a contrast to Marrakech, a city of brains as against brawn, Fes foots a stately measure, Marra spins a Dervish dance. The Arab word for these lands is *Maghreb-el-Aksa* (the land of the furthest west), a nice echo of Europe's *Cap Finisterre* (the end of the earth). It was slightly odd to start our venture by travelling to the furthest east of the country. Morocco is a corruption of Marrakch (Marrakech) and old maps have 'City of Morocco' against the town's site while the country as a whole was designated by 'Kingdom of Fes' and 'Kingdom of Morocco', the twin areas of central dominance historically.

The train journey, Rabat to Taza, took much of a day and was uneventful: dozing, reading, eating and watching the world go by: Kenitra, Sidi Slimane, Sidi Kacem, Meknes, Fes, the big Idriss I *lac* (dam), long ascent to the tunnel (one way of dealing with the constriction of the Taza Gap) and then the accelerating run down to Taza. With our baggage we were slow off the train so missed available taxis. One came eventually, two coffees later. The old Hotel de la Poste was expecting us. Our balcony door was secured with string and the plumbing was home to poltergeists. We were given an ill-spelt letter from Ali and he arrived after supper, having left Hosain mule-minding in the *medina*. "All ready; we can go tomorrow," he grinned. As we had expected a day or two in Taza this jolted us wide-awake.

Michael Collins, the pilot of Apollo 11 in 1969, described looking at our blue planet with its swirling cloud patterns and how he was able to trace the Atlas Mountains. A glance at any chart shows its distinctive line, like a breakwater across the northwest corner of Africa, holding back the oceanic vastness of the Sahara. The range runs from Atlantic seaboard to Tunisia but the highest, most spectacular part lies in Morocco. The early explorers called the mountains that look on Marrakech 'The Great Atlas'. Even with modern transport we took days to reach the start.

"Great!" I chortled, a touch of disbelief in my laugh. We'd been two years, thirty years, all life on the way to this sudden tomorrow. I could only echo *The New Road*:

'I would never take the nearer way anywhere, half the sport in life is starting and the other half is getting on the way, and everything is finished when it's done.'

When I had called in to check with my home doctor about updating any of the recommended jags for Morocco he requested me to stand on the scales, measured my height, noted my age (some well-meaning directive so dictating) and then looked up a book of words to pronounce on the findings. With a twinkle in his eye he commented, "Well Hamish, I have to inform you that you are a bit overweight for your age and height and therefore should suggest you take some regular exercise, something like a bit of walking..."

He thought the Atlas end-to-end would do nicely.

CHAPTER 3

Discovering the Middle Atlas

I saw in my dream, that when the shepherds perceived that they were wayfaring men they also put

questions to them, to which they made answer, as in other places: as Whence come you? and how got you

in the way? and by what means have you so persevered therein? for but few of them that begin to come

hither do shew their face on this mountain. But when the shepherds heard their answers, being pleased

therewith, they looked very lovingly upon them and said, Welcome to the Delectable Mountains.

Bunyan (*Pilgrim's Progress*)

Every invading army seems to have come by Taza, occupied the town, fortified it or knocked it about. When explorer Charles de Foucauld visited in 1883 he mentioned how the Spanish traveller Badia (in the guise of Ali Bey) had been there half a century before, seeing '*cette ville si florissante et si heureuse*' (this town so flowery and so pretty) whereas anarchy had reduced it to '*la plus misérable*' in his day. Nothing is ever static, whether it is the lot of an individual, a family, town, city or country; ascendancy and decay are the left and right hands of fortune. Islam came to Morocco by the Taza Gap, the Taza Corridor, *la trouée de Taza,* and various dynasties occupied it before taking dominant Fes, as did the Alaouites in the seventeenth century, the dynasty that still reigns.

At the end of last century the weak sultan Moulay Aziz faced a rebellion based on Taza, with Bou Hamara, the *Rogui* (Pretender), eventually declaring himself rival sultan and creating a decade of chaos. He'd fled east earlier and came back as a convincing charismatic holy man, gaining power over the superstitious Berber tribesmen. One trick was to bury a helper with a straw to breathe through, so he could be seen to 'communicate with the dead'. He would thereafter trample on the straw so the man smothered, then allowed the body to be dug up so the speaker was seen to be dead. Moulay Hafid succeeded Moulay Aziz and successfully destroyed the Pretender's forces. The *Rogui* was dragged to Fes and paraded in a cage. He was then ceremoniously given to the menagerie lions but they only had a chew so the man was shot and the body burnt.

The French insistence on not destroying *medinas* after their conquest has left old Taza poised on its limestone outcrop while a new town has radiated out three kilometres down the slope, with the railway station at the foot. Quite un-touristy, Taza is a pleasantly relaxing place and the *medina* deserves to be explored. Not that we could on that occasion; we were under orders. But, for the first and only time on the long traverse, we lost the mules.

Lost is perhaps not the correct word for we had still to meet our companions of the journey ahead and, if the day began with a communal idiocy it was to end with a personal one. If our ends are in our beginnings, Allah help us, I thought. The date was 28th March.

That we were *really* starting came home as soon as we dressed, for the clothes we pulled on were those of our march. The day sack was not for a snack on a train, but for the long walk west, the start of that tentative line that had lain on the map like a mesmerising snake for two years. We fixed up a rendezvous with Ali (or we thought we did) and he shot off in a taxi to unite our gear with Hosain and the mules. We then went in search of breakfast, which was easy, and a taxi, which was not. We spent half an hour vainly searching for a taxi only to find a whole rank of them at the back of our hotel block. We were dropped off near the old town.

As there was no sign of Ali, Charles guarded our gear and I walked up to the top of the straggling town's overspill. I walked past the 'Provence' to the Bab el Guebour, and down the sweep of road we'd come. From the fluttering gum avenue I had a fine view over the tawny plains to a *kouba* (domed structure, often over a holy site) in the valley below and the merloned walls of the old city above. The tawny cliff overlooking the road is pitted with troglodyte homes, well hidden by enclosed gardens and trees. There seemed to be mules-a-plenty down by the shrine but not our pair. I was about to walk back up the hill when a taxi shot past with Ali waving from it. We added Charles and the gear and drove out past the top end of the town. Not for the last time we had severely underestimated distances. "We can only improve on such a start," I suggested.

A grey and a dark brown mule stood below a thorny tree in a layby: Taza and Tamri, animals who would become distinct personalities in the weeks ahead. Ali and Hosain had had a complicated time making their purchase, as one came from a town thirty kilometres off. They had to be stabled securely in the old town, and panniers and harnesses purchased. They were the biggest single expense of the whole trip and by far our biggest and most constant concern. Taza was a douce female and Tamri a dark youthful male. Mules are almost always bred from a male donkey and a mare and, while offspring are sexually differing they are (with rare exceptions) sterile. While we were marking time at Rabat, Ali was chasing here and there to find suitable beasts, arguing prices (a hint of *our* involvement and the price would have soared), and, on top of all else, having to convince authorities, officials and the police that we really weren't a band of *kif* (cannabis) smugglers. With our bright blue tarpaulins covering the mules' loads we stuck out like a patch of blue in a Torridon summer. How do you explain people who go walking for the sake of it in a country where the first sign of affluence is to ensure one is *not* walking. One of the first questions in any conversation was always: "Where is your car?"

It was 1015 by the time our huge pile of baggage had been loaded on top of our honest beasts. They didn't quite buckle at the knees. We were to wonder on many occasions just what they made of our trip. Presumably they could not think ahead or make decisions based on predicted events. When the panniers came off they couldn't know whether it was for five minutes or forever. Though we soon had a general overall pattern of continuity, there were always days that were unexpectedly different. There were to be days when we weren't sure if the beasts would be fed and, after 96 days of this, the journey just stopped. As mules don't write their memoirs we will never know...

"*Hirrah!*" and we were off.

We set off on a very hot morning, wending through the lush green of spring barley, criss-crossing the tarred road and then steadily climbing a long rufous slope until our legs felt like lead. Even with the brolly up, my clothing was soaked with sweat. There's no escaping the harsh hammering of body and soul at the start. Even on a backpacking event like the TGO (The Great Outdoors) annual coast-to-coast across Scotland, the first few days are toilsome. After a week, the machinery is run in and functional, and then the crossing is over. This time we would be travelling far enough to stiffen the sinews and bear the ultimate fitness with us. There are no short cuts to fitness.

We could see the zigzags of the tarred road far below in a valley (headed by the dainty cascade of the Ras-el-Oued) then wending back and forth over to the left. A high knoll land-marked the heights we aimed for. A village indicated water, and rebellious bodies collapsed under some trees while the ever-active Hosain loped off to return with two five litre bottles of water. We consumed every drop over a long rest, long enough for Ali and Hosain to make and consume a *tagine* with a loud-voiced local. A steep gully took us up to meet the tarred road where urchins were selling the edible hearts from the fan palms that grew among the arid limestone crags. A hoopoe went whirring past, like a plastic whirler on a stick. An attractive *zaouia* (religious building) in the gut of the valley produced a deranged beggar who tailed us on up through oak forest and only vanished when we were hailed by a well-to-do family picnicking by their car. They asked us, "Where is your car?"

Just before the edge of the secretive world of the Dayat Chiker (*dayat* means lake, but the waters there have long gone apart from a small seasonal area) we stopped to let the others catch up and also for me to find four half bottles of whisky I'd left hidden two years earlier. Cache-ing whisky was not a common practice, but that year I had my Transit Camper and everyone seemed to leave some whisky so I had far more than the limit for entering Spain. My idea of doing a swap of *Red Label* for a Vévéy etching of old man's heads in Fes misfired when I was told to look at the booze shop round the corner: the price was considerably less than the UK Duty Free. Reconnoitring up from Taza I took an easy option and hid the bottles among the oak-scree slopes of the pass where we would come on GTAM—a vote of confidence in our expedition happening. My scrap-of-paper map led me to the cache at a second attempt but we left it *in situ* until Ali and Hosain arrived. We told them there was whisky hidden on the slope, and watched their looks of disbelief double when we found some. (The haul disappeared fairly quickly, oiling the wheels at Bab Bou Idir the next night; neither Charles or I made much use of it.)

The road split on the edge of the flat, hill-encircled plain. 'Taza 22' was a satisfying figure. The left branch wends south to Merhraoua (Meghrawa) and the right makes a dramatic mountain circuit through the Tazekka cedar and cork oak forests and then down again to the Taza Gap. We aimed for the best of both since to the right lay a cave system I'd explored on that Transit visit, which Charles just had to see, and Jbel Tazekka, the last real summit at that end of the mountains, just had to be climbed. We then aimed to wend south by Merhraoua to the Jbel Bou Iblane snows, well launched on our route.

The nearby Chiker Caves had been explored for five kilometres (by Casteret) but had to wait that day. Happily some locals at the fork were able to answer our questions about water availability and we struck right across the middle of the Dayat Chiker. A tiny stream drained eastwards but our water came fresh and pure from a well which shepherd boys indicated. They also raced off to bring fodder for the mules. Kids always appear, seemingly out of nowhere, and although in many countries they'd be an unpleasant menace, in the Atlas they are friendly and helpful, immensely tough and with the smiles of angels and the spirits of imps.

Our first day, a hard graft ascent in torrid heat, had been quite exhausting, which made the arrival of coolness welcome. While not yet desert-suffering from heat (that would come later) we could understand why so many Arab poets became lyrical about the shadowy hours of evening. The blazing fever of daylong heat can be tiring and stressful and one longs for the night to come with its kindlier cold. That was one reason why our encampments would become both the most reliable and repetitive pleasures of GTAM.

We had one of the few grassy sites of the trip, the whole area being grazing land in prime bowling-green condition. The only snag of being pitched on a snooker table was finding anywhere out of sight for functions one prefers to perform with some privacy. There was also the interest of pitching the new *Vango* tents for the first time. A large, domed, *Discovery* tent acted as kitchen tent, dining-room and sleeping place for Hosain, while Charles, Ali and I had a *Micro 2* each, following the advice of the Arab proverb, 'Keep your tents separate and bring your hearts together'. The high-tech aspects of the tents were initially daunting but before long we could pitch and strike quickly and appreciated their fine qualities. The *Discovery* inner was never used which considerably increased the space inside. Little did we realise how soon and often all four of us would be cringing inside it while the rain belted down. On the Dayat Chiker it was frost that came down, to give the coldest night of the trip when of course, while preparing for bed, I discovered my sleeping bag had disappeared.

I could last remember seeing the bag at Imlil so that left plenty of scope for the loss. An unlikely explanation was that it had been stolen for, despite stories one hears, I have found Morocco remarkably honest. In the fish market at Essaouira I once pulled out my handkerchief and scattered coins all over the place. There was a noisy diving and searching by all and sundry and grinning *gamins* (urchins) soon had my hands full of money, including those who a minute before had been giving me the classic greeting of "*Bon jour; un dirham*". In Agadir when a grocer innocently gave me change from a 50dh note instead of 100dh (he was serving ten customers simultaneously) the man beside me spoke up before I could open my mouth. I'm forever leaving things behind (spectacle cases, alarm clocks) but they always find their way back to me. As did the sleeping bag a year later, when I happened to be given the same room in the Hotel Central in Rabat that Charles and I had occupied before GTAM. I thought I might just check if I'd somehow left the bag there. I was led to the lost property cupboard—and there it was.

On arrival at camp, Ali ceremoniously brewed the first pot of mint tea he'd made since Taroudant: delicious and naturally on the sugary side of sweet. The distant sunset (*el maghrib*) call to prayer came half-heard from a remote village. After dark, when the frogs were machine-gunning the stars and the night reeled to the cicadas, we had a *tagine* supper and were ready for bed not long after eight o'clock. The pattern was set: plenty to drink, good food (none of your cement-mixer school of camp cooking) and long hours of rest.

I slept in all the warm clothes I could muster inside my bivvy bag, but the cosmic cold eventually chilled my feet. A surprising amount of mule traffic clattered along the road, but it was mostly sheer excitement that kept sleep at bay. In the morning every blade of grass stood on end, like hairs on the head of fear, gone white in the night. The tents were shining with tumbled stars of frost. I was up at six (in self-defence) but an hour passed before the golden sun found us. We discovered the one single deficiency of the tent material. On warm nights the flysheet material stayed taut but given soaking wet or hard frost—just the conditions when one doesn't like to go outside to tighten guylines—the material sags. This could lead to flysheet contact with the inner which could lead to wet penetrating.

The Gouffre de Friouata (Friwata) is a pot system of considerable interest to cavers. Originally the only entrance was the 20-metre wide hole on the hillside into which it would have been very easy to stumble (how much livestock over the years had done so?). However, in pre-war days a tunnel was angled in from the side and a flight of concrete steps was built on the walls leading down to a huge scree fan and down the scree to a 'squeeze' at the beginning of exotic passages, explored and unexplored. We stopped about 200 metres down.

Two years previously I'd been alone with just one poor torch which gave a certain edge to my explorations. Since then, a small café has been built by the entrance and we waited there for our two friends before going down. The *guardien* was astonished when our two friends arrived with two mules ("Where is your car?"), but with a *guardien*, we could all go down together which was pleasant. Head torches shone into many new corners, catching glittering red falls or white sculptures, pillars, draperies and pools, a fantasy world created over many centuries. Unfortunately, we got rather tied up with a party of flip-flop-wearing city types who latched onto us and our torches. What with a young male's posturing and teenage girls giggling, the ambience was rather spoilt. Wealth and education are by no means an unalloyed blessing as they lead to the loss of national characteristics—and happiness—and an acceptance of the noisy worst features of Western civilisation.

The *guardien* swung open the iron entrance door to what could have been a coal-cellar and we descended a flight of about fifty concrete steps to end at a hole in the wall of the great pit. What a theatrical revelation. One almost felt like applauding. Voices echoing led our eyes down to see *tiny* figures below; not trolls but tiny because they were a long way down. The steps, stuck on the sidewall, are a trap for the unathletic. The family who raced down puffed noisily back up in very different mood; at least the girls had stopped giggling. Looking up, the real size of the opening became apparent: 20 metres in ragged diameter with an odd blue patch of jigsaw sky. The descent was made into blissful coolness.

About 750 irregular steps led down the scree that filled the bottom. Perhaps the roof had fallen in, leaving one wondering what passages lay buried and undiscovered. One passage, a tight 'squeeze' down a vertical climb, had been cleared at the lowest point of the scree and odd steps either of concrete or cut in the rock led on through a tortuous maze. We spent an hour exploring without reaching the end of that main route, with some aids and worn rock or footprints in mud to guide us. At the furthest point we switched off our torches so everyone could experience complete darkness, a sky instantaneously devoid of stars, a heart thumping with blood…a girl screamed.

There were plenty of attractive features: waves that curled but never broke, lances that flung shadow weapons at us. One gleaming pillar looked like ice and I climbed over to check, but it was only translucent rock. Drips were forming new stalactites and stalagmites and there were some delicately rimmed pools. Sadly, features too accessible had been vandalised and graffiti was spreading, odd behaviour in a place which struck me as almost holy with tapestries of colour, bosses and capitals and pillars fit for a minister, echoing like a cathedral. The teenagers giggled some more as they pointed out to each other monstrous tits and rows of bulls' bollocks.

Outside once more we had cold drinks. Cool as it was inside, the climb up all those steps had us dripping with sweat. The whole plain below the *gouffre* was a patchwork of fields and terraces were being built up the gullies opposite. A pair of mules was refusing to cooperate with the ploughing of a field and the poor ploughboy was in despair as his team repeatedly took off in opposite directions. We cut right across the end of the plain and up through evergreen oak forest to reach Bab Bou Idir, a strange mix of development and decay. The map rather optimistically called it *Centre d'Estivage*. Taza scout troops were occupying the pinewoods and doing all the things scouts usually do with rope and wood and *dib-dib-dibbing*. Ali and I had to go and chat to officialdom. Tourists with mules were not something they had been faced with before. An old lag of a soldier took us up to a possible camping spot on a col which gave splendid views in all directions: out over the Dayat Chiker eastwards and over blue expected hills to Jbel Tazzeka. Below us the forest plunged down to the Taza corridor. We had endless visitors (word of the *Red Label* had got out) and a sociable evening in the *Discovery*. The scouts' cheery singsong went on until midnight, the sound coming up to us in wind-borne waves.

Jbel Tazzeka is only 1980 m, but thrusts out from the Middle Atlas to dominate the historic Taza Gap (the communication mast on top can be seen from the train). It is isolated enough that the magnificent crowning cedars are possibly a subspecies of *Cedrus atlantica*. Some of the larger specimens were young trees in the days of Moulay Ismaïl—or Cromwell. There was oak as well and west, on the road down, are forests of cork oak *Quercus suber* with their denuded trunks. From the age of 27 until they 'retire' at 75 the cork oaks are compelled to hand over their trousers every nine years. Some of the fields lower down were heaped with cork, high as coal bings. As well as cork products, the bark is a useful source of tannin, with Fes and its leather industry close to hand.

Natural forest like that teems with bird life and the ground was rich with flowers: pansy, minute daffodils, gagea, romulea and many more. Rather a contrast to the sterility of Sitka spruce plantings at home. We'd set off at 0600 and were home at 1400, a 29 km hike to 'bag' our first hill. We were rewarded with mugs of tea and hot, fresh bread with our favourite *Aicha* brand marmalade before we went off to find the charming official in charge of the Tazzeka National Park. We had mint tea and were shown around the visitor centre he'd been creating. The fenced areas we'd noticed are an attempt to reintroduce deer. Tazzeka itself is a cedar reserve while other areas are earmarked for different agricultural uses. Practical dreams: man as long-lasting partner rather than transient exploiter.

The wind had been increasing steadily all day and the quartz-sharp clarity had blown away. We went to kip with our torch beams ghosting through billowing mist. The pines surged like surf in the night with rain catapulting off the branches. It was like sleeping below a taut jib, going out at six was the equivalent of being thrown overboard. A couple of hours later Ali brought tea but he was the only one keen to set off after the rain eased. We bundled everything together and went however. The Governor of Taza was due the next day which may have encouraged us; Ali is wary of officials. Or maybe our nomadic encampment was a bit scandalous (we didn't even have a car).

The earliest account of Atlas travelling I've come across is in the writings of Leo Africanus, who was probably a Granada-born Moorish traveller captured by Christian pirates in 1520 and presented to the Pope, Leo X, whose name he took. He had travelled 'in the region of Barbarie' himself and describes fine woods and lofty trees though much was cold and barren. Even in summer, if you dipped a hand in a stream, you risked losing it! A party of traders travelling together ran into an October storm of hail then snow, were robbed by Arab bandits then all took shelter in some caves with some Berber shepherds. On the third day they descended, and found their abandoned carts had been pillaged and one of the party taken hostage. Leo, having his mount taken, went on three days by mule to reach Fes. The description of the area fits the Middle Atlas convincingly.

Our mules' accoutrements had been thoroughly overhauled while we were on Tazzeka and we held the bridles as the skittish beasts were loaded, then walked on to warm up. We turned off the tarmac on the road to Adman at a dip, the Bab Taka (the word *bab* meaning gate is used in that area instead of the more usual *tizi*, meaning pass). That village, using its local resources as all do, was into cork: walls were capped with cork, roof-eaves were cork, livestock pens were cork, even a child's toy lorry being pulled along on a string was shaped from cork.

There was a green and lush landscape, watered by seven *sources* and dominated by jagged rock *pitons* (pinnacle-shaped hills). There didn't appear to be a way through but we hit a clear winding stream, secreted between pink limestone walls. It snaked on through verdant glades and oak forest, the trees twisted as old men. Charles thought the area was just like the Yorkshire Dales. The weather certainly was, with the wind knifing us on the grazing lands we followed above the deep-set Oued Arba. South, in the murk, there was a hint of big, snowy mountains. Yet this was a peopled landscape, with charcoal burning in the forest. When the time came to stop we turned down to try and find shelter by the river. A cheery soldier with a donkey caught up and suggested a suitable place, and after sending his animal off home by itself, he became our pal for that day, finding entertainment in all we did. He brought fodder for our hungry mules. As we'd only had tea and toast for breakfast we had healthy appetites. Soup, bully beef with spiced vegetables and a rice pudding was our typical supper meal. A boy from the nearest farm had brought down a jar of buttermilk and huge, round loaves of bread. We enjoyed roughing it, brews in hand, with a tired moon leaning on the shoulder of the hill. There's a different level of restfulness in those circumstances. The normal world had orbited off into unreality while the weightless wonder all around becomes the centre of all.

Following the Oued Arba gave very varied walking and the landscape became richer, oleanders and olives choking the bank. It was impossible to be very sure of where we were on our map, as there was too much physical detail to crowd into the 100,000 scale and not enough names. Having gone ahead we also became concerned about missing the mules. An old man pointed ahead, saying "*Lalla Fadila*", but a few minutes later a youth gave the same place as being back the way. "Just follow the river", we'd told Ali. We stopped at a place where we could see both banks. A solitary figure on the hillside opposite was a red dot among white speckles—a goatherd and his flock. His dog barking indicated someone travelling below and our mules duly appeared. A man on a mule overtook, once we'd paddled over, then paused and asked if we'd like tea up at his house.

He had named his home Beni Raham, which actually agreed with a name on the map, while the Oued Arba had reconstituted itself as the Oued Beni Raham. The house was a huge grey sprawl with a flagged threshing floor surrounded by immense walls of stacked firewood. We lay on cushions on a rug outside, amused by wandering chickens, many-coloured goat kids, a puppy looking like a miniature St Bernard, and the usual shy (two-legged) kids. Later we went inside, kicking off Brashers and Reeboks, to enjoy mint tea and warm, crisp bread with *smen* (butter) melting over it.

We couldn't pick out the track ahead but after dropping down to cross a bridge for the long haul out of the valley we discovered why. The strata rose vertically and so did the path. We ground up to the Tizi Tafrannt and were looking down onto Merghraoua, quite a sizeable place with a fine mosque tower and an old fort on a guardian hill. There was also a *caïdat* (rural government office) at the end of the tarred road. A *piste* ran on into the Bou Iblane range to the south.

Our desire to explore the place was over-ruled by Ali who didn't want to have to spend time with the inevitable bureaucracy. We outflanked the town on the right to pick up a series of zigzags as the *piste* worked back down to the river again, the same river but now calling itself the Amezouarou, which had put in fifteen cliff-held twists and turns since Beni Raham, reason enough for our up-and-over route.

The mules took short cuts from elbow to elbow and cut corners off the river. Hosain enjoyed Ali putting his feet in the water and the wind blew my brolly away. I also left the map behind at one stage and went back only to be met by a bevy of giggly women who were bringing the mysterious object. They had black, lacy shawls over a glitter of *kaftans* and were not at all abashed at the stranger's presence.

We camped early, in the lee of a bluff, but it was a dusty, windy spot, surrounded by bare, ploughed fields and some of the oldest, thickest olives I've ever seen. My tent hardly flapped in the wind however and I took my brew inside and finished writing a short story which I'd begun the day before. We had haggis for supper. Both evening and morning were so grey and raw that, for once, I didn't have a picture of the site, probably the least memorable of the trip, except we did see our first Atlas (Moussier's) redstart. By the end of the next day there had been such a succession of pleasures that I found it hard to remember everything.

The day before we had travelled all day in a southeast direction, down-river, which seemed strange as we were supposed to be working up into big hills. That river had drained a vast upland area that was basically a desiccated plateau and now, coming to a real upsurge of hills it turned away to the northeast and, of course, changed its name, to eventually flow into the Moulouya. Our *piste* turned southwest, the general GTAM line throughout, heading for Tamtroucht, our next map name, beginning with a tortuous assault on the bluffs above. We left the *piste* to its endless frenzy of bends and braes for a gentle up-valley walk. A tiny *hanut* (shop) was welcome for drinks, mantles for the *gaz* light, and an introduction to *Taggers*, a chocolate biscuit akin to *Blue Ribands* and for which we were to develop a craving. We nearly died at the price quoted but then realised he was still working in the old system; rather like someone today quoting a price in pounds, shillings and pence he was using old *francs* or the more common *riyals* (where 20 *riyals* equal one *dirham*). Leaving the village one of the huge, fast, bright green metre-long lizards shot across the path. There was a south-of-France feel to the valley, hemmed in by limestone cliffs, with vines and olives and fruit trees as well as the chequering of little fields. We stopped to see an olive press in operation, a patient mule walking round and round the basin with a huge stone wheel pulping the black mess. Woven filters strained the over-scented oil and a black stain ran down from the site. Morocco is one of the great olive-producing countries; in the Roman ruins of Volubilis near Meknes there are 55 surviving olive presses.

Continuing, we came to an extraordinary pass, for all the world like a scree-filled Lairig Ghru only several times the scale. Unimagined labour appeared to have cleared fields, no bigger than tabletops, at the foot of the slope. We met a party of women staggering down under huge loads of firewood, bent double under the weight and using short sticks to act as a steadying third leg. The canyon wound on, sheer cliffs on the left, the oak becoming mixed with juniper. We reached cedar country again after a fearsome sweat up through white boulder-fields, passing the 1000-metre altitude we would hold for weeks ahead—probably until we drove down to Marrakech in 53 days' time.

We came to a col and, beyond, could see the fuscous flat of the Guelta Tamda (*tamda* meaning lake), which confirmed our suspicions that we had overshot the intended path off up to the Tamtroucht road. We yelled at the fast-disappearing mules and went back to the col for a well-earned rest, brew and a recce. Taza stood with her neck draped over Tamri's. The lake had dried out and when an ancient on a mule came up he confirmed we could continue over and then cut up to Tamtroucht, the next, last map name before we were right in the mountains. Had the lake held water (rare these last few years), going on would have been impassable; the crags rising from its wood-lined edge had a five-metre tide line. The *tamda* was an extraordinary mind-ambushing place ("weird and wonderful" in my log). We left a trail behind us as if we had been walking through black snow. There were goats on the cliffs with a boy herd above them who could not have been into double figures in years, controlling their erratic flow along the crags by voice and well-aimed stones. A British mother seeing her child in such a situation would faint or have hysterics.

We saw many groups of ruddy shelduck, an attractive bird with brick red, black and white combination of flight colours. We'd see them on just about every small lake in the Middle Atlas. The *tamda* went on and on then, beyond a banding of tumbled trees and branches, lay a flood plain which was being ploughed. There was a small farm perched on a crag above, chimney reeking, half-hidden in trees. We could have been approaching Arolla in Switzerland.

The cedars were magnificent and grassy spots among them cried out for our stopping. We walked up by a clear mountain stream called the Souf Igrane. Heaven is portrayed as a walled garden in many cultures. This was ours, and the walls were not made by hands either. A more delectable place we were not to see. We only went on far enough to try and obtain a fix of just where we were, then camped. It was quite important to find the path shown on the map which went up to Tamtroucht. (The place would be a sure location.) A very useful spot height helped the map and altimeter studies and I was chuffed to find the path where expected. Years of Atlas eyeing did the trick. I was doubly pleased because Hosain and Ali hadn't noticed and had gone past with the mules. Later I walked up a bit and met a man on a mule, leading two others, who was so astonished at seeing me he could only stutter out the usual "*La bas!*"

Our tents stood in a green glade among the cedars. Ali lit a fire and at dusk baked scrumptious bread on the girdle I'd brought from Scotland. (A flat stone would have done just as well.) We sneaked a few of Ali's round loaves, eating them hot and plastered in strawberry jam. Chicken with a cheese sauce went with the last of our Taza fresh vegetables. The day ebbed into a quiet dusk where the only sound was a solitary frog's pleeping. The wind had gone. Firelight lit a small oasis, roofed over with a web of branches, patterned with stars. In the morning, like the sailor in *The Coral Island*, I was to think, 'I've woked in Paradise!'

Nothing could have been a greater contrast than the following night's site however. It was a Sibelius world somewhere on the edge of nowhere, offering a scrofulous green patch to camp among jagged limestone, shadowed by freak rocks and looking along the miles of Jbel Bou Iblane's snowy flanks and the open strath of the Bled Tiserouine (Tisserwin). The air had the tartness of mountain cold and spirals of choughs shrilled overhead.

The first real view of Jbel Bou Iblane had come when we pulled up out of our magic valley to Tamtroucht. The forest had been denuded and only a few skeletons remained. The scene was a bit like upper Deeside in winter: the pines yielding to big sprawling hillsides, grey and patched with snow and the greater summits rising beyond in stark, laundered whiteness. We'd just reached the village, a tiny, unimpressive place for a name which had dominated our progress for so long, when a boy of about ten appeared, striding strongly along, his hand on the bridle of a laden mule. Behind him came a line of other mules, most being led, a few with infants perched on the loads, along with the hens. A younger boy drove the goats. This was our first meeting with a family migrating or, to be accurate we were seeing transhumance, which is the regular posting back and forth where a migration could be just one way. They went resolutely forward, eyes front, speaking to no one, and dropped down into the trees. Sadly, because of the late winter, we were to encounter few other families on the move.

'Transhumance' never quite conveys the thrill of meeting the process in operation, one which calls to us and blows the dying embers of romance in our souls into a brief warmth. In a world where everything is stereotyped, regulated and dulled by security such a sight is bound to 'remind us of heathery origins/And cave man doubts'. The pied piper is always ready to lead us astray. Then I laughed for weren't we on a similar journey—even more so—following no seasonal round, low to high, south to north, but a mighty east to west, the whole extravagance from end to end? And I quite consciously bit on this juicy apple of truth, knowing it would never come again. I didn't want to prance after the band on that occasion; we had our own procession.

As we left Tamtroucht there was a solitary, stately cedar on the right, the 'Tree of Reconciliation', commemorating where in earlier times the tribes, often hostile, rallied to the *Makhzen* (central government). For centuries the country had been divided into the *Bled el Makhzen* and the *Bled el Siba* with the sultans ruling a variable holding from Fes or Morocco (Marrakech) and making punitive *harkas* (literally, burning) expeditions against the tribes. This was a system well used by Queen Elizabeth or (more briefly) Mary Queen of Scots. They constantly toured the country and were given the hospitality of the great lords, thereby severely denting their wealth and restricting their opportunities to create mischief.

Perhaps the closest analogy is with the old Highlands–Lowlands situation in Scotland. The King of Scots faced exactly the same situation and, with varying degrees of success dependent upon character as well as force, controlled those clans who if they were not uniting against the government were quite happy to be fighting and plundering among themselves. Just as central government (by then in London) used the Campbells and other 'loyal' clans, the French used the 'Lords of the Atlas' to control the mountains until able to subdue the remaining dissident areas. There was no single Culloden to settle matters, however, and there were ghastly battles on mountains like Jbel Baddou or Bou Gaffer in 1933. Culloden was 250 years ago but I have picked old mortar cases or tins of *boeuf assaisonne* off the slopes of Bou Gaffer. The scene had been described to me by someone who was there, as a child hiding with the women in the caves while the men fought mortars, machine guns and aircraft with muzzle-loaders which—in style—predated Culloden. French toehold to departure was only a period of 44 years, which included both world wars. It deserves pointing out again that from Independence to the present is probably the longest spell of relative peace the country has ever known. They would not be clearing and ploughing the rusty slopes of the Bled Tiserouine otherwise.

Another similarity to the Highlands is that enforced peace and the corollary of adequate food has meant an explosion in population numbers and a scattering to the corners of the world. Morocco's population has exploded since Independence and the investment in expanding agricultural resources has an amount of desperation to it. There has been a huge shift of population to the cities, especially Casablanca, or to France (and Belgium) where many a little corner shop, the Moroccan *hanut*, will be in the hands of a Tafraouti. But young adults now make half of Morocco's population. Where will they go? Where will they find employment? The change, in my lifetime, has been nothing less than astonishing and I think history, which likes to record in sizeable chunks, will mark down the second half of the 20th century as something of a Golden Age.

New *pistes* appeared which were not on the map and luckily we were within hailing distance as Hosain shot off on a wrong fork. The correct *piste* tied itself in knots along bald flanks above the deep northeast drainage which, as ever, cut so deeply so suddenly. When others comment on the vast scale of everything, always emphasising the wide horizontal distances, I'm apt to mention the equally impressive scale of verticalities. There isn't much level walking in the Atlas Mountains. By such standards, the Bled Tiserouine is a plain—an elevated shelf of pastureland with long strings and scatterings of sheep and, like ink blots on a letter, the occasional dark patch of a nomad tent. Water was scarce despite the streaky snow on the flanks of Jbel Bou Iblane. We camped just above a well where the flocks came, in turns, to drink at the long trough. The map actually indicates one '*bain pour les moutons*' and Peyron warns of a well with a reputation of being poisonous. We took his word for it.

Facing our camp on the flank of Jbel Bou Iblane at 2000 m, were several sturdy buildings and a ski tow. I'm told there were grand plans for a ski resort there but development rather came to a halt. Whenever the conditions were right for skiing, the road in was always blocked, while in summer, there was inadequate water on site. We had hardly pitched our tents when a soldier came over from the buildings to say they were now the offices of the local *caïd*, and could we please report.

There was a feeling of unreality about our visit: outside was a scene that belonged to the time of Abraham and his flocks, whereas inside we were led past smart girls busily typing, into the *caïd's* office. His suit and tie made us feel somewhat travel soiled. He explained that there were plans to develop the area, that a new district (*caïdat*) had been created for this high wilderness. "Come back in ten years and you will find a town here", we were challenged. I said I hoped we'd be back long before then and, simultaneously, we said "*Insh' Allah*".

Ali was an assistant with a tourist agency and this always needed explaining. The company's brochure, illustrated from a selection of slides I'd provided, happened to include a picture of myself sitting in a group of happy village children. We were always amused to see the reactions when officials came on this: the long stare, the quick glance across the table, another look, the cry of "It is you!" and as like as not another handshake for someone who was obviously involved in their world rather than just a casual tourist.

"You are good friend to Morocco?"

"I hope so."

There is a dramatic change in relationships when questioners discovered one is on a return visit. There may be a certain suspicion that the question is loaded as, if you have been before, you are not so likely to be an easy mark for the taxi driver or tout, but that soon goes. You don't keep returning without good cause and, tout or *caïd*, you will soon be asked, "You like our country?"

"Yes, I like Morocco very much."

"How many times you been?"

"Nearly every year since 1965—over 30 times."

"Then, monsieur, you were visiting my country before I was born."

Some cards are easy to play.

At least they are for us. Officialdom can be heavy on ordinary men. Everything is regulated. The right papers can mean a world of difference. I've had a youth who'd thumbed a lift hauled out of my car and given a virtual body search and a verbal hammering because he was breaking the law by being with tourists when not 'officially' in the tourist industry. An opened wallet might have changed that ugly situation of course, or exacerbate it, one never knows—it is not a climate we understand very well. We gave the *caïd* one of our forms with all our personal details on it. This always went down well with officialdom. They worship forms. After all, when the French left Morocco they had four times the number of bureaucrats running the country as the Brits had in India.

Free contact with tourists has dangers, of course. Ideas can be swapped. There's never been a time or race when young men don't dream dreams (and we old men see visions). The tourist is a dangerous asset, much better corralled in Agadir or seeing the country from the goldfish bowl of an air-conditioned bus. What and how far to allow things presents one of these chewy problems for authority. There are extremists tugging constantly in all directions. Whatever one feels, Morocco has steered a middle course and enjoyed a peace, prosperity and a freedom found in few countries. The occasional annoyances (even horrors) may be tolerable for the overall *multum bonum*.

The tourist potential in Morocco is tremendous but not an easy concept to explain (never mind in broken French) to an isolated official with no tourist experience. The Jbel Bou Iblane massif is still *terra incognito* and while part of me delights in that of course, some wealth coming into the area would only be for the good of the local population. There's a certain arrogance in denying development when it could bring benefits such as schools, a clinic, decent roads and a *souk*, something more for people than the harsh minimum which many still face every day. That's a problem I've been masticating all my life and, likewise striving for a middle way, have drawn fire from the extremists. Truth never lies in extremes.

Charles was happy to depart at 0440 to climb Moussa ou Salah again, the first 'Munro' of GTAM (3172 m). Calling metric hills after the Scottish 3000-footers is a foible dating back to when I took school parties to the Alps. They wouldn't climb anything under 3000 m as they jokingly declared them not to be Munros. Charles slid the stove into my tent as he left but after an hour I set off, in full light after the fish scales of frost had gone, for modest Jbel Achlem Alem (2462 m). It is the highest of the breaking wave crests on the northern side of the *bled* (countryside), its limestone rock face wrinkled as an old face. The weather was cloudy but the main interest was the flowers: the yellowest of yellow raffenaldias and minute pansies which sensibly grew up through thorn scrub so as not to be eaten by goats. Higher, there were romulea, gagea and huge areas of *Ranunculus calandrinioides* with pink-tinged flowers, a species the professionals were desperate to see later. Horned larks, like busy mice, were rummaging around the dreich summit. Our intended route on, the Tizi Bou Zabel, had a long rising line of white leading up to it, indicating the direction of the track but also warning that the route was banked with snow. Back at camp I considered the alternatives if the snow stopped the mules using the pass.

I hadn't gone with Charles for Jbel Bou Iblane's summit of Moussa ou Salah (3172 m) as we'd done it previously. Jbel Bou Nacceur (3326 m) is the highest of this almost unknown area. Only Peyron had written about it, briefly, which lured Charles, Ali, Len and me to visit in 1992, backpacking and bivouacking over Nacceur and then obtaining a mule for Iblane out to Taffert— just along on the route we had planned for the following day. When the weather deteriorated on that trip, the muleteer quickly wove rope from grass to support the panniers between rocks as a shelter! We'd ran for our lives off Iblane as a thunderstorm swept in. Ali got a dose of snow blindness to add to his learning curve.

It was extraordinary how one *doesn't* see people on a big open slope. Charles was only 400 m off when we spotted him. A brew and we were off at 1100, up to a minor pass and then a stiffer climb to a higher pass. Conditions underfoot became claggy so I retrieved my boots from Tamri. There was some hail. Berbers are either born optimists or they are so fit that they are prodigal in expending energy, for the mules were driven on up that line of snow until it was quite impossible to proceed. Even then we were sent on to the *tizi* (2300 m) to see if the mules could win through from Taffert further on. We did not like what we saw. On a rather dubious Victorian era Alpine climb the guide Melchior Anderegg once gave his *führer* the comment: 'Es geht. Aber ich gehe nicht.' (It [the route] may go, but I don't). We were not going to risk Taza and Tamri. Spears of sun were piercing the armour of clouds and waving across the ridges as if looking for a place to wound. The Tizi Bou Zabel was closed to us.

We regrouped back on the lower track and wandered along to the Taffert *maison forestière*, a forestry building akin to all others in having a pitched roof of pink tiles, very French alpine chalet architecture seen in some of the few protectorate buildings that have been maintained. There was an avalanche of dogs but the place seemed deserted. The previous time we'd been taken in but only under sufferance, as we didn't have the local *caïd's* blessing (a bit difficult as his office lay two hours by car down the Fes road). However, the burly *haj* soon thawed and we had a curious night in the haunted atmosphere that would have served well for a horror film.

Rather sadly we went on, determined to call a halt at the first water. This proved to be just outside the cedar forest: a stream beside an orchard. We pitched on an *andrair*, a level threshing floor by a barn (with a pitched roof of cedar boards), a shepherd lad of about ten graciously giving us his blessing. By the time he'd watched us pitch, had tea and chatted with Ali, his flock had disappeared and he went off at a trot. Every village has several *andrair* for, like every part of agricultural or constructional work, threshing is done in concentrated fashion: the communal cooperation of crofting. Grain is laboriously cut by hand (usually by men) and carried home or to the threshing floor (by women). The crop is harvested at just the right time so the grains don't detach with all the handling but dries out to the correct looseness. It is then threshed: piled on one of the floors and trampled by the poor donkeys or mules tied to the central post, walking round and round. Forks of natural growth are used to toss the straw in the air so the chaff is separated; nothing is wasted. Explaining this to some female tourists, I was asked, "But what about the mules, you know, err, they err, might make a mess?" So I told her the remedy: "The mules wear nappies!" I don't think she believed me.

Tamri had developed a sore on his back so Hosain tried to re-shape the saddle to remove the pressure and Ali rubbed on some Savlon. The boy's dog came and lay patiently in hope of food. Soup, pasta, corned beef and onion sauce, apricots and custard, coffee and biscuits: not much for a dog. The dog had called up reinforcements for breakfast, but had even less chance of sharing our muesli. As we walked along the road the shepherd boy greeted us with solemn dignity.

Any hope we'd had of making a level contour around the western extension of the Bou Iblane ridge soon disappeared as the slopes broke into cedar-clad cliffs. We began to descend the road's zigzags but then cut off down a dry river bed to reach a spur beyond, up which ran a new *piste*, when we eventually found it. Before then the mules had descended ground never intended for mules and thrashed up through *maquis* (scrub) slopes. We were gasping as we followed.

A deep gorge and tiered crags showed our descent had been wise. "Better the devil we can see", canny Charles admitted. Off to the west a huge scarp dominated, down valley we could see the tortuous road vanishing in the foothills down to the Taza–Fes road at a place with the delightful name of Birtam Tam. A mule track led us up to Arbal, a village of neat stone houses and cedar shingles. We stopped at the *source* (spring) at the head of the village where the water was led off along troughs of hollowed cedar logs. Ali and Hosain couldn't get over such an abundance of wood. We brewed and had some warmed-up bread, making it almost as good as new (we also carried a simple toaster and a reserve of oatcakes should all other options fail).

The sky had turned the sad grey of an approaching storm and the atmosphere was stale. What should we do? On cue a local came down and asked if we'd like to stay in the village. As it was still early we dithered. There was a growl of thunder and several voices immediately replied: "Thank you", "*Chokrane*", "*Barakalowfik*". Taza and Tamri were loaded and we angled up into Arbal to be welcomed into a home which seemed to have an endless number of look-alike brothers all wearing identikit pullovers. A female carried off a loudly complaining chicken. "*Tagine au poulet*", grinned Ali, and nobody minded.

As mint tea is always served, many times a day sometimes, it may be wise to describe it. By the end of GTAM we regarded the beverage as the nectar of the gods. The British introduced tea from the east back in 1854 (Moroccans added mint), as well as the uniquely bulbous-shaped teapot. Some of the older ones may well have Manchester stamped on the bottom. The best brand of green tea has the slightly ominous trade name of Gunpowder.

Everything is portable in the uncluttered Moroccan home (we tend to fill space, they use space as part of the design concept). A girl brings in a low table with glasses, fat-bellied teapot, sugar box and tea, then a *kanoun* (a glowing charcoal brazier made of clay). When the kettle boils the teapot is rinsed and the glasses washed again. Tea is popped into the teapot and washed then the boiling water is poured in. Fresh mint is carefully washed, inspected, crushed and added, followed by an unbelievable quantity of sugar. Sugar comes in huge 2 kg cones and is broken by gently tapping with a hammer. The pieces almost fill the teapot to over-flowing. The pot is placed on the stove awhile, then our host tries and rejects several tastings and, eventually satisfied, pours the golden liquid into glasses from a great height with unerring aim, so the tea gurgles up with a frothy head. The glasses are passed round, one says "*Bismillah*" and sips. Tea is sipped scalding hot which is difficult for European tender fingers and lips and those hoping to drink quietly. Often home-grown walnuts, dates or cookies accompany the tea. There is nothing better to induce a feeling of utter relaxation and content.

The Arbal children were shy, never having seen strangers, never mind the like of us, but balloons and conjuring tricks soon had them laughing. A huge dish piled with layered pancakes was brought in. They were large, crisp and oily. We ate them with hard boiled eggs. "*Bismillah*".

Big eyes and snotty noses were pressed to the window grill. I did some homework on the route ahead and considered going for a walk but great goblets of gluey rain swept in. We were pleased not to be on the trail or setting up camp in the instant mud. We were cold inside the house, even with blankets round our shoulders. Going out for a pee required an escort, to keep the dogs at bay, a collection of fine-looking white huskies. Time rather dragged as it was too dark to read and we'd not been on the trail long enough to just float mentally when given the chance.

A mountainous *tagine* duly appeared: chicken, spuds, tomatoes all heaped in a spicy dish and eaten with huge flat loaves of brown bread: "*Mizyen*" (good) is a word learnt early on. The Atlas produces an unending variety of bread types, all enjoyable, besides the pancake-type goodies, crispbreads and endless honey-sweet goo-ey objects, all with unpronounceable names but *hobs* would always get us bread. There was refreshing *leben* (buttermilk) to drink. A *tagine* is a casserole-style meal (and also the name of the clay dish with the conical lid in which it is both slow-cooked and served), mostly vegetables and a few spices and meat to flavour. No two are ever the same and I don't think I've ever had a bad one. As they are left to cook for hours on a charcoal brazier, our supper came at 2100. We weren't used to such late nights. Our hosts, several brothers, had never entertained Europeans before. The remoteness of such villages is hard to convey. No wonder the Berbers call themselves *imaziren*, the free people. Hospitality was given to us as it would have been in the Highlands several centuries ago. Our first night under a roof would not be forgotten.

CHAPTER 4

Across Melwiya

Mount Atlas, a name so idly celebrated by the fancy of poets.
Gibbon

Shrill voices of children shouting the words of the Prophet in unison came from one house as we left the tidy village the next morning. Once the dogs had escorted us off their territory, we wandered on up into a slope of crowded cedars. With ravens on the crags, the calling of thrushes and the thin whispering of firecrests we could have been looking down on Rothiemurchus, although the comparison made me laugh outright. The scale is slightly different, Scotland has no nuthatches or Barbary apes, and there may even be leopards in the Atlas. Arbal on its spur appeared now and then and, beyond, the eye plunged down a thousand metres of forest, until the blue succession of fading tones disappeared in diaphanous whiteness. Nature's call separated us but we agreed to meet at the col at the end of the Bou Iblane ridge we'd been following for several days. When I next saw Charles he was doing an Extreme up a vertical mud slope. The hillside was seamed with gullies, mud, scree, boulders and piecrust snow, all at a steep angle. Paths were ephemeral. I described the trees as 'muscular'. (Something must have held them upright.) At 0800 we heard barking down at Arbal and assumed our other half was setting off. At 0900 we reached the col and I only had time to write-up the previous day's doings in my log when our boisterous team arrived.

The view along the flank of Bou Iblane was impressive: a skier's dream of white snow. Ahead, the landscape was hazy but the long shape of Jbel Tichchoukt thrust up, a rude gesture almost, putting us in our place with the 28 km we'd walk to just pass along its flank in a few days' time. Walking over horizons eventually stopped fazing us.

We made Tizi Ouiridene, about 2000 m, and followed a good path down shale-covered strata to a stream in the corner where all six of us were glad to drink. We then descended brown slopes, freshly ploughed and being worked over by black wheatears, one of the ubiquitous birds of drier parts. For several days we'd seen what we called the Atlas redstart, a cocky bird of black, white and brick red clothing (Moussier's redstart, *Phoenicurus moussieri*), which is only found in the Atlas Mountains.

Crossing a rise led us down to the well-scattered houses and fields of Tafadjight. Apples were growing in abundance but what made the place different from anywhere else were the houses, square in shape, with the north sides clad in cedar boards. From a distance, the effect looked like corrugated iron. Some of the more recent buildings were iron clad as the cedars are now officially protected. Balconies, complicated stairways and yards were all made of wood, however. A white mosque tower stood beside the *souk* but there wasn't even one shop open. Angling along between the oddity of wire fence and a vertical drop to the river, the mules' panniers made far too wide a load and Tamri was nearly bumped over the edge. Hosain therefore took down a post or two so they could walk along the field before returning to replace the fencing.

That huge hollow of life drained off into a deep gorge so we were forced up onto a stony *piste* which climbed high, away from the Oued Taferjit. The terrain was again uncompromising limestone, and, despite the warning of dervish-dancing clouds we went on strike after a shortcut over jagged rocks, bodies demanding food and liquid. As we hurried on up to regain the *piste* there was a dash of hail. The mules were sheltering below scrawny oaks waiting for us but as the hail continued to belt down and the thunder was cracking overhead, we donned full waterproofs. Our feet collected great dollops of mud as we slithered along the track. At the high point, Tizi Essous, the goo at least began to flow downhill. The mules were quite good at glissading on the mud which clung disgustingly to our boots.

Variant tracks were a bit worrying but we were never likely to be lost (head west and, perforce, we'd reach the Atlantic) but being temporarily mislaid was a nuisance and an admission that the machinations of the map had at last succeeded. We trampled short cuts among the fan palms or hopped along the spikes of weathered pink rock—anything to avoid the build-up of mud on our feet which would drag like a ball and chain, wobble us as on stilts and then collapse with a splodge like some pachydermatous excrement. Of all walking surfaces I find clawing mud the most revolting.

As to our destination, the general line was clear enough: the huge mass of the Tichchoukt bulked ahead, a sort of Schiehallion seen end-on, the cleft of our pass (thrice the length of Loch

Rannoch), the southern bypass of the hill. There were obvious army posts of no great antiquity visible on strategic points below and we discovered later that was a borderland where Berber and French forces confronted each other. We learned that from a charming man who confirmed the path towards our next destination, Tilmirat. As we were speaking to him an old lady rushed over from the house with a silver salver bearing cups of tea. In minutes we found out that she had a son living in Taroudant, who was known to Ali. The end result was that she sold us a turkey which then rode on top of Taza for the rest of the day, frequently being swiped by passing branches as we went up and down and over an arid *maquis* with oak and juniper and scented rosemary, a cheery river in the gorge below, lined with the spears of tall poplars. The heat hugged the slopes and, despite the clawing jungle, I used the *parasol*. Tilmirat proved to be just a few houses below path level, a cluster of well-blessed farms where even the dogs couldn't do more than lift heads to watch us pass. We descended another steep, harsh limestone slope towards a river.

There was an incredible complexity of rivers, meandering in sheer gorges before collecting together to become the broad Oued Maasser, soon called the Oued Sebou which flows on past Fes before reaching the Atlantic at Kenitra. We suddenly realised we had to cross this united flow. Where the path reached the bank the *oued* was wild so we fought the jungle upstream to a wider, but shallower, reach. We over-reacted, packing cameras away and taking off our trousers, and paddled across scarce up to our knees. However, it could have been the other way round, the water up to our necks, as the red, silty waters made a visual check on the depth impossible.

We camped on a terrace below olive trees, a *seguia* (irrigation ditch) beside us, and dined on fresh turkey served in a sweet onion sauce with bread brought to us by the owner of the idyllic spot. As so often happened, we were lulled to sleep by the music of the flowing river. Sun and water are the oldest gods of man.

Peyron gave dire warnings about what lay ahead, and Peyron is usually right. Any differences we noted were the result of seasonal changes. He passed that way after seven years of drought when things would certainly have looked different. The Atlas frequently suffers the manipulations of climatic extremes; but at least the Atlas has the saving grace of actually having seasons. Peyron's distances and descriptions should be regarded but a note of caution needs to be sounded about the times he gives. He was a lean and fit individual, exploring the Atlas year in and year out at all seasons. The untrained, over-indulged office worker going straight from city life to Atlas trekking is all too likely to find a twelve-hour Peyron route a recipe for benightment. For our trip, whenever Peyron gave treks of 10–12 hours duration, we automatically planned to take two days instead. We also had to read Peyron's descriptions backwards as his text runs west to east.

His warnings of the complicated navigation in descending from the long Tichchoukt pass were quite justified. For most of our ascending we could make little of the map or Peyron. We'd also had the doubtful guidance of the old man on whose terrace we'd camped. (He is forgiven as he brought some vegetables, four eggs and bread as well as the misinformation.)

The afternoon before Ali had ridden over the wide Oued Maasser perched on Tamri's rump, and the mule had not shown any concern for the big river. Come the morning, however, loaded and ready to go, he just would not cross the metre-wide *seguia* running above the terrace. All the considerable tricks of the trade from Ali and Hosain, from (literal) carrots to (literal) kicking, failed. They were determined Tamri would cross ("He has to learn!" an exasperated Ali explained), even to the extent of unloading the mule again. This made no difference but, for reasons of his own, he did eventually jump the tiny water channel as well as some invisible hedge about two metres high, landing metres beyond the imagined obstacle. This overkill—or over-jump—was an astonishing and entertaining spectacle. There are many *seguias* in the Atlas and only slowly did Tamri accept them for what they were and not treat them like a Grand National obstacle. Large rivers never bothered him at all. We began speculating what he'd do when faced with the Atlantic: probably treat the sea as a wider river and start off for the Canary Islands.

The *maquis* through which the mules were driven to find the promised good track was beginning to shred the tarpaulin covers and had also reduced progress to a dusty slowness, so when Ali saw a good mule track on the other side of the valley he opted to go right back down and find this. We'd meet at the valley head, *Insh 'Allah*. The valley on our side soon became a limestone scarp but a faint trail wended along the lip and eventually dipped into the red rocks of the gorge to end at an abandoned farm on the other bank, along which our mules had to come. We made the most of the water and washed top halves and bottom halves of our bodies in turn. A kestrel was working along the gorge and a chittering of choughs mingled with the stuttering of bee-eaters while the warm rocks were much favoured by brimstone butterflies. We were not long on the trail again when the mules caught up.

The valley bifurcated near its top, and still thinking we might reach the village of Mohammed Azeroual mentioned by Peyron, we took the left fork. Layers of cultivation kept forcing us higher and higher and suddenly we were above the tree-line, back in the freckled alpine world. Our gap to bypass Tichchoukt lay right ahead but the huge view was what really impressed all of us, and it takes something for Ali and Hosain to be impressed. We were beginning to worry about water, as Peyron indicated there was little or none on the day-long pass ahead. If we found some, should we carry an overnight supply? As soon as we voiced our concern we saw a *source* with a trough just below us so all six of us were soon drinking. While we ate bread and cheese with Cup-a-soups and coffee the mules made inroads on the fan palms, a diet which looked as nourishing as barbed wire. We set off again in the heavyweight heat, agreeing that we'd all stop up the pass at 1600, wherever that would be. We soon found ourselves on the edge of a deep hollow with no easy alternative but to go down over gritty disintegration. Being at the angle of minimal adhesion I had a good test of my sandals. Charles tried a couple of rolls and slides and used words I'd not heard from his lips before. We were led more and more across tiered acres of terraces and then forced up by a big house. We carefully tried *not* to intrude too much only to hear later that Ali and Hosain had stopped there for tea.

This 'arid valley with no water' (Peyron) proved to be so cultivated, right to the banks of the grey river of spate-boulders, that we were largely forced to walk along this pebbly riverbed. I suppose the track meant well but it was as tiresome as any pebble beach, only uphill. New houses were being built all along the valley, in quality stonework. The seesaw battle between man and rough nature always moves me in these circumstances. On the left flank of our ascent, the fields only ran up a few hundred metres, as far as a *seguia* could lead water from the stream coursing down the pebble walk. There were boxwoods and layered cliffs with the usual exuberance of choughs overhead. The new life delighted but I also wondered what would happen given another seven-year drought.

At 1530 we came on a newly cut *andrair* which would take all our tents together, and decided that was our site. A few minutes later the mules arrived. Hosain put a *Melolin* patch on Taza's sore back and had another session of saddle-adjusting. We had turkey, of course, but the dried mushrooms I put on to soak beat explanation or translation until I fell back on drawing them.

Years ago at a poor village in the Agoundis valley, which we came down to after a traverse of the Tazaghart Plateau, a drawing proved useful in communications. Not knowing the Berber for eggs I drew one and squawked like a hen which not only gained the desired provisions but had the listeners raucous with laughter. Later, I wondered if the failure to imitate animal sounds tied in with the Islamic prohibition on drawing people and things. I seemed to spend the next hour going through my entire pets and farmyard animal sounds before a growing crowd of villagers of all ages. The kids doubled over holding their tummies in an agony of laughing. They insisted we stayed (little did we know) and the solitary grey rabbit that had been hopping among our feet was grabbed and carried off to be turned into rabbit *tagine*.

One of the first signs of affluence in a village is to install grilled windows, which have a conspicuous white margin painted round them. Coming off the hill we'd noted there was only one white window in this village, obviously poor, which was another reason we didn't really want to stay. Four hungry climbers would be as harmful as locusts. We felt quite guilty about the rabbit. We were accommodated in the house with the one painted window and the bare room was given to us for the night. The day had been very hot and the mud-built house had absorbed heat over many hours so, when the temperature dropped, the effect was akin to having night-storage heaters, the heat radiating out again, not just to the starry sky, but into that small cell where we lay in our Y-fronts on top of sleeping bags and dripped in sleep-destroyed misery. Then we began to scratch. We began to scratch with the sort of crazed enthusiasm normally reserved for inescapable midge assaults. Our torch beams picked out the enemy—bugs, of scuttling, hairy repulsiveness, some cigar shaped, some round and flat, the latter being the airborne division for they crawled along the beams and then dropped on us. We built a wall of DDT powder round our Li-los and sat gibbering on those, watching the brutes wade through this defence which might as well have been caster sugar. We belted them as they came out of the cracks in the wall, we fought them on the floor, we fought them on our bedding and on our bodies, we fought them to the verge of sanity. It was a night to remember; only when the heat had dispersed and the frosts brought relief did we have a few hours of nightmare-ridden sleep. "Was it just a nightmare?" someone asked on waking. Then we saw the scores of purple blood blotches on walls and floor. It had been real enough. To reassure, that is the only such night we have ever experienced in the Atlas.

Years later, post DDT, I thought we might as well have some anti-insect powder for dusting sleeping bags, on the rare but annoying occasion when a flea came aboard. I happily went into my local Boots the Chemists and asked if they had flea powder. It was curious how the customers crowding round all took several steps back! I was told I needed the pet shop. Well, *Bob Martin's* does excellently. For GTAM I thought it might be a good idea to carry hair-clippers. City barbers are expensive and we weren't going to be in cities anyway while the incidence of ringworm and other nasties made the *souk* barber a doubtful option. Hairdressers at home gave up hand clippers long ago and I'd asked several before one gave the same answer, "Try the pet shop". So somewhere along the GTAM I could hand the clippers to Charles and say: "Pretend I'm a poodle".

Jbel Tichchoukt's highest point may only have been 2794 m but it was an 18-km sprawl. Peyron warned that the western end peak was off-limits because of military installations but we took this to mean the peak's summit, not the flanks which we traversed. Fortunately we passed on a Saturday while everyone was watching an important national football match on TV. We weren't arrested.

We took a couple of hours to gain the high point of the long corridor flanking Tichchoukt. The stream shrank very slowly and the landmark of a solitary dying cedar never seemed to come nearer. The col itself bore the name Foum Bessene (Bessam), a wind-seared *altiplano* with a cemetery unlike any we've seen elsewhere. The graves were all cedar board coffins, now above ground level, the wood dry and shrunk and the contents long gone. A sad percentage of those strange coffins were miniatures. A small dry stone hut had a half tree trunk as a seat where we had a rest out of the bullying wind. There had been cultivation during the ascent, and for the following two hours we walked through new green pastures. The vegetation was lush enough for brilliant poppies, adonis and other weedy flowers. The next two hours didn't appear to change the scenery, always the mark of big landscapes. New houses and a few grazing mules were the only signs of life. Our lunch stop was on another draughty watershed and we cringed by a ruin to eat oatcakes and *Kiri* cheese, feeling very small and immaterial, like a sweetie paper blowing along a promenade.

As we began to lose height the landscape became well watered, there was a confusion of new *pistes* and even signs of tractor ploughing. We found the correct path up to the county town of Boulemane and scored a big arrow and an H in the soil to indicate the route for Ali and Hosain. We passed an old oak with a vast girth that leaned crazily from the slope to give blessed shade. There were strong scents of box and juniper, the sweet and the tart, these plants seemingly enjoying the limestone slopes especially. Round a corner was a hidden cirque full of grazing flocks. A few trickles ran down before suddenly exploding into a huge flow with a strong resurgence. We marked some other path divergences up to a last pass from which a 3-km scarp-demarcated valley ran, steep and straight, down to Boulemane. A small saddle on this route held a cluster of military installations and oil drums. We tiptoed past and the mules came innocently after.

We paused just above the town at a *source*, almost afraid to cross a *goudron* (tarred road), the first we'd met since leaving Bab Bou Idir, being one of the great north–south routes from Fes to Midelt, the Tafilelt and the Sahara. The French had made Boulemane a garrison town, as a cemetery indicated, but traders, slavers and armies must have used the route over millennia. To the north and west lay a country scattered with many *dayat* (great bird-watching lakes) and the twin towns of Azron and Ifrane, built by the French in Alpine style with red-roofed chalets and palaces. In high summer, the government would retreat to these cooler hills just as the British would leave Delhi for Simla, a fantasy made sharper by seeing the cedars as deodars and the name Imouzzer-du-Kander on the Fes road came out as Kandahar. Hidden in the forest is a small ski resort, Mischliffen, where one of the tows operates on the inner slope of a volcanic vent. Years before, Charles and I had made a long ski tour over that landscape. Volcanic hills with snow was a strange combination and the unreality was made complete by having troops of Barbary apes trundling across our ski tracks. The P20 northwards goes through Sefrou (a neat and delightful town) before descending to the Saïss plain and Fes so Boulemane was once an important post on the royal *Trik es Soltan* trade route with the Sahara.

Thirst took us to Boulemane, down a pine-clad dell, to a cheerful café with a garden and tables shaded by gaudy umbrellas. The speaker was blaring out a tape of Andes music, which I recognised as one I'd bought from Peruvian strolling players in Warsaw! We had another coffee down in the square beside the mosque. There are no hotels in this busy market town and the tourist passes by; the very lack of pretension makes it interesting. We bought a load of vegetables and hot bread. Returning to the *source* we found Hosain waiting patiently. Ali eventually arrived with a small *charette* (barrow) with supplies. Taza and Tamri were glad to get stuck into some grain and straw. Their feeding is carefully regulated. Ali explained the details once but, never our concern, I've largely forgotten the facts although too much liquid and the wrong ordering of their food could have serious consequences. Mules, we were discovering, were as complex as motorcars. By Boulemane they were ready for servicing.

The owner of the terraces offered us an empty house but we liked the site so camped. It was strange to have the headlights from night lorries sweeping over the tents, lorries lit like Christmas trees with red and green lights. We were left to keep an eye on the *tagine* while Ali and Hosain vanished to the *hammam*. Hosain led us there later for our turn. The water went tepid but the room was still hot and steamy so our cleansing went well enough. We demolished the last of the turkey for supper.

Boulemane was supposed to be a rest day but we walked down the P20 to round the peak of Bou Beker and camp in a quiet valley rather than stay by the town. There were children about who were looking after a few grazing mules. They 'helped' us pitch tents, fetched water and were quite delightful. 'Rest day' meant we went mad washing every stitch of clothing, did some planning ahead, and much eating. Ali with a straw hat returned with a *charette* of fodder, and a shower had us rushing to rescue drying clothes. Ali dealt with half a chicken for supper. The other half hung nakedly on a hook from the apex of the tent like some weird votive offering. Planning wasn't helped by our next day's route not having a single name on the map.

Nor did much of the landscape agree with the map, but by teasing away at the navigational problems we eventually reached a long valley running south–southwest which led to the Tatyiywelt cultivations, at least mentioned by Peyron. Cows were standing knee-deep in a tarn. We had a day of bad encounters with dogs guarding isolated houses (a ski pole has its uses). Most dogs are being territorial but occasionally we ran into a pack roaming half-wild which were more threatening.

Tatyiywelt was a rare grassy site, coarsely woven and short in texture, with a *seguia* trickle meandering through. The flow was dirty but following up the course I found this was because the water had been run through a newly ploughed field, and not far above was a good *source* with water gushing out from a red sandstone gash. Having several 5-litre water bottles was useful on such occasions. Empty, they weighed little, and were tied onto the mule loads at the last minute where they would occasionally clonk against each other all day and drive the listener bonkers. If camping far from water Taza or Tamri were used to collect an overnight supply.

A cloud of about twenty ravens drifted over the site engaged in all manner of pair-bonding aerobatics. I saw the first cheery patch of *Convolvulus sabaticus mauretanicus*, so dark in colour as to be nearly navy blue. This is a well-behaved convolvulus species which forms a football-sized clump so is both a safe and colourful friend in my garden at home where it chums another blue flower we met the following day, the hedgehog broom (*Erinacea anthyllis*). Like many of the flowers thought to be rare in the Atlas, when you come on a flowering area there can be a profusion. I suspect a lot of botanists only go up one valley, find *one* place where, say *Narcissus rupicola watieri* grows, and declares this rare. However, had they gone up each valley along that particular range they would have found plenty, in every site with similar characteristics—and several apparently odd settings too. *Watieri* must be one of the most beautiful of all miniatures: a tiny pure white daffodil no wider than a 10p coin. This gem is so common in one area of the Atlas, that I once placed a bowl of them on the supper table and watched the botanists with me give the most violent double take. Plants have gone round the world as perhaps the greatest colonists of all. Fields in the Atlas are often hedged with prickly pear (*Opuntia ficus-indica,* often called 'Barbary fig'), a cactus which Colombus brought from America. (In certain areas there are what appear to be other cacti but these are a classic example of parallel evolution being *euphorbias*, purely African.)

We had stopped early at Tatyiywelt to be sure of water. We were too cold in the wind to hang around so Charles and I wended off independently and, later, chanced to meet on the hill slopes above the head of the valley. We went on upwards to see what we could see. It proved to be a complex mountain with secretive hollows, some ploughed, but with hosts of startlingly dead old cedars. Grazing had destroyed much too but we noticed the centres of the topiary-like bushes (stunted trees) were sending out fresh stems since the goats were now forbidden. Some herds of sheep were meandering along the craggy slopes. The summit—Jbel Habbid—was still tree-covered at 2447 m. Only Jbel Habbou (2488 m) a few miles off was higher, our GTAM route being chosen partly to take it in. The view was a bit hazy, a winter wasteland. The sky was like Pyrex. A strange knobbly area of marble lay north: white and ghostly. As the wind was knocking us about we lost height quickly and were back at camp in time for tea. Women in gaudy garments came and collected their bony cows from the meadow. The tents impressed us with their silent stability in the wind; even over supper we could hear the endless reeling of larks overhead, one of the day's consistencies.

Big winds usually are tailed by big wets and by the time we were abed (1930) the rain was smashing down—the sort of rain that would have Noah starting his round-up. I complained in my log, 'Two weeks, all unsettled so far'. Conditions became very cold and I was periodically aware of thunder, and of movement and voices from the *Discovery* end of the site. Some clattering of teapots suggested they were having a midnight brew.

Dawn hadn't so much broken as done a poor job of putting itself together again, and we discovered what a horrendous night the others had endured. We found Taza and Tamri swaddled in the blue tarpaulins and the lads asleep with exhaustion. Their night had largely gone fighting to save the mules. Taza had had her covering blown over her head, had gone down and been unable to rise, and young Tamri was in a pathetic state. In the tearing rain, sleet and snow ("It cried tears of snow", Ali told us) the mules had been fighting to stay alive. Sky-stabbing Tichchoukt was a white beacon and the snow greywashed the flanks of the valley beside us. Life was as unsmiling as a late Rembrandt self-portrait. We demolished coffee and jam sandwiches while Ali played his Irish tin whistle to cheer us up.

Just over a small col we came on the Lerkcheb huts as Peyron calls them, an occupied homestead with penned sheep set, like the Cheviot trig point, in a great goo of mud. We plodded past on a minor *piste*, new lines scoring in many directions, part of the effort being made to restore life to the forest. There was one big farm where seven mules were grazing on a meadow bright with buttercups and romulea. The inadequate map had us navigating carefully. Over one col we saw a steaming mud flat which helpfully pin-pointed a supposed lake on the map, and we hit the right track to head up and over the rolling, snowy watershed. We were given some bread and cheese, oranges and biscuits off the mules and they pushed on for kindlier levels leaving us to go off to climb Jbel Habbou. Climbing the highest peak in the area simplified navigation; at least one spot was certain. (There was a shattered trig on top.) In that unsettled weather we had to grab chances—'Our now/Which is all the place/We can ever be'. The whole area was covered in dead trees and, down again, we followed our mules' tracks over another long valley-cum-plateau that slowly tilted to a conical hill, Lalla Mimouna, beyond which we had told Ali they'd find our objective, the forestry hut of Aghbalou l'Arbi.

This stark *maison forestière* suddenly appeared over a green boggy meadow, red-roofed, with storks nesting on top and a line of poplars beyond. The setting would not have been out of place in *Dr Zhivago*. Morocco has such quantities of space, and variety, that it has been used for many film locations: *The Young Winston, Kundun, Hideous Kinky, Harem, Jewel of the Nile, Othello, Jesus of Nazareth, The Sheltering Sky, Sodom and Gomorrah, Lawrence of Arabia, The Man Who Would Be King, Gladiator, Babel* and *Kingdom of Heaven* are some I can recall.

Hosain came out to greet us; the mules had been stabled and tea was ready. Ali had used his charms on the forester and we were to stay. Tails of rain were soon swishing across the big screen. Ali kneaded out a basinful of dough as there was a fancy gas oven but after an hour of failing to make the contraption work, despite, or because of all the helpers, the resident old lady took away the big circular lumps to bake them in a fire. Pulled apart, hot with butter and honey, they were delicious. Bread is broken, not cut, because it is holy. When Ali spilt some flour he carefully brushed it off the floor so nobody would step on it, because it is the symbol of life. Later, noticing he still had two pairs of trouser on, I was told that this kept the inner ones clean for when he wanted to say his prayers.

We had a very sociable supper with the boss's son (the forester had gone off) and others of the family: a chicken *tagine* with a huge rice pudding with plenty of milk, butter, eggs and raisins in it and a nutmeg for flavouring. The locals added salt to theirs, sweet rice not being something they'd met before. The lanky, loquacious forester with his robber baron moustache joined us for coffee and was appalled at our planning to sleep on the floor. He opened up a room of his own house, which had a kitsch clock among lots of votive candles and natural history specimens. We were shown the map in his office with the optimistic forestry plans. Like all the foresters we met he seemed delighted with and proud of his work. Apart from the line of streamside poplars there were no trees anywhere near the house. A solar panel powered enough light to read as we sprawled on comfortable mattresses listening to the rain outside.

We discovered the effect of the socialising at 0500, when I found the door was locked and although we had a key on our side we also required an Allen key-shaped handle, which was missing. We tried a variety of substitutes from penknife to ice axe ferrule without effect. In desperation, we opened the shutters and knelt on the sill to pee into the night. At six I was wide-awake so, failing on the door again, climbed out the window and went for a walk. The neighbourhood dog was friendly. An old lady, seen far off in a black and white shawl, materialised as a stork. People consider it very lucky to have a stork nesting on the roof. When one bird flies in to join its mate on the nest they both throw up their heads in a loud beak-rattling ceremony. These Concordes of the air are often seen circling in the thermals. Old nests can be built up to over two metres high and while the storks occupy the penthouse suite, a dozen noisy sparrow families occupy the flats below.

As I could not climb back into our room (the window was too high) I eventually roused Ali and Hosain by banging on the shutters of their room. They found a handle somewhere else and freed Charles. Obviously there had been a very sociable night, part of which was ensuring we were well out of it. We tramped off across a plain to an obvious *tizi* in the hills beyond, and in that time a brilliant sunrise had turned to grey and cold. We really were becoming fed up with the endless poor weather. We took Peyron's 1½ hours to the Tizi n' Taddat and had a muddy descent to the Aquelmoun n' Sidi Ali, a substantial lake among the Beni Mguild's tribal pastures not far off the main Fes–Midelt–Tafilelt road, a spot often visited by ornithologists. On a previous May visit I'd noted marbled teal, ruddy shelduck, spotless starlings, pratincole, red kite, serin, shorelark, and several wheatears and plovers. For GTAM, the water shivered coldly and all the birds were black dots far offshore. Buzzards mewed overhead and there was a gossamer drift of lark song as we picked our way through huge flocks of sheep to the huge, derelict European-style building that was once a hotel. The only colour came from the erratic flight of a blue damselfly. Nobody was fishing for trout or char that day.

We found a spot out of the wind and all too soon picked out the blue dots of the mules coming down from the *tizi*. The lads were for pushing on and Ali was in a glum mood, which could have been partly the result of the late night. He complained the mules were starving, Tamri's back was sore again and Taza was limping on the rear starboard side. Hey ho!

We followed the lakeshore and passed a smaller lake, a water-filled crater. The sand was black and we had to pick a way through a whole array of jagged volcanic debris. We were edging along a wide strath where immense flocks of sheep were grazing. Nomad encampments were tucked in odd corners and seemed to be made of bits of wood and plastic sheeting. We paused for a somewhat subdued bread and cheese lunch. Eventually we stopped on a meadow by the Tizi Moudmam which we made 2130 m. The Col du Zad, the highest point of the P21 road to the south (2177 m), lay just a kilometre away. An old man guarding a donkey couldn't fathom what we were doing. He reiterated, "Tourists have cars". Several men were using the ubiquitous mattock to dig up the skinny roots of something like a parsnip but I only got a Berber name. The root is obviously a treat as I've seen it on sale at *souks* for a high price. Eventually Ali and Hosain went over to the road to hitch south to Zeïda in search of fodder for the mules.

Zeïda is largely a place of roadside cafés where the Marrakech road breaks off and wanders west between forested hills to the north and the huge Melwiya plains to the south, with a horizon of snowy peaks (Jbel Ayachi, Jbel Masker). We'd be cutting across new hill country to cross this road and the Melwiya plains to reach Aghbala, our next big staging post. There were a few surprises before Aghbala however.

The greatest traveller of all time came this way in the fourteenth century, criss-crossing the Atlas Mountains. Ibn Battuta (1304–77) was a Tangier Berber who set out in 1325 to make the pilgrimage to Mecca, journeying via Egypt, Syria, Iraq and Khuzistan. He then really began to travel, visiting East Africa, Constantinople, Caucasia, the Hindu Kush and India where he remained for some years serving the sultan of Delhi. He was sent on a lavish embassy to China but suffered shipwreck and disgrace. A second embassy succeeded however and he travelled to and from China via Sumatra and Ceylon. He escaped the Black Death in Syria and visited Moorish Spain. He'd been away twenty-four years! His story was dictated to the sultan's secretary in Fes and then he was dispatched across the desert (*Sahara* means desert), to visit Mali, Timbuktu and the lands of the River Niger. His journey back from the Tafilet by this *Trik es Soltan* was made through blizzards worse than any he'd met in Afghanistan. On the way he stayed with the brother of a merchant he'd met in China.

Ali arrived back in a cheerier mood from Zeïda and the mules snuffled into their food. To ensure fair rations, Tamri was given a new, decorative nosebag. Much of my time at this *tizi* camp was spent over Peyron and the maps, the former all too brief and continually using names that didn't appear on a more than usually confusing map. His west–east description reads:

'After the Kerrouchen outpost, forest trails go into some of the most thickly wooded areas of the Atlas; a matchless combination of rolling hills, stately cedars, grassy glades and murmuring streams, with Barbary apes galloping through the trees. Bivouac by the banks of the Oued Srou near Miwraghen Forestry hut. A gradual climb past wooden-roofed Timzought village onto the soggy, bird-haunted reaches of Luta n' Zad and from there to the Zad Pass and the main road.'

A longer French version of his guidebook gave more names and times so we worked out our theoretical route and had an ETA for Aghbala in five days rather than the 3–4 of Peyron. There were plenty of dots on the map to indicate human habitation, inferring water and supplies if required. Kerrouchen sounded like a minor town. The major Oued Serou could hardly be missed, nor the Marrakech road, and Ali had a tongue in his head! *Pas de problème*.

We still found it strange to hear the growl of traffic coming up to the pass in the night. There must have been a *souk* not too distant since on the Tizi Moudmam mules were coming in from all directions and being fed or tethered or, in one case, cavorting loose and raiding every other beast's food so there was much kicking and pursuing by the *guardien*, while the owners crowded into a minibus and trundled off. The *tizi* was the watershed and when our cavalcade arrived we left the *Trik es Soltan* and angled down to pick up a bold line of lakes shown on the map, a country which was lush and quite different from any we'd traversed. There seemed to be a super-abundance of water and the farms were large, with plenty of cedar boards in evidence, and pitched roofs which are seldom seen elsewhere. The first lake had shrunk to a mud patch and we swung along a big watercourse bordering a green vale, with regularly spaced farms. We could have been in the Tyrol, except for the battalions of cedar trees drawn up on the slopes on either side.

Tamri suddenly collapsed. His load had to be taken off and then put back. Ali said he was having trouble urinating and he had unsightly piles too, not a happy animal. Taza was still limping, from an inflamed tendon. We then became 'mislaid'. Our valley path should have taken us past a second lake and then round a hill to yet another. We found neither and could make no sense of the map but what we did find was a secretive hollow with a tidy village of pitched roofs, flag flying over the school and singing girls taking the cows out to graze. (In less lush areas they keep the cows at home and send the girls out to graze.) That place was not on the map either. Away to the left lay a huge area of green landscape which was no doubt Peyron's Louta n'Zad. There was a graveyard on one hill that we passed, ringed with sky blue flax flowers. The graves had proper markers and the knoll was defended by a fence. Often graveyards are barely noticed, with individual graves just a slight hump with, at best, a boulder at the head or foot, often overgrown, not being grazed by sheep or goats (of which the country has an estimated 30 million).

A cheery lad on a mule joined us for several kilometres in the required direction for Timzought, one name we could give being both on the map and in Peyron. We crossed a *piste* and our friend went off singing after handing us on like a many-legged parcel to a second man on a mule who said he'd be happy to go with us and also give us accommodation. He lived just below Timzought. "Did we want?" As the morning sky had been swamped with bog-cotton clouds and the first shards of rain were falling, yes, we wanted.

Our route led down a long spur between the Oued Zad and the Oued Serou and even the steadily-increasing rain couldn't detract from the beauty of the area: the slopes surged with cedars and an interweave of fields. Our host-to-be rode ahead, hunched into his *djellaba*, a dark shape below the pointed hood like some Tolkien figure. We slid and slithered after, enjoying a variety of colourful muds. The predominant colour was brick red, complementing the rich greens of the cedars. Even with waterproof tops, bottoms and brolly the wet began its insidious entry. The mules were soaked of course.

Down on the Zad side a pair of storks was perched on top of a solitary dead tree, like one of those religious fanatics on top of their pillar. Another big cedar was smoking among its branches from a fire which had burned right up inside the trunk. Enjoyment gradually oozed out of us. The rain seemed to be gutting the landscape. Our host never looked back. The down, down went on forever, and we were hot and sweaty in our protective gear. A village appeared. Hopes rose, and fell. Ali and Hosain drove the mules down skittering red mud and slabs on the edge of a gorge. At the foot Tamri played up at crossing the infant Oued Zad (here joining the Oued Serou) and refused a *seguia* beyond. A stiff pull up once across had me gasping and I stopped for a vital drink of water. Dehydration in a deluge was an irony I'd happily go without. A glutinous switchback followed. We dropped down to the river again, *wedeling* in the mud, but there our host came to life and indicated a farm perched above as being our desired haven. We plunged into the river to wash off the mud and squelched up to the house with the thunder banging overhead. If the initial four or five kilometres had proved four or five miles at least they had not turned into four or five hours. Time and distance are very European concepts.

Taza and Tamri were given straw in a barn then we sprawled in the guest room. Day old brown and white kids tiptoed in with us while we sat at the usual low table, painted with vivid geometrical patterns. A huge dresser filled the end of the room. Was it built *in situ*, I wondered. Scrumptious hot bread came with the welcome mint tea. There was a deluge awhile and then it just rained for the rest of the day. The snug house was roofed with huge lengths of cedarwood, still stippled with adze marks, and several wigwams of boards formed shelters for the oven, woodstore and anything else. A hollow trunk formed a trough. Later, when only drizzling, a girl went out to chop wood. She was thoroughly competent and handled her axe the way her British sister would have handled a doll. (In the Atlas, dolls are usually baby sisters who are wrapped on the back and are raced, jostled and hop-scotched without complaint.) The farm's goats had some shelter but the sheep were just penned in a ring of thorn bushes, being woolly and waterproof. I suppose human skins are waterproof too but there's a designer fault over our insulation efficiency.

The whole of one wall in the room was taken up with a loom on which a blanket was being woven, a hideous striped, Barbara Cartland pink colour. After the tea we all slumped on the cushions and snoozed but before the light failed I roused to write up some notes and try and make sense of our map and prospects for the next day. Not too far down the Oued Serou there was a bridge and a *piste* to Kerrouchen which was a name beginning to take on a kind of mystical significance. We began to hope the town might have a *hammam*. We demolished a roasted chicken and a mutton *tagine* with heaps of fresh bread, oranges and coffee. We had to have a chaperon for our late night pee call and the damned dog barked at ghosts for much of the night.

Our host gave us a discouraging forecast too—from their TV. Television is now a reality in some extraordinary places in the Atlas and the influence, as ever, is both good and bad. It can be manipulative but programmes on healthcare, improving drinking water supplies or agricultural advice probably balance appallingly bad Western movies or unending Egyptian soaps. The forecasts take no ultimate authority though and will end with *Insh 'Allah*, a let-out which the BBC might envy.

Nobody was very lively on waking. The morning mists were fingering a tapestry through the cedars and the sky was black and threatening. Surely not more bad weather? 'For heaven's sake! This is late spring in the Atlas!' I wrote angrily in my log: 'Wonky mules, manky weather, woeful walkers.' We were given ineffectual directions and at the village downstream, which could have been a group of alpine chalets with the cedar slopes above, we were hailed by a man who offered us *kebabs*—of 'pig'. They had apparently shot an *ilf* (wild boar) and were loathe to waste the meat, always something of a luxury. The man later attached himself to Ali and Hosain to become the unlucky charm of the day. Charles and I shook him off and then went astray in the forest as paths led us higher and higher before disappearing. The forest was magnificent but sprawled on a 45° slope of limited adhesion. By the time we'd slithered along and down to the Oued Serou we were at the road bridge, or bridges, for a new *goudron* crossed on a better bridge beside the old and wended up into the forested slopes. Before the sweat could dry on our backs the cavalry caught up. They'd met up with a party of Barbary apes so we doubly damned our diversion. I'd first met these monkeys (they are not apes but a species of macaque, *Macaca sylvanus*) when bird watching above Azrou. I was watching a nuthatch, a rarity to a North Brit, when there was a thump of something hitting the ground—and there was a Barbary ape having a good scratch just 20 metres away.

These are the same species as the well-known collection on the Rock of Gibraltar, which are on the army pay roll and whose presence on the Rock is indicative of the continuing British possession. If the apes go, so will the British. The irrepressible Tristam Jones (one-legged sea dog supreme and author of several autobiographical escapades) tells a yarn of how he made use of this by fixing a good price with the Algeciras police for kidnapping some of the apes. He sailed across the bay and a few days later returned with a haul of apes of all ages—a severe dent in the Rock's population. Well paid, he sailed on for Suez, noting Algeciras was yet another port he'd best not visit in future. They might just have found out that the ape population on the Rock was unchanged. He had sailed over to Morocco and purchased the apes there.

A couple of heavy motorbikes roared over the Oued Serou bridge; we could hear their din as they zigzagged up to the north. They were backed-up by vehicle support, a considerable overkill for such easy going. We agreed to meet up with Ali and Hosain in Kerrouchen. Our self-appointed helper knew a saddler there and he'd give us a room, which sounded perfect. Taza's saddle could be re-modelled and we'd have a roof if there was more rain. We ambled on pleasantly, writing a cursive route through the forest, up and up. We doubled round Jbel Tabarine, which we might have avoided had the map been clearer, but were however rewarded by the finest area of cedars of the whole trip: huge 300-year-old trees in park-like grandeur with much natural regeneration and areas of recent planting. Not for the first time we were impressed with the efforts being made to preserve this glorious asset. Looking back, the early weeks of the Traverse had two indelible memories—the Beauty and the Beast if you like—the richness of the cedar country and the continuous uncongenial weather. But eventually Beauty kissed the Beast did she not? Surely, some day, the sun would shine as the sun should.

The descent was on a *piste*, ready for the tar to go down. Shepherds clustered round a fire in the raw air. To save time, we cut off a big bend and wended down through the trees. A drizzle began and we realised we were astray again or rather that we could not fit in the reality with the map's imaginative delineation. We teased away at navigating (Charles's altimeter a useful aid) and were eventually sure again: there were motorbike tracks overprinted by boots and mule tracks. We cut more corners and came out of the gingerbread forest into wheat fields and grazings. We could see Kerrouchen. The sun shone—for that fraction of the day at least.

The sun soon grilled us and we had to take a rest and drink. The fields were edged with tassel hyacinths, tiny purple irises, poppies, rock roses, lupins and camomile. The *piste* became wickedly stony. We began to dream of a café in Kerrouchen, which sat on a compact ridge, topped by a mosque tower, and backed by a bruised, black sky that promised a thump of rain. We walked on what looked like man-made pavement awhile but was simply level sandstone strata. A kilometre before the town we came on the others. The saddlemaker seemed to have been a chimera and Ali wanted to avoid the hassles of bureaucracy so we were led off down fields and farms, well-watered and with good camping spots, to skirt below the town. We walked off the rim of the world into a jungle of oak scrub just as the thunderstorm split the curling clouds. Our 'help' said he knew a farm, and then got us all completely lost. He had light shoes and no waterproof gear or any belongings. "All mouth and no brain", was Hosain's concise observation. In a Terry Pratchet phraseology we had 'the sort of storm that suggests the whole sky had swallowed a diuretic'. The ground wasn't just wet, the whole surface was gushing water, a red flow that sizzled like a fire and tore whole banks apart to carry off earth and stones to the Oued Serou far below. The scrub tore at our clothes and ripped the covers on our baggage. We felt like we were loping through lasagne decorated with holly, becoming thoroughly depressed. So much for the comforts of Kerrouchen!

We found one farm (by chance) but they couldn't or wouldn't help. Taza was limping badly again but Tamri had more sense than baulk at a torrent of red water that we had to cross. This soaking was quite unnecessary as it was obviously going to rain at the time we caught up but I was beyond anger. A girl fetching water from a well at a second farm wouldn't take us in either as there was no man present and, for all she knew, we were *kif* smugglers or worse. However, she said we could camp in a nearby area of sparse trees and beaten soil. The rain eased long enough to rush up the kitchen dome tent and we excavated platforms and dug drainage ditches before erecting our personal tents. Ice axes make good trenching tools.

When I laid my ice axe momentarily on a hump of sandstone I did a double take for there on the rock was a small cluster of 'cup marks'. I let out a yell of excitement that had voices query if I was OK. I was thrilled, for these mysterious prehistoric carvings are distributed down the Atlantic coastline from the UK to Portugal and Spain but this was extending the range into Africa, so my excitement was justified. I've since come on them again in the far Western Atlas (Flillis), near Tinerhir, south of the mountains and on Yagour.

I forgave much for that serendipitous ending to the day but not to the extent of tolerating our unwanted guest any longer. He was sent packing. His presence had already delayed supper and our tin of turkey didn't disguise the flavour of burnt vegetables.

We went to our own tents with the rain still dancing on the roofs and puddles. In the morning we were able to dry out, the camp tree dangling sets of waterproofs as if there had been a mass hanging. The sun god obliged with horizontal shafts of light that picked out features in unnatural brilliance, delightful while it lasted. The man of the farm had returned so came over and had to be entertained awhile. We drew water from the well, lowering a rubber bucket (recycled motor tyre) on the end of a hairy rope, hand over hand. Ali went over to the farm and returned saying there were 'bad people' about and we'd best leave. As we left he was giggling and I asked what the joke was. "In my sleepy state this morning I tried to light the stove with a *Knorr* cube box instead of the matches."

The road on was a corkscrewing in and out and up and up before plunging down to a new *goudron* (a road into Kerrouchen from the Khenifra side). The cloying *hamri* (red soil) constantly built-up under our boots so progress was purgatorial. Charcoal burners were sending up smoke signals. Oleanders in the eroded gullies indicated a drier climate was normal and the fields, as usual, were bright with flowers. Among the many tassel hyacinths, I spotted one of the strange brown-flowered 'bluebells' (*Dipcadi seritinum*). We had almost descended north to the Oued Serou again, while we really wanted to cross the long, rising flanks to the south to reach the Moulouya plain and Aghbala where, come hell or high water (or both) we would stay in the town and have a day off.

We tackled the slopes from a scattered but affluent-looking village with a big school, the village as red as the soil it was made from. The southwest gables of the houses were defended from the rain by overlapping layers of oleander branches. Pitched roofs were still the norm although, after that day, there were no more. Only in a few corners of the Western Atlas was there anything comparable. Architecture is never static. Leafing through the books of the early Victorian embassies to the court of Morocco there are many illustrations of what look like simple grass huts, rather like wigwams, but I have never ever seen one.

What is very attractive today is the way, even in new towns, a distinctive style of building is adhered to. This creates a harmony we have lost in Britain. History comes into this of course. In the past, rural life was so uncertain that a crude hut was ambitious enough when there was no guarantee of taking in the next harvest or surviving the next *harka* (raid). Architects are expendable in survival situations! Climate helps too. Open courtyards, high balconies and arched terraces don't really go with our home weather. We, of necessity, enclose, look inwards and draw curtains. There, air and space are part of the scheme and the kind sun allows an orange tree or fountain in the court and walls bolstered with a shock of bougainvillea. There's a simple elegance that even opulence doesn't destroy; palaces are just such places on a larger scale and using finer craftsmen and more extravagant materials.

Such musings were soon forsaken. If clinging *hamri* mud was bad enough in descent we squelched and scrabbled and stumbled up endless field edges, periodically falling off our stilts of goo or angrily banging our boots on the stones to be rid of the tiresome weight. Rounding a spur we found we were looking down on an intermediate valley of great lushness. A woman, unasked, gave us a big round loaf of bread, hot from the oven, and refused any payment. We paused to eat it, with spiced sardines and *Kiri*. A nightingale sat on a fig tree a couple of metres overhead, throat throbbing out the variable music.

We planned to angle up to a col beside a bump which was given a spot height; I wanted a check from Charles's altimeter. But no Charles arrived. There had been a fork where Ali had built one of his thin *homme des pierres* and scratched an arrow on the path but Charles had walked past the signs. First Hosain and then Ali went off to try and retrieve the stray. Hosain and I traversed some fields to be more visible and eventually Ali and Charles joined us. The lack of a check led to a real mix up. We were aiming for a village, Arrougou, and, despite nobody about to confirm directions, we assumed Ali knew where we were going. Zigzags led to a hamlet I assumed was Arrougou, but the cavalcade went on and on and up and up, in a biting wind, crazily off course. When a figure was encountered Ali went to check and merrily led us downhill again. We lost hundreds of metres in height which we had to come up again the next day.

Fields and oakwood gave way to a steep glen into a bigger valley. Some *moussem* (festival) had obviously been held at the confluence as, from there, we were swept on in a flow of people, as if borne along in a home-going crowd after a football match. The valley was dominated by a huge scarp (not on the map) and two dots of houses (on the map), forming a compact village around a central square. A big water channel led us to it. So much for our easy half-day. The best we could do for accommodation was a couple of cell-like empty shops opening onto the public square, one for Taza and Tamri, the other for the four of us who slept as packed as puppies. The cells had the musty smell one associates with old French books.

When Ali was being shown the stables the door collapsed onto an old man so we had to plaster his shaven head. This led to a general first aid session, not that we could do much for the many *goitres* in evidence. A gusting wind made us pleased not to be in the tents. The village swarmed with children, the boys football daft but not at all camera shy and the girls with bright dresses and brighter smiles which vanished anywhere near the camera. There was no loo of course but I did not regret the early walk out of the village. The elder bush I hid behind had a nightingale going full throttle, in competition with blackbird, chaffinch, the ubiquitous cuckoo and a whole squabble of sparrows. Knowing the route only too well we set off long before the mules were ready, accompanied by some children keen to practice their French. One pointed out his little brother as "mon soeur". The cuckoo was still calling—*kou-kuk* they called it. On being told there were plenty of *sanglier* (wild boar) I asked if they shot them. A thoughtless "Oui" was at once given an over-ruling "Non" and the child received a lecture from big brother during which I heard the universal word "police". Well, poaching is the third oldest profession in the world.

Just beyond our high point of the day we cringed beside a well of icy water to wait for the mules. Girls came up from a hamlet to fill water jars and a solitary man in a red *selham* (cloak) rode down on a mule, muffled up against the cruel wind. The clouds were skimming overhead, but the landscape of the Oued Serou was also patterned with dark oakwoods, viridian fields, red soils and golden stitches of sun. Someday I'd like to follow the river all the way from source to plains, as the river runs through magnificent country and the navigation would be so simple.

The mules went storming past and we had to yell to stop them on the col. The Tizi Mouchentour was a mere dip in the crest, where cloying mud had me again swopping sandals for boots. Charles and I boulder-hopped field edges up to the wreck of a trig point at 1933 m. Windy or not, larks were singing in the grey. Pity there was no far views for big hills are hoisted on the horizon. I took a while to work out our onward route and we found the mules grazing a moist valley bottom, glad that they'd paused to ensure we were all heading onto the big plains together. From a rise we could see the road from Zeïda to Marrakech, an old, familiar route. A small *douar* (hamlet) beside it had a miniscule 'shop'.

These little *hanuts* have increased in the last decade but the stock can be limited and not necessarily on the correct side of a use-by date. However, wormy biscuits and oxidised sardines are no longer the norm and, joy to us, remote spots are likely to have some brand of *coca*. In one village I once wanted to replenish candles and asked for *bougies*. With a twinkle in his eye the shopkeeper handed us a packet of spark plugs. As there was no road, within half a day's walk this seemed an unlikely product to have in stock. (*Bougie* is both candle and spark plug in French.) GTAM had taken in, or would take in, several weekly *souks* by intent and we never ran out of supplies, but burning up energy at our rate any topping-up of sweets, biscuits, chocolate or drinks was welcomed. I am sure we came to know every brand of confectionery in the country.

Crossing the road we walked over the next horizon to Azerzou where we stopped on a grassy bank below the stark houses to picnic. A stork had set up home on a lamp with the light shining down into the nest: all mod cons. A good *piste* led us on and the day was suddenly intensely hot. Huge cumulus clouds boiled up over the plains. Our cavalcade appeared as tiny dots miles ahead to give the landscape scale and reassure us as to a common choice of route. A moving house-sized mass of brushwood materialised into a poor over-laden donkey. For a kilometre, the verges were domed with my favourite sky-blue convolvulus then a rise gave us the first true view of the vast scale of the Moulouya plain: east and west it ran as far as we could see. The map, incorrectly, gave another Azerzou below our perch. We caught up the mules by the grey flow of the Oued Moulouya, the longest (400 km) Mediterranean-bound river and the boundary between Middle and High Atlas ranges. Tamri slipped in the mud and went down so both mule and all our gear was given a coating of greywash. An over-hasty loading led to the gear soon tipping off again and to a sore rubbing on Tamri's back. The *oued* was patently undrinkable but a youth said there was good grass and a well on the other side. The *oued* was wide enough for Tamri to cross without objection. We humans paddled.

Jbel Masker and Jbel Ayachi bound the plain to the south, their snow-covered flanks visible. Ayachi to the Berbers is the 'mother of the waters' and was first climbed by an outsider in 1901, de Segonzac, one of the early explorer surveyors of the French penetration from the northeast borders. But Ayachi was almost certainly mentioned by Herodotus (400 BC) and loomed mightily for a Roman general (AD 42), Ibn Battuta (14th Century) and others on the *Trik es Soltan*. Its snowy bulk was once thought to be the highest peak in the Atlas. Early maps often put Mount Atlas against Ayachi but they also speculatively put Mount Atlas to the south of Marrakech or towards the western end, locations where snowy peaks could be seen from city or sea. The secret of the highest would be kept for centuries. Charles, Ali, a friend Len and I traversed all the summits of Ayachi in 1992, being chased off by the mother of all thunderstorms. We also climbed Jbel Masker. These, backing our view south that day, are of such longitudinal scale that they extend over the horizon to both the east and west.

Midelt, then Jbel Ayachi, was the start of a notable Willison journey in 1983. In some ways, the town of Midelt marks the eastern end of the main Atlas, but we wanted to extend our route further to take in the new Middle Atlas country. John Willison was an army officer and hit on the idea of an independent Atlas traverse. His route often differed from ours, or Peyron's GTAM, though both Peyron and he stopped (or started) at the Marrakech–Agadir road. Willison stated: 'after that only the purist would walk finally to Agadir'. The logic of this starting/finishing point eludes me. We never considered anything other than reaching the sea; after all the mountains do so! Accompanying Willison was 'a young lady of sporting inclinations but no great walking experience'. Four people commenced but, not for the first or last time, coping with Jbel Ayachi took its toll and the others fell out. With inadequate maps, no Atlas experience and a punishing summer season John and Clare Wardle had quite a rough time but, again and again, praised the kindness and hospitality met along the way. (A few years later John was killed in the Alps but his father has kindly let me quote from his journal.)

The Melwiya only irrigates a narrow swathe in this wide barren wilderness, the course marked by slim trees, lit like torches along the banks. The well was an oil drum set nearly flush with the grass but from the depths came pure, clear water. We had the tents up in a flash and a brew on when an old man came down from a nearby farm with mint tea and bread with olive oil. Ali had been rather reluctant to make contact. We'll never fully understand all the ins and outs of social life. They are a very complex people with family breeding, religious affiliations and wealth and official status all playing a part. A whisky-swilling Shereef (descendant of the prophet) with the lowest of employment may be given an esteem we'd find surprising but I'm sure a Moroccan would find the nuances of British etiquette equally baffling.

Behind us, the Middle Atlas was covered by a black pall so there was a feeling of thankfulness to be over Moulouya or Melwiya, which is how it is pronounced. (Foucauld had Mlouïa.) Our first three weeks or about 400 km looked quite substantial when seen on a road map of Morocco. Even illiterate Hosain was impressed. With the crossing of the Moulouya we were really done with the Middle Atlas, the area we'd known least.

I was pleased that, despite all the difficulties, we were a day ahead of our schedule—but the picture could change once into the mountains again. Beyond Imilchil we had long days at altitude and there would have been snow, not rain. I teased away at logistics, sprawled on the grass until a pitter-patter of rain sent us inside, destroying our hopes of a day when it forgot to rain. An explosive sunset burned golden behind the supplicating upreach of riverside poplars. Out of the north came the complaint of thunder. 'How long, oh Lord, how long?' I wrote then lit a candle and wrote for an escapist hour or two. In the morning when I shook the flysheet to spray off the raindrops I found they were clinging beads of ice. The sky was the colour of a clear mint.

Charles and I followed the Oued Moulouya for two hours, marking any junctions with arrows, but the mules still went a variant route. A small shop produced drinks and *Taggers*. The *hanut* was topping-up its stock; like a West Highland village store it didn't have much of anything but something of everything. Inadvertently I dropped the plastic snake and the large crowd of kids round the door vanished as if vapourised. There were far more paths than the map showed and we were dithering over the route when a young-looking female spoke to us—in English. She was from Rabat and was one of the local teachers. Sadly we turned down an offer of tea and, at the next ford in the *oued*, luckily chanced on our companions. The obvious peak of Toujjet to the south, which we'd half-planned to climb, never seemed to come level with us and there was another two hours of sun-tramping to reach another recognisable map feature, a side stream, the Oued Guelgou. Here we left the *pistes*, determined to cut along more directly. We also discovered a small gap between two of my photocopied maps which didn't help to bring horizons any closer. We lunched on an arid knoll. Hosain produced a forgotten radio and, perched on Taza's load, broadcast western or Moroccan/Egyptian pop to the empty world. We let the mules on ahead.

We had been gaining height steadily all day and the oasis feeling of the river shrank away for a splendid aridity. The mountains grew closer, and the huge cauldron-boiling cumulus grew blacker. We touched the Arghbala *goudron* (tarred road) briefly but walked a parallel mule track rather than a road which was spoiled by ugly power poles. This tilted plain held the upper sources of the Moulouya and ended in oak-covered crests beyond which lay Arghbala. The peaks of Toujjet and Ariba cringed below a textbook thunderstorm: the black cloud trailed long streamers of rain and the lightning flashed regularly. We quickened our pace but the tail of the storm caught us, racing in at an audible canter. A few minutes later the world was deafened and drenched by the downpour. As we could not travel quicker than the flashes we said *Insh 'Allah* and plodded on. Wearing *Berghaus* 'Lightning' jackets seemed all too appropriate. A strange monument was passed and I could only guess at a French creation marking some past battle. They were rather keen on them. We swung towards the *goudron* and a break over the rocky crest, keen now to walk a firm surface for our boots were heavy again with the instant mud. A steep pull up set the thighs screaming at the effort then we went downhill, downstream, into Aghbala of the Aït Sokhman.

The higher town had one-time French barrack blocks and there were other tiled roofs in the lower town. Being the day before the weekly *souk*, plastic café-tents were going up. On other days the *souk* area doubled as football ground. The main street was like a river and at the first café Ali dived into the insalubrious interior while we stood and dripped along with Taza and Tamri. Ali squelched back and suggested we stayed there while the mules could be stabled elsewhere. We would have agreed to anything in that discourteous wet.

Our quarters were through the spartan café (which nevertheless sported a picture of the king) and up unfinished stairs to a big concrete area with breeze-block walls. A smelly loo under the stairs and animal quarters below added a rustic atmosphere. Seedy or not, the presence of a light bulb in a nest of dodgy wiring was a luxury. We'd camp there well enough. As ever, from quite unpromising sources came food that was excellent. There was even central heating in the form of a converted oil drum, a not uncommon feature in remote places and surprisingly efficient. When Charles, Ali and I had been chased off Jbel Ayachi, a house in the remote valley to the south lit one of these stoves and with no more than half a dozen lumps of wood had the top glowing red hot so our saturated clothes dried overnight. While Hosain and Ali went off with the mules to find stabling we ordered coffee and demolished *baguettes* and strawberry jam. Later we sat on an upstairs café balcony in the centre of the town to watch life go on, rain or not. Being so utterly non-touristy a town, we were either ignored or given friendly greetings; there was not one "*Bon jour monsieur, un dirham*".

The unseasonable bad weather was worrying, for me at least, for I knew the mountains ahead and was already presuming that, beyond Imilchil, our planned high-level route would be impossible and a major diversion would have to be made either south or north—which might take us off the maps we possessed. I could spend the next day on logistics while a saddler was making a new outfit for Tamri. The poor beast was rubbed sore in several places. Reddish-brown *djellabas* seemed to be the Aghbala fashion and our café filled with as ruffian-like a crew as could be imagined: swarthy faces and bandit moustaches, exotic garb, a ready-made cast for a pirate movie. Even after all those years I find a touch of the unreal when such characters prove to be kindly, generous folk.

We took our last coffees upstairs: the roof leaked, the byre smelt, our tents (hung up to dry) dripped, the breeze blocks crumbled. Another stray man put down his bedding but was shortly scandalised by Charles's night performance which sent Ali into a fit of the giggles. Our roost may have been a dump but was dry, well dry-ish and we felt quite at home. Daybreak brought some leaking but we had a busy day. As well as a new saddle for Tamri, we had to sew up a failed zip on the big tent, buy a new basin and stock up with food supplies. Charles and I made a brief recce for the following day's departure and came back to the 'Aghbala Hilton' with built-up red mud-soles. The barometer was well down and by mid-morning the streets were rivers of 'redwash' again. When we bedded we were subjected to a timpani concerto of drips landing on dixies, pots, lids and anything else that could catch water. With minor orchestration, a modern composer could have conned us into believing we heard music. The wail of weather died out in the night, probably from exhaustion.

Sleep came with the sound of the indestructible female voice of Oum Kalthoum whom I first heard in her native Egypt fifty years ago. She died in 1975, but her tapes just keep selling and selling, far beyond numbers ever dreamed of by our painted posers in the west. This cruiser-weight figure with grey hair tied in a bun, singing to strict traditions, has outsold The Beatles. Colonel Gadaffi postponed his coup so as not to interrupt a charity concert she was giving for the PLO.

Wednesday was Aghbala's *souk* day and while Ali and Hosain and the mules took off over the first hills we went, like iron filings, to its magnetic pull. The walled area was filled with scrawny livestock and we were thankful we didn't have to buy local mules. The large number of women taking part was unusual and I don't think I've ever seen so many lorries at a *souk*. The women all wore the Central Atlas striped *handira*, a blanket wrap-around. Every *souk* has its own character but the practicalities are the same, simply being an outdoor hypermarket, selling meat (slaughtered on site), fruit and vegetables, oil, poultry, bread, spices, nuts/dates/figs, eggs, salt, mint, *sjinj* (doughnuts), new and used clothing and footwear, household goods, pottery, floor-covering/carpets, radios and cassette players, tools and windows. There are also services: cobblers, barbers, restaurants, repairers of radios, etc., while more luxury goods or gift items are available according to the area's affluence. There will be itinerant minstrels, cookie sellers and Berber jewellery touts.

Few tourists I'm sure ever see this particular *souk*. We received brief nods or were ignored but I caught the word *Roumi* meaning foreigner (the Highland equivalent would be *Sassenach*). This word has roots in the word *Roma* (Rome) which indicates the country's long independence and resistance to outsiders. The word *Nazrani* is more specifically anti-Christian yet the Berbers themselves were largely Christian before Islam arrived. (Tertullian, Cyprianus and St Augustine were all Berbers.) Quite how the three 'Religions of the Book' rub along is an ever-shifting and complex matter; the said books can be quoted to justify almost anything.

The *souk* area was tacky with the mire, but was nothing compared to the traverse along the slope across the valley. There were times we could barely move for the mud which had been well-churned by mules heading to the *souk*. A litter of floppy dogs greeted us on the col and swallows were skimming through, heading north. "They should have more sense," Charles commented.

CHAPTER 5

The Lhasa of Morocco

*The earth was originally flat and unsteady so God stuck mountains into it to keep it steady; thus
mountains are the balance of the world.*
Arab tradition (source unknown)

We had our last look at the cheery town of Aghbala sprawled below its hill, an untidy, unpretentious, practical place which we had found friendly and helpful. A man on a mule tried to give us directions, but however the paths wended down the broken slope with its scrub and erosion gullies, the eye was led on to Ksar Oumichcha. This is a town of grey-earth, with towered *ksour* (fortified hamlets), architecture more akin to the southern side of the Atlas. A swarm of kids were on the grey mud of a football pitch, the mud so clawing the ball never bounced. We found Ali and Hosain with everything off the mules, modifying Tamri's new saddle and redistributing the gear. By now we were a slick, efficient team and wasted little time with such practicalities or the regular camping.

On arrival at a chosen site we'd grab our ice axes and clear a large circular patch of its stones and thorns while the others unloaded the mules and saw to their needs, then we'd all thread the poles through the *Discovery* tent's sleeves and erect it with one of the three doors facing downwind. After GTAM, Ali got someone in Taroudant to add a snow and rock valance around the bottom which, while adding weight, made an even sturdier mess tent. We had two large gas bottles as well as a couple of small Camping Gaz stoves so in a very short time after the tent was up, there would be mugs of tea available. By then we'd have erected our personal tents. Ali and I would have a brief chat about that night's supper and then we'd largely leave Ali and Hosain to the preparing and cooking, very willing to acknowledge their superior culinary skills. Basically

63

we had soup, some form of *tagine*, and fresh or reconstituted dried fruit and coffee with cake or biscuits. To eat well is advisable. Not to eat well is merely bad organisation.

Sometimes we'd have a novelty like tins of spicy *Grant's* haggis—for which Ali had already developed a liking on previous trips. Pork products were off-menu for Moroccans so seldom practical for us, which perhaps influenced an enthusiastic indulgence in bacon butties once home. Our choice of drinks included several varieties of black or green tea, coffee (ground and instant), chocolate, *sirops* and pure fruit juices. Though using a fresh mantle every night, after supper the cooking head on one of the big gas bottles would be replaced by a long-stemmed light unit so we could read, write and be sociable in something better than candlelight. Back in my own tent, I often lit a couple of candles to write-up the day, or work on my book. After I knocked a candle over and melted a patch of inner tent, half a metre of silver duct tape singled out my tent from the others.

We had *Therm-a-Rests*, a sort of semi-inflatable roll-up mattress, both for insulation and comfort. Next to good eating comes good sleeping and our heavy, aging bones really appreciated the unbelievable comfort of *Therm-a-Rests*. Our simple *Arthur's Seats* were a last minute addition which became another everyday blessing: a simple foam-padded canvas back and bottom, with adjustable straps to vary the angle between, which formed a seat (with back support), thus making sitting around far more comfortable. We used them outside the tents, during supper and in our own tents, carrying them about and as attached to them as French tourists to their bottles of *Sidi Harazem*. Ali and Charles had good sleeping bags and I should have had one. Somewhere along the way Hosain had bought some horse-blanket material to go under the mules' saddles and I made up a rough 'bag' of this to counter the cold spot under my hefty hips, otherwise I just donned all my thermals and slept in my bivvy bag. Only on a few nights was this inadequate. The others didn't know of my lack until long afterwards.

Ali, Charles and I all had *Petzel* head torches and the usefulness of these was constantly being noted so when the first group left we arranged for one of them to leave Hosain his head torch too. Both Charles and I had *Opinel* knives, simple blades, with collars to stop accidental closing. We'd acquired our knives in the Alps decades before and, as Ali and Hosain were constantly borrowing these for everything from cleaning carrots to harness repairs, we brought two back from Spain for them during our break. A year after the trip Ali commented that one of the special things about GTAM had been our equality in equipment and clothing as in anything else. Everyone felt they mattered.

I was usually first up in the morning, a sin which my companions tended to tolerate as I'd take them a cup of tea in bed, but this in itself is a crafty method of rousing people: hitting them in the bladder. Usually the items required were left handy and I'd light stoves and brew without rousing Hosain, take Charles his pint of tea and then we'd chomp our way through our bowlfuls of muesli, a gastronomic challenge to start any day. If we were lucky there was fresh bread or old bread toasted, with plenty of margarine and *Aïcha* the popular marmalade. By the time we'd struck our tents Hosain was usually stirring. Hosain was always busy, a cheery hyperactivity, thank heaven. Ali was not so good in the mornings and it was best to agree the day's doings the night before. We were always surprised on how many nights some local—or locals—would join Ali and Hosain in the large tent and there would be endless rounds of mint tea and gossip long into the night. The Berbers are a marvellously sociable people anyway but Ali has a special talent of making friends wherever he goes and his choice of Hosain, as our fourth party member, was perfect.

In many ways the long trek must have been an extraordinary venture for Hosain, a middle-aged, illiterate, small farmer responsible for wife, four children and parents but nothing ever fazed him. He became very dear to all of us. Staying in Hosain's delightful home a year after the trip he and Ali would reminisce by the hour, the memories wrapped in happy laughter. Nothing would ever be the same again for any of us but only after that interval did we realise just how special the trip had been for them.

Charles and I liked to set off early in order to break the back of the day's walking before the heat became too punishing. Often enough there would be a demanding *tizi* to cross or a big hill to climb and going east–west, the sun would be on us soon after rising. Walking west–east, many hot slogs could have been avoided, which we knew, but still preferred to walk to the sea, a psychological and romantic decision we never regretted. Two or three hours into the day, however, we'd invariably glimpse the distant dots of blue that indicated the mules catching up. They didn't appear to hurry but they moved faster than we cared to. Sometimes we would then travel together or keep in touch at least, share a picnic and brews but, in the afternoon, they would shoot off ahead and we'd meet up at an agreed camping spot. There was often an amount of uncertainty about this in country none of us knew but Ali and I seemed to almost read each other's minds and we always ended on site. There was never any rigidity in our days and it was a measure of our confidence in each other that we could have such flexibility. We had a deep respect for each other, and for the tough world we journeyed through. We deserved each other.

From Aghbala we were aiming to intercept the road from the north (Kasbah Tadla and El Ksiba) to Imilchil. Aghbala is on a tarred spur road off this, a loop which continues to the Zeïda road though few maps show a *goudron*. The tarmac on the Imilchil road continues some way beyond the Tizi n'

Isli and then ends*. The *piste* onwards is of variable standard and condition. Water is the engineer and, quite unexpectedly, that day was to see water dominate progress.

We crossed a bridge beside a water trough on leaving Ksar Oumichcha to undulate through oak forest without going astray. There were distant views of Jbel Masker and white Ariba in a tumble of cloud before the path twisted down to the Assif n' Ouirine, a wide grey flow which Tamri crossed with no hesitation at all. Ali and Hosain perched on the rumps of the mules to cross dry shod and we were left to paddle. Charles is not happy with river crossings but I tend to regard them as a welcome cooling of sweaty feet. My feet are also more attuned to hard use as I go barefoot whenever possible. Charles's sandals were on the mules and his slow *pas de bas* across made a useful foreground for photographs. Luckily there was a gravelly-sandy riverbed. Over a spur, which was simply a crest between confluences, we repeated the performance with the Assif n' Ougheddou, river number two.

The continuation looked simple enough on the map: the path crossed the *oued* and then passed one gully to head up the next. However, there had been some large-scale reclamation work with new fields carved out from the bend in the river and we crossed higher up than expected. Seeing a clear path heading up, Ali and Hosain went charging off for this. The appearance agreed enough to fool us all but when the path had twisted high up a spur through oak and juniper and bore off left we knew the route was all wrong. A cliff edge on the right confirmed this. The mules were pretty effective but 400 metres of abseiling might daunt even them. We looked from a great precipice over the Ikassene valley basin—our objective—but there was nothing for it but to wend all the way back down again.

There was a unanimous call for a break as we were hot, sweaty and disgruntled. Ali sat over a *Casa Sport* (cigarette) and the others just sat so I headed up the shingles of the gully behind us with a mix of logic and intuition. The shingles had been newly laid by a spate and ran up between sheer walls but there was one set of prints and, on a ledge on the right wall there were mule droppings. A path. There was also clean, clear water. I returned in a happier mood and we headed off up, mainly on the bed of the gully but, where blocked, there would be a twist of path on the flanks. We drank our fill. The late afternoon sun was desperately hot so the climb was exhausting. At the eventual col the cairns were made of a mix of juniper wood and stone. Beyond, lay a world as bleak and barren as could be imagined and, while all we longed to do was stop for the day, we had to thread endless bumps of grey shale and shingles, with remnant oaks and a few of box and never a sight of drinkable water. Even Ali seemed weary and asked me what we should do. Across the Assif n' Ikassene I could

---

* It is now tarmac almost all the way to Tinerhir.

see a house so I suggested if people lived there water had to be available. We could ask. "Maybe it is empty", was the discouraging response but, as if on cue, a puff of smoke rose from the interior. "But the river!"

"We have to cross sometime so now's as good as any."

So the third major river of the day was paddled. I don't think one member appreciated a book describing such crossings as 'jocular'. We found a threshing floor which would make a good site and Ali soon made contact with a local and found the essential *source*, a supply ten minutes downstream, so while Hosain went off to fill every container possible we went into the usual routine of pitching camp. We'd downed our welcome pints of coffee when the hospitable local came back with a tray of tea and fresh bread. After a second pint of coffee I went for water, a slow process as only a mug could catch the small flow. The day's route had been quite a yo-yo, trekking at its best, and would have been perfect without the energy-sapping erroneous ascent. Big cumulus skies had dominated all day and we nearly had rain. However, the heavens cleared meaning we were able to take the lamp outside and relax over supper. Silent lightning flickered to the north, and Bou Guanfou—the hill which we'd half climbed—formed a black wall to the stars.

A warm night with heavy dewfall was a novelty. We ambled on separately, my route taking me down to a newly planted onion patch by the river's edge and a hollow trunk acting as a *seguia* bridge across a side gully. I was always impressed to see how every possible corner that could be watered was brought into use. I followed the gully up but the eroded interior was just as difficult as staying by the big loops of the river, so I was forced over to walk the Imilchil *piste*. Proper roads felt like arrogant assaults on our pedestrian peace. Two yellow dogs were playing 'tig' through the boxwood slopes below and several rollers were working along yellow-flowered berberis bushes. The *piste* twisted up to a village: Ikassene.

We'd once lunched in a nomad tent there. The tatty tent had gone but the Café Atlas produced a 1½ litre bottle of *coca* and sardine sandwiches. Round the school came a boy on a donkey with rubber-tyre jars for water slung on either side. Exactly the same had happened five years before— and it was the same boy. The lad at the café must have wondered how many more were coming as first Charles arrived, and then the rest of the gang. Tamri lay down, fully loaded, which was not a welcome gesture: it meant an extra unloading and loading would be required. Five 4 × 4's drove past without even a glance from the occupants. A chuckle of choughs was pleasanter company.

The whole area is dotted with a mix of natural woods and forestry plantings, which mercifully are never planted in the claustrophobic ranks of home. Each tree is set in a small, rain-catching hollow, often in a scar gouged across denuded slopes and eroded wastes. The forestry officers have done immense work in stabilising the landscape by planting pine (Aleppo pine mostly, a species that can stand drought) which are now beginning to look like real trees. Here and there the web-like nests of unwelcome pine processionary caterpillars are noticed, a Mediterranean pest. Jean Fabre's book, *The Life of the Caterpillar*, is worth reading to learn about their extraordinary habits of nest-building and going for long walks in a line, all nose to tail. They are highly poisonous, a practicality noted by the Borgias, while the hairs are used in itching powder, enjoyed by generations of nasty schoolboys.

We continued on in steadily deteriorating conditions and had to paddle a wide gravelly side stream that crossed the *piste*. The mules went past with their accustomed nonchalance. On went waterproofs. Five bikes snorted northwards in a gorge section where the *piste* had been largely washed out. There were many such sections making the route a much tougher proposition than on the previous November. Where fields could be carved out, fruit was growing. A couple of hours later we stopped for a stand-up bite beneath a thorny tree, keeping the picnic food dry under my brolly. Somewhere nearby we must have camped by the Assif Tassent on our previous trip but I couldn't recognise the site, so much had been washed out.

Two boys hovered about, too shy to speak. We hoped they were messengers from Ali; they were but more effective in conveying the message was the Ali-style *homme des pierres* by the side of the road where there were some houses. A house? Praise be! From feeling like flounders on a fish merchant's slab we were soon in a comfy guest room sipping tea and juggling with bread which was too hot to hold. Ali and Hosain had been welcome the more readily because our host had noticed us all at Boulemane. The guest room had sturdy beams on the high ceiling and the dresser on the end wall had been painted in brilliant diamond patterns. We looked at family photographs and were made very welcome, as ever. The rain continued on and on, into dusk and dawn. Camping would have been rather unpleasant. We felt honoured with such hospitality, in a house most passing tourists in their 4 × 4s wouldn't even glance at. Dervla Murphy in her cycling epic *Full Tilt* makes the point when describing a poor Afghan house: '…What some might describe as poverty…I prefer to call simplicity, since poverty denotes a lack of necessities and simplicity a lack of needs.'

We set off in a breeze, warm and young. Above, the stark trees were tearing at the shawl of mist on the crags. The river was flowing like an over-watered concrete mix, both in texture and colour. As we strode out (for warmth) the clouds began to move, teasing in and out of the rocks and revealing striations of snow not far above. At Tassent, the atmosphere changed instantly, our valley twisting sharply south and the eye being led up many steep side valleys with gushing waters and clinging attempts at life. On the previous trip, I'd seen a huge herd of camels at the foot of the Assif n' Tassent gorges and we'd walked up until the sheer rocks barred all progress before toiling up a goat path to regain the motor road. The *piste* sufficed this day, however, and we cut some corners and played dodging games with overloaded *camions* (lorries) grinding up for the next day's *souk* at Imilchil. There were always yells and greetings and good-natured banter from the people perched on those tough vehicles, which have so frequently displaced camels and mules.

Some cyclists coming down into Tassent from Imilchil told me of a near fiasco they'd had: there was a chain across the road so tabs could be kept on motorists but the bikers coming down at speed only saw the chain at the last moment. They took avoiding action that had some up the bank to the right, some off the road to the left and one just making the narrow pedestrian gap. Our quiet passing failed to rouse the *guardien* but he came running after just to say hello and welcome. ("Trekking very good.") There was a *maison forestière* and some grassy flats below an area of mature black poplars with silvery-white trunks that would have made a delectable campsite. Odd granite boulders lay on the slate-covered ground and, across the valley, there were thin, high falls and vertical strata accentuated by the touch of snow. The long climb up went easily enough in the coolness. However, the traverse thereafter impressed as the edge of the road just dropped sheer to a churning gut of water among the dark rocks of a gorge.

The Tassent traverse ends at an old monument, quite a viewpoint with a valley of unrelenting barren-ness running up into the hills to the south. The whole area gives the impression of a geography class who'd made a complete mess of sticking a model's contoured layers together: strata bandings stand on end or twist and contort as if tortured in their creation while some form complete circles. "What a land to travel through", Charles commented, "So very different from anything north of the Mediterranean". Louis Neltner's much-quoted comment was: '*Il n'est plus beau ni moins beau que les Alps, il est autre*' (It is neither more beautiful nor less beautiful than the Alps, it is different).

The road turned up a long valley to the east below a rugged scarp, the 16 km Bab-n-Ouayad, whose snowy crest kept in cloud. There's an old watchtower on the crest normally visible from everywhere, while a new mast serves to bring TV to yet another corner of the innocent earth. Water, mostly run-off from the snow, cheered the gradual ascent for us. Nearing the top of the valley, the *piste* lurches off to the south to break through and suddenly, movingly, reveal the blue disc of the Tislit lake below. 'The lake is the most beautiful thing I have seen, a deep deep blue, horribly incongruous in this desert landscape', wrote John Willison on his epic 1983 trip.

What had us staring this time was the quantity of snow covering the long east–west sweep of hills beyond Imilchil. Our planned route, so carefully studied from Peyron, went along the crests in places and was obviously not possible. Though half-expected it was still a shock, but not for the practical implications (I was resigned to making changes) but because it was so spectacular a sight—crazy ice-cream poured onto mountainy *kebabs*! Willison and Wardle went on from Imilchil to Zaouia Ahancal by the route we were abandoning because of the snow and, in July, their main concern was finding water and carrying it. (When we did that crest route later, every afternoon ended in a thunderstorm: not good on the nerves when we were the highest objects for many miles.)

Tislit is *fiancé* and nearby Isli *fiancée*, derivations lying in a folktale of thwarted love, the lakes being the tears of the lovers denied happiness by family feuding—the Berber version of *Romeo and Juliet*. The area is a famous pasturing ground with the local name translating as 'celestial fields'. Each September, there is a marriage festival when young people can come together and become engaged. If it doesn't work out, then this can be rectified without the usual channels—a most unusual set-up. The *moussem* fits in with the end of the harvest and is blessed by the *marabout* (holy man) of Sidi H'mad ou Lemghani. The girls wear sequin-covered hoods and striped *handiras* (blanket cloaks), their faces rouged and heavily bejewelled. The boys appear in spotless *djellabas* (robes) for a much-photographed scene, which has become rather a tourist spectacle. When we saw the festival (and camped there) we reckoned 5,000 people were involved besides innumerable mules and camels. It had become a final *souk* for the year as much as anything, stocking up with goods (metal troughs, stoves and lamp stands) and selling the surplus beasts before winter closed in. The scene at night was thrilling with the slopes dotted with fires, around which hooded figures grouped for supper and stories. A medieval army besieging a castle must have looked just like that. Government agencies had tents and there were endless rows of tented stalls and cafés, dominated by an eight-metre high mock *Coca-Cola* bottle. The *moussem* was a mixture of trade fair, Highland show, Harvest Festival and Crusaders' Camp. The only people who did not seem to be enjoying themselves were the male children facing circumcision.

We were puzzled by a *ksar* standing on the west side of the Tislit *lac* for there hadn't been one there when we'd passed before. This proved to be a new *auberge* of character where we sat on the terrace over welcome drinks and enjoyed watching the noisy erection of a nomad tent preparing for the tourist season. There seemed to be six workers, ten gaffers and a hundred opinions. I suggested our *Discovery* was a much easier option. We paddled among homely coots, grebes and redshanks. A black kite ghosted along as we watched the two blue dots that were Taza and Tamri descend from the *tizi*. They grazed while Ali and Hosain joined us for coffee. Tamri disgraced himself by lying down again. The lads didn't spare the rod. "He is young mule and has to learn", Ali explained. "Bloody teenager!" Charles added.

With considerable regret we left the Auberge Tislit but we had carefully planned to be in Imilchil for the *souk*. They are always an interesting sight and we could re-provision mules and humans for what could be difficult days ahead. An hour's walk took us to Imilchil and the Hotel Atlas which stood right above the market area. We unloaded and Taza and Tamri were led away. Over drinks, the patron slowly thawed when he found I was a contributor to *The Rough Guide*, knew Peyron and Zaïd (a local) and had been there before. He even suggested we might like baths. We liked. The bath proved to be a huge galvanised basin into which buckets of hot water were poured. This was set up in the loo cubicle (the usual hole in the floor variety), so we could splash away without restraint. Apart from the icy draught we all enjoyed our baths. My description of Imilchil being the Lhasa of the Atlas brought chuckles to two French cyclists who were half-way between Paris and West Africa. They couldn't even afford the hotel but were having some repairs on their cheap bikes as they weren't taking the hammering too well. One bar bag was also needing repairs—a supermarket hand-basket. I worked on forward plans until called to supper, which was an enormous *tagine* liberally sprinkled with olives, then retreated to work on in bed as someone had managed to make the dish aerial work. The TV on full blast made conversation and even thinking impossible. The Lhasas of the world are becoming dreams again; banal TV is the reality.

The *souk* (Saturday, 22 May) was in full swing when I went out at 0630 with the area immediately below the Hotel Atlas crowded with the buyers and sellers of sheep and their docile beasts. The sheep sale was a casual, friendly affair with knots of figures coming and going, chatting and quoting prices until happy. This would be followed by a slapping shake of hands and a few sheep would be dragged away by a string tied to a leg. Most of the men wore the dark brown *selham* (cloak) with here and there a startling red. They were lean, hardy figures with faces as weathered and hard as the landscape itself yet they had the manner of kings. Red Bedford *camions* were arriving continuously and off-loading people and goods. Many metal boxes are left permanently on site to save carrying in goods every week. We were amused to see the variety of old oil drum or unused sardine tin sheeting they had been made from. Stoves, made from old barrels or paint pots which are popular across this end of the Atlas, were on sale, in all sizes. An armada of tents in raw canvas material was arrayed in haphazard fashion and, beyond, rows of gaudy clothing displays.

Hosain helped Charles buy a dark brown *djellaba*. I sat in a corner café for an hour trying to photograph the girls, each wearing a striped Imilchil *handira*. Later I bought one for myself and Hosain gave me full marks for not paying too much. Since female garb is invariably draped and belted or pinned with a hefty *fibule* (brooch in decorative work), there is little knowledge of sewing, which tends to be done by men at these weekly gatherings. (In the Bou Guemez the men traditionally wore striped woolly long johns in the winter and, like farmers in Scotland a century ago, they were donned when the frosts came and stayed on until the spring.) The heavy jewellery often has magical numbers and patterns involved, the number 5 for instance being regarded as powerful and exemplified in the stylised Hand of Fatima motif. What people wear changes, however. Photographs taken a century ago show men in *haiks*, like Roman *togas*, but this garb has gone. Few now wear the baggy trousers (*sirwal*) which, in Turkey, I was told were so designed as people believed the scriptural prophecy of the Messiah being 'born of man' was to be taken literally. In my lifetime, the *djellaba* has been adopted by women for street-wear and the wearing of daggers and satchels (*choukkara*) has almost disappeared. ("Say, Wilbur, it's cute; out here the men have the handbags.")

Hosain and Ali did the provisioning necessary to see us through to Zaouia Ahancal. We had two weeks to win through to the Bou Guemez to meet up with the first of the groups of friends who'd join us along the way. At Imilchil we were 300 miles up and had completed a third of the journey although we didn't know it at the time; statistics were only kept out of duty and for retrospective interest.

We had a filling *cous cous* for supper, a dish which can have endless variations. The grain often marks some of the year's domestic ceremonies, for example *cous cous* (uncooked!) being thrown over newly wed brides. Replete, we crowded around the barrel stove in the Hotel Atlas: Moha our host, Zaïd, a local trader, we four and the village idiot who took a shine to Charles. Zaïd had been a lecturer at the School of African and Oriental Studies in London for some years, but now runs a butcher's shop in Imilchil, considering his life all the better for the change. The promise of the big city proves a lie to so many.

Years ago, when Charles and I were coming out from climbing M'Goun we stopped off at one of the first villages in the hope of hiring a mule to take over the rucksack-carrying. We interrupted Koranic school lessons to be well entertained by the teacher over tea and then a *tagine* lunch. Our host had surprisingly little French so a boy who had gone to school in Casablanca was fetched from the next village to act as interpreter. The lad kept admirable aplomb, even when translating the convoluted dirty stories. From the teacher, we learned of America's bombing of Tripoli and, when we asked what he thought of that, the reply was a shrug and a comment on the lines of 'a plague on all their houses'. He had lived and worked elsewhere but had sought this spot in the end for the quality it gave to his life. "I have peace, messieurs." Lucky the man who knows it.

Our journey perhaps gave us something of the best of both worlds. The telephone didn't ring very often! But time and again I hated moving on from a site or place which was unusually beautiful or interesting, despite the poor weather. An amount of pertinacity (bloody-mindedness) is a necessary part of an expedition such as GTAM. There's a French saying I often take out of context: 'The young aren't onto it and the old aren't up to it', which left us in happy possession. Another saying I trot out regularly is that 'Experience is the sum of near misses'. We'd come through and were now on a plane of fitness (bodily and mentally) which we'd probably never known before—and would never know again. We'd taken in quite a few holes in our belts.

As Imilchil is located in an east–west lying valley, it experiences sunlight both early and late. The grey and tawny towers take on a romantic brightness touched with reds and golds, and the riverside poplars turn to flaming torches. A fair number of these old *ksour* (fortified houses) survive with imprinted patterns round the tapering tower tops. Modern government buildings have been built in matching style. The smoke rising from early morning fires gave weird *contra jour* effects—out of which came Taza and Tamri who'd been stabled in the next village east. They were given some wiry grass to eat while their loads went on. Taza managed to reach round and steal some from her own pannier. The two boys who helped Moha reminded me of the lively pair who served T E Lawrence in the film (some of which was shot in Morocco): one had a long nose, was gloriously ugly and swanked about in a red *selham*. (Cloaks were much in evidence over our stay because of the icy winds.) The boys scrounged some money and cigarettes on parting.

During our first hour or two we headed westwards where the villages were regularly spaced along the valley, their surroundings green and loud with spring birdsong. A Moussier's redstart (*rubiette* in French) flickered ahead of us. The river was already wide and deep, the *Assif Melloul* (White Stream), a river of great character which drains the country of the two lakes and other big basins lying through the hills to the south. Simply following the river west was not an option as some of the wildest canyons of the Atlas gulp down the river and the diversions are never less than difficult, even without the wintry conditions. Our original route crossed the *oued* three miles out of Imilchil and climbed to the crest of the long watershed ranges lying to the south, staying more or less high (when not on the crest itself) to pass remote Tafraoute n'Aït Abdi, and then a tough pass to Zaouia Ahancal. Tafraoute must be one of the most isolated hamlets in the Atlas. The whole country between Imilchil and the well-known Bou Guemez contains some of Morocco's wildest and most spacious landscapes. We were glad our fitness had gone up to a higher plane; the landscape was doing the same. There was also an option of outflanking the snowy crests by going much further south, touching the upper Dadès country and Msemrir but, having had many visits to the marvels of the M'Goun, Dadès and Todra Gorges and their peaks, we chose the unknown northern bypass from Imilchil—to be well rewarded.

Our major sadness lay in missing any encounters with the nomad families, a feature of the

Central Atlas, who would now be drifting up from the desert south. To meet a whole family on the move, their tents, belongings, infants, puppies and poultry on camels and mules, everyone else afoot, with accompanying flocks and herds, is to step back centuries. Thus Abraham must have journeyed thousands of years ago. But even this system is changing; the previous autumn we met a *camion* descending the Todra Gorge which had all this array on board, the beasts in two layers and all the family goods on top. Perched at the rear a superior-looking dog gazed down his nose at we pedestrians left in their tail of dust.

After an hour of easy walking along by the Assif Melloul we began to swing up dry country leading to scarps and towers of red rock. The other pair caught us up but four heads still couldn't make the map clear. We seemed to be on a route from nowhere in particular to nowhere at all. The path shown on the map ran on to dip into and follow a valley to a village Tastaf; instead the path we were on curved up behind a flat-topped conical hill, then zigzagged up a scarp onto a big, open plateau where the air was fresh and the terrain was bright with flowers. There were flocks grazing and shepherds' houses made of neat stonework. The views were immense for this really is the Tibet of the Atlas. We were joined by a direct up-and-over path from Imilchil which Peyron described. For most of that day, however, Peyron was merely another distraction as he used endless names, none of which appeared on our maps. We went over a small *tizi* and then down a stepped shaly spur to discover Tastaf and, there, away down the valley to our right, was the monument on the Tassent road we'd passed two days before! The path beyond Tastaf was shown on the map as going up the spur beside a gorge, but the spur was a rocky bulge and patently impassable. A shepherd then told us the continuation was up the gorge itself which proved to be delightfully small-scale with the path criss-crossing the stream and with odd corners of green tucked below the high walls. We were seen on our way by a bevy of excited girls and had a minimalist picnic once out of the gorge: ageing bread with sardines or *Vache Qui Rit*.

The sardines were our favoured spiced ones and I told Charles of an odd experience above Lake Titicaca in South America. We were eating sardines and one of the gang, noting their piquancy, commented they were just like the spicy Moroccan sardines we knew. On turning over the tin I was astonished to find MAROC stamped on the bottom. On that same trip we visited Arequipa and when we went into the monastery we stopped in our tracks for the place looked completely Moroccan, which it was, at a couple of removes. The Spanish conquistadors had obviously come from Andalucia, the part of Spain that was Moorish (Moroccan) for 800 years. What was more natural then for Moroccan architecture to be reproduced high in the Andes?

The valley above the Tastaf gorge produced sward after sward, rather like the upper Oued

Nfis which we all knew so well until, using the compass as a check, we split off right to rise over a crest. This revealed another huge basin, a cone of hill in its heart and backed by the high, huge crest of Imghal and Messafragh. A sudden revelation like that could still shock for what we viewed was our immediate continuation: dropping down among the grazing flocks, skirting the rocky hill and toiling up to the dark crest—and then some more. There can be a glut of viewing Promised Lands.

Several of the shepherds strolled over to shake hands and give the familiar string of greetings. They had hands with fingers tough as twigs and smiles that always broke across faces of marvellous natural strength or, often enough, a completely false ferocity. No wonder the Berbers were always renowned through history for their lofty independence. The story of the conquest of Morocco by the French and Spanish is a sorry litany of heartbreaking Berber bravery as they faced new and unknown odds. Yet, who wins in the end? Two world wars and so much greed and anguish and, all the while up there, through the generations, the flocks have been led (not *driven*) by men like these. Ali shared a cigarette with them and chatted as only Ali can while we plodded on. The mules soon caught up and, on the fierce climb, were reduced to two tiny blue dots on the crest before we'd gained a second wind.

The horizontal banding near the crest eased the path's steepness but snow lay around, the wind cruel and the sky pewter. We could see the hills west of Aghbala and, beyond, the Middle Atlas looked as if it was being well irrigated from on high. The mules were waiting below, out of the wind, where there was a choice of paths and we had to decide which to take. As everything on that side of the crest drained to the Assif n'Tafenda the choice didn't really matter but we did like to feel that we knew what we were doing, sometimes. The path we took traversed along and then down a long spur. On the flank, a red band of rock intruded into the grey and the path along this joint of shale and sandstone was seeping water. Our boots were covered in mud in an instant. At the same moment, two Barbary partridges went squealing off as if mocking us. The village of Ouaghad lay below so we stopped when we found an area of springs. One *source*, on the slope opposite the tents, gushed out of the hillside as a considerable stream and cascaded down into the valley. We camped with the sound of water and the fluting of owls in our ears yet again.

Two unhappy-looking scorpions were lurking under a boulder that I moved as we smoothed the ground around the tents, forming a sort of dry moat across which scorpions wouldn't be happy to pass. That was the theory anyway. As these were the first scorpions we'd seen, and would be about a quarter of all we saw, they were not a regular concern. The reality is that they are about as dangerous as adders are in the UK. The *mogreb* (sunset) call to prayer came faintly on the breeze from the village down in the main valley. God is invoked a hundred times a day in Muslim life, directly or indirectly, and we found ourselves whispering *Bismillah!* or *Insh 'Allah* like everyone else in the comfort of compliancy.

We had a hard frost and I was glad of my Imilchil blanket. While out for a pee at 0300 I found a night of stars such as I've seldom seen; they seemed to be billowing in a cloudy haze. At 0545 I heard the clatter of pots but fell asleep again until 0615. Obviously Hosain did as well, for when I unzipped the tent the steam billowed in a fair imitation of a *hammam*.

Not far down the valley there was another gushing spring which watered an isolated farm. A man digging just about took his foot off as I loomed alongside him in the angled sunlight. Whether turning-over fields, clearing *seguias* or building houses, the standard tool is a simple *amadir* (mattock) with a randomly-shaped blade. Whacking towards one's legs means self-injury is not uncommon. I've had to patch plenty of shins and feet over the years. Strangely, this implement, known from South America to the Far East, has been quite superseded in Europe and North America by the spade. I waited on a spur where choughs were strutting and squawking about like fussy clergymen. A red-stemmed berberis edged the path. Away up left were the snowy crests of Mouriq, like a breaking wave running away along the beach. I noted, "And tonight we will end *beyond* it! We cover so much in our little day's walking and still we pull horizons to our feet".

Once our cavalcade was assembled we went down and forded the stream into Ouaghad, a village of cream-coloured stonework of immaculate workmanship. People swarmed out to see us go past. As the sun had not yet reached the village the flocks were still penned. There was a lorry and we found a rough *piste* but if the road's escape was out to the north the map didn't show it and, if it was down to Anargi we were thankful to be afoot. Not far along, the valley constricted into a gorge and both *piste* and old track twisted down like a broken spring. A cantilevered bridge caught our eye and Charles and I stood for minutes out of sight of each other, waiting for the other to cross and make a foreground figure for a photo. As soon as we'd given up a man in a green *djellaba* rode his mule over to make the perfect figure. The valley opened out to a rich carpet of field patterns before Taghzout, a village of purple-washed houses hung on the spur beyond. We stopped to let the mules catch up and, regretfully, turned down invitations for tea. The village stood on an intersection of valleys and we turned up the lengthy, resonantly named Assif n'Tafenda, a valley of colourful strata and jagged bumps. We kept to riverside paths rather than the *piste*, having been left some lunch by the faster part of our team.

The last village was Tasraft, a straggling grey-coloured village with a long sunken main street where we picked up a tail of a hundred kids. A woman tried to sell us some gaudy woven material. Our tail slowly thinned as we patiently plodded on up the valley until only two boys were left, one in a smart *djellaba* and wellies, the other in tatters. They weren't begging, just endowed with enough curiosity to walk an hour up to a pass with us. A solitary building high up may have been a shelter or hospital of sorts as we found ourselves surrounded by some very odd teenagers, who were desperate for cigarettes. There were plenty of springs nearing the pass so the cultivation tideline ran high. Mouriq was big and bold above us, a huge horseshoe crest (four tops over 3000 m) that drained down to Anargi leaving the exposed flanks and shoulders mantled with snow. The kids repeated the Mouriq name to us so unusually map, Peyron, locals and ourselves were all in agreement.

A hill stood on the col and we passed to pick up the infant Assif n' Tezgui which meandered for several miles through the finest acres of green meadows we'd ever seen in the Atlas. Peyron commented sadly how drought had 'brought a parched and tired look' to those grasslands—just a decade earlier.

A small gorge ended the pastures and the *piste* swung over to start an upward traverse of the hillside. We cut straight over and found, by their prints, that our mules had done likewise. The *piste* had been deeply pitted by mule feet when wet mud and had dried into a surface that made walking tiresome, the afternoon sun was hot and Anargi was still 1000 m down in the gorges of the Assif Melloul. On our right the Tezgui became Aqqa n' Tezgui; the word *aqqa* is only used of canyons and gorges. Charles paused and noted tents down on the right. They were ours! We could easily not have seen them and were none too pleased to lose hot height gained to reach them. Ali explained Anargi was only half an hour away so he'd stopped where there was water. The time was nearly 1600 so it was all for the best. The tents needed drying out as well. Some shepherds shared our tea; they had shown Ali the pools which were our water supply. With the shepherds wrapped in cloaks and the snowy bulk of Laqroun (3117 m) filling the sun-hazed depths of the aqqa the camp enjoyed a singularly romantic setting. The shadows chased the flocks over and up the flank opposite, housed in an *azib* (goat shelter) tucked under the top limestone overhang. When out at night I saw an extra star indicating their howff. A little owl called plaintively and the frost sneaked back for brief, black hours.

The descent to Anargi was entertaining; we left the track at what we hoped was a Peyron-described path (a very minor path initially) that seemed to drop over the edge of creation. The Atlas not only has impressive heights but balancing depths—and there are no elevators between. Plateaux and gorge bottoms may give some periodic walking of an easy nature but most walking is up or down and always determinedly so. Although we were well accustomed to this, certain descents and ascents could still impress. This descent certainly did, twisting down 1000 m to Anargi and dominated by the Dolomitic tiers of the Melloul gorges, themselves topped by Laqroun. There was one farm tucked in a corner then the path inched across gullies, built-up Himalayas style, with stones and boughs of wood. A water pipe ran down to Anargi from a high spring. Another perched hamlet, Aït Aïssa (*Jesus tribe*) had several fine big houses, often so set into the slope that the roofs were indistinguishable from above. (I trotted onto one unknowingly.) Vine-shaded terraces and neat vegetable plots added a homely air. A last switchback took us over to rejoin the deviously descending *piste* and into Anargi which I immediately mispronounced as Anarchy, 'one of the most isolated village clusters in the Atlas', according to Peyron.

The *caïd* saw us signed in and there was much of the usual chatter, repeated again when Ali and Hosain caught up. We seldom told the full story, being suspiciously incredible, but merely indicated the current section of the trek. Zaouia Ahancal as a destination could be understood, Tamri, never. We were scoffing tea and biscuits in the *souk* when Ali and Hosain caught up. Not being Thursday *souk* day there was only one shop and one café open and the café owner had to nip across to the shop for what we ordered. Once a child returned with eggs, we had omelettes and noon had passed before we set off down the Assif Melloul, big box canyon country but with a well-made *piste* which snaked along the bottom. The going was hot and hard on our feet.

A couple of hours passed and we were uncertain as to where we were. We'd noted four existing and two wrecked footbridges, which hardly agreed with the map's description of two bridges. A spot 1317 m with the canyon easing off gave us a more reliable fix. Somewhere up above was Adendoun for which we wanted the correct crossing and a camp by the first water possible. An hour passed. We didn't fancy drinking the sedimented waters of the Oued Melloul, waters which we'd been on at Imilchil, which seemed decades ago. A crowd at a mill were able to confirm our turn-off but while the mules crossed, forged on and seemed to wend back and forth on cliff ledges overhead, we went on strike. We stopped for a rest, some intake of food and liquid and the chance to dry our sweat-soaked shirts. Ali and Hosain will go on all day without rest, or they'll stop and picnic at a whim. It's all much the same to them with their super-fitness. As there were plenty of flat places and even a *source* beside the river we were not best pleased at a final upward toil but we should have known better. When we topped the lip of the crags above the river we found the tent already pitched and a strange new world.

There were a couple of soaring peaklets beside the site which gave us the feeling of the camp being pinned to a Japanese screen. Bonsai-like pines clung to the crags and exploded out of the rays of back lighting. The slopes above were heavily forested with feathery Aleppo pines and the soil was brilliant red. Ali found a huge black scorpion which Hosain spat on. He claimed that would be fatal, some people having this odd ability. (I've read that, in Japan, human saliva can be fatal to centipedes.) Hosain rode off on Tamri to try and find some mule food at Adendoun, the need of mule food being the main reason they'd climbed up out of the valley. Taza was quite upset at Tamri going off. The night was warm enough to sit outside for supper. There was no moon so the stars were brilliant, the sky a shattered candelabra of lights, echoed by houses and caves on the other side of the valley. A lad stepped into the gas light with a gift of fresh bread for us.

Like a peal of bells the changes continued next day. Often travel abroad, in Africa for example, has a monotonous sameness for days on end, even when speeding along in a vehicle. I've always asserted Scotland scores so well because of the rich and constant variety of scenery but Scotland is relatively small and the Atlas big, yet there is the same surprising discovery as one moves on from day to day. To be so big *and* so varied is richly rewarding.

Just as we had circuited Mouriq, we had to do the same with Laqroun, a tighter circuit for we were technically on the slopes of the hill all day. The Tizi Hammadin, which we climbed up to then descended from, was simply a shrug of shoulder running down to the Melloul depths. We were cutting up and over rather than following down to a confluence with the Ahancal, which we would then work up. The *tizi* name was written rather casually on the map, however, and there wasn't much in the way of paths shown. But we did have Peyron and, initially, people who could be asked for directions. To begin with, we went too high and a garrulous woman shrilled directions at Ali from her rooftop. Adendoun wasn't so much a tight, cubist village but a scattering of small farms; the mix of fields, pines and jagged pink crags was outstanding. Both spotted and green woodpeckers were active and the morning chorus could have been recorded at home. There were some interesting architectural details in the tower houses, many still in use, like rows of herringbone work or dog-toothed ventilation slots under the eaves and even a big bow window on one occasion. After a long, gentle-angled traverse we looked down on a big hollow with isolated *ksour* perched among the fields: a fairy tale setting.

We then faced a hard toil upwards. Brightly garbed women were herding goats along the crags and we could hear their raucous singing while we filled water bottles at the Aghbalou n' Hammadin, the usual old sardine tin being used as a spout. Charles was in talking mode which ensured a steady pace. We pulled out of the last shaly funnel to find Ali and Hosain asleep and a pile of nibbles laid out for us. Tamri did a lie-down which roused the lads.

There were odd fields, no clear path and the crest had endless bumps and hollows, along which the name of the *tizi* was spread with more enthusiasm than accuracy. Peyron however gave a height so we wended up and up until common sense—and what was plain to see—blew a whistle on continuing. Charles had got all het-up as he'd lost sight of us while doing up his laces, stumbled among the *grykes*, twisted an ankle and broke the umbrella he'd never used for protection against the sun until then. (I used mine a lot as I dislike anything on my head.) Hosain rescued the remains of the brolly and when we stayed at his house a year later I noted the same short-stemmed brolly was used by the girls during dashes across the courtyard from kitchen to storeroom in the rain.

From our Tizi Hammadin spine we could see down to the huge feature still named *La Cathédrale* on the maps, which faced Tamga on the near side of the Assif n'ou Ahancal, where we were bound. Peyron's *tizi* height was still further up the ridge and obviously wrong. When I'd explained this, Hosain was all for a direct descent from where we were, a pushy characteristic which had already been noted (and a year later was a major cause of Taza and him both going head over heels down a hillside). When Ali said we'd go back to easier ground they had one of the few tiffs of the trip and hardly spoke to each other on the descent.

I could have wrung all their necks at that moment for the view was one of the most glorious of the whole trek, a huge panorama and, closer, facing us, towered a startling Gothic cathedral. More practically, we were being given a clear view ahead and nobody seemed very interested. The view was a sobering one for the peaks of Timghazine, Azurki and Arroudan were white as sea marks and the Tizi Yllaz, our gateway to the Bou Guemez, could well be a disputed barricade. The 'Flower' gang coming to join us might not make our meeting point by road, and they were flying out in little over a week. That our diversion had been correct was obvious as the whole southern horizon was a long white-cresting roll of peaks. 'Crazy amount of snow', I complained to my log that night, and wondered just how we were to keep the momentum going. Although we didn't know it then, that day was the start of a real improvement in the weather, and snow can ablate and melt with surprising rapidity. The scene was so uplifting (we'd never seen so far ahead at any viewpoint until then) and the day so perfect in blue clarity that I was high with delight and neither the uncertainties ahead nor my glum, unseeing companions could spoil the moment for me.

We backtracked and picked up a trail which dropped down to Tamga village (not to be confused with *tamda*, a lake), along spur and flank with a deep valley to the left. The mules' loads swished through tangy juniper and the voice of a child carried on the clear air as she sang homewards under a heavy load of brushwood. (Some of the twisted old junipers are thought to be 5000 years old!) Tamga lay on open, sunny slopes, almost parkland in character, the fields so green (the colour of Islam) they appeared neon-lit with many an isolated classical *tighremt* (fortified house), all in immaculate condition. Late in the day when the horizontal sun picked them out, the effect was vividly romantic.

Ali pushed us down to camp in rather uninspired wasteland by the river and we were there early enough for Hosain, Charles and I, in turn, to wash just about every garment we possessed. Ali said the lunch sardines had given him a headache and was 'out' thereafter. I did a major repacking of my belongings and then spent the rest of the afternoon swotting rather desperately over the possibility of problems ahead. A gentle up valley ascent to Zaouia Ahancal and two days there would give a semi-break before essaying the route into the Bou Guemez. A walk up before supper reconnoitred the route onwards and gave a close-up view of the Cathedral, soaring across the valley, an exaggerated Suilven of naked rock. The darkness always treads so quickly on the heels of sunset but the night was balmy and we dined under a walnut tree with a nightingale serenading from the riverside jungle. A few million stars canopied the site. Our diversion was proving to be through superb country. Both Mouriq and Laqroun were notable peaks, the Cathedral astonishing, the Melloul Gorges quite mind-blowing. Needless to say we've been back several times since GTAM, particularly to climb the Cathedral, Mouriq and Laqroun.

Since Tamga to Zaouia Ahancal is one of Peyron's 10 hour days (in descent) we decided we'd take two days, and good days they proved to be as the Ahancal valley was a grand highway back to the heights. My recce paid off and, as Peyron's down-valley route description was too complex to understand, we generally kept to the *piste* which must be one of the most convoluted roads ever built. We were up at 0500 and off an hour later with Hosain still asleep and Ali feeding the whinnying mules who'd already had some stale bread from us. They recognised us all right but we rather felt it was more in hope of food than with affection. Ali is one of those people who can charm animals and I've seen him quieten a kicking, terrified mule by voice alone when no one else could go near. Much of the mules' 'talking' is done with their ears as they lack facial expression. Taza and Tamri obviously had a good relationship; whenever one was away for some reason, the other would be distraught at the separation and loud in welcoming the others' return. Taza was a sedate female and Tamri a youthful male, still growing the last of his adult teeth and with a decidedly teenage appetite. Given the chance he'd always steal Taza's food before eating his own yet would object if Taza tried a similar game. Ali had originally led Taza but now he preferred Tamri for the challenge of teaching him the tricks of the trade.

The early light descended the sculpted east front of the Cathedral like water on a wall, a Turner view seen through the frame of pines above camp. I reckon we made the right choice as Ali said later that we'd gone by the old mule route (they saw our tracks), which followed a shallow gully for over an hour of unrelenting ascent. A woodman passed, axe in hand and his sack clanging on his back, and we came on him later brewing by the track. Would we like some tea?

We'd cracked the climb before the sun was high enough to find us, landing on the *piste* as it turned from wiggling up the hill to just wiggling along the valley. The endless twisting of road was hard on film as views kept being given new angles. I went through a film in each camera, wide angle and telephoto. If the Cathedral (west of the Oued Ahancal) dominated early, on our eastern side a huge scarp rimmed along above the route for two whole days, each jut a soaring Dolomitic tower, the whole a golden band hundreds of feet high, topping off a pleated skirt of trees. One area we passed was covered with acres of euphorbia, that African parallel to the American cactus, sap-filled fingers bunching up in many thousands of fist-like domes six foot across.

There was a mine on one spur. We cut the next spur and then baled off to go down-and-up instead of following the wandering *piste* through a succession of loops. Charles being a canny Yorkshire lad always has two minds about following my short cuts but to me the complicated challenge, with the possibility of erring, is irresistible. A nice safe *piste* is my last desire. As we went down at an angle of minimal adhesion and traced exposed goat tracks over shale with a similar uncertainty we stirred the adrenaline in a way the road would not have managed. Back on *piste*, the day became hot and at a side stream, the Assif n' Tagourt, we had a lunch stop and dipped feet in icy water. Two tiny tots stood and watched in solemn fashion. We gave them some sardine on *Henry's* biscuits. Their father came to see where they'd got to; they'd been suspiciously silent. Apart from two people earlier who, after asking us "Where is your car?" obviously marked us as nutters, we met no one all day.

After another short rise the walking was all gradually downhill, drawing ever closer to the Oued Ahancal. The bends were endless, however, about 16 hairpins or loops in a couple of kilometres, as the snipe might fly. We took one short cut in hope of finding water and, after an initial disappointment, found a brief resurgence and sink. We drank water. We paddled in water. We poured water over our heads. We thanked God for water. *Hamadula.*

A bulldozer was working at creating a *piste* on the far bank, then very close but when we found a cheery side stream we looked about for a possible campsite. A flattish area covered in thyme bushes under a big pine was not to be denied. Every time anyone moved the air became rich with the oily aroma. We'd no sooner built cairns and scraped directing arrows on the *piste* when the others caught up. Being only 1330 we had a very leisurely brew and relished not being under any pressures. Not a vehicle had passed all day. I meant to do some writing but somehow, a proper all-over bath in the mocking river, reading-up the route, creating a mince dish with our spices and taking photos of the site, saw the day slip away. The mules had been ridden off to Tifwina, the next village, to buy straw and a few items from the *hanut*. The last of our fresh vegetables went with the *Mince Ahancal*. Frontal clouds built up. "You don't expect two days without rain?" I mocked. "We'll have rain in the night." We did.

The Ahancal valley was altogether charming. The eastern scarp presented endless 'Table

Mountains', which reared up out of plump, ripe clouds, while the valley was one of the most intensely cultivated—wherever water could be led. The Ahansal cliffs front the Koucer Plateau of the Aït Abdi, one of the weirdest upland desert plateaux while the Talmest area to the west is still grazed, above tree level, by nomadic Aït Atta. Near Amezraï (upper of two so named) a *seguia* not only stalked over a side valley on concrete legs but also crossed the main river to water a prosperous-looking farm. We dipped hot feet in the flow waiting for the mules to catch up. They meandered along the *piste* while we took paths by the alpine torrent. Perched houses had the atmosphere of Border keeps. The valley closed in below wild mountain towers.

A dipper whirred ahead of us into the village of Zaouia Ahancal or at least to the *souk* where a corner café had cold drinks, a rare treat. Not being *souk* day there was little open and the haphazard red buildings looked like Lego that had fallen from a schoolboy's satchel. Eventually we saw some officials and did what shopping we could before returning to the café. Between *souk* days the choice of food on sale is apt to be limited but we were being fed for the next two days, we hoped, at the home of Moha Amaghar, at Agoudim, a separate village a mile further up the valley. The café was noisy with card playing and we soon went on. I'm sure John Willison found the same café back in 1983 when drinks were even more welcome. Of the card playing he wrote, 'I join in with no knowledge of its intricate rules, but twenty minutes of inspired guesswork leaves me eleven matchsticks better off.'

On the wall outside I found a huge hawk moth which must have been about 15 cm across. There are several hawk species to confuse identity. Morocco is paradise for the lepidopterist. Shepherd lists over 100 species of butterfly.

Agoudim is one of the most architecturally interesting villages in the Atlas, comprising a cluster of tall, tapering *tighremt*, many with fine decorative detail. Several houses are official *gîtes*. I estimate every rural home in the Atlas has been rebuilt or extended in my lifetime. Breezeblock and cement may be used as well as stone or simply *toub*, which is *pisé* in French. (There is no English word for this mud mix construction—not with our climate!) The proportion of earth, gravel, stones and straw depends on the vicinity but the work is just like using cement with shuttering, the mix tamped down, dried off and then another layer added.

Moha is a rotund, cheery, relaxed character with a large family. The youngest followed us about, wide-eyed with wonder. The guest room had been repainted since we were last there and a light bulb hung from an incongruous plastic doodah. The walls were a garish green on the lower half and white above, the beams on the ceiling carved and decorated in geometric patterns. Hanging from one was a miniature plough about a metre long. I wondered if it had ever been used, since I'd read how the seasonal ploughing once began with a small plough cutting the first furrow, pulled by dogs or such-like. One of my own prized souvenirs is a 15 cm miniature plough, perfect in every detail, made from twigs and roadside wool, coloured by biro and sold to me by the maker for one dirham at Tahanout *souk*. The craftsman must have been about four years old. I've seen libations being poured out at a sacred tree or rock and pieces of cloth tied to bushes, superstitions not so unknown in Europe, even today. Most recently at a *source* supposed to cure infertility we noted a crowd of women at the cave mouth, a cloth held up to prevent male eyes seeing the optimistic Bathshebas. Sneeze in Aroudane, as in Aviemore, and there will be voices saying "Bless you!"

We were staying in one of the many houses of the 'saints' of Zaouia Ahancal, the descendants of the eponymous founder. Sidi Saïd Ahancal reputedly travelled from the western seaboard and stopped there because his cat jumped off a mule, which was taken as a sign. Like Moses, he struck the rocks to bring water gushing forth (as it still does) and became venerated as a holy man and miracle worker, a *baraka* which descended in his family. Zaouia Ahancal became the spiritual centre of this remote area and its leaders the arbitrators for the fractious tribes. (Ernest Gellner's study *The Saints of the Atlas* covers this fully.) The authority of the saints was such that the local tribes united under their leadership to successfully defeat Glaoui advances into the region. The various mountain tribes formed a mosaic pattern which could easily be broken and inter-tribal wars were frequent while nobody wanted outside controls. Tribes were made up of various clans which in turn had various *ighs* or family lines. With great store set on clan loyalties and the communal *touiza* system of work cooperation, it sounds just like the Highlands of Scotland. The shrine of Sidi Saïd Ahancal (and graveyard) lies just outside the village, a plain white cube with a roof of green tiles. Green tiles are historically used only for holy places or regal dwellings. The village has tremendous atmosphere, as if haunted by the ghosts of its past. Zaouia Ahancal is a place where few, if any, Europeans had set foot before the 1930s.

CHAPTER 6

To *La Vallée Héreaux*

"You can't get there from here."
It came like a message, bent.
"You can't get there from here" –
So that's the way I went.

We had planned two nights at Agoudim and, the next day being a side trip and not part of our traverse, I suggested we allowed ourselves to *ride* Taza and Tamri up to the village of Taghia for a picnic. Ali thought, and Charles hoped, I was joking about this as the former had never known me to give evidence of any previous experience and the latter is a cautious lad. I was given Taza and Charles was put up on Tamri—two beginners together. Not far into our ride the inexperience showed, and Tamri put a hoof on a sloping slab in the stream and went down, luckily with no damage to man or beast. Charles bravely remounted and as the miles passed his desperate grip, fore and aft, slackened. "Hey! This is rather good"—especially for splashing across the river which we had to do several times as we wended up-valley. Mules don't have to keep taking off their boots and socks. I thought we were a bit like the pair in Don Quixote. (Incidentally, Cervantes was captured by Barbary pirates and made a slave, as was the fictitious character Robinson Crusoe.) Like the don and his servant we rode on, with a certain excitement, for the scenery up to and around Taghia is reputedly the most spectacular in the Atlas, a claim few would dispute.

Agoudim is a worthy start with clustered castles, green-roofed *marabout* and the cliffs of Aroudane hanging above. Not far along the way the sun picked out a massive wall of light off to the right, the *berg* fronting the Aqqa n' Tazaght. That meandering, many-branched canyon was simply the start of more and more impressive faces and spires of soaring limestone. Filling the view for much of the way ahead was Jbel Aoujdad, a buttressed and tapering symmetry of glowing rock, nature swanking as supreme showman. Taghia lies below this spire but, just as in New York bigger and grander skyscrapers followed the Empire State Building, here Aoujdad is flanked by gorges which are squeezed out like narrow streets by bigger and grander rock skyscrapers.

We dismounted below Taghia and walked on to where we'd once camped. The mules rolled about and kicked dust in each other's faces. Freed of their loads at the day's end there was nothing they liked better than a dust bath, a sight I always found incongruous. They are not built for rolling about and a mule, feet flailing in the air in an effort to roll from port to starboard and back, is a ridiculous spectacle. Taza and Tamri then began to rip up grass with gusto and an old crone came and raised hell over this. Later, her hen-pecked husband arrived, so Ali gave him a cup of tea, soft talk and ten dirhams—and the mules could eat what they liked.

The others shot off to see the start of the Aqqa n' Taghia to the right, the gorge dominated by a 600 m wall of Dolomitic character, the Tagoujimt. I went into the left fork, having had my thrills of the former before. What I found was not mentioned in any book I'd read so came as a complete surprise: the river didn't girdle Aoujdad but came out of its flank in a score of gushing *sources*, as dramatic a resurgence as any I've encountered. Some of the holes were six foot in diameter, quite a force of water, while others were a mere hand-span. All sprayed and stuttered down over rocks and screes in ponytails to create the river proper. I went up to another fork in the gorge, the prow of Taoujdat like a spear thrust of rock aimed at the clouds, pinioning the sky, while the gorges, left and right, were like prison doors. The *aiguille* of Taoujdat gives a handful of 500 m high-class climbing routes, put up in the seventies. Dippers were diving in and out below a boulder, bearing food to their well-protected brood.

My explorations over, I turned to scramble down again and a stone whizzed to crack on the spot I'd just vacated. I let out a yell in case human agency was at work but the culprits were goats grazing away up on the ledges below the sheer cliffs. Later I spotted two little girls who were herding the flock, who looked about eight years old. I'd the brew half ready when Ali appeared on the slope opposite and simply skittered down the scree and scrag like a Barbary sheep. Charles appeared half an hour later and thirty years slower. We envied Ali.

The Taghia *aqqa* must present one of the most spectacular paths in the land, the way across the cliff often created by wedging branches in cracks and piling stones on top of this insecure foundation. A vivid imagination is not an asset under these circumstances. Peyron describes the path as 'hair-raising…a Berber *via ferrata* in places'. The Gellners while staying at Zaouia Ahancal on their years of study joined up with Wilfred Thesiger and an Oxford student, Colin Pennycuick, to explore the Taghia gorges. The explorer, hearing thunder, persuaded the group to make an unwilling retreat and, safely withdrawn, they watched in shock as the gorge walls filled house-high with a dirty, roaring spate in which boulders weighing tons grumbled along as if they were chickpeas. They also tried a rock climb up Aroudane's great face and had to abseil off to avoid benightment. This was Thesiger's first climb—and abseil. They'd met up at Boumalne des Dadès and made a crossing of the high plateau country to reach Zaouia Ahancal.

At Taghia we once had our worst scorpions encounter: several were running about under the stove as I cooked supper and we zipped bivvy bags tightly that night. I was sure the hard frost would send the creatures underground—or under Karrimats. I don't think I helped by saying that scorpions were preyed upon by lethal spiders. Years earlier, a Club Alpin Français (CAF) member had reassured a visitor by writing in a newsletter: 'The High Atlas scorpions are not mortal (*sic*) but the bite gives great pains and serious disorders. Never has a member of the Marrakech Alpine Club been bitten (*sic*) by a scorpion…'

One of the female scorpions had her back covered with pale miniatures; they carry their young for the first few weeks.

Returning from our Taghia side trip, I went on ahead of Charles and the mules hoping to take photographs and walked most of the way back, only waiting for a mule lift at the last big ford. That time I was left to ride Tamri who only went well when he lost sight of Taza and broke into a panic trot. Our host laid on a vast *cous cous* for supper and, one by one, finally in droves, the family came in for photographs—even matriarchal granny. Ali and Hosain smartened up for a night out while we retreated to an eleven-hour kip, lying on our sides as our tummies were bulging and our backsides sore.

Jbel Aioui, which has been renamed Jbel Aroudane, is one of the most spectacular climbing cliffs in the Atlas. It is strangely unknown or visited by British climbers who tend to want their routes both accessible and pronounceable. Peyron gave a sketch which shows a mere nine routes on this 3 km long cliff, 600 m in height, but he warns: '[Aroudane] has attracted rock gymnasts of various nationalities, with occasional fatal consequences'. Issues of *La Montagne* show that a score of notable routes of all grades have been added; there's plenty room yet for new lines. With miles of cliffs and gorges beyond Taghia or down to Tamga and scores of other rivers, the climbing possibilities are endless. There's more rock thereabouts than in the whole of the UK. Aroudane looms over a deep glen to the north, the Aqqa n' Illissi runs up to a *tizi* of that name and over to a devious *piste* from the outside world, Aït Mhammed, and Azilal. West of Aroudane, eye-catching Jbel Azurki is also flanked by this *piste*, a branch of which skirts Azurki for a pass into the upper Bou Guemez valley. After the Tizi n' Illissi we hoped to outflank Azurki on the other side but it had looked snowbound when seen from the Tizi Hammadin a few days earlier.

Our walk up to the Tizi n' Illissi was a delight in the cool of a 0615 start (Moha had brought in hot bread at 0545) and I'd learnt some of the quirks of the track on other visits so we didn't waste time and effort straying. A finger pinnacle fore-fronted the distant view of Azella and the Tafraoute peaks we had to bypass. Where the valley grew steeper, we stopped for a snack below a huge, spreading juniper, then flanked up to a watered alp hidden away behind a spur. A snarling dog got a surprise when I scored a direct hit on its ribs with a stone—so, I may say, did I. There was no sign of the mules so we took a lazy route up to the *tizi* through slopes of boxwood. The white fin of Azurki suddenly surfed over the horizon. The *piste* drops to Oussamsouk, a small Tuesday *souk*, where the drainage from both flanks of Azurki, and several gorges and hidden valleys to the south, all converge. By cutting across we could drop into the first of these valleys to camp on a grassy sward, a site we'd christened Azurki View. The traverse path had helpfully cleared of snow in the last day or two. From there we'd see if the Tizi Yllaz (Azurki bypass) was practical. We ate bread and sardines waiting for the others. We could see back to Laqroun and beyond, a satisfying retrospective. It wasn't long before the mules came; we'd only been given a two hour start!

I showed Ali the rising traverse line off from the *piste* and we let them go on to give some scale to the scene. Azurki put a cloud scarf over her head for the camera. Jbel Azurki is perhaps best known as a ski-mountaineering challenge, as the northern slopes catch and hold the snow, an impressive sight from far on the Demnate–Azilal road. The southern slope is a steep, tiered, scree-covered horror. The *source* pools beside the camp were full of toads' spawn so Ali built a small dam on the stream beside the tents and had the water spouting from a cut-down *Sidi Harazem* bottle. Our big tent was invaded by flies and almost as many choughs seemed to argue their way through before rain drove us inside. Our supper of potatoes, onions, green peppers with beef slices (tinned) and a cheese sauce wasn't so bad for a night using up leftovers. Later the weather cleared up so there was a slither of moon, as if a fingernail had pressed on the black membrane of sky and let through a golden glow from whatever lit beyond. A big moon simply quenches the stars but, at new moon periods, the sky throbs with stars like a pulse.

Chancing that the Tizi Yllaz would be passable, we allowed ourselves a side trip and ambled off for the top of Aroudane next day. We rose steadily under a rock bulge, Waousramt, and met another path higher up where there was a large and very soggy sort of plateau on the 3000 m mark. We swung up to follow the west ridge, dodging as much of the snow as possible, enjoying the odd sharp limestone edges. After a false summit, we found ourselves on top at 3358 m. Ali, who had given us an hour's start, was snoozing when we arrived. The map and Peyron indicated we were on the summit but Charles insisted we went along to another bump in case it was higher. The altimeter gave the same height! I was content to be the coo's tail, dawdling behind, as I wanted to study what we could see especially as clouds were rolling in.

Jbel Ouaougoulzat (gargling helps with pronunciation) at 3763 m to the southwest is the eye-catcher from there, a succession of snowy summits with gashed drops inbetween. From a camp by the Lac Izoughar, a small group of us from the Eagle Ski Club had made a ski ascent in similar conditions, except there was water in the lake to act as a reflecting pool for Azurki. South from Aroudane lay rolling shaly domes and the great *aqqas* of the Taghia area. Beyond them lay another long crest of snowy domes 'of some of the loneliest and driest high altitude desert in the country' (Peyron) which we later explored on autumn trips at the time the nomads were loading-up and heading south to winter quarters. A southern bypass on GTAM would have to have found a way through that mountain maze. Looking ahead, the Tarkeddid crest was smothered in snow and M'Goun looked more Antarctic than Atlas—a no-go area for certain, but one we had really wanted for GTAM. It was a strange world, layered worlds within worlds really, with life in the valleys, seasonal flocks on the plateaux, and a few peaks like Azurki or Aroudane lording over all. The scale still shocked with its magnitude.

Azurki is grazed by the Aït Atta, a long way from their southern home of the Jbel Sarhro range. Tradition has it that Sidi Saïd Ahancal called on Dada Atta to help quell his neighbours. They took as reward the right to summer grazing on the hills. John Willison and Clare Wardle went around the south side of Aroudane on their traverse and were astonished to find so many flocks. One child sitting on a mule (facing the tail!) led about 400 beasts, all purposefully heading for the heights. Once the Bou Guemez is reached this plateaux country ends, as does the traditional transhumance lifestyle.

Ali was saying the mules were low on food which riled Charles and me for we had emphasised we should take a good supply. He suggested a raid down on the Oussamsouk *souk* the next day, so we gave him a shopping list of human requirements as well. The weather was still playing up and we were in and out the tents with Azurki clouding over steadily. In the middle of the night, Hosain began a loud inter-tent conversation with Ali (whose tent was about 50 metres off) and I stuck my head out to see if the mules were involved. They were quietly grazing, tethered to our ice axes hammered in the full length of their shafts, a use I'm sure the manufacturers never envisaged. Hosain had heard a rummaging under the pile of panniers, which lay covered by plastic sheeting just outside the mess tent. Vehicle lights on the flank of Azurki looked strange, but top evening entertainment was some rummaging of our own to catch a mouse discovered in the kitchen case. I eventually caught the terrified creature by the tail and whizzed it out the door. If the mouse had hitched a ride from Agoudim it faced a long walk home. A jackal sang me back to sleep.

A rather bored sunrise greeted us, but Ali was off at first light and we weren't long in leaving either, traversing west with some (dry) obstacle watercourses to cross before joining the Tizi Yllaz track from Oussamsouk. At the valley head, the snows had blotted out the *voie normal* track up to the *tizi*. This was obviously a regular annoyance, as there was an alternative track zigzagging up on the snowless eastern side—quite a relief after days of worrying if we'd get through. The *tizi* was cold and windswept but the view of the strung-out wave crests of Ouaougoulzat and mighty M'Goun were as astonishing as ever. The crest of Ayachi ran away over the horizon. We wandered about but there was no water in the immediate area. Charles stayed to keep an eye on the *tizi* while I ran down the dusty valley eastwards hoping for a *source* seeing there were so many *azibs* visible. Eventually I found a proliferation of small gorges running with water and sending the melt, as it mostly was, down into a deep *aqqa*, with Aroudane rising proud behind. Of course I'd left cameras with Charles and by the time I'd rejoined him the weather had changed its mind about being friendly. We ate, then saw the mules charging up not far below. "*Hirrah! Hirrah!*" we shouted, urging them on. They always seem to go at slopes *hard*, which certainly wouldn't suit us. The mules had ample food which was what mattered. And no doubt our companions had had a sociable *souk* visit.

We followed my prints back to the streams and carved out individual tent sites on a ledge above a gorge. The horizontal banding had shattered into thin slabs, which we used to pave tent entrances (an anti-dust measure) and even make troughs for Taza and Tamri while every guy line was fixed round a stone. A good wash removed the dust of our labours. After a brew we each wandered off. Charles, the summit ticker, headed for the nearest peak (Ifrilzene, 3171 m), one of the nearer and bigger of the swelling bumps of this vast plateau country). Ali and Hosain took the mules to graze a wet grass patch on a higher level. After seeing a whole lot of fake carvings (modern, mostly footprint outlines), I was eventually rewarded with one faint, decorated prehistoric disc which looked genuine. I then went a long traverse in and out the gorges, each better than the previous for sites and water. I explored a long leak line, came back up the gorge to camp and made the tent ten seconds ahead of a storm of rain. The north was black, with trailing showers.

'What a season!' I complained to my log. 'The flowers here are at the stage of Iblane and that was a month ago…A simple tagine, tea and biscuits our meagre repast while the rain drummed on the tent at our ears. Shorelarks and wheatears the only sign of life. Retire early.' Thinking out the next bit of storyline to my book was always a sure way of sending myself to sleep.

Despite the spitting grey clouds of dawn we decided to give Azurki a go, arranging to meet up with the others over the pass by Lac Izoughar which, despite the wet, was brown and dried out like an overdone pancake. We wended back to the Tizi Yllaz and then along and over tedious rises to reach the steeper slopes above. A ridge led straight up which improved with height but was abominably loose and held bottomless sugar where snow-covered. Eventually, scrambling from one ledge to the next, we came up under the ledge carrying the corniced ridge. This ran off for miles to the west, and down for a long way to the east. Charles started to kick steps up while I tried ascending with the initial help of a ramp. However, this led to a vertical wall of snow and I wasn't tackling that without some protection so, when Charles backed off his line, I went up to have a look and battered on to gain the crest. I realised at once that that was far as I was going. The miles of ridge were edged with a curving wafer of fantasy cornice and the north side was hard snow, requiring crampons. *Sans* rope, *sans* crampons it was *sans* hope but at least we'd made what could be called the East Top at 3640 m.

Shelley called mountains 'the naked countenance of earth', and they don't come much barer than Azurki, sacred summit though the peak may be. Even colours were stripped away that morning to leave the world white, black and grey. We retreated carefully. The local legend has Azurki as the chosen spot for the burial of the Prophet Mohammed. When the camel bearing the body arrived, however, the poor beast was frightened away by the din coming from harvest eve at the Bou Guemez, where the fields were noisy with everyone scaring off the birds. So, to the local loss, the camel headed back to Arabia.

We followed a ledge east below the cornice, lunched, and then descended snow, scree and other rubbish. We even sat and slid to try and hasten the descent, frightening a big brown hare. We floundered in soft snow over to the summer col, traversed to springs and began the long, gentle-angled descent to the wide valley, almost a plain, which ended in the Lac Izoughar (Izourar), a seasonal lake dependent upon rain and snowmelt.

Nearing the *lac* I was a bit disconcerted to see its size. I felt like an ant which had made Wembley a rendezvous. A blue dot in quite the wrong direction gave a moment of dismay until a look through the telephoto lens showed plastic on an *azib* roof. I printed steps over a smaller dry *lac* and climbed up to a *refuge*, a well-designed and sturdy building which had appeared since our last visit. However, the place was a wreck inside and, with no sign of water in the immediate area, seemed a bit of a white elephant. I began to wonder where our party had vanished to. Over by some *azibs* to the south, where a broad valley ran up to the *chantilly* of Ouaougoulzat, I could see a mule and figures. I lit a prickly bush to send up a smoke signal— and was replied to at once.

Charles arrived wearily and suffering from a headache (more usually an Ali complaint) and we had to hurry to pitch the tents while still dry. A sneaky wind puffed dust over everything, dust which was 50 % soil and 50 % dry goat-shit. We had one of the less-liked camps: in or by *azibs* seldom satisfy for many reasons. Once or twice we've been desperate to get into an *azib* out of a storm but, if itching to get in, we've usually been scratching to get out. The rain eased later so I had a look behind our row of *azibs* and found a track that led up to a spur from which there was a view—and a track—down into the Bou Guemez, a major pause with known comforts. By the time we were eating apricots and custard (sprinkled with wind-borne additives) the wind was blowing hard and did so all night. Dust seeped in and swished over the tents like brown snow.

We had realised that Ighil M'Goun (4068m) was not going to be possible this time but I'd been up it more than once, the last time with Charles, so Ali was the one who would miss out. In 1972 when I'd my VW Camper in Morocco, a gang of us tried to drive in to the Bou Guemez. The road was in such a horrendous state, however, that I gave up after bouncing over bare limestone pavement to Tamda, an abandoned French outpost. The road beyond was snow-blocked anyway.

Alistair and I were in the middle of a world-roaming sabbatical and lacked the Munro-bagging spirit of Eric Roberts who was set on M'Goun as the only 4000 m summit he'd not bagged in the Atlas. So Eric and Donald Mill set off for M'Goun and I was delegated to be at Skoura on the south side to pick them up several days later. They ran into foul snowstorms and, after three nights, still had formidable M'Goun to cross and 50 km of unknown tracks to find the van, passports and flight home. The traverse was covered with deep snow and the winds were the coldest which either had ever faced; they were thankful to escape to the south.

Darkness ended their twenty-hour traverse, with the scale of the walking out only dawning on them. No map names seemed to mean anything and there was still 45 km to Skoura and the tarmac. A mule lift took off a few kilometres next morning and, over a meal in a house, they heard that a blue vehicle had been enquiring for two people the night before but had "gone back to Skoura". They set off for a weary walk and, round the first bend, found Alistair and me picnicking by the Camper. They caught their flight. Only later it was noted that was the first British crossing of M'Goun: in 1972! Sadly Eric was to be killed in an avalanche on Annapurna and Donald was drowned trying to cross a Highland burn in spate one Hogmanay. Just as well the gates of M'Goun were closed to us on GTAM perhaps. The ascent is long and tedious rather than technical, but the weather is always dodgy and nobody makes the summit easily.

It was much easier recalling memories than rising from our snug beds. Everything inside the tent was filmed with dust. Dust grated between my teeth and clung inside ears and nostrils. Tea and muesli sufficed for breakfast. All we wanted was to be away from the disgusting dust. Two mules crossing the dry *lac* provided a scale to the scene. I sat up on the ridge waiting for Charles, firing a bush to keep warm and was amazed to find optimists carving out fields. Once down steep zigzags and refreshed by a thorough wash in a *seguia*, we followed the south side of the Bou Guemez valley. Every village seemed to be rebuilding the older, attractive buildings (in the process of crumbling to dust), with neat stonework. This cannot be regretted, and is simply the same thing that happens everywhere. In Scotland the old thatched blackhouses of the Highlands have been replaced by an aesthetically unpleasing mishmash. For a decade in Ireland the best-selling book was *The Bungalow Builders' Guide*. At least what goes up now in Morocco, urban as well as rural, still has a style and suitability. The Bou Guemez is somewhat regarded as the Shangri La of the Atlas and is certainly a beautiful and productive vale with attractive villages. Conditions can be harsh in winter, however, hidden away in the mountains and often cut off from all outside contact. The valley is unique in being long and wide rather than the usual narrow strait.

Spring had caught up on us at last. We sat for a nibble by some scented thuyas to watch a field being ploughed below. The whole valley was covered in what looked like carpets in all shades of green, a patchwork of neat fields. Potatoes were being planted. Sadly, the standard greeting from kids was "*Donnez moi un stilo*" without even a "*Bon jour*". Teachers and/or parents do the kids no service teaching them to beg, nor tourists in giving *stilos*, *dirhams*, *bonbons*, or *fennig*. The latter puzzled as it sounded *pfannig* and one wondered at a partiality to minor

German financing but *fennig* is just the local word for *cadeaux*. Here it seems the first verb learned in schools is *donner*, to give. Pestered with *donnez-moi* demands I've occasionally asked "*Pourquoi?*" only to receive blank looks. Turning the tables and begging off them can be rewardingly disconcerting to the little beggars. As the Bou Guemez follows Toubkal as the most popular trekking area in the Atlas I'm surprised it remains so unspoilt.

Above the village of Ifrane the *piste* from Aït Mhammed gains the valley floor but it is quite possible to walk field paths and riversides without trailing along the hard, hot road. There is plenty of opportunity for straying, but serious errors are unlikely. Several of the villages we passed through had a solitary standard street lamp, powered by a solar panel, often set up in the most incongruous spot. The official *gîtes* in the valley invariably have solar-powered lighting and probably hot water showers from a gas supply, havens of peace and traditional hospitality often in superb settings. "When I'm old I'll come here for weeks of pleasant indolence", I said to Charles, after we'd looked at one *gîte* and had tea from giggling females, the master being absent.*

We had a last snack below a wood of silvery-barked poplars with an overpowering scent of apple blossom in the air, before cutting over to a traditional *tighremt* to circle round to Iskattafene (Imelghas). We could see Taza and Tamri at a door and Hosain waving from an arcaded balcony above. We felt as if we were coming home, as this splendid *gîte* was the home of Mohammed Achari, one of the most experienced guides of the area, and an old friend of ours. When Charles and I made our first visit to the area we drove to Aït Mhammed only to find that the road on past Tamda was blocked by snow. (Now, there is an alternative road winding in to the lower end of the valley, less at the mercy of the weather.) We were assured—at noon— that we could cut across country via Sremt and still reach the Bou Guemez that day. We did as well, but that route is a reasonable two-day walk including a high pass, and we arrived utterly exhausted. Luckily we had a mule to carry our rucksacks. We even rode for short stretches but found being perched on a mule in the dark skidding downhill was more frightening and energy sapping than walking. We seemed to pick up strays too and ended up with about seven people, one mule and one semi-functioning torch. When we debouched onto the valley road (at 2100) the torch beam picked out a brass plaque on the first building. 'Mohammed Achari. *Guide des montagnes*'. We must have been tired. We were beyond eating, even Charles.

That assault course into the Bou Guemez was never regretted as we discovered the classic way to approach the valley of valleys. The miles of open plains from the tarmac reveal the reality of time and space. Sremt as an overnight stop is a gem of a place, with diverse towers

---

* A decade later, the Bou Guemez had electricity and is reached by a spectacular tarred road.

on hills and riverbanks. The majesty of the mountains is exploded on the walker by the Tizi n-Aït Ourïat, as no other approach can do. M'Goun rises as a long white crest like a seventh breaker curling in on the Atlantic seaboard.

I've often been asked how to avoid all contact with the locals in the hills—as if one could! Television and mass tourism (while having their good aspects) must be among the most pernicious destroyers of ethnic cultures in the world. Travel programmes are usually as trite as the rest. The wastefulness of western ways is using up everyone's world and it's the only one we have. GTAM gave me a fierce, deep, almost desperate love of the Atlas mountain people. Thank God they have had this last half-century of peace. Even prosperity bears the seeds of destruction, like red poppy warnings among the green corn, as *pistes* penetrate the furthest glens. I suppose many of the problems arising between tourists and local contacts are due to the limited time and opportunity to create any relationship: the former only has a brief goldfish bowl swim, the latter an instant for their fishing.

A year after GTAM when some of us were back in the Bou Guemez our host, Mohammed Achari, spread a colourful display of carpets and local blankets on the courtyard of his house and said they were for sale if anyone was interested. He had one sale and while Bob was tempted, they couldn't agree on a price. Two afternoons later we were at Aït Mhammed, having walked out via Sremt, when a car and a Land Rover approached our camp. The latter was the *Caïd* of the Bou Guemez who wanted to meet me, the former our host who, of course, knew we'd be there. (We had his mules.) While the youthful *caïd* and I talked I noticed Bob being led over to Mohammed's car and, a few minutes later, he returned carrying the *kelim* (carpet) of his desire. "He'd put it in on the off-chance." Bob apologised and laughed at his own glad surrender. "These people! They're just bloody marvellous, aren't they?"

The remainder of the Bou Guemez rest day was hard graft with the hundred and one tasks needed to keep our caravan humping westwards. Mohammed Achari arrived and said his Land Rover would be bringing the 'Flowers' gang the following day. One more mule than was first ordered was "no problem" and he confirmed that heading for M'Goun and the Tessaout was out of the question with the deep, unconsolidated snow. Our onward itinerary also had to take into account the coming of Aïd el Kebir, the Sheep Festival when, like Christmas, every family wants to be together at home. While disappointed at not taking in M'Goun we'd simply be deflected to more new country and the thrill of novelty.

M'Goun is a huge east—west whaleback with arid, difficult approaches from the south so is most often approached from the Bou Guemez. The base is the Tessaout/Tarkeddid plateau, snug under the mountain's northern corries. It is a magical meadow of *sources* and meandering streams, the banks starred with gentians, but quite a trap. The Oued Tessaout, flowing west, drops into one of the country's most fearsome gorges, the Wandras. Flowing east, it drops into a big dip and eventually breaks out to the south by more magnificent gorges. From the dip, the Arous gorge slices northwards down to the lower Bou Guemez. Mules find the Arous a bit much as paddling and abseiling are required, and gain the *sources* plateau by a devious route over the high ridge of Tarkeddid. Between M'Goun and its westward continuation lies the Tizi Oumsoud exit to the south but it can be impassable to mules until the end of June. The great historical pass south is the Tizi n' Aït Imi which joins the Assif M'Goun to either follow and wade its length through grand gorges or exit over other high passes southwards, trekking routes *sans pareille*. We once watched sixty mules cross from the M'Goun villages carrying potatoes to a Bou Guemez roadhead, yet a single lorry now carries more over the Tizi n' Tichka than what a whole caravan crossing the range could carry in the past.

Most people tackle the Wandras Gorge in ascent and there are exposed pitches of up to V. Diff. standard to tackle. John Willison's account of their descent is worth quoting in full, a case where the bliss of ignorance was somewhat retrospective. Willison had had a bout of serious dysentery from which he bounced back for a long traverse of nearly all M'Goun's many tops, several over 4000 metres.

'The concept of walking along a ridge for 40kms is difficult to imagine, but when it narrows to a knife point it is quite spectacular and the view magnificent. We do all the minor summits, believing each to be the best yet, and finally stop on the main top at 4068m. The ridge then snakes round several giant corries, each perfectly scooped out and with towering 'soldiers' of rock standing up against the back walls, and descends via another succession of minor summits. We have come to a point where I have neither map nor photocopy, and tiring of this splendid ridge we come down from it early, over extremely steep and difficult scree. The plan is to follow an apparently harmless valley to arrive in Amezri for late evening.

'Our valley starts with a beautiful green bowling green of a meadow with the amazing sight of hundreds of skydivers [swallows?] whirling around in a great cloud only inches from the ground. The valley suddenly narrows and we follow what has by now become a large stream down through a tiny gorge—the stream quite fills the gorge and we have to jump carefully across boulders. Soon it is some twenty metres high with the torrent becoming stronger. At one point we have to climb round the vertical walls of a pool.

'All the time the gorge becomes deeper and deeper while the river develops into the most powerful we have come across, carrying along rocks the size of footballs. Every fifty metres or so we are faced with a fresh problem: usually the sheer smooth walls of the gorge close in and we have to choose between some tiny ledges, often wet with spray, and climbing high up the side walls, out of reach of the torrent but totally unprotected. Sometimes there is a third course involving a big and accurate leap to an almost submerged boulder and immediately another leap to the opposite wall. The noise is deafening and we have to communicate by signs as we explore the separate alternatives. Another hour of this very slow but deliciously adventuresome progress and it is nearly dark. We are halted for some twenty minutes by the most testing problem so far, only to be followed instantly by an even more difficult one. We just have to solve it: neither of us could face going back for the best part of a day, besides, many of the waterfalls would be far harder in reverse.

'This one is the end; the walls are too smooth, sheer and high to be climbed even without sacks, and the waterfall is a drop of some twenty metres. Eventually in the dark I find the equivalent of an inland blow-hole, wide enough to squeeze into and narrow enough to bridge my way down. Partly wet, the first few metres are not too bad, but then it narrows and the sack has to come off and be jammed in the crack above me, thereby removing the faint light I had. Slither on down, and at last a ledge, I grope around some more and find that I am coming out of the roof at the back of a cave, with a soft silt floor, level with the next bit of river. I return for the sack and to guide Clare, and we've made it. We sleep there on the silt; lovely and dry, although still with the deafening roar of the waterfall to lull us to sleep.

'We start relatively late as the bottom of the gorge receives little light. Only ten metres further on we arrive at a long drop which looks well beyond our capabilities, so we climb out high to one side, to follow a wide ledge along the side of the gorge until we find an easy way down. For a kilometre it holds well, although the bottom of the gorge falls away fast and soon we are stranded at the dead end of a ledge with some 300m of sheer rock both above and below. I remove my sack and tentatively traverse on a ledge wondering whether Clare will want to follow and if it does let up whether there will be worse to come. It widens to a terrace once more and I explore further. Sure enough after another 400m it peters out for good. Back to Clare and then return to the start of the day's walk almost, and to our surprise we find three sheep. How they got here I never shall know; we chase them to see if they know a way out, but they just retrace our steps and then wheel horribly near the edge and gallop back to the start. Suddenly we hear faint shouts from deep across the gorge, and after some methodical searching we spot a tiny Berber waving a stick at us.

'Ten minutes of wild arm signals later we manage to bring him more or less beneath us; he seems to be pointing to a way down but neither of us can see any possible descent. Finally I lean over the edge as far as I dare. He is motioning us to come straight down where he is; looks absolute madness but we haven't come up with anything else in four hours. I gingerly dangle a foot over the edge, having removed my sack, and to his cries lower myself further. Just as I feel at my point of no return my foot touches down on a tiny hold and I can breathe again. Another couple of metres of this and it gets marginally better. The Berber has come up to join me and assists Clare; we can now pass the sacks down; still there are stretches of almost vertical slithery loose rock and a good deal of it ends up below as we scrabble down. We will never forget that Berber. Shaking with adrenaline, on to Amezri except we had underestimated the length of the valley and only reach Amezri after six in the evening.'

From Amezri they descended the Tessaout valley by mule, both riding the same beast when not falling off or sending it skittering in terror at their rolls of yellow *Karrimat*. They kept well north of the main Atlas crest to cross the Tizi n' Tichka road at Zerqtene (Zerktane) and on through to Setti Fatma, mostly on foot but with some mule lifts and the help of a *souk*-day lorry.

The 'Flowers' contingent arrived late the following afternoon (6th May) via the Oued Lakdar (lower) entry rather than the now seldom-used Tizi n' Tirghist (upper entry), towards which we'd been tempted to walk to meet them. 'Flowers' was just my shorthand for a group who came out every year or two to spend weeks exploring the alpine flora of the Atlas while trekking. We kept returning to particular areas in order to see the seasonal variations, while also exploring new places. Some treasured flower could mean a bum-in-air posture for half an hour before the petals stopped blowing in the wind and the shutter could be clicked. I remember one incident when six flower fanatics were all nose-down, rear-up around a solitary rare orchid found by a field path. A group of wide-eyed children viewed this novel form of worship with wonder and as soon as the group had moved on rushed in and took their places, peering intently, utterly baffled, for they could see nothing of interest at all about the grassy patch.

When we show pictures of daffodil meadows or hillsides blue-acred with hedgehog broom there is almost a feeling of awe in the audience. The Bou Guemez is often, justifiably, called *La Vallée Heureux*, and this verdant swathe among stony mountains, lit by spring blossom and shining waters, poplar rows, orchid meadows and darting black damselflies, can astonish. Our Flowers gang arrived in a state of suppressed excitement.

David had been head gardener at Branklyn Garden on the outskirts of Perth, a Himalayan garden created by the Rentons between 1922 and 1968 when it was bequested to the National Trust for Scotland, Francis was in charge of the gardens on the Berriedale estate in the far north of Scotland and Charles was from Kendal where he followed another profession but was no less knowledgeable on alpine flora. He and David were to follow up this trip with articles in relevant journals and visits to universities and botanic gardens to study herbarium specimens, generally bewailing the lack of accurate information on the Atlas flora. This professional seriousness was balanced by Lorraine from Perth and Nicola, Irish, but working in Luxembourg. They had all been wandering in the Atlas before and were delighted to be back. You never visit Morocco *once*.

We had the pleasure of using the house's *hammam*, a small cell with a barrel of water brought to near boiling point by an external fire underneath and a tap in the wall for adding cold water to our buckets and basins. Within minutes, the room was billowing steam and every pore in our bodies was at work. Later, we were taken to the main guest room for a superb *cous cous* supper. Eating by hand can be a messy job and even Moroccans these days tend to use spoons. Old accounts write *seksu, seksuksu* and other variants. Although instant versions can be bought even in UK supermarkets, the real preparation is a long, skilled task. The vegetables and meat are boiled in a bulbous pot on top of which sits a steamer containing the *cous cous,* cooking in the aromatic steam. Even the best can be rather bland so a peppery *harissa* sauce is often available for the bold or the innocent.

Mohammed's guest room ceiling and upper walls were decorated in bold primary colours and geometrical patterns, the work of an itinerant artist. A cartouche on the end wall bore an invocation to Allah and the date. Above, another hand had drawn lifelike horses. Looking kitsch and out of place were some *Fête champêtre* prints of eighteenth century court life and a fat stuffed lizard a metre long. Charles, with new, willing ears, recounted our past doings by the hour. I spent as long sorting out gear and food, wondering how gear manages to accumulate, and had a huge bagful to donate to our host and a bigger ungainly parcel for him to deliver to the Hotel Ali storeroom sometime. David managed to get himself locked out although no one noticed for some time and Nicola took her bedding onto the terrace to escape the prime snorer. We had a windy, bangy night, and I hoped the weather wasn't loosening up for another assault by rain. There's nothing more depressing than a wet weekly *souk*.

I woke to a nightingale concerto and rose at six to do my own packing. Ali produced brews and then Mohammed bore in tea, coffee, hot brown bread (loaves almost a metre across), fresh butter and honey. Even David, a strong eater, was satisfied. Mohammed's hospitable *gîte* was to be the only three-night stop on the whole journey and, in retrospect, the sites where we repeated nights tended to be recalled with greater affection. While driving the journey forward was important, a part of us constantly desired to linger in such beautiful, natural caravanserai. If others are tempted to stray all or bits of the Atlas, note our experience, and linger over the journey—as one would sip a good malt.

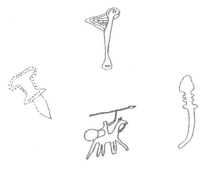

CHAPTER 7

Rounding Rhat

I had made up my mind, most learned Vogel, that henceforth, as long as it shall please God to let me live, I shall every year climb a few mountains, at the time when the flowers are at their best, so that I can examine them and combine a grand exercise of the body with enjoyment of the mind. Is that not true bliss?

Conrad Gesner (1541)

With the sun swanking up the sky we wended through the fresh fields to reach the *Souk el Had* at Tabant. I was glad the party had brought in more film from our Marrakech store. Sitting unobtrusively in a *souk* one can often capture photos of people. Here, the camera didn't seem to concern most adults while the kids reacted with everything from fear and flight to strutting and posing. There were rows of off-white canvas tents tiered along the *souk* area. Mules were tethered all around and above the site among the pines. A stylish *poste*, shut for Sunday though most of the Bou Guemez was in town, a modest *caïd's* office, forestry huts, permanent shops selling everything from kid's gobstoppers to fierce rat traps, ubiquitous *Tide*, clothing and farm implements, all made for a colourful scene.

There were a surprising number of butchers (indicative of a wealthy populace) who used broad cleavers with more energy than finesse, smashing through bones and flesh with indiscriminate vigour to make up the required weight. Long ago we learnt to treat *tagines*, *harrira* or anything else with care; they are apt to contain shrapnel. Olive oil was decanted from oil drums into all manner of proffered containers. Our oil went in *Sigg* bottles since, honey apart, there aren't many things less pleasant to have leaking in one's belongings. (We've had most over the years.) All our pots and pans and such risky products travelled in an expanding suitcase, the same one which had been used for several seasons, testimony to its robustness. One holdall carried all our plates, mugs, cutlery and tins of tea, coffee, drinking chocolate, sugar and the like. Our only GTAM mess was when a lid on the turmeric jar came off and managed to stain everything nearby bright yellow.

The Tabant *souk*, as any other, had its spice merchant with small sacks of colourful goods spread like a carpet around his perch. Cumin is one favourite spice, used in many soups and *tagines* or simply as an additional flavouring with the usual salt and pepper. Salt and cumin is very popular with hard-boiled eggs, for example. Coriander is another favourite and Ali and Hosain went through paprika, cinnamon and ginger steadily. We also had saffron and its cheap alternative, turmeric, the latter always in *harrira*. Moroccans use spices with gusto yet skilfully, combining flavours that complement.

Even more colourful than the spice stalls are the displays of kitchenware for these are in gaudy plastics: scores of piled buckets and basins or glittering pots, pans and fat teapots. Some of the basins are huge but, equally popular, for women washing clothes by a river, are cut-down oil drums since these can be perched on stones over a scrub fire. In the eastern end of the Atlas, batons are used and clothes are beaten clean. Everywhere clothes are spread on rocks or bushes to dry, like colourful gardens of garments.

Once our spice jars were topped up, we retreated from the dusty *souk* to sit outside a café under the shade of poplars. We enjoyed hard-boiled eggs with rounds of bread, cake from home and melons. Locals came and scooped handfuls of water to drink from a *source* which gushed into the stream beside us. Two boys were deeply involved in playing knuckle bones with pebbles. *Café au lait* orders had a youth despatched from the café to the *souk* to buy a tin of milk. While competing shops seem to be overstocked to a surprising degree, cafés seem never to keep anything ready. They'd sent out for our bread as well.

The Bou Guemez, like Gaul, can be divided into three. The lower valley is dramatic, rather than beautiful, where the hills are almost tortured in appearance. To the south, they take on a more aloof form. The river has cut through horizontal layers of ancient sediments in a tell-tale of the geological past, leaving little room for cultivation other than in the crooks of the river bends. Eventually, the river plunges down into the deep Jorro gorge of multi-hued rock, studded with Aleppo pines. The clinging ruins of Tighza are reduced to broken fingers reaching up to the brassy sky. The waters join the Oued Lakdar at the foot of what is the Bou Willi valley leading up to Abachkou—our continuation—and by flanking the Oued Lakdar north the new *piste* (now *goudron*) breaks over to reach the outer world.

Heading up the Bou Guemez this barren lower part ends at Agouti, a sprawl of houses below some dust-coloured spires, the combination of nature's carving and the remains of mans' work. The strata still loop along on the northern flanks but the bluffs of Ighil-n-Igoudamene stand well back to the south so the valley is suddenly wide and verdant. Just up from Agouti, nursing the village of Idoukaln, is a symmetrical cone of a hill half-planted with pines and crowned with a tower. Near Tabant there is another cone with a grander structure on top (the shrine of Sidi Moussa) and between these two markers, the real Bou Guemez lies: wide, rich and lush—the result of a one-time lake bed accumulating the alluvial deposits behind a landslip dam at the western end of the valley. A spur, Adazane, pushes Tabant into a side valley at the head of which the great 2905 m pass of the Tizi n' Aït Imi leads to the south. This spur narrows the main valley, still green and mile-stoned with attractive villages for many miles, the upper Bou Guemez in common parlance.

Stepping westwards, our walk went from one guardian cone to the other. A good mule track runs along the middle of the green fields and made a hard choice for the photographers as colourful parties on foot and mule were still streaming to the *souk* and equally colourful flowers were beckoning from the meadows: oversized orchids, drooping cerinthe, woad, buttercups, rest harrow and *muscari à toupet*, or tassel hyacinths. There were quails, warblers and the noisy nightingales to please the ear and a large raptor circled overhead. Tucked into a corner below a smaller hill were a dozen pairs of nesting storks, their presence heard before seen, with the pairs greeting each other with ceremonial beak-rattling. I've seen the valley look like paddy fields, the river having overflowed after heavy rains.

Ambling through the flats of the Bou Guemez is a constant delight at any season for the walking is gentle, the scenery varied and human activity constant. While there seems to be no great effort being made, the acreage under cultivation is prodigious (and expanding) and something is always happening in both the fields and the villages, most of which have been largely rebuilt in the last decade. The thumps and cries of builders tamping earth on new structures is almost as common a sound as the multi-programmed songs of the nightingales. These birds are everywhere and easily seen as well as heard. I can recall the thrill of my first positive identification in the garden of the Hotel du Toubkal at Asni since they are a rarity to a Scot. Another guest watched me checking-out what I saw and heard. "Yes, it's a nightingale", he smiled and we talked awhile. I commented that this hotel and others strung over the Atlas would make for a happy honeymoon. He laughed and said, "I'm on the next stage. I'm celebrating my divorce".

We found Taza and Tamri had been joined by two other mules and were installed in a *gîte* with hostel-like facilities. There are now several *gîtes* in Agouti alone and over a dozen in the whole valley. A woodcarver has a workshop in the village and a small olivewood bowl joined my Imilchil *handira* as a souvenir of the trip. The Bou Guemez blankets are a natural white colour, sometimes with thin coloured lines or sequins added. After a while, one can recognise local styles in blankets, carpets and pottery just as there are subtle differences in building styles in different areas.

Most *gîtes* have attractive pictures or posters on their walls, but private houses can have very odd reproductions: *kitsch* Watteau-like scenes, bathing beauties, Reynold's Child Samuel or the Mona Lisa. Clocks are an odd status symbol. The dining room at the Hotel Ali for instance has five antique wall clocks for show rather than practicality (none work) while the devout have donated so many to the tomb of Moulay Idris II in Fes that the shrine appears half a *zaouia* and half a clock museum. Modern technology has brought in wall clocks in glitzy plastic, battery-operated, and playing tunes on the hour so one can be dipping into a *tagine* when 'Frère Jacques' or the 'Blue Danube' strikes up to be followed by Big Ben chimes. I've yet to hear a clock or mobile phone ring with an Arab tune.

The lower Bou Guemez has special memories for Charles and me. After our first visit to M'Goun we came down to the valley there. On the descent we had to stand back to back to fend off a pack of vicious dogs, an experience thankfully never repeated. We hoped to hire a mule but the one we obtained was as feckless as its driver. At least we were free of rucksacks and could enjoy the riverside walk along the Oued Lakdar. We'd turned up a side stream hoping to reach Sremt and the known exit to Aït Mhammed but it looked as if the gorge would beat us. The muleteer knew nothing. At that stage a man appeared, dressed in flowing robes and *selham*, on a well turned-out mule. He was a splendid if ugly figure, like Auda in the *Lawrence* film, and greeted us enthusiastically from his restless mount. He confirmed there wasn't a way through to Sremt and told us to go up to join the new *piste* which would eventually lead to Aït Mhammed. He showed us a track and soon vanished up it. Having been on the go for ten hours we followed at a considerably slower pace, which was still speedier than our mule's. We camped by a solitary farmhouse after two hours of ascent and the next day set off along the *piste*.

At midmorning, we were overtaken by our helper of the previous day, given a great welcome and hijacked into a tea stop. He went to a poor house to borrow a *kanoun* (brazier), teapot and a bulbous copper kettle full of water, then set about making the brew. (He had tea, mint and sugar in a saddlebag.) It was princely hospitality. We set off together but our plodding pace called forth imprecations on the muleteer and finally he gave us a flowery farewell and rode off at a canter, only slowing to deliver a mighty kick on the rump of our beast. Out of sheer astonishment the mule broke into a panic trot lasting all of 50 metres. Later, we saw a magnificent black stallion break loose and go galloping through a village then over the fields—with the same effect as releasing the bulls in Pamploma.

At the lower end of the Bou Guemez we abandoned the river for a mule path which went directly down to the valley below. At the bottom we had a break in the shelter of a big walnut tree and watched a French party descending, one of the two tourist groups we'd see on the traverse. The *piste* was avoided as much as possible as we followed up the Bou Willi valley but paths gradually petered out and we had a *seguia* scramble before cliffs overlooking the water channel intake barred progress. We had to paddle back across the strong flow, in quartets, lined upstream, and naturally were in midstream when first our mules and then the French party passed. We lunched while dressing, which became a scramble as our chosen patch was suddenly invaded by irrigation water. Not far on, the *piste* forded the river so we had a second paddle.

At the ford there was a small *source* that bubbled out at river level. The French were filling bottles and having a stylish picnic under the trees. We envied them for the hard *piste* onwards was in full sun and even with a brolly I suffered. We could tell it was hot for some boys had stripped off for a noisy swim. We envied them also. There was a fine village across the river, Taghia, where half the towers were red and half were grey, depending on the soil that had been used in their construction. Nearing the *souk* a squat tower on a spur dominated the up-valley view with the distant snows of Jbel Rhat beyond. We found a small café open and downed the complete stock of soft drinks.

Our destination was the village of Abachkou and I set off for there leading the way, only to be waylaid by Hosain who insisted we went up a side valley. As I'd been raving about the tall, tapering *tighremt* among the walnut trees where we'd stayed once before I was none too pleased and we ended up pitching our tents in the shadow of a red fort where the map and the locals agreed to differ. The village was called Tarbat n' Aït Moussa on the map, but Targa by the locals (the map name of another pretty hamlet). The ground was like iron, so erecting eight tents took a long time, skinned knuckles, much cursing and many bent pegs. The wall surrounding our spot became lined with shy children, mostly girls in rainbow raiment and with the faces of angels. We may not have been in Abachkou but I wrote in my log: 'Still, a new site and rather fabulous…looking over eroded red slopes to bold Jbel Tifdaniwine and the crazy crest of Tarkeddid. We perch above a dizzy drop to a stream with another stream on the other side, a defensive position reminding me of Castle Campbell in the Ochils'.

Charles A. and I went to recce the route for the next day. A thorn hedge covered in drying clothes led down to the river and a good bridge, upstream of which spouted the village water supply. A water channel was led off to feed four mills, perched directly one above the other. The way on was obvious so we returned. I spent some time re-sewing my mule-blanket. I'd hoped my sleeping bag would turn up with the Flowers but it hadn't. The loss was more a bore than a deprivation; it meant having to don endless layers instead of taking clothes off. We dined sitting on a tarpaulin by the dome tent: thick, fresh tomato soup, vegetables with ham and corned beef (according to faith and fancy), oranges, coffee and biscuits. That took us into dusk and a large moon floodlit the castle beside us, the clouds dispersed, and the peaks glowed eerily. We declared Targa the most romantic site of the trip.

Our recce and an early departure gave us a good start next day and we soon climbed to the highest Bou Willi waters descending from the Tizi n' Tighist (2399 m). There were steep zigzags and plenty of wending about before the slabby col was reached. We were there by 0930 so were able to spend much of the day exploring the finest concentration of Neolithic rock carvings in the country, *hajra mektuba* (written stones). The red sandstone slabs have carved or pecked-out pictorial studies of shields and weapons, scenes of hunting and battle and weird abstracts and presumably religious or ceremonial features, some of life-like naturism, others beyond understanding. There are further sites round Jbel Rhat, and one wonders what significance that vast mountain had to those unknown people. Comparable sites can be found at Oukaïmeden (easy to see) and the Yagour Plateau, north of Adrar Meltzen (Ourika) while smaller sites or solitary carvings are found in many places in the Atlas or southwards. Most are on high pastures in spectacular mountain settings, facing up into the sky and the sun, slowly flaking or wearing away, alas. They have tentatively been given a date of 4000 years ago.

Ever since the Flowers had joined us they'd been talking about one flower above all others that they longed to find. I did a rough sketch. "Yes, that's it!" was the response. "We've seen it everywhere", Charles grinned. On one of my circling searches for carvings I came on a poor specimen. The experts wasted half a spool of film on the miserable flower and for the rest of the trip saw acres of it. *Ranunculus calandrinioides* became a sort of mascot for the Flowers trip, so much so that I can even remember the Latin name. This beautiful flower, a bit like a *Dryas octopetala* or a wild rose, has several white to pink flowers clustering above crinkly, lanceolate leaves. It grows in various habitats, especially where able to snuggle down among the hollows of a limestone pavement but is equally happy—and pinker—on open screes. The most photographed flower of the trip, I now grow it at home in Scotland.

Having found the ranunculus we went our various ways, Lorraine and Nicola calling into the village of Iskad to teach the grannies indoor volleyball with a balloon, while Charles K. and I wended over the slopes finding a few other carvings. We regretting not having the book with us to pinpoint the several good sites listed, but the *tizi* was not on our original route.

Over at Iskad, a white mule broke loose and cantered from terrace to terrace with half the village in pursuit. A small col brought the rich red buildings of Tarbat n' Tirsal into view—but which one was providing us with hospitality? The green aprons below the town were covered with white *djellabas* stretched out to dry in readiness for the next day's feast. The men would all climb two kilometres to the holy spot on a small col, pray and recite the Koran in unison—an impressive spectacle even at a distance. I decided to go up the valley circling south of the village in hope of being spotted and, sure enough, I heard Hosain's welcome shouts. The fields were dotted with St Bruno lily. Tea was very welcome, so was washing socks but dank clouds settled on us and the socks didn't dry overnight. Our girls arrived next and were given an extra welcome by the young girls and women of the house.

The house belonged to the deputy headman who gave us a formal welcome over supper. The house, like most, had been reconstructed periodically and 'grew' up the slope. The mules were in the lowest yard (Tamri stealing the resident's food), cows in the next, we were above them and the rest of the house sprawled overhead. A tiled passage led in from the street door with a spacious toilet/*hammam* off left and a cooking area near the guest room door. Our room was covered in red carpets and the usual firm cushions provided the usual minimalist comfort.

We had two nights there, as the next day was Aïd el Kebir when everyone tries to be home. This was a bit difficult for Ali and Hosain but at least we could stay put and negotiations began for purchasing a sacrificial lamb. Since mutton is generally favoured, our beast proved to be a mature (and expensive) ewe. It took a week to eat her. Once again I was struck by the rich graciousness of our hosts. Islam is so much a garment of the soul that it can be worn lightly. We were welcomed, not just tolerated. The deeply devout can afford to be gracious.

Jbel Rhat slowly lifted her veils and the Aïd el Kebir became a day of perfect clarity. A wild shooting off of film began as everyone was in best clothes: the men in white *djellabas*, the women and girls in hues that would dazzle a rainbow. With the men away to the *musalla* (outdoor prayers' location), the women were not slow in coming out and Nicola, Lorraine and I had a hilarious time with them. Much of the traditional lore (and superstition) is kept alive by the women, who are by no means inferior. We made a very sociable circuit of the picturesque village. Many of the houses had old features surviving or copied, there were dark alleys and passages built over, decorative windows, towers and secretive stairs: a living film set. At the end of our circuit we watched the men streaming back from their devotions.

Meat is expensive so normally used sparingly, often a *tagine* will be 90% vegetables with the meat and spices merely acting as flavouring. For feasts however, a family will lash out on a sheep or, if poor, a goat. The festival commemorates Abraham's offering of his son and God's provision of a lamb instead. Slowly and surely a purer Islam is spreading, every village now has an artistic mosque tower while in Casablanca the new Hassan II mosque is one of the wonders of the modern architectural world as well as a bold gesture for all the world to see. Morocco is, statistically, the most Moslem country in the world. The king is not only the country's ruler, but is also its spiritual head, descended of the Prophet and so venerated as *imam*. Morocco maintains the Sunni orthodoxy although with its own distinctive characteristics. Not surprisingly, a portrait of the king hangs in every public place and private guest room.

The whole family, with Ali and Hosain in borrowed white robes, gathered on the rooftop for the ritual slaying of the sheep which was carried out in a clean, efficient manner. Bled, decapitated and disembowelled, the back legs were broken to criss-cross with the tough tendons and the animals hung up to be skinned. The whole process could not have taken more than half an hour.

Having shot three spools of film that morning, I wrote in the afternoon. Those of us at the house were called in for the first taste of our sacrificial beast: unrecognisable parts, *kebabs* galore, served with fresh bread and plenty of mint tea. *Bismillah*. We were left flattened so went off for a walkabout which ended on the steep soggy meadows with David in search of flowers.

The two Charles's had gone off early to try and gain the crest of Jbel Rhat which, while laudable, left most of us wondering why? We'd plans for Rhat later after all and might never be so closely involved in Aïd el Kebir festivities again. They reached their objective at 3500 m. Jbel Rhat's summit (3781 m or 3797 m, depending on the map) lies miles beyond the crest above a chunky bluff, instantly recognisable from afar, while the centre of the mountains is hollowed out into a tortuous valley. Peyron describes an ascent from lower down, below the rim at Iskad, as a 7–8 hour ascent and as much in descent. Geologically, the hill is a huge syncline feature, meaning that the jam roll strata so clear in the M'Goun corries had collapsed in on themselves, and the valley had subsequently been eroded out while the rim maintained the jagged broken edge of the volcanic jam roll.

After dark, a large salad and *mechoui* followed a strange but tasty soup to ensure we went to bed replete. *Mechoui* is simply a large hunk of mutton (a whole sheep even) cooked very slowly over a fire and often served with a dusting of cumin. The flesh crumbles at a touch and is absolutely delicious. There were no vegans in our party, Charles is no mean trencherman and both Lorraine and David had the capacity of JCBs for shifting food. There were some invalids in the morning however, with David and Charles A feeling under the weather and Lorraine completely choked with the cold she'd brought from Europe.

We were seen off with noisy enthusiasm and wound up through the fields below Jbel Rhat, lost our path and followed a *seguia* to gain a good mule track up-valley. We had several descriptions for that day's planned route, but the map was quite deficient in the names used. Jbel Rhat is such a monster of a mountain that to merely make a summer circuit would take four days of demanding walking. With snow, the massive structure can be picked out from the Haouz Plains round Marrakech. Those going to see the Cascades d'Ouzzoud are often astonished to see such a brutal snowy mass, but melting snow off the hills helps to feed that most beautiful of all African waterfalls (to be visited in the afternoon when the sun will often set a rainbow in the heart of its gathering plunge).

Our track led clearly up the valley and onto a *tizi* which agreed with the height given for the Tizi n' Kark (2850 m). Pale pink domes of alyssum dotted the harsh landscape and tiny hooped-petticoat daffodils crowded a line of seepage. The col where we lunched gave a view along the west flank of Rhat, with our thread of path looping across the screes between small spurs of rock. The steepness below didn't impress from the map but did so in reality, our eyes dragged down a multicoloured world to dwarfed hamlets. Giant Anghomar to the west had a streaky bacon look. Francis suggested Anghomar looked a bit like An Teallach. When I pointed out the peaks of the Tizi n' Tichka and Toubkal areas this brought something of the scale home to Ali. We were seeing 'mountains kissing high heaven' (Shelley). The muleteers demolished some fruitcake and pressed on. The cavalcade quickly became little beads strung on the path, necklacing the girth of Jbel Rhat.

Both David and Lorraine were going painfully slowly so we had a conference on the last spur (below the 3584 m top) and decided to drop down to first water, towards Imazayn, one of the villages below. The path for several hundred feet was just sand which I didn't enjoy in my sandals. We had a pause for the weary and to fill bottles at a *source* but then came round to a big grassy spot below improbable pink, sculpted sandstone towers, made more impressive as afternoon cloud began to creep among them. Ali yelled up to query stopping and we all echoed, "Yes! OK!" Everyone, for varied reasons, thought we'd discovered a superb spot. Charles made it 2490 m.

While the kettle boiled I built a dam in the stream so Ali could make a spout for filling our water cans easily then, lower down, I scooped out a gravelly pool and washed all my clothes and all of myself in turn. Time flew with food to organise, medications for the invalids (including our doctor!), taking pictures of the site before the sun dipped, boiling eggs for the next day's picnic, swotting the route (such as was possible) and writing-up my log. We had mutton for supper, overeating to bursting point. I couldn't sleep as a result but was quite content. I even went and sat on a knoll under the swinging stars for a while, in amazing peace and silence, the only noises being the stream, the clink and munching from the hobbled mules and the wind eavesdropping around the tents.

Being mutton-stuffed was a good thing as next day we were on the go from 0700 to 1900 with a fair ration of doubts and difficulties to sup on. We cut round and up onto waterlogged daffodil meadows fed by a *source* that we'd noted the previous day from above. At an *azib* I nearly gave a shepherd heart failure when I jumped on a rock to obtain a better view and found him lying on the other side. When asked for the Tizi n' Iblouzene he pointed up rather than along which helped, we hoped. Traces of path led us to the edge of cultivation where a big switchback path headed over spurs to the wall of Jbel Aguensou n' Issis. There, we found a long spur off Rhat which we had to cross at some point if we were to gain our destination of the Iblouzene col between Rhat and its higher but less dominant neighbour Jbel Tignousti. However, we spotted the 'high-level transhumance path at 3000 metres' (Peyron) and decided that would be a simpler level at which to traverse across. This line worked out all right, although David and Lorraine were still moving very slowly. David has a tradition of gut trouble on every Flower visit (often the only one in any season) and goes down with a wallop but bounces back again strongly.

Charles A (fully fit again) and I teased out the route ahead, too far ahead as Charles K took the invalids too high and they were a long time catching up at an *azib* where we lunched. Charles A and I hit one bare patch of sandstone which nearly defied adhesion but at its edge was a leak line brightened with gentians in flower and beyond were the finest pink *Ranunculus calandrinioides* we ever saw. The mules came across noisily and were just going to pass when I yelled at them to wait. "Our destination is just over there," Ali countered. "Where shall we camp?" They were not pleased to learn there was another high ridge to cross, the Tizi n' Iblouzene, still a long way off.

An improbable and, to us, invisible track crossed over to a scree ridge (out of which gushed a big *source*) before mounting the Issis ridge. I raced after Taza to grab my boots; sandals do have limits. We off-loaded our ice axes too, just in case. The Issis ridge anywhere lower down was a banded cliff and the hollow beside it, up to Rhat's crest, was mobile scree. The mules rapidly became tiny dots and we lost them on their Issis ascent, although we could hear the faint calls of "*Hirrah!*" as they were driven on.

They obviously had no problems and neither did we, except we became a bit strung out. Charles A, Nicola and I sat on the Issis crest for half an hour before David and Francis appeared. Charles K was apparently shepherding a very puggled Lorraine, a long way back. This was a bit worrying but if the doctor was happy to go off and give Rhat a bash then so were we. Francis waited with David but the latter decided he'd have a go too so Charles K, always the gentleman, was more or less volunteered into going on and down with Lorraine. She was gummed up with cold and needed three long rests on the descent. I didn't like not knowing exactly where everyone was so hurried after Charles A and Nicola and caught them where the Issis ridge abutted Rhat. Peyron's description of an easy ridge had us going straight up to bands of crag assuming there would be an easy break. There wasn't, and a look along to the right showed steep snow and cliffs. We traversed left onto vile scree and disintegrating rock bands. Nicola suggested waiting while we went on (it was menacingly loose) but was encouraged to continue. ("You were a schoolteacher weren't you, Hamish?" she sighed.) Eventually we pulled over the small crags of the Rhat rim. The summit lay several undulations off over black rock and the odd wet snow patch.

The view was exceptional in both scope and quality during the hour we were there, improving constantly. Only necessity sent us homewards. The valleys were seeped in a milky haze so the world was arrayed blue tint beyond blue tint; like opening Russian dolls the progress went on forever. Our camp would have a somewhat similar view to the west, and the blue turned to royal purple at dusk before burning up in flames as the sun disappeared. Sirwa was clear and Hosain was thrilled to see something he actually knew. Toubkal was held up like an offering in pilgrim hands, and the fortress fastness of Anghomar could be seen. It was our next objective, and had chased us off on previous occasions (as had Rhat). This was another summit to induce the horizon consciousness of our progress. A horizon only limits when we stand still—walk to any horizon and there are more and more horizons beyond. Horizons are for going over.

Looking back, M'Goun and Tarkeddid were still very white and unapproachable but the sail of Azourki showed some of the snow had gone. To see from peaks above Zawyat Ahancal to peaks beyond Toubkal makes Jbel Rhat one of the great viewpoints, perhaps only surpassed by Igoudamene in the Bou Guemez which, oddly, only receives a single sentence from Peyron. Tignousti was studied more practically: the curving crest, snow-edged, from the Tizi n' Iblouzene looked attractive. Over the long west ridge the symmetrical cone of Tizoula was very eye-catching, one of several peaks about which little has been written. (I would find prehistoric shards of flint on its summit.)

After GTAM I was often asked: "Is that you done with the Atlas then?" It was not a question anyone acquainted with Morocco would ask and on Jbel Rhat we looked out on several lifetimes of potential exploration. The really big and dominant hills probably number a score or so, but the sheer complexity of the landscape thrusts up an inexhaustible number of peaks and ridges, moated by valleys and gorges—and all attractive, all beautiful. To me a spring wheat field, bloodied red with poppies, is no less beautiful than a big view of any peak. In sweeping majesty as well as minute detail the Atlas Mountains are blessed so, in Norman MacCaig's words, 'There's a Schiehallion anywhere you go. The thing is, climb it.'

Perhaps wonder sharpened our appetites and we demolished every morsel of food and drink on the summit rocks. We reckoned it was a first on Jbel Rhat for Panforte Bianco, Scottish oatcakes and Orkney cheese! As the time had passed 17.00 we set off regretfully. Two hours to camp was good going, but the bad screes allowed a skittery fast descent back to the Issis ridge where we picked up the mule track down into the valley draining the Tizi n' Iblouzene. We assumed the track would angle down to the camp site so had one rest on the long flank (where I unintentionally left my brolly behind) then from a small spur had the shock of seeing camp right at the head of the valley, still a long way off—and up.

There were masses of gagea, buttercups, speedwell, forget-me-not and, on the wetter 'greens', a starring of gentians, which always lift the heart. We had had a long, hot day and leaving camp that morning Jbel Rhat had not even been on the agenda. We drank and drank and ate and drank and by the time a big moon had been hung over Tignousti and the colours switched off in the west we were abed. For once I didn't even make any notes in my log, just relished the remote peacefulness, the silence where one hears the wind draw breath and the stars singing.

The tents were pitched not far below the *tizi* where we'd levelled off platforms in the stony earth with our ice axes. A small stream of melt water ran through the camp from the snowy flank of Tignousti while, 50 metres off, was a *source* where Ali had built a dam and spout. A twist of green growth marked the spring area. There was a frost overnight—we were at 3000 metres— and I watched with amusement as a bleary-eyed Charles A came over from his tent, toothbrush in hand, and stood blinking in incomprehension at his vanished water supply: the melt stream had turned to ice. David's rapid recovery the day before was matched by Lorraine's that day. Despite being sick in the night and still gummed-up and weak with cold, she came with the rest of us. Charles K shifted into top gear and, as we wended off for Jbel Tignousti, he headed straight for Rhat—and added Tignousti later in the day. A determined hill-bagger is our Charles.

We managed to be off at 0700 and were on top at 0930. "Peyron time!" someone purred. The first stretch from the Tizi n' Iblouzane was easy although steep and loose, the red soil changing to dark volcanic rubbish. There was an unstable roughness as if a tower block had been blown up and we were climbing the pile of rubble. There was a knifing wind and we crept up on the edge of the east face to avoid the assault. There was just enough rock to scramble up on the edge, as the face fell away in a fine curtain of fluted snow. Higher, there were just shaly bulges and snow bands, easy walking. The cairn on the big dome declared we were there—3819 m—and so easy compared to Jbel Rhat. There's a Moorish saying, 'A climb with a friend is as easy as a descent'.

Being early and bright we opted for a long way home. The slopes had acres of regular frost-combing patterns, a feature several recognised from the Cairngorms. Some snow patches allowed us to 'ski'-slither down fast off the summit dome to gain the long west ridge. South, the ground fell away to a plateau which was dotted with the brown stains of dried water pools. Beyond this were the cliffs falling down to the Oued Tessaout. In area, Tignousti is even larger than Rhat, but the mountain is secretive and seldom noticed while extrovert Rhat appears a dominating upstart. If one were to sex them, Tignousti is feminine and Rhat masculine. The first note of climbers on Rhat and Tignousti is by the great Polish expedition of 1934 which bagged M'Goun, Toubkal, Imaradene, Tinergwet and other major peaks.

A path descended to gain the Soufskmoud stream which drained our valley. It led to slopes ablaze with buttercups and, by the water runnels, galaxies of gentians, over which David and Charles were bottoms-up in photographic worship. I flanked a gritty red slope to reach the main stream leading back to camp, this too starred with gentians. I defy anyone not to stop and photograph gentians in such settings. I was also thankful that the Flowers pair had seen such prodigality for I'd been telling them about the gentians on the wending stream by the Tessaout *sources* plateau under M'Goun, and that paradise had been denied us. The weather, the snow cover and the seasons can make predicting the availability of any flower species a gamble. We found this a year later above Taza when we went up Tazekka a few weeks later than on the start of GTAM. I was hoping to find the mini-daffodils in seed, instead they were only just shooting up their thin leaves, weeks behind schedule. All the alpines were weeks and weeks behind whereas floods, rain and snow had exploded plains and desert into a madness of floral extravagance. In the desert, some seeds will lie dormant for many years waiting for rain to trigger germination then, within a day or two, spread a carpet of colours under the sun before withering and dying a day or two later. There's a desert snail that can remain dormant for years waiting for rain. *Berber Village* by Bryan Clarke has a story about some of these 'coming to life' after years on display in a museum cabinet, after the cabinet received a wash.

Charles K was last back to camp, grinning from a brick-red face among the fuzz and so enthusiastic as to suggest he'd go up Rhat again next day with Lorraine, early, and then catch the rest of us up. The wind died away and a full moon swept down the slopes like a tide. The mules had eaten their way up the slopes above the *source* and refused to come down for their supper despite much calling and waving of their nosebags. The grazing must have been good, as normally they were all attention as soon as there was the rustle of the grain sack being opened, pawing the ground and straining at their tethers or, if free, clattering up to nuzzle in as the supplies were prepared. Ali said it was midnight before the strikers were fetched down.

Strangely, Ali was not knowledgeable about the stars, a surprisingly common lack among the Berbers who have such a skyscape to study. Most can't recognise individual stars or constellations and Ali was, I think, a bit overwhelmed by some of the information I poured out but the practicality of finding north by using the pointers on the Plough appealed and was learnt at once. "Good for working out the direction of Mecca," he grinned.

The following morning Lorraine was hardly able to speak as the cold had gone into her chest. She coughed and coughed, so "that was Rhat". Having risen early my reward was to see the majestic moon world slowly transform into the jewelled glitter of day. I half-packed the food and communal gear (and my own) before rousing everyone else. Lorraine was sent on ahead but instead of going slowly she went off like a startled hind and I had to go pell-mell after her, for miles, before I could catch her and stop her going straight down a gorge. Despite lighting many warning bushes the Flowers fanatics almost went straight down the gorge too. Smoke signals don't work for those with eyes on the ground in a valley ensnared with flowers.

A score of mules were grazing freely on the large meadows, what I'm sure they regarded as their annual treat, the only time of the year when they are not needed for ploughing or carrying manure to fields, stones for houses, *souk* supplies, harvest-home or tramping out the grain. The high Tizi n' Maradal offered a more direct but somewhat demanding alternative to following a day-long loop through gorges, but we wanted to explore. The ground was as hued as August heather moors with a tiny cranesbill and there were plenty of yellow raffenaldia, attractive speedwell, sorrel carpeters and many of the treasured ranunculus. I smiled when I thought back to the excitement over the solitary tatty specimen I had originally shown those flora twitchers!

We carried on down and after a couple more strata humps we found cliffs ahead. There was a path off to the right, however, which we (correctly) assumed would lead us down to the river. None of that complex detail is possible on the map of course. Charles K stayed back and yelled down that he'd wait for David who, as usual, was miles behind. We lit a few navigational smokes

Ali, the key member of the party

Hosain loading Tamri while Charles speculates

The magnificent cedar forest on Jbel Tazek

Ali with the puppy during the
tea break at Beni Raham

Off to school, Moussa ou
Salah in the background

rossing the dried up Guelta Tamda

Taza and Hosain battling
through the flooded scrub
below Kerrouchen

The welcome repast out of the
rain after descending to the Oued
Serou

Tea stop with a friendly nomad
near Imilchil

Jbel Laqroun from the camp above Anergi

The worrying view of Jbel Azurki; our planned route obviously snowbound

Tamga and the Cathedral at the lower end of the Ahancal valley

Jbel Azurki from Jbel Aroudane

On the walk up to Zaouia Ahancal

Mohammed Achari welcomes Charles and Hamish to the Bou Guemez

At the Tabant *souk*

Mist in the upper Bou Willi with Jbel Tifdaniwine and the crest of Jbel Tarkeddid

The 'Flowers' camp on the Targa threshing floors

dangerous snakes. They remained at a safe distance and edged back every time anyone walked near them.

I don't think I have ever laughed so much as at one camp when some of us were washing and brushing teeth at a *seguia*, with the usual crowd of kids watching every move with kestrel intensity. One of the party reached into his mouth without any thought and pulled out his set of false teeth. There was something between a moan and a shout and the children went screaming up the slope in horror. They were slow to return and stood tense and well away from this dreadful person. When another of our gang repeated the act the reaction was similar. The children fled for home. Someone commented, "Pity nobody has a glass eye".

Our Tessaout water supply was a *source* which rose in the edge of the river itself. Without local contact we'd never have found that spring. Villages are quite fussy about clean drinking water. Earlier in the Tissili we'd filled bottles at a side stream only to have an old man yell at us that the water was not good. Charles dutifully poured out his water (and was dehydrated later) but the rest of us simply doctored ours with *Potable Aqua* pills, something we were quite unable to explain to the emphatic old Berber. Ali and Hosain went off on Taza to buy gas mantles, bread and large bottles of fizzy drinks—a craving we never had at home. We always ate well and made sure of taking plenty of liquid.

Several of the tents when struck next morning had toads under them. Mine was the biggest I've ever seen: six inches long and built like a Sumo wrestler. The local children regarded toads with the same superstitious horror as kids at home. They won't touch chameleons either. There was plenty of creepy crawly life under the stones which we were happy to leave in peace, although I couldn't resist bringing along a giant millipede, seven inches of shiny black-bronze shell walking on a wave of legs. David found a giant-sized calling cricket—eventually. Three hawk moth caterpillars completely denuded a euphorbia clump by the tents overnight.

Ifoulou reputedly had a *souk* that day at a site a kilometre down-valley, but only a handful of the tight row of shops were open. We had a thorough hunt for toilet rolls, since Lorraine was using about one a day thanks to her streaming cold. We ate hot doughnuts at the Hitelatlas (*sic*). The scenery was still on a grand scale. A big valley comes in from the south from the major trans-Atlas *piste* of the Tizi n' Fedghat where we had originally planned to go on this trip. Even from Ifoulou we were tempted to go up the Tessaout to visit Magdaz, a perched village of notable architectural fame, and make a high traverse to the Tizi n' Fedghat while the mules came round. The Fedghat pass linked on rather deviously with the *tamda* under Anghomar for Anmiter and Telouet, but the passes are high and if we found them impassable for mules we'd be in logistical trouble. Getting through was still our priority. (In 2006 we were astonished to find a tarred road from Demnate to Skoura had been routed over the Tizi n'Fedghat.)

The prow at the confluence was dominated by Toufghine, a new-looking village, its houses large and built with immaculate stonework, including a *gîte*. Several mules and pedestrians were running up and down the Oued Tessaout, like disturbed ants, before essaying a crossing, those afoot taking off their shoes and trousers for the brown flow. The heavy traffic crossing the river was because there was a proper *souk* in full swing at Aït Allah, not far along. No wonder Ifoulou couldn't compete. Itinerant farriers were shoeing mules as we joined the busy two-street *souk*. The girls tried every likely and unlikely shop in search of tissues or toilet rolls. We had drinks and Nicola used her Irish charm to obtain bread as, strangely, there wasn't a baker. The street was cluttered with tethered mules and a few *camions* had come in from Demnate.

Our *piste* continuation wended through the dappled sun and shade of Aleppo pines. Wood had been piled on the verge and a lorry heaped high with timber and people growled slowly past. Peyron suggested the riverbed as an alternative to this higher route but it was well awash from the fierce snowmelt. There was a noticeable regular rise and fall in the river level but the simplistic Alps recommendation 'cross early in the day' wouldn't have held here. The high tide was the previous day's melt up on distant mountains around the Tessaout plateau. Tessaout, oddly, translates as 'thirst'.

The temperature soared once the shade ran out. We had a pause beside a morning blue clump of convolvulus. Women staggered past with huge loads of grass, their clothes a riotous mix of reds and greens and gold, every bit as bright as the feathers of a dead roller I found on the bank. We stopped to drip-dry at a hamlet, Taglast, where men were sitting in the shade of the arcaded shops shelling walnuts, some of which they gave us to go with the *Fantas* and *Colas*. The shells formed a deep litter beside the road. With minimal languages in common we enjoyed a social break. One child took a sweetie paper discarded by a luckier friend and ardently licked at the minimal reward.

Some trekkers suddenly appeared round the bend: mostly female, in very short shorts and vests, "A French eyeful" as someone later described them. The local men told the crowding boys to move at once: they wanted to have a lecherous look. Comments were made (just as one might have heard in a chauvinist setting at home) and what I found delightful was our being included in the banter, as part of the locals! Apart from a brief "*Bonjour*" the rucksack-laden, white skins just walked on. One mule trotted behind and the bantering comments danced between muleteer and spectators. One of our lassies said, "Now I know why you insist on everyone dressing properly out here", and the other commented that there would be some severe cases of sunburn that evening.

For girls to appear dressed like that is scandalous and what astonishes me is how completely unaware they are (as on that occasion) of what they are doing but, such types are seldom making any real social contact or reading-up beforehand about the social mores of the land. What is surprising is the blindness to the effect created yet how they'd scream when their stupidity leads them into trouble. Don't people dressed like that feel *odd* and out of place when they look about them?

There's also the practical point that any people evolve the clothing suitable for their setting and in hot, dry countries covering-up with light, loose clothing is the norm; natural nudity is a thing of the dank jungly places of the tropics or, in certain cases where hot and dry, there are peoples with exceptionally dark-black skins. I'd be happy to roam the hills at home with little or less on but in the Atlas I consider rolled-up sleeves quite bold! I want to merge into the landscape and be part of it, not parade as an arrogant intruder, whether at home or abroad. The real cause of such gaffes is a lack of thought; many outdoor activists simply bumble along with brains set in neutral. In all the years I've introduced kids or adults to the hills, my endless message has been to "Think! Think! Think!" and if I ever write a book on the subject the title will be *Sense and Sensitivity in the Hills*.

We were slow in setting off again and the *piste* climbed steadily, a long pull up during which the sound of the river dropped to a whisper. Ahead, the hills were covered in powder puff trees, a landscape akin to Asni, semi-*maquis*. At the highest point, a *source* was indicated by both Peyron and the map, but the hoped-for water had been concreted over and piped off. We scrambled up the bank to sit in the shade of a juniper and eat lunch; the mules passed and went trotting on for Aït Tamlil. The barley slopes below our perch were 'white unto harvest', and the sun throbbed like a headache.

The map showed a path cutting across to avoid several wiggles of the *piste,* probably the original mule route since mules usually took steeper gradients and more direct lines than any mechanically propelled transport could. Where a *piste* had been built on top of an original mule track (whether or not then used by vehicles) a beaten mule-trod would soon snake its way along the *piste* in a gracious mark of condescension. Unfortunately, a battalion of mules had used this short cut when it was muddy (no doubt heading for the Aït Tamlil *souk*) and the resulting pitting had dried as hard as concrete: a recurrent annoyance. Looking back, southwards, over the deep-set Oued Tessaout, there was a view to Jbel Tissili n' Warg, a big tabular *berg* with immense scree skirts, topping the 3000 m mark and hiding mighty Jbel Anghomar, 3609 m. The circling of those peaks would occupy us for several days ahead.

Through a gap we dropped down to what the map marks as *Mais forest*, another red, pitched roof establishment of the *Eaux et Fôrets* department. Many of these *maisons fôrestières* are sited pleasantly and are surrounded by tall stands of mature pines. We half expected to see the kitchen tent under the shade but there was nobody about, not even children, nor could we see anything across the valley where Aït Tamlil sprawled from a low-level *Souk Tleta* area to houses high on the road out to Demnate. We made a big loop to the *souk*. An old man there said he hadn't seen any mules but a shopkeeper had and, sorry, he had no *Sidi Ali* or *Coca*. We cringed in the shade and left our reunion to Ali and Hosain's initiative, quite prepared meanwhile to do nothing and rest afterwards. We had completed our tramp along the Tessaout.

Hosain retrieved us after ten minutes and led us a dance across huge fields to a delightful corner where a gritty, dry, flat stream course below a bluff forced the tents into an orderly row. I pitched on grass, always a rare treat. A bigger treat was a spouting *source*, the jet about three bath taps in volume, and with our basins and *Tide* (pronounced *Teed*) I washed every garment, even pile clothing, and also myself from head to foot. There hadn't been much chance of such thoroughness for a long time and since descending into the Bou Guemez the weather gods had forgotten about rain. We had quietly slipped into the blessed normality of largely settled weather and the bliss of certain sunshine, a happy presumption I've always felt. We gloried in the sun and had no further rain for the remainder of GTAM.

CHAPTER 8

Tessaout to Telouet

Regions mountainous and wild, thinly inhabited, and little cultivated, make a great part of the earth, and he that has never seen them must live unacquainted with much of the face of nature, and with one of the great scenes of human existence.

Samuel Johnson

I was happily presumptuous in assuming everything washed would be dry before bedtime—and appreciated the climate that made this possible. We strung lines and hung our washing between the pines. I went over our supplies and made a shopping list for Ali. At 1700 he rode Taza off to the *souk* which, being eve of *souk* day, would have some shops open. Somehow Tamri freed himself of his tether and set off over the fields after them with Hosain in loud pursuit, teaching us some new vocabulary. From a knoll above camp I watched them vanish towards the *souk* (about 3 km distant), Tamri giving Hosain a good canter. No doubt Tamri would soon find Taza, his companion, and receive a good hammering from Hosain. Some nasty flies at that site actually drew blood on the mules—the only such I've seen in all my Atlas years. A scented hawthorn by the cook tent was in blossom and attracted dancing flies, wasps and hornets and when we dined in the light of the moon, there was a flirtation of crazy moths.

That night I was able to enjoy the magic of lying out under the stars, such a cobweb of stars and the fairy lights of glow-worms. The soft noises of the night included winds whispering in the fronds of fan palms, the sharp voices of a fox or jackal and the muffled clip-clop from a late traveller. The only drawback to sleeping out is a lack of privacy: sleep late and you're likely to wake to a ring of silently observing children.

If all days were equally good, some were more equal than others. And we were slipping pieces steadily into the jigsaw knowledge of the Atlas. Shipton, as a young man exploring the Alps regularly, wrote of how he 'began to have that exciting feel of connected knowledge of country'. This is something those who ask questions like "Why climb the Munros over again?" or "Haven't you done enough in the Atlas now?" know nothing about. There may not be visible excitement but the deep satisfaction of knowing what one views from a summit or meets along the journey only increases with the passing of time; one starts to possess the land, not wander through.

The new day was to insert abundant fresh spice into the cake of our 'connected knowledge' and prove one of the best days of GTAM, 'an extraordinary day' I was to write in my log, very late, by candlelight. I added, 'I don't remember such non-stop, dramatic *uphill* ever. Fit, thank heavens, so able to enjoy life'. The *varied* landscapes we travelled through I now remember as special.

We wandered through magnificent Aleppo pine forest initially, the way cheery with people riding in for the *souk*. We'd ascertained that our path was now a *piste*, curving down to the Oued Tessaout and on to a village, Tallent, but the mule path cut corners as ever and we descended a steep little glen quite beyond delineation on the map. On a prow before the final twists down to the flood plain we studied the wide flow of water. People were crossing at two places and we chose the upper. We took off our trousers to splash across, like the locals, with varying degrees of skill and enjoyment and plenty of comments from the spectators who'd probably never seen such wimps or such white, female legs. The Berbers, while showing a modest rectitude normally have few inhibitions. If a girl is trampling her washing in a stream she is quite happy to show a great deal of leg. I recall an incident at Imlil where a man was rebuilding a terrace wall washed away in a spate and, having to actually stand in the water to work, he, quite unabashed, took off all his clothes to do so.

Charles A nearly went up the first valley south, towards Jbel Tissili, whereas our route was initially downstream for the long Assif n' Terga (which outflanked this huge chunk of mountain and the western thrust of Anghomar) then over a pass to reach the Azib Anfergal and to connect with the known country of Peyron's GTAM. The brevity of Peyron there and the unreliability of the map were to ginger the day on several occasions. The valley was intensely cultivated and the spring flowers a joy, the path edged with cistus, euphorbias, broom and dazzling, genuine *Erodium guttatum*, brilliant as Juba's robes. Even the common daisy is *Bellis rotundifolia caerulensis*, i.e. tending to blue, which hardly conveys the delicate mauve tints of the flowers.

I quoted Peyron: 'Descend towards the meanders of the Tassawt (Tessaout) river. A little before the hamlet of Tallent, splendid views are obtained towards Jbel Rat. The river is fairly wide at this point and in winter/spring crossing can be troublesome. To keep dry feet, organise a mule shuttle', to which someone laughed "How useful! Our mules are probably drinking mint tea back at the camp". (Thumbing lifts across rivers on a mule is something we have done often enough and I'm always astonished at how one always seems to appear at the right moment.)

Our trouble began when we realised Tallent was shown in two different places on the different maps and the path up to Terga (Targa) had been abandoned because the *piste* now continued further down the Oued Tessaout to a bridge near a village, Tiwghza, and then zigzagged up to Terga direct. We knew nothing of the new bridge and *piste* and, already across, worried away to find the Peyron line. At one stage the path we were on ended in someone's yard where a toddler went bawling off at the sight of us. We were at once invited in for tea! The man of the house then insisted on showing us the way which meant he ambled ahead of us all the way up to Terga. As half the party was lagging badly and could miss the complicated and decaying track I suggested he went ahead to get the kettle on and find some bread for us. A village was overspilling a cliff-girt thrust of crag in one of the river loops far below while Rhat and Tignousti dominated our backward glances. Only on a last crest before turning into the Terga glen did we see the *piste* snaking up and our cavalcade as remote blue dots on the lower bends. The whole area appealed immensely. My log gasped, 'Sun all day. Just love it. Flowers. A very heaven'.

So was Terga. '…an imposing village cluster…nestling at the foot of austere arid slopes. A few poplars and the usual patchwork of fields bravely attempt to strike a gay, verdant note.' was Peyron's restrained description, although what we found astonished. The valley was massively cultivated and there were several large villages on both flanks of the valley, an unexpected oasis ringed with habitation, the people noisily friendly and helpful. We were ushered into one of the first houses and sprawled in the coolness of the guest room. My hands were given a wash then a tray of glasses was placed before me to make the mint tea. My brew met the approval of our host and was welcomed by our laggards and then by the mule lads. A big vegetable *tagine* suddenly appeared with plenty of fresh bread rather like *naan*. The far wall had a frieze of what looked like little coloured flags but were the labels peeled off flat torch batteries. There was also a portrait of the king (of course) and a bouquet of dried flowers. Nicola commented: "Add the Pope and JFK and it could be a cottage in Kerry".

We dropped steeply into the valley and up a spur opposite to end in a confusion of houses. An old man raced ahead to show us the way but when he saw the mules coming there was a right old barney and they were sent back down to take a route on the other side of the valley; it appeared our demanding track had tight places where the mules wouldn't pass with panniers so once more we made a hopeful rendezvous with Ali and continued our upward way. We didn't see them for the rest of the day and when they appeared, they were on the opposite crest, tiny dots lost in the austere aridity. The Assif n'Terga cut down continuous gorges yet wherever there was the slightest relenting in the wildness, a path wiggled down to tiny cultivated plots or grazings. Flocks wander everywhere so one must never trundle boulders—even if goats have a habit of doing so onto people.

Our track traversed determinedly along and up. We had an escort of about a dozen (two-legged) kids. They showed us a small pathside *source* with the usual old sardine tin left as a cup for the wayfarer and we lunched on a breezy crest. At a side-valley a man heading down rescued us from their eager attentions and, walking out on opposite banks of the side-valley, we exchanged waves and ever fainter "Bye-byes!" The exit from the side-stream was up bare gravels with little adhesion then we flanked in and out an extensive hollow under a dominating wet overhang, dramatic at every step, to eventually reach a natural big red wall we'd seen from afar. Kestrels were keeking about as we zigzagged up and over into another discovered paradise.

Dominated by the screes and scarps of Jbel Issermad, this west flank produced a surprise of springs rushing out and down the slopes, like kids released from school, to water a huge area of secret cultivation. Peyron noted rock carvings with small meadows, but the meadows were lush, extensive and rich with flowers which so excited all of us that we quite forgot to look out for the carvings. There were plenty of people too, mostly planting potatoes in this alpine market garden. There were sheets of colour: orchids, star of Bethlehem, vetches, asphodels, campions, clumping alyssum, salvia, thistles, hyacinths and chrysanthemums—among those I recall or can name. Beyond the meadows, bare red spurs and *pitons* (pinnacle-shaped hills) contorted the onward track. There were several streams, and with plenty of water and well fed we enjoyed the hot day without any dehydration worries.

I left Francis and the girls at one stream to push on in hope of seeing the mules. When finally spotted, they were tiny dots coming steeply down the other side of the valley, competently displaying their skill at scree running. A long *seguia* tapped a distant *source* and led the water round to tumble down in an artificial fall. Once the mules were down, they had to follow the main valley, stream and path often synonymous, while our path continued to weave in and out the lofty spurs, dotted with remnant oak forest and a few pines. From a final spur we looked down onto a flood plain with *azibs* and terraces and many feeder streams, the ground painted yellow as rape fields with a small ragwort. Anghomar bulked hugely at the head of the valley, the high horizontal banding vertically broken by snow-filled gullies creating the familiar streaky bacon effect and the lower slopes grey, unrelenting screes. Though the flat was over 2000 m, Anghomar still dominated, a huge wreck of a mountain, the summit 3610 m.

Ali and I actually met on the first terraces—perfect timing. And there we camped. We'd left Aït Tamlil at 0715 and it was now 1715, although Peyron covers not only all of that day's route but also crosses the big pass under Anghomar, deals with a gorge and camps in the valley beyond, in one 10-hour day! We put in two camps and felt we'd done well, and I can only reiterate the warning that if Peyron gives a long day the normal walker will be well advised to consider it as a two-day stint. This was our fiftieth day on the trail and by the following day, we'd have covered 500 miles. The site is chiefly recalled from sharing accommodation with two fat vipers, spotting a third as we set off.

The Koran has the eloquent picture of the dawn 'breathing away the darkness' which described perfectly our mornings in the mountains where first light came like babies' breath and the cold shadows rushed off in hot haste. They say that in the desert, day is despair and night made welcome, but in the mountains the biting night is feared and day the delight. As we had plenty of sleep our dawns were certainly highlights. We set off with Anghomar dark against a golden sky. "Just another bloomin' sunny day", a comment on our first-ever trip, which once more became a bit of a catch phrase.

Bits of stringy path and plenty of boulder hopping focussed the mind; care had to be taken to follow the correct side valley for our pass. Grazing paths went off everywhere and there were many side valleys. A slow-moving caterpillar line of sheep and goats moved across the screes opposite. The 50,000 map, usually so bad on names and paths, was more helpful on that occasion and we turned off, correctly, to begin the ascent of a valley which led to a solitary, smart *azib* where we sat in the sun awhile. Two youths, just into their teens perhaps, jumped when they rounded the building and almost stood on us. They were having a quiet brew at that last water when we left but they soon passed us on the *tizi* and sped off beyond. The climb up to the pass was scree and soil set at the maximum angle possible and we rested at the col to dry off our sweat soaked shirts. We had three maps, and all gave the 2800 m col a different name. The gorge on the way down had two names. I commented, "We could do with Harvey's maps out here. Or even the OS, bless 'em. I'll never complain about our home maps again". At least we had maps, for it is virtually impossible to buy maps for trekking—even when going to the Rabat map offices in person.

This 2800 m *tizi* lay between mighty Anghomar (3610 m or 3581 m, depending on the map or Inghemar 3609 m in Peyron) and Jbel Taghalliyn (Tighaline) (3310 m or 3326 m) and a path of sorts led round to the southeast ridge of the resonantly-named peak, across slopes which were dotted with dainty blue flax flowers. We wended in and out the bumps on the ridge, the floral differences between north and south slopes very marked and at one stage I yelled for David as I'd found something I'd not seen before. The flower was the same as our old friend *Ranunculus calandrinioides* but instead of wavy sword-shaped leaves, these had leaves the shape of table-tennis bats. Anghomar has quite a known flower reputation and David reckons variations occur on several of these huge brutes of hill simply because they are as isolated as islands. *Matthiola* (stock) was also plentiful on Tighaline and, for once, I (and David) reached the summit last. Lorraine had gone ahead like a gazelle.

From the summit we could see just about everywhere we'd been since coming round the Rhat: M'Goun was still white though less so, ahead villages by Anmiter and Telouet could be seen, as could the large dam south of the mountains at Ouarzazate. Jbel Siroua and Toubkal were visible. North, below us, lay a huge hollow strangely ringed with circles of exposed strata while to the west lay Peyron's 'sizeable chunks of uninhabited uplands'.

I'd observed the mules reach the *tizi*, but was then puzzled when they crossed on our track to the next col, dithered, and then angled along rather than down. This was not the plan so I grabbed a salmon sandwich and some Christmas cake and raced off down a scree of knuckle bone sized pieces to intercept them as they wended along, rather aimlessly, on the crest of the ridge above the valley into which they should have descended. The explanation was that Ali had taken the two names of the one col I'd given him as being the names of two cols and was taking both, only there wasn't a second. They went on over easy ground and cut down to the Assif n' Tamda while I took a more direct route down, brutally steep but assisted by the moving surface.

Lower, on whitish rock, a marble perhaps, there was a happy abundance of flowers: flax, a miniature rock rose (*Helianthemum*), ornithogolum, blue hedgehog broom and chrysanthemums, one streaked with scarlet. Out of this dry hollow (corrie) the Assif n' Tamda suddenly burst as a full-blown stream. (I don't understand why it is named Tamda, which means *lake*.) Cold as the water was, I was glad to splash in it after my sweaty sprint and I lay sunbathing to dry afterwards. The valley was ungrazed and lush, the blue broom forming huge cushions two metres across, but slowly the valley turned into a gorge with a faint track on which I could see the marks of our mules' passage. Relishing another paddle my eye was caught by a line of tiny blue dots wavering among the grass stems, which turned out to be ants carrying the wings from a couple of butterflies. They looked like a line of miniature blue sails. A dipper scolded past and an eagle hung on a curtain rail of cloud.

From habit I noted possible campsites and one extra good *source* then, well down the gorge, saw tarpaulin blue ahead, the loads off the mules and the muleteers having tea—welcome as ever—but not what was expected or wanted. Looking down between the gorge walls we could see the Azib Anfergal fields where we intended to camp, less than two kilometres off, but now quite beyond reach through the gorge as far as the mules were concerned. The path had been washed away in a spate and several boulder overhangs and tricky slabs where a stony pathway had once been were now bare. So, the mules actually had limitations. "Haven't you taught them to abseil yet, Ali?"

As it was already 1500 and the next day was a shorter, lazy day (which would be quoted back at me) the best thing seemed to be to camp where we were. We retraced quarter of an hour to the good *source*. On the way I saw what looked like a toadflax growing on a wall in creamy white drapes and later led the delighted experts to *Sarcocapnos baetica*, one on their list of 'hoped to see' rarities. Trying to write at the tents was made difficult by thousands of ghostly moths battering about. When we lit the lamp they flew into the mantle and broke it almost at once. For days afterwards moths appeared out of the most unlikely places in our gear. Polaris lay right up the 'V' of the gorge and a satellite passed over, later a fat and jealous moon dimmed the stars and glowed like a lantern light down the cliffs onto the site.

Porridge was our popular breakfast alternative to muesli. We briefed Ali and then set off with David not well again, a recurring nuisance. The cliffs where the mules had been stopped from descending the gorge were hanging gardens of *sarcocapnos*, this exciting rarity now being seen in plebeian plenitude, as always seemed to happen. There was some nice scrambling and route picking down the lowest section of the gorge where vertical strata fanned up like fossilised palms. Cutting corners to gain the upper Ounila valley gave us a tedious steeplechase, except I rather like teasing away at a challenging route (tedium to me being an easy walk on a marked way). As David had not been seen for some time we perched on a knoll for an hour till he and shepherding Charles K appeared.

Charles A and I wended over to explore some marshes, Peyron's Aghbalou n' Ougerzram: a round pond and springs that feed the infant Oued Ounila not far above the Anfergal meadows. The pond was a frog and toad bedlam (*Bufo viridis* can change colour like a chameleon) and the drier banks were studded with the pale blue thistle-buttons of *Carduncellus pinnatus acaulis*. On another visit, we watched a snake eating another snake here. I suspect a muleteer had killed one by a blow on the 'neck', and the other was being an opportunist cannibal. The victim had been grabbed several inches down its length so swallowing a double thickness proved quite a mouthful but, as we watched, the unhinged jaws sucked in the last of the head and the elongated thickness moved along an inch or two at each swallow. We left it to a long meal, speculating on what would happen if the snake it was eating was longer than itself.

We sat on another knoll for an hour, to see and be seen. Doctor Charles A went off to investigate if there was anything he could be doing to help. Eventually, I followed the others. An old man was bringing down such a huge load of grass on his mule that it appeared to be a mobile green stack on short legs.

Over on the left were *azibs* under a huge cliff and further on, tucked in, was 'our' *azib* where Charles, Vi, Inge, Mohammed from Anmiter, his helper and myself had once survived a night of heavy snowfall. We spent some of it in the frozen bell tent (eating) but were then thankful for the spacious shelter of the low-roofed *azib* (sleeping). That storm effectively put an end to our first Anghomar plans but we struggled on up to the *tamda*. The scenery under snow was so startling that, out of devilment, I included a slide of the frozen waters in a lecture on Spitzbergen, and nobody noticed. This defeat (and warning) motivated our circling approach on GTAM, cutting out the high Tizi n' Fedghat which might have been snowbound.

Peyron describes the up-valley going as tiresome with tussock and scree and the path difficult to find in places, but we found the path was excellent and the going easy. There were a few short steep sections and in general the place looked very like the Pass of Ryvoan in the Cairngorms, even producing a Lochan Uaine on cue. The *lac* came unexpectedly soon, a brilliant, startling blue like Viking eyes, so cool among the warm tones of the surrounding screes. I cleared the stones off an area for the cook tent and my own then walked around the *lac* and explored a grassy spur back a bit but failed to find a *source*. (The water supply proved up-valley; an odd, short length of stream which didn't reach the lake and had started as a resurgence.) We lunched, those of us present, the temperature over 80°F in the shade, except there was no shade.

About to go off on another water hunt, I returned at a run as Charles K and the mules had arrived but not David or Charles A. Apparently, the mules had passed them without being seen and David and the doctor were still down the valley, the former incapacitated according to Charles. As soon as the mules were off-loaded, Hosain and Charles rode off on Taza and one of Mohammed's mules to find the others while we pitched all the tents, a task that left us dripping. The tents were like ovens, so we made frequent drinks to survive in the open. Ali and muleteer Hassan rode off for bread as an alternative to baking some and, I suspect, to enjoy socialising. Eventually the stragglers rode in: Charles K supporting David on one mule and Charles A behind Hosain on Taza. David came off his mule like a sheriff shot by an injun arrow in a western, except we caught him. He was dumped in his tent with both ends open for a hint of a draught.

Lorraine had been up the valley and returned to say there were two more lakes, one really big. This was interesting. The 50,000 map did show two *lacs* but the smaller one didn't exist if this by the tents was one of them. Slowly I realised that there were really just two *lacs* and this one, possibly seasonal, wasn't on the map at all. The altimeter rather bore this out. In our winter visit we'd only been aware of one *lac* and looking at slides, that was obviously the upper pair, recognised from the large flat cover of ice and snow. Of the lower there had been no sign, simply being buried under snow. Others have been misled. When Charles de Foucauld crossed the Atlas he saw Djebel Anremer (*sic*) and wrote: '*C'est de cette montagne que sort l'Ouad Jounil. A son sommet est un étang, toujours rempli d'eau .....un object de vénèration profonde pour les Musulmans des environs*' (Its from this mountain flows the Oued Ounila. At its summit lies a lake which never dries out...an object of deep veneration by the local Moslems). Walter Harris heard there was a crater lake at the summit. I wonder if they were being misinformed on purpose, to keep them away. Anghomar was often called Jbel Ounila then. Even today, a thousand people will gather for the August *moussem* and goats and sheep are sacrificed at the top of the mountain. Of course, a *lac* couldn't exist at the top of any mountain here and, interestingly, the *source* above our camp didn't come from the main *lacs* but spouted out at a higher level. Not surprisingly, this odd location has lured us back several times since GTAM.

Once the heat of the sun had ebbed slightly I walked to the far end of our *lac* and dived in fully clothed! I then washed all my garments and myself and splashed around very pleasantly. Eventually most of the others followed suit. The water was not at all cold but harboured hundreds of toads who provided a noisy *continuo* overnight. Ali and Hassan didn't turn up until 21.30, long after dark. Young Tamri had led the way back and Ali was quite impressed; mules obviously have good night vision.

All except David were up for an alpine start, 0300, and off at 0345. Although the moon was nearing half, the light was so bright we hardly needed torches as we walked up to the *lacs*, glad of Lorraine's recce the day before. First light found us on the long flood plain beyond, a treadmill of gravel tramping that seemed interminable. There was light enough to spot the path zigzagging up on the right to reach the Tizi n' Taghaghayt or we might have boxed ourselves in the gorge which had spewed out that plain. The *tizi* at 2838 m was gained in time to watch the changing tints of dawn, a scene enhanced by the *hamri* red landscape in front of us. The scale was brought home when someone pointed out there was still the equivalent of a considerable Munro to climb. Anghomar (or Inghemar, meaning *elbow*) is a dozen kilometres long with most of the south flank an endless succession of scree slopes. However, from the eastern end, an arm runs out and down over several bumps to the *tizi*, then round to Zarzemt (3113 m) south of the *lacs*. By heading up that crest we reckoned to miss most of the screes (Anghomar and Zarzemt being the A to Z of screes). There was a little scrambling on the crest then we were able to skirt to keep in the shade, enjoy water from a stream and have a snack with a sunrise view of where we'd been the previous week. We climbed ever-steeper and higher, but with easy going, and found ourselves at the iron trig point on the summit, arriving with that sudden joy like opening a door to smiling sun.

Anghomar is the highest summit between Jbel Rhat and Taska n' Zat so the view was extensive. Charles K suggested going along the long summit ridge westwards which most did but I had my eye on Zarzemt so, with Nicola, I set off down by the ascent route initially. A good way down we met David! Twenty-four hours before he was barely conscious so we were astonished to see him there. Nicola bluntly told him he was daft. We cut down to the stream in the corner and managed to find a long traversing path I'd spotted at dawn which led back to the Tizi n' Taghaghayt. It soon became clear the 'path' was an old *seguia* carrying water round to the arid south. Running under boulders, squeezing tightly between rocks, no mule could have passed. (A year later Ali, having missed out that time, did Anghomar and used the *seguia* line as well.)

At the *tizi* I suggested Zarzemt and Nicola rather doubtfully agreed. Initially, we had some good scrambling on the shattered ridge of dark volcanic rock, but the going was tiring and Nicola decided she'd had enough. She turned for home down easy ground to the *lacs* where she had a swim. The *lacs* were vivid blue, the sort of colour that would be bad taste in clothing. I watched Nicola with a touch of envy as I headed on up but the final upthrust of crag was superb rough limestone which gave enjoyable scrambling. Crimson-winged finches were working the scrub. Beyond lay what Nicola would have described as Burren country: a plateau-like tilt of caramel-coloured limestone pavement, pockmarked and savagely carved, not a place to make sudden contact between bare skin and bare rock. The rock was like sharks' teeth. Like the Burren, the plateau was a natural rock garden. I was quite irritated reading an old guide that night, which stated that alpine flowers are not abundant in the Atlas, Anghomar is not really worth the effort, and our beloved Tichka Plateau of not much interest.

The ridge down gave periodic glimpses of the various *lacs*. Choughs were sporting along the scarp, diving so fast their wings thrummed like thrown stones. A deep glen cut off the end of the ridge but I used a traversing path to swing round to just above our campsite, giving me a bird's eye view of the colourful dots of tent. I chuntered down slopes as crumbly as cheese, right into camp. Tea or drinks that had been cooling in the edge of the *lac* were instantly offered. Most of the afternoon I spent by or in the *lac*. The traverse group came up-valley and David came down the screes to camp. Our appetites being pretty good after the big peak we had fish soup, haggis, with plenty of vegetables and Christmas pudding for supper. At my urging, everyone decided to tackle Zarzemt the following day. Anghomar sprawls like a big grey rhino, Zarzemt its horn.

The following day's camp was established back down-valley at the Azib Anfergal, flat fields between a crag and the river with a water channel by the tents. Anfergal means 'place of a thousand dead', and records a 14th Century battle. A few years previous, there was a bit of a tushie over tribal grazing rights and a couple of men were actually killed, which explained the moribund agriculture. (Both sides were banned.) Charles K and the girls were in first after climbing Zarzemt and the botanists long after. A stiff *chergui* (desert hot wind) had most people cringing in a cave at the foot of the rock wall while the interior of the cook tent provided a good imitation of a *hammam*. Only one of the three big gas cylinders was functioning, so cooking was slow even with small back-up stoves. Ali and Hosain had gone for a romp to Anmiter and were expected back the following day. The wind, perversely, dropped as soon as we'd eaten and it was a warm night again, the 'moth-like stars flickering out'. Finally, we could take layers of clothes off to sleep; it hadn't been that long since we were piling on thermals. Being warm is rather pleasant.

A reasonably early departure paid off for the easy and beautiful walk down the Oued Ounila valley. When David went to fill his waterbottle a snake dived into the tempting hole presented—and stuck! Snakes were rather common on that site. There were goats being driven along the slopes, producing a weird cacophony of grunts, groans, bleats and yells as they went, their dust kicking up against the golden sunlight so it rose in fiery-edged clouds. The Zat snows appeared tantalisingly distant down the 'V' of the valley, our next objective, beyond the Tizi n' Tichka.

We had a long pause by the stream as it threaded through a jungle of oleander below fields, purple-hazed with orchids a metre high. At the first village, Ighourzane, we found the mules tethered by a small village shop that seemed to sell everything except the items we wanted. We scoffed chocolate *Taggers* and *Cocas*, though. The view down into the valley was a sea of green, upon which a perched village with a fine *tighremt* was balanced. On our previous visit, the 'sea' had been foaming white as the trees are all almonds—a spectacular sight.

We followed a sturdy matron walking with the week's washing in a huge basin balanced on her head, the ubiquitous packet of *Tide* perched on top. When we swung down to the Tighza school we found our lads sitting against a wall with tea and walnuts on the go. After we'd indulged, we continued to a confluence of rivers (with several springs) where there is always a gathering of women washing blankets and clothes which are then hung on the layered banding of the cliffs, a colourful spectacle like warships dressed over all. Small girls romped about the cliffs as sure-footed as goats. Nicola and Lorraine went over to say hello and there was a great deal of laughter and banter.

Ighris is a bigger village with some architectural interest and a new mosque tower. 'In recent years this has become a road-head for expedition vehicles that pick up or deposit cargoes of package tourists at regular intervals throughout the summer', complains Peyron while giving praise to the 'picturesque castellated kasbahs of Anmiter'. The trekkers now tend to be using the fine Tighza *gîte* and Anmiter steadily loses its architectural gems. Charles A and I were so far ahead that we lost touch with the others. We rebelled at the hard, hot *piste* and turned off to wend paths through the lush fields and river edge. The air was sweet with the smell of wild roses. Our route was a bit of an obstacle course but it finally brought us along a concrete *seguia* right into Anmiter below Elyazid Mohammed's house where we were to stay. We could see the others striding down the hot *piste* on the other side of the valley and we had consumed several glasses of sweet reviving tea before they joined us, their local—unwanted—guide being astonished to see us there already. This character claimed to be the *guardien* of the *lacs* but had been sponging off us since the previous night's camp and obviously hoped for a lift to Marrakech. When he found we were staying for two nights, had no car and planned to *walk* to Telouet, he disappeared! A lunch *tagine* followed and most of the gang flaked-out in the cool, rooftop-level guest room until the temperature eased off after 1700. We gathered later on the roof, squatting around the low table set on a spread of brick-red carpets and blankets. *Bismillah*. We broke bread for a vast, scrumptious *tagine*. (You rarely encounter a poor *tagine*.) Most of the gang chose to sleep on the roof.

The following day was grimly hot and stuffy, yet Charles K led everyone on a long hike down the Oued Ounila until they rebelled. With Flowers' time running out I stayed and dealt with mail and logistics so our 'couriers' could carry letters home. The Flowers gang hadn't found my sleeping bag at the Hotel Ali (or Imlil) so Lorraine kindly agreed to leave me hers, a very light *Snugpak* which reduced to half the size of a football. Hosain and Mohammed had been to Telouet so supper was served at the latest for the whole trip. We found an attractive praying mantis, green with spots. Several people were startled in the toilet chamber by a noise at the window, only to find a broody hen ensconced on the sill.

Much of Anmiter (pronounced Ani-meter) is red: soil and buildings alike. The village must have been very impressive a generation ago but many of the *ksour* and *tighremts* have fallen and others are decaying. Some, on the edge of cultivation, have been restored rather than supplanted and soar, strikingly handsome, with geometric brick patterns and rising towers, to castellated tops. Several of Majorelle's paintings on display at the gardens in Marrakech are of Anmiter. The Ounila valley down from there has interesting villages and then becomes a gorge with spectacular settings, with mosque and *zaouia* buildings and decaying *tighremt*. There are some cave dwellings on cliffs, largely abandoned now, but once used for safe storage and refuge. The green thread of well-dressed valley lies far below the rim where the rough *piste* runs. The gorge ends at the tourist trap of Aït Benhaddou, a village of character, partly restored as a film set and all too accessible for the massed tourism based on Ouarzazate. Busloads of the overweight and underdressed debouch for a ten-minute tour, an expensive mint tea, and depart.

Peyron comments: 'Talwat [Telouet] to Anmiter is a road; 2½h. on foot; ride a truck or hire a taxi', which we considered both heretical and unnecessary as there is an alternative track offering an excellent walk. The road itself passes through an area where salt was once mined and white stains still seep from the slopes. (Salt mining was the origin of Glaoui wealth.) We made an early breakfast but our hosts kept producing further types of bread and bowls of *taghboula*, the standard gruel-like porridge, with first tea and then coffee. By the time we escaped the day was already shimmering hot, the view reduced by a clammy haze so one strained to see anything, as if viewing a painting in an art gallery from too far away. As we walked, we stirred up clouds of dust, fine as talcum powder.

From a short way down the Ounila valley we were able to turn up into the hills which run northeast–southwest like swooping herds, parallel strata, undulating but easy to walk along. At one hollow, paths led off to the four cardinal points of the compass and, not for the first or last time my spirits soared at the sight of new roads leading I knew not where. I cursed my too many lazy years in the Atlas when we did little new and over-much that was repetitive. Pity I couldn't swap a surplus Toubkal ascent for days of novelty. But I wasn't quite ready to 'hang my hat on a pension', and the decade following GTAM would prove the most active and rewarding of all.

Eventually, we turned north to break through the parallel crests and reach the Anmiter–Telouet road at its highest point, the Tizi n' Tanbdout. We dropped down through an area with the appearance of rocky acne, a violently weathered landscape which nevertheless gave some odd flowers. There was a skullcap and an astragalus with bladders like papery Chinese lanterns. We were led off-road to investigate a brilliant red patch which turned out to be a vetch, then stuck to wandering mule tracks rather than *goudron*. Areas were snowed with a white rock rose and then we wended through a brilliance of *Erodium guttatum* (storksbill), the air scented with thyme and the river banks hazed with tamarisk; altogether a more interesting walk than expected. On a subsequent trip, we headed westwards for longer up in the hills, to descend directly into Telouet which was even better. The Tastwiyt hills backing Telouet are fascinating but seldom visited. (The Scottish explorer Joseph Thomson climbed one in 1888.)

We kept to the riverbed (resurgences) and only crossed to reach the green-tiled *kouba* of Sidi Wissatane (the local patron saint). It looks down on the past glory of the Dar Glaoui and so to the welcoming *auberge* (Chez Ahmed), where we found the Berber contingent sprawled on the couches under a brown nomad tent. Greetings were exchanged:

"*La bas!*"

"*La bas!*"

"*Las bas alik.*"

It had to be time for tea.

Lunch was a Berber omelette *tagine*, rather like glorified scrambled eggs. A youngster was sent off on a bicycle to the *souk* area to buy the eggs. A few cafés and shops and a large empty square *was* Telouet, the residential villages sprawled out around it. We tried most of the cafés at one time or another but ended that day with a walk around the mosque and a track between the village and the fields leading over to the stark Glaoui palace-fort. The village had a mediaeval feeling, quite in keeping with the lord's castle. After dark, we were entertained by some of the locals. Young girls in glittering *kaftans* danced while an ever-changing group of instrumentalists beat out rhythms and any and all joined in the raucous vocals: a music of wind and water wildness. Not a few dancers had marked negroid features, doubtless the descendants of Glaoui slaves in the not-so-distant past. There was an interval to allow us to demolish *harrira* and chicken *tagines* and, after a few more dances the girls vanished into the house to consume their share of supper. Payment was made by tucking 10 dh notes into the girls' headbands.

Lying on the sagging couch inside the huge guest tent that night, I thought it another strange place to be passing through. The moon was picking out the towers of that secure eyrie of one of the most extraordinary raptor families in modern history, in whose dungeons the traveller often ended. T'hami El Glaoui had been the despotic ruler of the Atlas and south on behalf of the French, an extraordinary mix of mediaeval ruler and European playboy, feared rather than loved. Everyone had been to the Dar Glaoui at some time that day to marvel at the decayed splendour, the swank and pomp of power reduced to rubble. Death doesn't omit to call on the dictator and if the rise of the house of Glaoui was dramatic, its fall was even more so, the story chronicled in the bloody classic *Lords of the Atlas* by Gavin Maxwell. I had the privilege of reading some of this in manuscript, and the author inspired me to visit the Atlas for the first time.

We first visited Telouet over thirty years ago, and the place had changed very little in the intervening years. As in the case of healthy old persons, the decay is insidiously invisible. A tile falls here, a beam cracks there, a fissure spreads, a wall leans. The warning notices not to explore should be heeded. Where the roof is sound there is survival of a sort but the older parts—the outworks, mud-built and roofless—have reverted to their elements, levelled to the ground or left behind as stark hummocks and spikes like the towers of termites. Half the buildings seen in old photos have vanished, yet Telouet is still a vivid throwback to the Middle Ages. Less than fifty years ago, black guards stood at the huge door, chained prisoners starved in their cells, barbs lined the stalls of the stable and boar-hounds yowled in the night. The setting is now no less desolate, distant and distressing.

Over in the open ground above the Dar Glaoui we'd passed three *khaima* tents and while we sat over refreshing drinks, a stream of 4 × 4 vehicles drove up, nose to tail. They were numbered and obviously drove in order, each following the number displayed on the rear window of the predecessor (if it could be seen for the dust churned up). There were only two people in each vehicle. Eventually, there were *sixty-seven* 4 × 4s lined up along the slope by the tents, like some strange other-world armoured division drawn up in battle array, ready to assault the mediaeval fortress below. They certainly invaded the Dar Glaoui (armed with *Sidi Harazem* bottles) and were all back within half an hour, another site on their itinerary ticked off. They then invaded the two dining tents for a Berber lunch, the waiters scurrying from the third (kitchen) tent with endless *tagine* dishes, being filled from vast vats of simmering stew. Others carried in conical baskets containing bread. As soon as they had eaten they were out again, into the 4 × 4s, and away.

The golden early light on the old *kasbah* saw me wandering off with my camera before breakfast. After checking our onward route we gathered on the square for a second breakfast at the Café Ropos (*sic*) the owner insisting on treating us to tea. (As soon as we'd walked in the day before he'd commented "Ah, you must be Hamish; we knew you were coming".) The tea was perhaps to stall us, as the coffees took nearly an hour to come as they had to await the arrival of a taxi from Ouarzazate bringing the milk! Both *Pepsi* and *Coca Cola* lorries arrived together and we counted something like 1500 empties being taken out to the rivals. Some years previous, one of the firms put it about that the other used pig's fat as an ingredient in their product which, not surprisingly, severely dented the sales statistics of the opposition. They regained the lost ground, however, by putting about a counter-claim that the others' drink made men sterile.

One year I kept a note of the menu misprints in cafés. There were Quoissongs with the morning coffee and you could dine heartily on Stick and chaps, Scheese omelit, Herbet omelit, Plan omelit, Hana borger garnied, Roost chicken, Lamp stew, Spare rebes, Orange whit shugr, Flambed pan keses and Fruids salad. To drink: Bootled water, Green or Black pee and Coffee all calor. At the foot of one menu was written, Mercy!

The square was livelier with the *souk el Khemis* due the next day and we sat in sweet content just watching life go by but, eventually, our minibus arrived to bear us off to Marrakech (after another Berber omelette in the tent). We also took farewell of Taza and Tamri. Mohammed from Anmiter was offering them stabling while we were away on our necessary but short intermission. We felt decidedly odd whirling along in a vehicle again.

The line of the modern road over the Tizi n' Tichka was chosen in order not to intrude on the Glaoui HQ of Telouet. Imagine the surveyors faced with a virgin barrier such as the High Atlas and the engineers having to create the route, or the thousands who toiled (1925–39) to give birth to the reality. The road brought commerce, the real conqueror, so while the Dar Glaoui crumbles an echo on the breeze brings the hungry purr of *camions* on the pass.

That day (24th May) was hot and close and, with the best will in the world, we all failed to stay awake for the scenic run down to Marrakech from the Tizi n' Tichka. The hills quickly reeled back into haze. Our first port of call was the ice cream parlour behind the Hotel Ali for mammoth *coupés*. Those going home could relax—and did—but Charles and I had an assault course of logistics to deal with: organising tickets and plans for Ali and Hosain, going over plans with Aït Idir Mohammed for the next stage and paying for the bus. A mammoth re-packing was required, with gear to join us at the Tizi n' Test–Ijoukak stage via newcomer Graeme, clothes and other items for the very end, our own needs to organise, some items for home, some for Imlil, some to the Base case in the Hotel Ali, and films (about 30) to make ready along with the rest of our mail. By the time we'd washed clothes and ourselves it was 0200. Walking was the easy part of the expedition. We resumed at 0600 with various letters to people who'd be joining soon and only after seeing everyone off (the Flowers to the airport, Ali and Hosain for a bus home) were we able to deflate ourselves over a coffee in the Iceberg.

We were in Marrakech because the GTAM was going to run for over three months and tourists only have a three-month allowance, not that many are aware of this. The Tizi n' Tichka, the most famous pass over the Adrar n' Dern (the 'mountain of mountains' as the Berbers call the Atlas), was a very natural place to make the break and we'd decided to visit what was Moorish Spain for a short break and then re-enter Morocco. With hindsight I'd have taken even longer on the traverse and spread the journey over two late spring seasons, thus gaining better weather and the chance to climb more along the way. We could have made the trek within three months, but that would have introduced an element of artificial hurry, alien to our desires. To Spain we would go then, except our minibus driver told us the railways were on indefinite strike.

CHAPTER 9

Mostly Zat

That way
Over the mountain, which who stands upon
Is apt to doubt if it be indeed a road;
While if he views it from the waste itself,
Up goes the line there, plain from base to brow,
Not vague, mistakeable! What's a break or two
Seen from the unbroken desert either side.

R Browning

Buses all the way to Tangier would be tedious and we were at a bit of a loss until Charles suggested, "Why not fly?" We did so the following day, to Gibraltar. We slept in La Linea and then took the toy train up for a few days in Ronda. Playing the tourist was not unpleasant, but flying back to Marrakech on 1st June was a blunt resumption of GTAM. It was out of the flying pan into the fire, as Marrakech was boiling hot and blue with fumes and it was as necessary as pleasant to eat on the roof terrace of the Hotel Ali. Graeme, who was due to join us at Ijoukak, drifted in. He wasn't due to join us until the third week of June, so went off with some French lads for the Bou Guemez in the meantime. If they climbed M'Goun I'd not be surprised if Graeme joined us for Toubkal! The new quartet of big John Barnard, Max and Chris Huxham and Chris Bond clocked in, and Aït Idir was there to see we had transport back to Telouet. Finally, Ali and Hosain arrived from Taroudant, relieved to be heading for the out-trail again.

When we returned to Telouet, we repeated the highlights from our previous visit: a good lunch and supper *chez* Ahmed at the Auberge Telouet, a visit to the Dar Glaoui and dancers after dinner in the *khaima*. There was a boy dancer too, once he'd been persuaded to perform. Solemn-faced and in a blue *gandoura*, he jiggled up and down with disciplined gusto. Several of our newcomers joined in and a good time was had by all. Being back was deeply satisfying for the four of us of the team, and as Elyazid Mohammed and other Anmiter lads had arrived (with Taza and Tamri, who had lodged with them) we were suddenly quite a crowd; the *auberge* turned into a real caravanserai. We were travellers in the way of a long tradition.

That first night back on GTAM, after Ahmed had produced a huge brace of delicious *tagines* (one mutton, one chicken), he laid on a larger *ahouach* evening, several musicians with tambours (*bendir*) and one huge leather drum which was thumped with a length of rubber piping, its bass boom sending shivers up the spine. A lone voice would call out, followed by a brutal, solitary note from *bendir* and drum, a process repeated several times then, after wild *you-yous* (ululations) the score of women would be off in song, slowly tramping and swaying around the musicians. They were dressed in shimmering layers of almond white and pink and their heads were bound in scarlet tasselled scarves. One of the girls bore the same striking features as the boy dancer. What I liked was the obvious enjoyment our muleteers had at the spectacle while several rows of local children sat, silent or clapping in time, utterly caught up in the scene. One of the joys of Morocco is the lack of practised prejudice based on tribe or colour, a refreshing change from so much of bloody Africa south of the Sahara, never mind elsewhere in the world. Of course there is still pride and competitiveness but now one sells to a neighbour rather than raiding. "Arab and Berber are just like English and Scots", as Ali would explain.

Sleeping out was pleasant; the moon, smooth in a baby skin, rode the gauze of stars and the gum trees shivered around the angular tent lines. The short break in Spain might never have been—it could be compared to an eye blink on our tortoise journey. I sometimes looked on our doings with a sort of disbelief. Was this really us? Then the moon would rush out of shadows again. Who dares sleep under an Atlas moon?

I was awake early and amused myself watching the ants carrying off the supper crumbs from the carpet. When I finally had to rise I followed the busy line for 50 metres before finding the underground nest entrance. I've often wondered what happens under there when the heavens open. There's no sealed door. These were minute ants but they could carry crumbs larger than themselves. One morsel had been grabbed by two ants and, as neither would relinquish hold, they progressed with movements somewhere between a waltz and a tango. There were also some huge black ants and another medium-sized species which moved in sporadic darts and stops.

When they make their dashes, the speed is such their legs become a blur of motion. None of the species is very interested in humans, thank goodness.

We trekked off from Telouet across the plains towards a dome of hill, passing through a village with a mosque tower that had some childlike drawings on it, including vases of flowers. Oddly, the date of construction was given according to the western calendar. Several of the party had brought walking poles and the click-clicking of those made the party sound like a convention of the blind. We joined an *assif* (stream) beyond fields scented with roses and began the real climb, putting in long rising traverses on another decayed *piste*, until breaking off onto a mule track that took us up by the black pylons that rather disfigure this historic pass. The slopes were flocked with the pink alyssum domes and blue hedgehog broom while just about every flower we'd seen to date was blossoming, a wall to wall carpet of colour, the red soil a delight to every species. (The north slopes had a cover, acres in extent, of brilliant white cistus.) If anyone wants to marvel at the range of mountain flowers in the Atlas they could do no better than walk up to the Tizi n' Telouet in mid-June, an easy three-hour tramp.

The wind made the *tizi* itself untenable (Harris and others found similar conditions over a century ago) and, not far below, the cavalry caught up with us and went skeltering down a corkscrew of a track, hard to envisage as a major caravan route in the not-so-distant past. Odd damp patches produced greens, buttoned with the blue of carduncellus. The valley-head is a complex and jagged ring of peaks, jutting out in prows and walls of tottering strata, many-hued and barren beyond belief yet, over on the east, spur after spur falls in fans of green terracing due to a high *source*, the thread of water being captured in a *seguia* which contours with arterial importance to spread the life-giving water to the fields below.

After a steep, dusty, corkscrew the going changed to grey, the path and the pylons undulating along an elephantine crest that led down to a confluence of streams. Even by Atlas standards this is a grim pass; de Foucauld's description of a century ago still stands: '…de tous côtés s'élèvant de hautes montagnes de grès; tous est roche; le chemin, sans être difficile, est très raide et très pénible' (…on all sides rise high mountains of sandstone; all is rock; the route, while not difficult is very steep and very tedious). Joseph Thomson compared the valley head, with its burnt and blasted aspect, to a volcanic crater. He noted the work of glaciers in times past and kept his head down looking for flowers as he toiled up. At the Dar Glaoui, his party was met by a scary *fantasia*. History often rather overlooks this explorer but his 1888 Atlas trip covered more ground than most. He climbed into the Atlas from Demnate, crossed the Tizi n' Telouet twice, climbed a

3000 m peak (Taourirt) from Telouet, then explored extensively from Amizmiz, reaching the main crest south of Ijoukak (therefore gaining a third crossing of the range), climbed Igdat and, later, the Tizi n' Likemt above Tachddirt. He also crossed the Bibouan Pass and returned by the coast route from Agadir to Mogador (Essaouira). How quickly things change though. As the century ended, Isabella Bird (Mrs Bishop) and, later, Lady Grove made what could be described as safe tourist crossings of the Glaoui pass to Telouet. By the time the Glaoui entertained Churchill and Lloyd George at Telouet, the Tizi n' Tichka road was in place.

There was no sign of the mules when we came down to cultivation level, so we took a track over fields to pause above the village of Titoula, now mystified at no contact having been made. We sat waiting; eventually we would see or be seen. We soon noted some people waving and we descended to a pantomime request to follow. We edged down by the side of the village, conscious of stares from grilled windows and toddlers fleeing indoors at the sight of us. We passed some huge walnut trees and edged fields above the eroded riverbank to eventually cross to a *seguia*-path and, round a bend, there was the camp set up on a grassy terrace under the fingery shade of walnut trees. It was a truly idyllic site: noisy with green woodpeckers, chaffinches, nightingales and blackbirds. Pools allowed baths and a riverside boulder provided impossible climbing problems, until shown how by a girl in plastic shoes with her baby brother tied to her back. A smiling hunchbacked lad and many others watched our every move. We entertained them after supper, when the lamp was lit, by producing shadow shapes against the wall.

Our new GTAM group took twice as long as usual to get going from the Titoula riverside and I girned in my log, 'I wish I could buy back the hours others cause me to waste'. Tamri then lost his footing on the gritty path up to the *seguia* and rolled back down to the campsite, and both Taza and one of the temporary mules cast shoes. "One of those mornings", Ali shrugged. In the end I went on through the three-dimensional fields, enjoyed trim Ta'ayyat village, where the neat stone houses have painted window surrounds. Cows were being driven out and wended along the hillside paths. An older man was giving a younger one a screaming which only stopped at an *azib* in the gorge when he took to throwing stones at a dog to protect our passage. After we had sheltered under boulders from a shower near the *azib*, he offered us mint tea.

A hamlet down-valley is Idirl, the village where an Oxford student party was based in 1955. The book *Berber Village* by one of their number (B. Clarke) is still worth reading for the background to village life and their travels to and from Telouet. They were joined by Wilfred Thesiger, a regular visitor to Morocco. Unfortunately, the book doesn't do more than mention the trips Thesiger made to the east and west. To the east, he went via the Ounila valley, the *tamda* and along the southern foothills, drove to Boumalne des Dadès, then, linking up with the Gellners, traversed north to Zawyat Ahancal. This is a much less demanding venture than I'd always been led to believe, but was the first of such a nature for a long time and at a period when conditions were far from safe. They also set off to walk to and climb Toubkal, but the route is not described. They probably passed below Yagour, with its many prehistoric carvings, then up the Oued Ourika.

The tea *azib* was in a secretive side gorge of character (the Assif n' Tizgui), with the path rising and falling over spurs and criss-crossing the stream for the easiest option. Being at an easy angle and in the shade, it was doubly relished. Women were coming down with colossal loads of alyssum bushes on their backs. The gorge ended on grassy slopes full of flowers (a year later we listed over 70 different species) with nodding sea pinks (white), stately thistles, a white thyme, gladiolus, pinks, rock roses, vetches, St Bruno lilies and endless puzzling compositae. A big adder-like snake was skulking in a pool where I was considering a paddle.

The saddle of the pass itself, the Tizi n' Telghist at 2200 m, was a long, wide, close-cropped green sward quite unlike anything elsewhere. Animals were grazing there and among the multihued slopes above. Chiselled crags walling the south were interspersed with springs and 'greens'. The Tizi n' Tichka area is ruggedly bare (to the bus-borne viewer anyway) yet hides some of the most beautiful *sources* and meadows: a very special place among the green corners of the earth. The peace was shattered by a near-war between two gangs of female cowherds, as one had allowed her mules and donkeys to get among the others' cows. As they were trying to mount the cows, this was not popular.

We bore left from the meadows along a shelf and then descended into the valley (Talat n' Taynast). A steeper, more direct descent could be seen on the other side, running down across black shales. With a boy and a cow for scale, it looked quite dramatic. We crossed to join that track, had a pause by water under a walnut tree and rounded several spurs to reach the large village of Issiyrs (Izikhs) which was being rebuilt at a great rate. We picked up a swarm of not very friendly kids, so took to wending on through fields and watercourses. Several times the kids were warned off only to return, and when we stopped to eat in the welcoming shade of mature walnuts, one boy remained. He threw stones, urinated and cursed at us—despite various women (taking fodder home) telling him off or trying to chase him away. That was the only incident of such a kind I've ever had, but it left a bad feeling.

A little owl perched on a boulder nodded us off, its sad call carrying a surprising distance. I once drove past one perched in the crook of a hairpin bend and its eyes swivelled round as we passed until I thought its head would screw right off. You remember little incidents like that. The little owl often nests in ruins, so has acquired the Arabic name 'umm al-khirab (mother of the ruins).

The descent of the Issiyrs valley was a good tramp, very steep at one point, down shaley black slopes then through fields with the grain ready to harvest (the men cut, the women carry). Most of our gang simply walked down the piste but I'll do anything to avoid its unremitting hardness. One of my diversions took me through the only other village, Tamguingant, where everyone was most friendly and the children shy as mice. The houses appear scattered as randomly as sprouting mushrooms, and my path ran through a passage where houses had extended over the public way. Like a Giotto Madonna, a tiny tot and mother eyed me through a barred window.

Suddenly the main road was below us, with heavy loaders and artic lorries grinding up the Tizi n' Tichka (2260 m), the main road south from Marrakech over the Atlas for the dreams beyond Ouarzazate. We once went over the tizi just before the king visited the south. The mosque towers had been painted like candy sticks and every roadside hamlet hung out welcoming carpets (rather than flags) and royal portraits, a very colourful gesture. I've also crossed a few times in winter conditions and was impressed by the canny driving of the big CTM bus. The driver was so familiar with the road that he would slow for certain bends knowing that around them he would find a drift. The road is seldom closed for long since snowploughs are stationed on both sides.

I never tire of driving over the Tizi n' Tichka: a scenic treat and a spectacular piece of engineering. After crossing the Haouz plains from Marrakech, the road comes in high above the main valley, which is then flanked with a huge balcony view before reaching river level. This is followed in endless convolutions and easy gradients to Taddart where the buses will always break the journey for a tea stop—very civilised—before the final fantasy zigzags and elbows up a desolate spur facing utter mountain bleakness. Summit meadows (in spring) are a surprising floral extravagance but Tizi n' Tichka translates as the 'pass of high pastures'. We once stopped my camper van to fill the water bottles and shepherd boys appeared like magic—as they always do. Requests for dirhams changed to smiles when they heard the tape I was playing. It was a Berber song which they knew, and soon they were chanting, clapping and dancing along to the music. We spent the night nearby, the view dominated by Jbel Bou Ouriol, and they spent hours looking at a picture book of Morocco. They had just moved up from Taddart the previous day, to graze the summer pastures.

Taddart is one of our regular stopping places too. Over the years I've bought some fine crystals there and a white silk *kelim*. Originally we had thought of spending a GTAM night at Taddart, but the *auberge* was rather pricey and the hamlet too urban for our absorbing *pèlerinage*. We hit the main road a few kilometres above Taddart where a new cluster of transport cafés has sprung up in the last few years, a sort of New or Upper Taddart. We piled into the first café to consume litre bottles of fizzy drinks and mint tea. The day was very hot. I spotted a possible campsite just ten minutes walk back up our side valley, and we weren't there long before the mules arrived. Ali and Anmiter Mohammed rode off on a shopping spree to 'big' Taddart, the others re-shod one of the mules and we prepared bivvy spots for the night, under a spreading tree. The yellow lights of lorries sweeping the hillside and the growl of their passing was strangely evocative; after all, the Tizi n' Tichka was a very big landmark across our east–west progression. Mohammed burst into the very song which the children had sung and danced to on the pass two years previously. In theory, we only had the Toubkal Massif and the Western Atlas to traverse but, while the Toubkal Massif is relatively small in area, it is a brutally vertical world and horizontal progress would be slow. Our next area, the country of the Oued Zat, is some of the least visited in all of the Atlas, being very cut-off and difficult to reach—and we'd never met any outsiders in the Western Atlas.

The following morning, while we were walking down the main road through several nerve-wracking loops, Charles and I dubbed the others of our party the 'Phuds'. They were all PhDs, yet to our now smoothly operating expedition, seemed fussy and inefficient. All too often, groups coming out brought the hustle and hassle of western ways with them and needed a week or two to simmer down and relax in a world more in touch with the rocks and flowers of reality.

Before reaching Taddart we turned off onto a new *piste* beside a cylindrical water tank and wended up the steep valley flanks to gain a col on the enclosing crests. The *piste* contoured along, the sky colourful as a fuchsia hybrid, the slopes of hacked oakwoods shivering with morning mists. The *piste* led to Afra, a village perched on barren ground, the starkness changing when we saw the apron of green valley below. Up-valley, a jagged peak dominated the north side of what was Jbel Bou Ourioul (now Adrar Tircht) at 3578 m, west of Tizi n' Tichka. The upper end of the Afra valley is verdant with melt water meadows and a path loops on under crags to reach the Tizi n' Tichka. Adrar Tircht from the *tizi* of the main road is a long, unremitting slog up remarkably even-angled slopes, so maybe one should test its other name as 'peak of the donkey' and ride up. As we passed through Afra, ovens were smoking and a hen high-stepped past with a mouse in its beak. The *piste* died not far beyond, among farmland and walnut trees with the local school perched high above.

At one time, a *téléférique* system ran through in connection with manganese mines. I can recall the eyesore line in the 60s but all signs have disappeared, although one new guidebook still has the line shown on a map! The Oued Afra drained this tight valley and its side streams into the Oued Zat, a large river, which the Tizi n' Tichka road (P31) crosses at the beginning of its climb into the mountains. It was complex country made even more difficult by being divided between various sheets of two different map scales. A drift of goats was heading upwards, a speckled smoke on the landscape. All day the views upwards impressed. We took a goat trod through wet fields, which led to an impasse of crag falling into the river and, after trying the crag, we realised the path was the river. Girls were carrying huge loads of grass as all the fields were being cut. We crossed to the south bank of the narrow glen, contouring high as the river fell away. Dropping down to the village of Assads (or Acadç on the idiosyncratic 50,000), a spur jutted into the *oued* with the buildings overflowing down both flanks.

We found a way through, and took a path along the south bank to a small flood plain above where we thought we saw the track we wanted which was shown on both maps. This led to the Tizi n' Wakel (1836 m) and cut off a dogleg to join the Oued Zat beyond. The path either did not exist or had vanished from disuse as mule traffic now goes the longer, safer route on down the valley and then up the Zat valley which has a good *piste*. While decrying our shortcut I'd still recommend the pass, only follow a perfectly good track from Assads that runs around and up to a higher village, Assaka, from where a good track angles along to the Tizi n' Wakel—*pas de problème*. The path down from the *tizi* to the Oued Zat at Wimmadsan (Wimadzen), however, is no longer safe for mules but gave impressive walking. Peyron gives the village name as 'the wood of the blacksmiths'.

Navigation is, of course, much easier by hindsight. We tried to find the declared path for the Tizi n' Wakel, but such goat trods as there were soon ended and we slithered on gritty granite scrag among cloying scrub and battered trees in an exhausting heat. The rockier areas, as in *maquis* country, provided the only respite, and we scrambled up and eventually into the Tizi n' Wakel, a cruel toil made more annoying with the clear route from Assads to Assaka coming into view across the valley. We drip-dried and drank our cheese sandwiches on the *tizi*.

There appeared to be a choice of paths beyond and we opted for the higher, which contoured with a dip, to a spur overlooking the Zat valley. One section had been washed out in an avalanche. Adrar Meltzen (3595 m) dominated the view from the col onwards, a cleft peak with a high valley running towards us. Miles of crest ran off to a far thrust of summit facing the Oued Ourika and the plains of Marrakech. Lt Washington on a mission to Marrakech in January 1830 made a three-day expedition to the Ourika, and managed to reach 1950 m before snow turned the party back. This is the earliest real mountain attempt by Europeans that I've discovered. The fine tent-like sweep of Meltzen as seen from Marrakech often tricks people into assuming it is Toubkal. North of Meltzen is the scarped Yagour plateau which has many sites with the sort of carvings we'd seen on the Tizi n' Tighist. 'Meltzen the magnificent', we dubbed the peak, climbed on an earlier exploration, escaping from the slavery of Toubkal—a typical raid of the kind we've always relished.

The path into the Zat valley often angled down over grit-on-rock surfaces at a very steep angle, and I worried about how the mules would cope. However, nearing Wimadzen (roughly the pronunciation) we saw our blue-burdened beasts trotting along the *piste* below. They didn't condescend to wait for us and, after we'd filled water bottles at the village supply tank, we hurried after but failed to catch up. The *piste* was hard and heat-blasted. They angled down to a spur before Tizart and we thought "Good! Camp", but Ali was on the road to explain that with the *piste* wending high the mules could go more easily along the Zat bottom—which was their turn to make a bad choice. I went down to the mules with Ali (anything to avoid the punishing *piste*) and they all shot off over the end of the spur only to become entangled in all sorts of bother down at the river. I could hear curses and much crashing of oleander bushes but a long time passed before they escaped and were visible paddling up the river. Deciding *oued* was even worse than *piste* I sweated back up to the road. The others were talking to two young urban Moroccan students who were making a multi-day trek round Adrar Tircht with minimal gear and experience but no lack of initiative and enthusiasm.

We were led high and the *piste* disintegrated on the outskirts of sprawling Tizart, a village with a view of Himalayan grandeur. We went on contouring round the valley flank until we came to a big side valley, the Oued Ansa. We angled down just as the mules reappeared below, still largely splashing up the riverbed or thrashing through the verging oleanders. The Ansa ran out a wide flood plain of grey boulders, and camping looked problematical. However, a bridge led over to the hamlet Imergen (Imyrgn) at 1534 m where, among tight fields and an abundance of irrigation channels, we squeezed our tents onto a few bare patches below the trees. The mules got some newly cut grass and Tamri did his best to steal Taza's. Ali was huffy because of the muleteers' erroneous diversion, and I was a bit huffy too when pre-meal drinks were of such vital importance when help in preparing supper would have been appreciated.

The meal ran on into darkness, the lamp casting weird shadows among the branches overhead. The fun would really start the following day. I read out Peyron's down-Zat description to them, a man not given to over-statements: 'With its quaint houses and friendly inhabitants, and dominated by lofty ridges some 1600 m above the valley floor, we leave Zerwon, descend again to the Zat and follow the river bottom for some 5 h—at first through a dramatic gorge hewn out between Meldsen and Tafoughalt; the only way to remain dry-footed on this stretch is atop a mule; otherwise wear old gym shoes to cope with repeated river crossings alternating with stony paths wending past small cultivated patches and walnut trees…at the gorge exit lies the tiny hamlet of Imergen…a popular place for angling (permit required).'

Bats flickered about the Imergen site. Identity was not even attempted: there are 26 species of bat in Morocco. There are near 50 species of geckos, lizards and skinks and 23 snakes. The most surprising over-abundance is for orchids: 40 species.

About ten minutes into the next day, before any difficult terrain, I had a stone turn underfoot and ended up with both feet wet—which relieved me of worrying about wet feet thereafter. Then came the promised fun. After a first crossing there was a traverse of the sidewall for about 30 m but Charles, who will do anything to avoid water, and John managed to spin this out for 300 m and still had to wade eventually. The details blurred by the end of the day, as hours slipped by wending along wet verges, *seguia* channels, and criss-crossing the river at various depths so often that it was easiest to go barefoot in sandals and shorts.

There were only traces of mule path but at every possible corner fields and walnut trees were lodged like green river flotsam. A bluff had a *seguia* built round it and led to a larger area of cultivation. A good path came down from another village, also named Assaka, which perched high above in a side valley. After waiting twenty minutes I waded back in case anything was wrong but the others appeared and Charles yelled they were going up to the track (a stiff climb up to join a path angling down being water-avoidance *in extremis*) so I retraced my route and joined the track at Zat level. I waited to catch sight of the others then wended on, the path excellent. A few men were riding mules. There was still plenty of criss-crossing. At some houses on the south bank I zigzagged up to pass the hamlet only to have a local yell at me to go down, giving a splendid mime to show the higher track was all up and down while the lower was easy and level. Sure enough, the locals were all using the lower route, which was more in the river than out of it. With the gorge at last relenting, we began to lose the blessed shade the high walls had afforded. The path on the south side did all the local had said and wended away up only to twist down below Zarwoun (Zroueun) where we waited for the anti-water contingent to catch up.

Continuing on, a good path led determinedly up, the only stiff ascent all day as we climbed from 1534 m to around 2020 m. In a corner, there was a rock basin where we were glad to drink, as were the mules who caught us up at that point. Ali and Hosain had been quite impressed by the route, there being nothing similar west of the Tizi n' Test. Round the next corner the twin villages of Taghazzirt and Ouniyd pincered a tree-choked tumble of fields, an amazing vertical slice of productivity in that remote wilderness. We wiggled through the first village but then lost sight of the mules, a useful guide, so stopped for lunch by a big boulder in the cool shade. A dozen children sat at a safe distance like a row of parakeets, chattering over everything we did. We must have seemed like strangers from Outer Space visiting among the soaring peaks. Some of the bolder followed us through Ouniyd and ensured we didn't go astray.

Any hope of high traversing vanished when we saw the tiny dots of the mules hundreds of metres below, splashing off up the next bit of gorge. The mule path took to the Oued Zat and, so, perforce, did we, to paddle a good proportion of the rest of the day's route. The kids followed for a surprisingly long way, hitching up *djellabas* and splashing about like spaniel puppies. They and the cultivation gradually fell away as we followed the golden flow on and on up the gorge, so closed in there were no views—and precious little sign of our mules either. We slowly regained the height we'd lost. 'Very enjoyable', I wrote in my log but I suspect, as our variable speeds indicated, the day was enjoyed by some more than others. After a rest we came on some *azibs* which appeared on both sides of the river and, on the biggest terrace, we found camp half-up, brews on and Hosain busy shoeing mules.

These were the *azibs* of Azib n' Tilst, as lonely a spot as could be imagined yet an *azib* just upstream was occupied and grain was being grown as well as the normal herding of sheep and goats. The gorge had given way to a more open valley and somewhere above lay the Tizi n' Tilst (around 2800 m), our exit to the north (Ourika valley) while south, a tortuous side valley ascent led to the Tizi Tazarzit (3110 m) and the desert country south of the Atlas. That southern crest rolled westwards like ocean waves, rising higher to the final sweep of Taska n' Zat. Its triple peaks register 3818 m, 3912 m, 3850 m, then, circling round to enclose the springs and streams of the infant Zat, it rises to Arjoût whose rock-bound hulk dominates the upper Oued Ourika and Setti Fadma. Peyron notes that nothing was written about the Zat summits until 1908. This was very much *terra incognita*, and still is, as hard graft is needed to penetrate the Zat fastness.

Our progress was made to look pretentious and cumbersome by a gaggle of men and two bare-legged boys who strode down past the camp, mere bundles slung over their shoulders, before vanishing into the gloaming: a majestic simplicity. I had a busy evening of logistics and planning for the days ahead.

In the morning I rose with a dicky right knee and hobbled through breakfast for our 0615 departure. There were a surprising number of *azibs* up the valley and if the barking dogs indicated our passage, the human contacts were friendlier. I wonder how many years per European for the upper Zat gorges. After an hour of gravel crunching, the walls closed in again for a mixture of boulder scrambling and waterfall-dodging that sharply focussed the mind for the following couple of hours. Fun though it was, I didn't dare trust my knee.

A big stream came in and eventually, with much map, compass and altimeter study, we pinpointed our position and were suitably humbled. The next stretch took us up to a spot Peyron recommended as a bivouac site (2467 m on the map), below a stream descending from Tougroudadane (3320 m). (The peak falls to Setti Fadma on the opposite side, a drop of 2000 m of wild, harsh rockiness.) Despite being such an idyllic spot it seemed ungrazed. As well as masses of yellow woad, there were hundreds of pink alyssum clumps, erysimum, blue-tinted daisies, wallflower, silvery thistles, golden thistles, erodiums, cerastium, forget-me-nots, scarlet pimpernel and bold stars-of-Bethlehem.

I was able to make that listing since, at the start of the next succession of gorges, I decided not to go on: an athletic and demanding sideshow was not worth jeopardising the main GTAM route. The tendons were caught at the knee or over-tight meaning I couldn't fully straighten my right leg, so I think not forcing myself on was wise. I'd already traversed the Zat crest but regretted missing Arjoût (the moon) which had been high on my list of desirable objectives ever since our 'Ridge of Dreams' high-level traverse in 1979. That quality trip had started at the Tizi Tagharhat (of Hooker and Ball fame) above Sidi Chamarouch and taken in all the summits from the *tizi* (3456 m), over Iferouane (once 4001 m) to Taska n' Zat and after six bivouacs over 3000 m, we'd escaped south and (one more bivvy) out to Ourzazate—just as the weather collapsed.

We brewed coffee while I sorted out some food for myself and retained the old coffee pot for my cooking and brewing. The others then continued up the Oued Zat and I hobbled back to find a good bivvy spot by the river, on which I played the lizard for much of the day. In the Atlas there isn't much chance of removing clothing for a more extensive tan so I made the most of it—perhaps to my undoing. Most trips I finish with only my face and forearms a deep brown and with eye-catching white-brown stripes on my feet from wearing sandals. I revelled in the day of solitude and read a short story every hour or two, using the pages to help light a scrub fire to boil coffee water after. One of the stories gave me an idea which was to develop into another children's story, and would keep me busy at odd moments for the rest of the trip.

Supper was a thick mushroom soup into which I added pasta and dried vegetables, scoffed along with a tin of spiced sardines. Bread and cheese and coffee rounded off the repast, all cooked with wood from skeleton juniper. A few stunted survivors decorated the crags that soared up in every direction apart from the valley up to Tougroudadane, a peak which surged in and out of view among blowing cloud. Some animal or animals were afoot up the gorge and I hoped I'd see *moufflon*, now so rare. The ticking of hooves was clear but I saw nothing. (*Moufflon*, the wild Barbary sheep, are being introduced in the valley west of Imlil but the easiest place to see them is in the Bird Garden in Agadir!)

At 2020 there was a minor earth tremor, half-felt, half-heard as I woke from sleep. Later I had the company of a half moon and half a million stars. A saturating dew then had me pulling on some clothes inside my sleeping bag. The dew also dampened my store of wood and, the morning being completely windless, the breakfast fire just sent up a pillar of smoke and turned the sticks into charcoal. To my flower list I added campanula, rampion, poppies, thrift, a minute campion, a white campion with 'reversed' petals, a gaudy thistle, a mysterious baby's breath-like flower, mullein, bedstraw, a camomile-like species, various chrysanthemum types, trefoil, knapweed, lavender, valerian, broom, a shrubby rose, milkwort, mallow, kidney vetch and a carpeter of 'everlasting' nature besides others too exotic to recognise. Birds were few: wagtails, dippers, choughs and a redstart being the poor total. As my leg was still not completely sound I resisted dashing off on any ploy and headed back down for the *azib*. The descent was both easier and faster than on the ascent, the benefits of hindsight and being able to look down on problematic areas.

At one section I had to keep under cover for twenty minutes while a flock of sheep and goats threaded along the crags above, knocking stones down into the gorge. (The roar of water made warnings of any falling stones impossible.) Near the end of the gorge, I ran into Ali and Anmiter Mohammed heading up so we made some coffee together. I found Hosain and Mohammed-2 up on the cliff facing camp; camp had become largely untenable from a disgusting plague of flies inside the tents. We kept to our eyrie until the evening cool had removed the visitors.

Other wildlife was not so unpleasant. We found moths had mobbed the wet path by the adjacent *azib*, carpeting the muddy section in a puzzling suicidal manner. Before supper, we removed sixteen long-legged spiders from the tent while inch-long crickets and huge slaters kept crawling in. In the night, a tickle on my back turned out to be a glow-worm. Our water-supplying *seguia* was full of dashing trout. A chough had me racing in panic when it did an excellent imitation of a falling stone. My knee felt better but my legs were breaking out in lumpy spots. Later in the day I retreated to another eyrie and worked out ideas for the story. Waiting for supper, I wrote the book's concluding paragraphs!

Everyone drifted back down from the heights next day, Charles and Chris B only at 1930 as they'd traversed Arjoût and Tougroudadane to the Tizi n' Tilst then descended from there, despite Charles still fighting off a cold he'd probably inherited from Lorraine. The party had camped by high springs the first night and Charles and Chris B had gone up the North Ridge of Taska n' Zat, the others (not all in the best of health) had climbed easy Arjoût which has a grand view to Jbel Toubkal. Ali and Mohammed joined them and, to their common joy, Ali spotted a tribe of Barbary apes up on the crags. I'd never heard of these anywhere in the Toubkal massif before.

CHAPTER 10

High Passes, Formidable River

What have these lonely mountains worth revealing?
More glory and more grief than I can tell...
Emily Brontë

North or south, the escape route from the Zat valley would be hard work so the route was never a major crossing of the Atlas. Our start was rather ineffective, since although we were up at 0500 we didn't set off until 0730. I sneaked up on the wrong side of the river to dodge dogs, but was ambushed by two above an *azib*. The sun was already on the slope as I wended in and out of the trees up the 'gunbarrel' that began the haul. We then moved well left (as had been suggested) but only to find scrubland, dusty in the heat. Goat trods allowed some rhythm, however, as I gained height to pop out onto a fine crest with huge views across to Zat and the upper valley. Topping the crest was exhilarating and the Tizi n' Tilst (2800 m) lay not far along, a couple of small nicks on the ridge which undulated on and on over an intermediate top Louah, to soar up as the south ridge of Meltzen the Magnificent. There was a clear view of the path across to the south over Tizi Tazarzit (marked by an odd flake of rock) to start one dreaming of future ploys. As the others came up they all, in turn, posed with Taska n' Zat behind. We demolished an early lunch (fruitcake the highlight) and watched the mules struggle up, by yet another variant route. Hosain was in front, as ever, but had to run back to help Mohammed-2, in trouble with a shed load and an upside-down mule. "*Hirrah! Hirrah!*" The muleteers, as well as their charges, arrived in a lather.

The descent outdid most with endless zigzags on rough, steep ground (bright with delicate forget-me-nots). On a slight spur, places for camping had been levelled, close to an icy source surrounded by tall purple marsh orchids. Mules and humans drank their fill. The path descended the prow on harsh granite, then used more open slopes but at a ferocious angle. At the next trickle we dipped our hot feet in a pool and splashed water about generally. The mules caught up and we moved together awhile. I changed into sandals thankfully. My spotty legs were not affecting walking muscles, thank goodness. On a big trek like ours, lying-up for long just wasn't possible. One has to walk-off any ailments (like my knee) though I'm glad to say none of us ever faced the accumulation Nick Crane faced on his eighteen-month walk on the watershed of Europe (told in *Clear Waters Rising*): 'I woke with hay fever, an aching tooth, stomach cramps, a cold sore on my mouth and a throbbing calf. The soles of my feet were so bruised that I had to crawl to the sink. I did not feel well.'

We kept to the boulder-strewn valley bottom, by-passing Agouns while, up on the left, we could see the works—and a hole—of the abandoned site of a Protectorate plan to take a railway tunnel right through the Atlas. The approach of civilisation came with "*Monsieur, un dirham*" from the kids. A last high track above a small gorge and we were back onto a *piste*. Amlouggui on the opposite side of our valley was very affluent in appearance, no doubt from an input of city wealth (second homes). In the last couple of decades, every village has sprouted a mosque tower and many of these are stylishly designed and decorated. The *piste* was descending a bit too far down the valley to reach a bridge over the Oued Ourika so I cut the corner, quite happy to paddle and scramble up the far slope onto the tarmac. My knee had been well tested.

Setti Fadma had multiplied itself over and over since I'd last been there and was an endless line of hotels, cafés, stalls and shops, all a bit unplanned and tatty with the *goudron* giving way to a *piste* once more. I walked to what I thought was the end of the village and, having found no sign of the mules, returned. I met Charles and Chris B ambling up, having had a coffee stop. As they'd come round by the bridge and not met the mules, the cavalcade had to be up the road somewhere. Charles and Chris were hot enough to stop for another drink with me in one of the many small cafés that perched between road and river. As Setti Fadma had just happened over the years there was a chaotic liveliness, the (Moroccan) tourists far outnumbering the needy or devout coming there for the *marabout*. The annual festival of Setti Fadma is in high summer, when pilgrim holidaymakers occupy every space. Tents and vehicles were scattered among the grey boulders and the colourfully costumed people seemed like flowers in the brightness. Little did we know as we sat over our drinks, what would happen in August, two months later.

The village seemed to straggle on forever and we picked our way up the wet *piste* still wondering where everyone was. We found them all at the last roadside building, the Auberge Bella, beyond a stretch with no buildings (where I'd turned back). We sat round a table by the river, the numbers slowly accumulating as two lads arrived and said they were Mohammed and Omar who were muleteering to Imlil for us, replacing the Telouet pair, then Aït Idir rolled up in his ancient Renault 4, with fresh fruit, vegetables and bread. We were thirteen for supper that night, in a tiled room with a delicately carved and painted plaster ceiling, Berber music and the cheery river as background sounds.

The *auberge* was fairly new and was a fascinating mixture of building site and appealing craftsmanship. We were there a year later and the inn was much the same, the chief addition being the wooden ceiling in the main dining area. It had been painted in rich reds and greens, utilising explosive geometric and floral patterns: an immense labour. The inner part of the balcony had a plaster ceiling, the intricate patterns picked out in pastel shades of blue, cream and brick. Out of their attractiveness snaked a bare wire and an empty socket for a light bulb. For dining, a light bulb was borrowed from elsewhere (and had gone again at breakfast time). The main difference, however, was in the river. We could hardly hear ourselves speak over supper because of the solid roar of water coming down the Oued Ourika.

The rush and roar of the river produced another folk tale concerning the Oum er Rbia, one of the longest rivers in Morocco. It rises in the Middle Atlas from many gorge-held *sources*, a cheery enough setting yet strangely atmospheric. The river has a bad reputation, with people believing that every year forty people will be drowned to placate the guardian *djin*.

This dates back to a time when the evil spirit stopped the flow of the water entirely, holding it back underground in the mountains so all the crops in the fields along the banks failed and there was poverty and starvation from the Atlas to Azemmour city at the Atlantic outflow. The sultan of Azemmour took himself to the mountains to plead with the *djin*, who demanded the sacrifice of forty scholars as the price of setting the Oum er Rbia flowing again. The sad ruler called his best poets, singers, writers and musicians together and explained the situation to them. They all, one by one, found excuses why they could not sacrifice their lives and departed, leaving only one old man, Sidi Rahal, known for his piety as well as his learning. He merely said, "As Allah wills", and set off to find the *djin* in the mountains.

The other thirty-nine followed, ashamed, and when they came to the gorge they hesitated to go further into the fearsome place. Guiltily they knelt to pray for Sidi Rahal's success and safety. Because of his piety and whatever magic he used, the *sidi* did succeed. The waters came gushing out in a hundred places so it piled up like an avalanche and swept down the gorge in a mighty spate, sweeping away the scholars in the red torrent. Every year since, apparently through ill luck, but because of the agreement with the *djin*, forty people (all kinds of people for scholars are in short supply) drown in the waters of the Oum er Rbia.

Water on the rampage is formidable and nowhere was this better understood than in Setti Fadma. Most of the village would be wiped out that fateful August following GTAM and hundreds of festival visitors would be swept away. All the cafés where Charles and I had stopped for our GTAM drinks disappeared. The ground floor of the Bella was inundated, but at least the inn remained standing as did other better-built buildings not in direct line of fire. The *piste* was gouged out and piles of boulders were left when the spate finally abated. It was a major horror, largely because it was the festive season and the thousands of visitors included many urbanites who ignorantly pitched on the riverbanks and flood plain. When the mass of water rushed out of the gorge like a hundred express trains, they were simply obliterated and half the village buildings with them. Imlil, base for Toubkal and like a second home to me (with Aït Idir Mohammed) suffered in this catastrophe also. Of the popular Café Soleil, only a corner survived with a tilt of roof dangling by reinforcement rods like a broken limb. Of the friendly walnut trees, which filtered winter sun and gave shade from summer heat, nothing remained. Boulders and a natural imitation of concrete half-filled the CAF *refuge* to the ceiling of the ground floor.

Aït Idir Mohammed had just returned from Marrakech in his Renault 4 when the rain began. Assuming a shower he dashed for a café, planning to unload the car later, but then watched in horror as his car and over 40 others were swept away. Many, including his, have never been found, no doubt buried under the heaped boulders which can still be seen during the drive up, despite the rehabilitation of nature and man's determined labour. A sleeping bag of his, pulverised into rags, was found eight kilometres down the valley. The work of rebuilding, both buildings and fields, has been astonishing. Those sitting in the new *Café Soleil* find this recent past almost unbelievable. One local recently smiled that Allah had been kind to him as none of his fields had been washed out and the spate had delivered on site all the boulders he needed for a house extension.

That was the result of a cloudburst in the Toubkal massif that did not last an hour. With hindsight, our GTAM year was a happy choice, the early wet and diversions a mere nothing to what we'd have faced a year or even a couple of months later. El Niño was thought to have been a contributing factor.

Had GTAM been a year later I would have missed out on a pleasant day working up the

Ourika gorges (two months later, the *piste* up the flat valley would lie metres deep in a mix of rock, silt and water.) Nobody else wanted to risk wet feet so they kept to the ascending track and I went up the gorges alone. Their large track zigzagged up to a spur (with a spectacular view down the Ourika with Meltzen in the background), before looping in and out side valleys, the last having a waterfall hidden in a cleft of rock in its heart. The Oued Ourika is regained at Anfli. The walls of the gorge are sheer and some of the wildest, rockiest, most jagged landscape of the Atlas lies above. Yet even in this landscape, there are hidden villages reached by the most tortuous of paths. In the gorge I could not see far or pinpoint anything; there was only a world that reflected the colours of Morocco's flag: red and green, rock and walnut trees—and a stitching of silver river thread.

Initially a girl walked ahead, picking a way from side to side or along field edges, beautiful country all to be destroyed and left scoured bare by the flash flood. A confluence caused a moment of confusion, for both rivers were of a size and equally impressive but I decided on the right fork: if wrong it would just take me to the up-valley track earlier than desired whereas if the left fork was wrong it would lead me into that vertical wilderness and I'd have to retreat and try again. A check with the compass backed the decision and then I had the first of many views of castellated Angour (3616 m) at the head of the Ourika valley. I had a pause after an hour, and by the second hour had cleared the gorge for the extensive flat fields of Anfli. Every margin had been won for cultivation over past decades and there were many spreading walnut trees, willows, and a plaid of walled fields. The gorge had been both grand and restful—as going alone so often is.

The Anfli fields were nearly ready for harvesting and the path went around the edges in a succession of right angles, a sort of maze on a grid, with a few walls and ditches to cross for good measure. The pattern led me up to the straggly village, fascinating with corners and details, passages and yards. Balconies are popular up the Ourika and, with everything having to be brought in on mules, local materials dominate. The next village was very similar but had a tall finger of a mosque tower pointing a message of eternity. (The Ourika towers are picked out in brown with the apex balls coloured blue). Exterior house stairs were frequently formed from a leaning tree trunk with steps cut out by *amadir* (adze) and struts nailed across the fork at one end. The path dropped down through the village and traversed above field level before leading round to Timichi. Mules were streaming up as it had been *souk* day at Setti Fadma; panniers held sacks of flour, cones of sugar, vast *cous cous* platters or *tagine* dishes, rolls of plastic sheeting or new *djellabas*. At a pinch, most villages would be almost self-supporting, with tea and sugar the main imports.

In the Atlas, recycling is a practical necessity. The red dust bore the improbable marks of tyres except the vehicle must have had a kangaroo in its tank for they were only impressed intermittently. They were, in reality, the tread of sandals with motor tyre soles. Buckets at wells are often made of tyre rubber as are panniers for carrying soil and the rope of a well may be an inner tube, peeled like an apple, to make a single long strand. An exception to such thrift is that wood from buildings that have fallen down is not re-used or even burnt. Perhaps a superstition prevents pillaging of the old home.

A dog too lazy to rise barked feebly. Below, the cultivation was wide enough for several football pitches and a large, solitary tree by a resurgence of the river would have made a good campsite. This seemed to fit where Aït Idir had suggested we camp, but as the mules and everyone else were still behind I wandered about Timichi. 'Rather a wreck of a place', I noted, but with one tawny *tighremt* which was a *gîte* and another across the valley. There was a CAF hut at one time, but in the fallow years of the 50s into the 60s, the absence of mountaineers saw the *refuge* begin to decay. Now I couldn't even recall which particular wreck it was. Timichi straddles several shallow gullies, which would either be gouged deeper or become heaped with great tips of boulders in the spates that were to follow, the destruction often metres from ancient homes. They must have had a terrifying experience.

I went back to a perch above the wider reach of valley to wait. (A year later that solitary tree, de-barked for five metres on the upstream side, stood in a wall-to-wall spread of grey boulders. The fields had gone.) The path was overhung by the smiling faces of pink erodium, one of the commonest flowers of the trip, always growing in vertical fissures.

After half an hour the walkers appeared and after another hot half hour we *heard* the muleteers. They are always cheerfully noisy on the march! Ali had a swollen cheek from a bad tooth (years of drinking sugary mint tea was catching up) and it would have been best to have it extracted as soon as possible. To add to the team's medical worries, Tamri was limping because of an infection in his hoof. We were learning the hard way that such a continuous journey was not good for mules: their hooves couldn't grow fast enough to take regular re-shoeing. If doing a GTAM again we'd hire for sections (as our groups joining did), which would work out no more expensive than buying beasts.

We camped in fields just below Timichi. That night my legs itched maddeningly and I had little sleep as a result. In the morning I found I had sprouted hundreds and hundreds more lumps down my legs below the knees. Running my fingers down them was like feeling an old-fashioned washboard. I'd dismissed the incipient itch as being an irritant from brushing against some nasty vegetation, or an encounter of the biting kind, but it looked liked it was some form of sun rash from my over-exposure the other day on the upper Zat. But why the shins? Charles was on antibiotics, Chris H had not been feeling too well and John threw up after supper. Were we all disintegrating?

Ali's face was still bad next morning and half the gang seemed to be walking wounded. I kept my own problem to myself and got on with things but the group never seemed capable of setting off in less than two hours from rising—twice the time of most groups.

"*Zid!*" ("Let's go!")

The initial haul led us up above Aguerd n' Ourtane which, being on the spur between the valley split, had a quality view down-valley, delicate in the morning light and the golden harvest fields. L'Ibassene was a bigger village, 'amazing dollops of terraces among the red rock towers' according to my log, where a St Kilda parliament seemed to be in session on the red street. I was given directions, which was as well for the path sneaked *up* before continuing along. I sat to wait for the others who then went into a pow-wow over Ali's state of health. One of the party suggested that, as Ali's employer, I should be taking care of him! As he had taken it upon himself to dish out drugs and act the doctor with no reference to me I thought the comment somewhat rich. Ali and I have a very special relationship and he'd bring his innermost worries to Uncle Hameesh as he'd do with no one else. We'd already been talking about his teeth problems and the options open to us, one of which was followed as it proved. We had time in hand if necessary—and they might well be needed with Big John and Chris H weak, Ali in agony and me with itching limbs, not to mention a mighty pass to get over that day.

The path contoured up through typical Ourika wildness with the serrated crest of Adrar n' Ineghmar (Anghomar) looming above and ahead. This peak has alternative names which helps confuse it with the one above the *lacs* east of Anmiter. Names are duplicated out there for the same reasons the Highlands are full of Ben Mores ('big hills') and Sgurr Deargs ('red hills'): they are named by local people, unaware others are doing the same. There are half a dozen Imlils (meaning *white*) in the Atlas for instance. The same peak will have different names as viewed from different angles: Jbel Toubkal was long Jbel Tifni for those living south of it. Like the Gaelic, too many names have been so bastardised in time and transliteration that they mean nothing to Berber speakers, never mind us. This Ineghmar or Anghomar was first climbed in 1924 (de Prandières), had a winter ascent in 1925 and both first female ascent and the Atlas's first fatal climbing accident in 1926.

Our GTAM path reached welcome water where the valley split with the path turning more to the west to zigzag up to the Tizi n' Tachddirt (3172 m) with a gushing, thistle-bound stream never far away. In the autumn after GTAM, we returned to camp at that gentle corner only to find the site obliterated, the grassy spots buried under new scree slopes and boulders heaped up as if a tower block had been brought to the ground. Anghomar presents a very rocky aspect throughout the plod up to the col (a far kindlier ascent than the Tizi n' Tilst) and the mountain's ascent is a climb rather than a scramble, on good granite. Heading for one of these climbs once, we met a shivering shepherd boy who begged some matches off us, set fire to a dead 'hedgehog' bush and then stood over it, *djellaba* spread so the smoke percolated through his patches.

We lunched after a steady uphill hour out of the Ourika Valley then took the final zigzags to the spacious *tizi*, a thoroughly satisfying pass. Two hours later we were setting up camp on the slopes across the valley from Tachddirt (2314 m), where a gasping cold surge of water comes out of the hillside, draining the barren corrie up to the Tizi n' Likemt between Iguenouane (3882 m) and Aksouâl (3910 m). Over the years both campsite and Tachddirt's CAF *refuge* (built in 1926) have had many happy visits. My log of February 1965 describes the GTAM's setting equally well. 'The village at sunset was busy with herds coming in. The houses are all huddled on top of each other, built of mud or stone, flat-roofed and with few windows—in the better ones these are painted white round an iron grill. The beasts are herded in at night (warm farm smells). Fires are of scrub, which is carried home in huge bundles that bow the women double. Women are unveiled and favour orange colours in their garb. The men wear *djellabas* and tattered *selhams*. The children are very poorly clad. No lights go on at night and there is no sign of life until the sun hits the village at 0930. Blue smoke leaks out then and the animals wend off to scrape food from the barren slopes.'

We based ourselves at Tachddirt frequently in early years as it offered such good climbing with Angour on one side of the valley and Aksouâl on the other: a rock peak and a snow peak. Angour dominates the upper valley with huge cliffs, on rock ranging from good to god-awful, and was first ascended by Lépiney and de Prandières. We put up some routes in the mid-sixties, routes which I found quite terrifying with the then minimal protection. We had a couple of slings and nuts, just garage nuts with the threads bored out—not much support. On one occasion, partner Roger's careful pitch-by-pitch description gave up with 'Climb straight up for 600 feet. No protection'.

Being south facing, Angour can offer rock climbing all year round. Aksouâl on the other hand is north facing, and its vast sprawl of ridges and gullies holds the snow and can give classic alpine ascents. There isn't much ice because the frequent freeze-thaw required rarely exists. After heavy snowfall (and attendant avalanches) the snow largely ablates rather than consolidating.

Tom Weir records an early climb on Aksouâl. They headed up through the soggy snow for 1000 m to the obvious high rock *arête* leading to the summit, which they gained at 1430 after eight hours on the go. 'But something ominous was happening to the weather', he noted. Aksouâl's summit is a long way from home. The rock towers of the crest were passed by exposed traverses or direct assault with the clouds rolling in. Eventually they headed off down what they hoped was the right gully. Glissades came to a halt at a drop and they had to rope-up and climb down. On they went, finding they'd been in a mere side gully. They slid another 300 m into the main gully, in darkness and in battering hail as a thunderstorm let rip. They were soaked, and the going was difficult as the snow ran out but 'electric storms can have a reinvigorating effect on tired men', and fourteen hours after they'd set out, they reached the hut. They could not open the locked food cupboard, so went supperless to bed.

Tom Weir's enthusiastic account of the Atlas in the 1957 *Scottish Mountaineering Club Journal* (and his slides) was another of the spurs that took me to the Atlas originally and he uniquely captures the flavour of these times in his autobiography. In 1966 Colin Firth and I set off to make a first ascent of the next ridge along from Tom's on Aksouâl, one which was to have extraordinary similarities. To shorten the climb, we floundered over to bivouac at the foot of the climb. A miserable night of cold-denied sleep made dawn a relief. We were on the go for a gruelling 23 hours. We started well with a two-hour climb up an *arête* to gain the main ridge, which was excellent throughout and very mixed. Colin dropped his axe to give a half-hour diversion. (A few days later he managed to bash his head with the axe and received first aid from Gavin Maxwell at Imlil).

All I can recall is snow slopes, endless rock towers and lots of AD climbing standard with pitches of III. Even skirting the last tower, we only reached the 3910 m summit at 1700 and, innocently, hoped to make the Tizi n' Likemt before dark. Once dark, we brewed and went on by torchlight. '*Gendarmes* of every sort and fine scrambling I suppose', my log sighed. Colin was exhausted so in a sandy corner we prepared our bivvy and slept for two hours until the sky milked over and a sneaky wind made the cold unendurable. We brewed tea, had apple flakes and went on. Eventually there seemed to be a gully running down so we took it, glissading down funnel after funnel and just praying the brakes would work if a vertical step intervened. My torch was dying and it was my turn to feel shattered, so we had another extended brew stop before continuing. We found the *seguia* which we followed to the Iminene gorge and the path into Tachddirt, setting the dogs yowling and reaching the *refuge* at 0415. The hut was locked, of course, so we were forced to bivouac outside the door.

Those more into marathon walks could attempt the Three Tizis Walk: from Tachddirt over the Tizi n' Tachddirt down to Timichi, Agouns (one can cut the corner by walking from Ibbassene to Agouns), the Tizi n' ou Attar to Oukaïmeden ('the meeting place of the winds') and back over the Tizi n' ou Addi: a 12 hour tramp, with some tough uphill hauls. We did this one spring when glissades helped descents but snow also made the ascents hell. The meadows of Ouka were ablaze with colchicums and daffodils, the ski slopes of the resort reduced to mere runnels of snow.

Tachddirt's GTAM camp pitched, having walked 600 miles, I spent several sessions in the icy waters of our *source*. My spots were spreading, however, right up both legs, on my back and on my hands. Both Ali and I needed servicing. There was endless discussion among the rest and Chris H remained indecisive, making a hash of logistics and my planning of necessary rations. The mules were turned loose and ate their way high up the Tizi n' Likemt gully. Both Ali and I found scorpions on pitching tents and gave the others warnings. The valley has a reputation for them. Quite why some areas are popular with the beasties is a mystery. Richard Gilbert, camped above Tachddirt with a school expedition, noted, 'Scorpions dominated the conversation and our dreams...Beneath these stones lay scorpions. Hundreds of scorpions. Big scorpions (2½" long), small scorpions and families of scorpions. The local tribesmen said their sting could kill...Ed put his hand in his rucksack and was nipped, not stung. Paul D shook one out of his sleeping bag, Paul H slept on top of a huge boulder until he found that a scorpion was sharing it with him.'

Our site below the Tizi n' Likemt looked down-valley into the sunset. The cone of hill above the Tizi n' Tamatert was a bold shape in the painted golds and reds of dusk. An owl gave its sad, repetitive notes, and chanting drifted over from the glow-worm village. I creamed and creamed my estimated thousand spots and slept better. The moon was so bright that I almost rose at 0300, thinking day had come.

Charles and I were almost driven mad by the interminable discussions about who did what. Ali and I were heading for Marrakech, that was certain, and in the end John and Chris H decided on a day recuperating while the rest went off to climb Aksouâl. Charles had already been up to the Tizi n' Likemt on a winter ascent when three of us (Charles, Keith Skeens and I) optimistically hoped to walk south from there to climb Jbel Siroua. The whole route was snowbound, with avalanches abounding. The flounder *down* from the col was pitiful, every step breaking thigh-deep so we ended up pushing our sacks before us while semi-swimming. The Tizi n' Likemt and the summit of Bou Iguenouane had also given us good ski-mountaineering ascents, this branch of mountain activities popular with the Swiss especially. (Half the Imlil guides have cast-off Swiss skis.)

The Tizi n' Likemt (the grandfather of all Atlas scree slopes) was first reached by Joseph Thomson in 1888. He was expecting the pass to be the main crest with the empty south beyond so was astonished to see the upper Ourika drainage instead—with miles of mountain country before the southern plains. He also noted one hill which appeared to dominate and hazarded, correctly, that it was the highest in the Atlas: what we now know as Jbel Toubkal. Almost 50 years would pass before Toubkal was climbed. Now there are only a few days when it is *not* ascended. Aksoûal was climbed in 1928 by the strong Lépiney–Stofer team who traversed the towers to the Tizi n' Likemt and went on to add Iguenouane and Anghomar (Inghemar). A year earlier they'd traversed the entire Ouanoukrims ridge above the Neltner (Toubkal) Hut.

My sympathies with Ali's toothache were amplified by personal memories. The first time I took the beautiful Tachddirt–Iminene valley walk down to Asni was with raging toothache which, amongst other inconveniences, had made eating almost impossible. So I set off at 1740 after some potato broth and seven fried eggs to find a dentist, walking into a flaming sunset, eventually sleeping by the path when it was too dark to see. A four-hour walk took me to Asni the following morning. At 1500 that afternoon a huge cavity was being filled by a Gueliz dentist who worked surrounded by three attractive young ladies, and I was dreading what the visit would cost. The bill came to the equivalent of £2.50—even 30 years ago that was a bargain. Maybe the modest charge was a softener since the dentist had a sideline in selling slabs of polished fossil rock (*Nautiloidea*) from the Tafilelt. The first time I had my own camping van in Morocco, I came back with a slab which I used to make a table top. The slab weighed nearly a hundredweight and, being impossible to shift, I had to sleep on top of it every night on the journey home.

What with all the pow-wowing none of us set off early from the *source* camp. We took Hosain (who needed a cobbler) and both of the Imlil mules as Taza and Tamri had set off for the Tizi n' Likemt with our pedestrians. The mules left me trailing by the Tizi n' Tamatert

(2366 m) but, being familiar territory, I knew the short cuts so we all reached Aït Idir's house together.

The road from Imlil up to the Tizi n' Tamatert was built in 1968 when the forest was planted by an army of workers that was based on Imlil. 'Army' is the correct description, as they were paraded each day, all very noisy and cheerful, with latecomers being made to double up and down. The trees often mask an approach so Barbary partridges (*hedjel*) go off squealing at one's feet, leaving the victim trembling with the explosive surprise. Several times on GTAM, Ali showed me partridge eggs. The Tamatert col gives a magnificent view up to Angour and is a natural spot for a pause. On one occasion we all jumped at an explosion and turned to see smoke rising about 100 m off. Investigating, we found a small *adit* for mining silver. There too, in the 60s, we encountered a migration of painted ladies and some of the butterflies we 'marked' for someone's Ph.D. were recovered in the West Country.

Aït Idir was not at home but Ali was greeted like one of the family. After a second breakfast we caught a minibus to Asni and a taxi to Marrakech. Lunch in the El Bahja was not to be missed, a back lane café behind the Hotel Ali providing an unbeatable menu selection at ridiculously low prices. The *patron* has even been on a British TV programme, one of a series shot in different countries. The lively female presenter obviously enjoyed Marrakech and we enjoyed her enjoyment. The *haj* from the El Bahja produced a *tangia*, which really takes slow cooking to an extreme. A clay amphora-like vessel is filled with meat, *smen* (butter), onions, garlic, ginger, salt, pepper, saffron, cumin, coriander, lemon juice and some water (to quote one recipe), the mouth sealed, and the pot carried along to the local *hammam* to be buried in the hot ashes of the fire for several hours or even overnight. The girls jokingly refer to *tangia* as a 'bachelor dish' as it requires neither kitchen nor cooking facilities to produce.

Ali had a 1600 dental date and I set off to find a reputed English-speaking doctor. Failing, the tourist office gave me the addresses of two dermatologists. I sat in the waiting room of one for two hours before being seen. The French was not easy to cope with and many pages of grisly illustrations were pored over. He was very keen for me to have been eating celery, which was one food we'd never had. Something must have sparked off the reaction. Locals blamed the water (all that paddling) but he favoured the sun (of which I'd had a ration). Only a series of tests would clarify and there wasn't time; his advice of "staying in the shade and resting" wasn't really practical either! Our trek was quite beyond his comprehension but interested him enormously so he conversed at such length that I was starting to panic at the likely consultancy bill (which came to £15). The chemist next door charged twice that for two tubes of cream and two bottles of lotion to be applied several times daily. They probably did help, since the marks and the itching faded then eventually vanished over the following week or two.

There's nothing like turning ill to good so being in the Gueliz, I went for a big *Coupe Azilal* before taking a taxi back to the Hotel Ali. Ali returned with a bloody mouth, one tooth less and a date for the following day to lose two more. I enjoyed a buffet and Iceberg coffee, even if gap-toothed Ali didn't. First thing in the morning I went onto the Hotel Ali rooftop to gaze at the southern rim of peaks. Rhat could just be made out, with a whole jumble from there to Telouet and Meltzen, tent-like, was looking quite the highest that early travellers thought it to be. The Zat crest and Angour led the eye onto the huge sweep of Aksouâl and the pyramid of Toubkal with Afekoï nestling at its flank. What almost shocked was the panorama onwards. Still to be tackled was the Tazaghart mass, the Tizi n' Test dip, Gourza, Erdouz, Igdat, as well as what lay beyond the horizon leading on to the sea. Known and unknown, it thrilled. I left Ali to the mercy of the dentist, visited the bank, did some shopping and, relieved, took a place in a shared taxi at the Bab er Rob for Asni. The run across the Haouz Plain had led to so many Atlas adventures. Roll on the rest.

Back in 1966 we bought an old Bedford van (costing £60) for our Atlas expedition and, while driving the bumpy roads of Spain, one of the bulbous headlamps fell off. We hadn't even noticed as driving was hair-raising enough in daylight without attempting any night driving. On one occasion, down from the Atlas, we drove into Marrakech only to be stopped at the approach roundabout and told we really should have two headlamps. We said we'd see about it. Of course we forgot and the next time down to the city ran into the same policeman at the same roundabout. We explained we never drove at night, that the lamp had fallen off in Spain and Bedford parts weren't exactly common in Africa. But he was insistent. Had we known the creative skills of local mechanics we might well have done something but we drove straight back up to Imlil for a last climbing visit. Unthinkingly, setting off home, we approached the same roundabout—and there was the same policeman. "Fair cop!" we felt. But there was a very Moroccan solution. As we neared the roundabout the official found something extremely riveting in the view towards Meltzen and only turned his eyes back on the road to Asni after we were heading to the Bab er Rob.

CHAPTER 11

Topping Toubkal

For the first time we saw the Atlas before us in all its kingly elevation; now the eye roamed from its
dark forest-clad base to the snowy masses which broke through the clouds that softly swathed its
upper zones and above them gleamed against the blue sky, seemingly not of the gross earth at all.

Joseph Thomson, 1889

Asni is a wedge of green thrust into the red world of the mountains, lush with fruit-growing and the
setting of a huge Saturday *souk* which draws villagers from up on the Kik plateau and all the valleys
draining from the high peaks. For the rest of the week, it is Sleepy Hollow although the changing
post for leaving the Tizi n' Test road and heading for Imlil. The view is made bolder and wider for
anyone prepared to walk the Kik Plateau edge, that rufous Stanage Edge that dominates Asni.

We've often patronised the local youth hostel. It occupies a scenic site by the Oued Mizane,
with panoramic views up to the Toubkal massif, surrounded by old olive trees. The dark or dappled
light explodes here and there in outbursts of almond blossom and rows of translucent white iris.
Facilities are fairly basic but clean and the family that runs the hostel are friendly and helpful. They
are relatively new, a previous family having been there for most of the forty years I've known the
place. They only gave up when the warden's illness forced a move to Marrakech. One of their boys
was mentally handicapped and could rather surprise hostellers. He tended to sleep in a cellar which
was also used by roosting hens and a store for straw bales, reached by some steps from the hostel
yard. The visiting hostellers could be having breakfast with the serins and bulbuls calling the day
awake, when there would erupt, seemingly from the bowels of the earth, a raving figure dressed in
rags, straw and feathers flying, voice roaring. I've seen unknowing hostellers take to their heels, but
the boy was harmless enough.

The bane of our life there was the dog. He was friendly and would come long walks on the Kik Plateau with us but he too grew old and his limbs arthritic and painful. 'Nice doggie' he may have been but when he sat outside the dormitory window and barked all night he was called stronger epithets. Poison was the favourite suggestion for dealing with the problem. One night ten of us, ragged from sleeplessness, were about to consume my whole supply of sleeping pills when I hit on a simpler solution: we gave the dog a sleeping pill.

A rattle-bang-stop-start run in a minibus took me the 17 km up the Mizane valley to Imlil. There were 17 people on board (two on the roof with the baggage), hens and a sheep under the bench seats. The sheep leaked. The road up was built in the years 1931–34, saw little use in the war and in 1947 was severely damaged by floods and only re-opened in 1952. Before that, one took mules from Asni to Aroumd (the original CAF *refuge*). With the building of the sturdy CAF *refuge* (1954), Imlil was born. One benefit of this mountain tourism has been a greater number of local children can remain in the area, for almost anything would be better than being forced off to Casablanca and its illusory streets of gold. Heading west from Imlil we would not encounter another European for the remainder of GTAM. I recovered from my journey in the Café Soleil.

Imlil is an important staging post on the Toubkal trail and Toubkal aspirants would do well to overnight there. Asni is 1150 m, Imlil 1740 m, the Toubkal *refuge* 3207 m and the summit 4167 m, so acclimatising is sensible. However, I saw one lot of Italians, straight from Marrakech, loading mules to go to the high hut there and then. Once they'd gone, though, the peace returned. The muleteers played cards. I had another *café au lait*. A chatter of young city women, half in western clothes and teetering about in high heels, half in brilliantly coloured *kaftans*, were enjoying an adventurous day out.

The tourist tends to encounter only the male-dominated activities but, in reality, everyone has their place. The men sitting playing cards are not idlers, they are muleteers, waiting for their turn to be engaged. Their behaviour is no different than waiting London taxi-drivers doing exactly the same. Looking down from the eyrie of Aït Idir's balcony the fields are seen to be dotted with the colourful figures of women or girls gathering fodder or keeping an eye on a bony cow. Once I heard the comment from a visitor. "Seems only the women work the fields." My retort was a brief "And who do you think *built* the fields?" A couple of generations ago the men had to be fighters before anything else. Imlil, like most valleys, is dominated by a fortified site (*agadir*), which bears a close similarity to home defences for Border warfare or clan feuding. Men are also the traders and travellers so, naturally, the women stay at home and run things and see to the crops. As did Rob Roy's wife. Highland life has many similarities: life at a saner pace.

Staying at Targa Imoula the women prepare our meals yet, on the trail, both Ali and Hosain were the expert cooks. Mohammed's wife Ayicha in fact is not the best cook I've known, although she is improving with practice. Ayicha cooked, did the laundry, looked after the kids, cared for the cow and made rag rugs. Mohammed was a mountain guide, a crofter, a trader. Both *worked*, and hard but, bringing the cow back at dusk, there was time to stop and chat with a neighbour, comparing the babies on their backs, planning for a wedding day, chaffing with a travelling tinker who sat mending their pots and kettles—always with plenty of noisy laughter. I judge a country and its people by how much laughter and singing I hear.

Ayicha's rag rugs were quite often sold both to visitors and locals. On one occasion I took an American quartet up to Mohammed's house for supper and one of the company admired the rag rug on the guest room floor, saying he thought the bright and glittering colours would look swell on his sunny ranch-house wall. Would I enquire about his buying it? I did and had to inform John that that particular rug had been made for the guest room and wasn't for sale. But he wanted the rug and money talks after all. Mohammed kept refusing, however, and John's constant asking was really a social *faux pas*. At one stage Mohammed rolled his eyes at me in a despairing gesture. I could only shrug. When John pestered our host to name his price Mohammed, seeing a way to end the conversation, quoted a figure about ten times the going price for such a rug.

"Done! Great!" was the instant response.

Mohammed's face was a study. He shot me another look and it took some self-control not to burst out laughing. After the third glass of mint tea he began to roll up the rug and at that moment Ayicha came in to collect the tea tray.

"What are doing, dear?" came her startled query.

"Tell you later, dear," whispered her red-faced husband.

His glance didn't miss the quiver of a smile on my lips and his blush deepened. None of the others noted any of these undercurrents, I may add. We made our formal farewells and John bore off his trophy into the dark. As we wended homeward, down through the walnut trees, I could hear Ayicha's voice screeching her displeasure at poor Mohammed: she was giving him hell.

One commercial venture at Imlil has stood out. Catching the eye, as one looks from Aït Idir's terrace, is the old fort on the conical hill that dominates the valley and the view towards Toubkal. This was the old *agadir* or fortified granary where the locals would store their grain and treasured possessions in the bad old days of clan feuding and outside attack. As a one time *caid*'s base too it had been slowly crumbling away like a sand castle lapped by the tides of time, before being bought by an English company, Discover Ltd, to be turned into a field study centre and now classy hotel. The restoration was entirely the work of local labour, the result being beautiful in the extreme. For the grand opening they had a major celebration for all the nine high Mizane villages. A friend Jill and I had tea with Omar, the steward, the day before the opening. The women had baskets of chickens and one terrace had all the innards hung up to dry like washing.

We had to fly to the UK, alas, so missed the feast but later heard all about it. Prayers and readings from the Koran were made the day before by way of blessing. Two cooks were brought from Marrakech and all the villagers streamed in, dressed in their finery, chanting and singing as they came. They were given dates as the traditional welcome then feasted on chicken *tagine*, mint tea and cakes in one of the salons. As one group departed another would arrive. All the time the ladies sang and danced in the central tiled yard, a scene to assault eye, ear and nose. In the evening there was a feast of *mechoui* and more dancing into the night. The consumption was 900 loaves of bread, 152 chickens, 135 kg meat, 4 sheep, 4000 cakes, 100 kg sugar, 40 bundles of mint and 4 kg tea.

Martin Scorsese's film about the Dalai Lama, *Kundun*, used the Kasbah du Toubkal for the monastery of Dungkar (to which the Dalai Lama fled). The rest of the filming was done at the Ouarzazate studios, Morocco's answer to Hollywood. For filming, the *kasbah* was clad with fake stonework, wooden doors, Tibetan domes and prayer wheels. Three weeks were needed to set up the scene before 33 4 × 4s and 10 *camions* invaded Imlil and everything was carried up to the site. The location was covered in snow (Epsom salts) and the filming took just three days. The sun shone and snowy Toubkal as the backdrop was no fake. The last scene in the film, the Dalai Lama looking back to the panorama of the Himalayas, is the view of the Atlas from Asni.

A return to Imlil is like coming home. Apart from the CAF *refuge*, the guardian's house across the road, and the bare space of the Parking I have seen every building go up and, as like as not, have known the builders, and probably 'kent their faithers' too. The heartbreak of the spate was still in the future as I returned from Marrakech to resume GTAM. I was so mobbed by local friends that I forgot to pay the *camionette* (pickup) driver so Bari, the tout of touts, gave him my fare and chased me up later. Bari is a lanky lad with the rubber face of the practised comic and is expert at selling souvenirs to visitors who'd no intention of buying them in the first place. "Berber credit" he grinned once at a victim: "Pay half now and the rest at once". In all these situations I maintain strict neutrality. I warn parties of the practices and procedures but then leave them to it: if they want to pay idiot prices that is their affair. My sympathies are with Bari's four children who rely on his selling skill for their daily bread.

At 1600 I bought fresh bread and headed for Mohammed's house at Targa Imoula. Passing the school the kids grinned and called out "Bonjour, Hameesh". Mohammed didn't appear for hours but I 'made the *burnous* sweat' with a major unpacking and repacking from the stored bags, squeezing in a meal and a *kaab el ghzal* (gazelle's horn pastry) with the family.

I'd done several hours of work before 0800 the next day so sneaked down through fields fluttering with a mock of magpies. I managed to creep close enough to see the sky-blue 'eyebrow' that distinguishes the Atlas species. I wrote letters in the *Café Soleil* and left trousers at the tailor's for repairing. Mohammed brought over an English-speaking lad, another Hamish, who said he'd grown up in Scotland.

"Where?"

"Oh, you'll never have heard of it."

"Try me."

"A wee place called Gartartan."

I could only smile. "Two of our party live at Gartartan Lodge."

There was also an Atlas connection for the drive from Gartartan Lodge led to 'the big house', once the home of Cunninghame Graham. His adventures in Morocco from a century ago are told in *Maghreb al Acksa*. We chatted over an extended lunch and I was about to head 'home' when Graeme arrived on a *camionette*, having traversed M'Goun, descended the gorges and enjoyed a quick visit to Essaouira since I'd last seen him. We had another round of coffee and were about to go when Ali also climbed down from a *camionette*, to be greeted by half of Imlil.

The fields were being ploughed and the maize planted for autumn harvesting. Autumn is a bad time for hiring mules as they are all working: walnut, apple and maize crops all follow hard on each other and the fields are then manured and sown with winter barley. The walnuts are harvested in a single week during which there's a patter like rain throughout the valley as every tree is climbed and long poles are used to bang down the nuts. If timed correctly, the fruit hits the ground and the impact bursts off the outer fleshy covering. Contract labour, grannies, unemployed teenagers—all are pressed into this frantic harvesting.

This Mizane valley and Tachddirt's Iminane meet just above Asni to form the Oued Reraiya which gives its name to the watershed-held tribe. In the Aït Mizane, the tribe is made of four clans: Aroumd (largest and most superior), the Aït Takhsin (Imlil), with the Mzik to west and the Aït Souka to east, the last newcomers after the original large Aït Takhsin village was swept away by a flood around 500 years ago. After that disaster, people radiated out to settle on the rim, like Targa Imoula, or above Imlil where the mosque tower stands. Haj Brahim donated the site for the first Imlil mosque, just a room opposite the *refuge*. Each clan is democratically run by its own *jemaa* (council) who arbitrate when needed with local problems, such as water distribution. All irrigation is made in turn and an example of natural cooperation is that Mzic villages can tap in to Imlil water if need be, in return for work in the fields or other services. Everyone helps others and can claim help in turn; this *touiza* is crofting by another name.

While we had been to Marrakech, the rest of our GTAM gang had gone over the Tizi n' Likemt to camp by the *azibs* beyond (Azib Likemt, Azib Tifni) and had begun a high-level traverse from the Tizi n' Tagharat to Toubkal where, if our timings worked, Ali and I could join them for a summit bivouac, something I'd wanted to do for years but had never hit the necessary benign conditions. (Toubkal, like many 'highest' summits is a notoriously fickle, cold and draughty place.) While they launched themselves on the traverse of Tichki (3753 m) and Afekoï (3755 m), the mules descended by Sidi Chamarouch to Imlil.

Hosain thought he'd be helpful and left most of the mule loads at Sidi Chamarouch to save carrying them up again. However, I wanted everything at Imlil for sorting out the gear into: needs for now; Neltner *refuge*; what was to be abandoned and what was needed for continuing GTAM. Taza and Tamri were to be rested while local mules could yo-yo up and down to the Neltner hut, now renamed *Refuge du Toubkal* (as the Lépiney is now *Refuge Tazaghart*). Louis Neltner and the Lépiney brothers were famous pre-war French climbers, part of a sort of Gallic Creag Dhu, who did much in the Alps. They were fortunate to work in Morocco awhile—as have the main explorers since, such as André Fougerolles, Roger Mailly and Michael Peyron, though they have been general wanderers rather than climbing specialists.

Graeme, Ali, Hamish G and I set off with four mules the following morning at the rather late hour of 0800. My legs were no longer itching but looked disgusting. We kept ahead of a French cavalcade of about thirty people and as many mules. We paused at Sidi Cham (where Hosain had stayed overnight), which gave me a sweaty hour to sort gear. We wanted some for the hut, some for the Phuds who were to be at the hut an extra night, and some to go down with Taza and Tamri, the latter to have an operation on his infected foot. Tamri demonstrated the hardiness of mules that night; he was laid on his back, bundled up like a parcel, while the inside of his hoof was scooped out and filled with cauterising pitch, yet a few days later he set off to trek to the Atlantic.

Sidi Chamarouch is a strange sort of place. In the 60s the hamlet didn't exist apart from the sacred saint's boulder, but this didn't prevent the muleteers brewing in its shelter and sharing their tea with us. Now non-Moslems are not allowed over the bridge and small shops, stalls and rooms line the hillside, not to catch the mountain tourist (that's a bonus) but the Moroccan pilgrims.

There is a big annual *moussem* now to the *marabout* and the flood plain at Aroumd becomes spread with tents for this August festival with supplicants going up and down to the shrine or staying overnight. Nearly every *marabout* is regarded as worth visiting for women who cannot conceive, but this one also has powerful *baraka* for mental illnesses and cripples who may make the tough ascent on crutches. The atmosphere has something of Lourdes or Badrinath, only on a smaller scale. The site dates back to around 500 years ago. A mythical spirit Chamarouch visited Aroumd in a terrifying manifestation to indicate where he wanted his hundredth 'house' built (100 is a magical number). The shrine has been in the custodianship of an Aroumd family for centuries.

Graeme and Hamish G went on while I sorted out the food and followed with the two local mules, one of which would descend with Charles, Graeme and myself, the other with the Phuds a day later. We spotted snakes on the slabs overlooking the zigzags above the *marabout* but were too late in the season to see the snowmelt greens bright with gentians. The French crowd were camping, fortunately, with two *caïdal* pavilions and a dozen identical sleeping tents. I'd never seen that before and decided winter had much to recommend it, even if the hut can be a broiler house with bodies sleeping on or under the tables and meals being taken in shifts, the floor soaked with melted snow and the walls sweaty with condensation. (Now, there are two high-class mountain *refuges*.)

Being a landscape created by demolition teams and dumper trucks, I try to avoid the Toubkal Trail in summer. However splendid the setting, I've come to know it rather well over several decades but the highest summit had to be included on GTAM —not by the Tourist Route though. Toubkal is quite splendid really, as is the array of peaks on the other side of the valley—which is why the *refuge*, built in 1937–38, (3207 m) was likely to be overcrowded. There are two passes at the head of the valley. The Tizi n' Ouagane (3750 m) drops to the Agoundis Valley and, with Ras (4083 m), Timesguida (4088 m) n' Ouanoukrim (the highest local summits after Toubkal) and later the Tazaghart plateau all to the west, sweeps round to join the Oued Nfis at Ijoukak. The second pass beyond the Neltner, the Tizi n' Ouanoums (3665 m), leads directly to the Lac d'Ifni which is, erroneously, often referred to as the only lake in the Atlas. (It is the only lake near Toubkal.)

Atlas weather in spring (when we are usually there) generally gives long spells of immaculate conditions with frontal upheavals in between. The fronts are often of text book creation, building up to snow and blow for a couple of days after which there's a return to blue skies and afternoon clouds bubbling up out of the valleys. While once enjoying a bivouac at the *lac*, a front blew in so we packed up and headed for the Tizi n' Ouanoums as fast as we could. Racing up in winter, with heavy packs, trying to beat both storm and darkness, was exhausting. High in this icy Cresta Run, Brian who was not experienced in winter mountaineering, gave a thick icicle a cheery whack with his ice axe. The icicle, thick as a tree trunk, broke off and went shooting down the fall-line of the gully, zipping like a toboggan. We could only yell a warning to the pair below. Luckily they heard us and stood aside to let the thunderbird pass. Brian was aghast but no harm had been done. The Neltner Hut was reached in the last of the daylight, the wind already swirling snow into the air as the blizzard began. One of the party was so exhausted at the supper table that he fell forward asleep and put his face down into his soup. This was only amusing later on; he was quite nastily scalded.

The Lac d'Ifni was first reached by Louis Gentil in 1924 after he'd been up Toubkal. A Segonzac party had ascended Iferouane in 1922 hoping it was the highest summit in Morocco but the ascent only confirmed that Toubkal was such so they decided to have a CAF 'meet' the following spring with Toubkal their objective. This was washed-out by bad weather, but in June (1923) Segonzac, Berger and Dolbeau made the successful raid. This spurred on rather than hindered explorations and all the Toubkal massif summits probably fell by the late 20s.

At the *refuge* I spent another hour sorting (food mostly) and at 1300 Graeme and I set off to climb the summit of all North Africa. I found this odd as normally I'm off before daybreak to crampon on frozen snow and enjoy the early sun at the top, and am back before the snow turns to porridge. Nobody else does this so we can always cook supper early, in peace, then be in bed when everyone else is fighting for meals. We like to rise to a sleeping hut, be off untrammelled and return to an empty hut. Early rising never worries me, especially when it makes life easier.

Two hanging valleys are held between the nearest enclosing arms of Toubkal's ridges. The Ikhibi Sud is immediately above the hut and the Ikhibi Nord is slightly down-valley and, as a result, seldom taken though I've always considered it the much pleasanter way up. Before the Neltner Hut was built, the northern corrie was the tourist route. One then took mules from Asni to the refuge at Aroumd and set off from there so the nearer Ikhibi Nord was naturally followed. The ridges are generally ignored except the classic 1927 OSO Arête up from the Tizi n' Ouanoums. This route was pioneered by Bentley Beetham, a prodigiously active British alpinist who grew tired of the Alps, found Morocco and made several visits to the Atlas. In the 60s we followed the jagged pink crest between the two *ikhibis* (valleys) and had a superb alpine traverse—and all of this lies on just one side of the mountain. There is quite a path up the Ikhibi Nord although this hasn't the penal nature of the Ikhibi Sud. Once up the steep flank we stopped on the lip of the hanging valley for some lunch, enjoying the peace and quiet, shared with an emerging cluster of broken skeletons.

To explain these I'll go back to April 1970. I'd been ill so headed off alone up Toubkal as a rest-cure. Two friends followed, to ski down. After ascending the Ikhibi Sud and sitting a full hour on top with a completely clear view, I went down the Ikhibi Nord. On the descent, I took in Immouzer (Toubkal NE, 4010 m), a Cuillin-like scramble with its own TD Gap. The next summit, Tibherine (3887 m) had an odd golden sheen to it which turned out to be the result of thousands of rounds of ammunition scattered down the slope. The summit cairn had been replaced by an aero engine and reeked of oil with all the smashed parts clean and fresh. Nosey-ing about I found a pair of jeans still in their packaging, which I took to give to Aït Idir. There was a pack of biros too and I took a few working wheels and cogs for souvenirs. When I almost cramponed onto a smashed box of high explosives wedged in the rocks my nerve rather failed and I picked a canny way off, before tobogganing well down the corrie on a bit of fuselage. In the hut there was a Moroccan family up for the skiing, and I gave the boys most of my souvenirs as I'd weight enough for skiing down to Sidi Chamarouch the next day. We flew home a few days later.

Reading the ABMSAC Journal many months later, I came on a note from a party who had been refused access above Imlil in April because there was a big search on for an aircraft which had crashed, while flying arms to Biafra. By chance, the next visit, I met the same Moroccan family of skiers. They had still been at the Neltner when the military arrived and sent them down. I'd never given a thought to the crash not being known about (after all, it's not the sort of thing one stumbles on very often) so was quite glad to have got away before all the hassle. I'm just relieved I didn't stumble on any of the six crew. They were carried down and buried on the lip of the Ikhibi Nord, but began to surface again a few years later. A doctor in one of our parties pointed out obvious signs of impact injuries to some of the bones.

For the first time ever we met a few people descending the Ikhibi Nord as we climbed up. They no doubt wondered what on earth we were doing heading up so late in the day, without even rucksacks. (Porters were carrying them up the Ikhibi Sud.) We did have large *Sigg* waterbottles and some empty *Sidi Ali* bottles which were filled at the last likely water source and we enjoyed scrambling up the stream bed and wending about to look at the scattered wreckage so we landed on Tibherine very quickly. We didn't linger long, as I'd like to have done, as there was a strong wind with a considerable chill factor. We looked down and along the secret corrie to Afekoï.

Somewhere down there (Tizi n' Immouzer) the others presumably bivouacked the night before. (Later they reported an enjoyable traverse of the peaks and a good high bivouac as there were plenty of snow banks providing meltwater.)

From most viewpoints, Afekoï is a perfect cone in the lee of Toubkal (first climbed in 1927, by A. Rand Herron), and for a long time the peak was the only distinctive summit in the *massif* I'd not climbed, largely because we were winter-into-spring visitors and the corrie approach had barring bands of ice-draped cliffs. However, a few years back one late spring, I'd scrambled up the crags south of the corrie and cut in above the rock bands, all a bit hairy with a heavy rucksack, but the reward was great for I found a well-watered secret place and Afekoï gave a delightful scramble on a day fresh as Creation. In the back of the corrie lay a wheel and other sizeable pieces of wreckage, hundreds of metres below Tibherine: it was as if a plane had crashed on Scafell and wreckage lay by the shores of Wastwater *and* by the River Esk on opposite sides of the peak. I bivouacked by a large waterfall in the centre of the sunset cliffs.

The gentle slopes over from Tibherine to the final upthrust of the Toubkal peak are stony yet quite a few alpine flowers thrive in that hostile place. These include a minute pansy (*Viola dyris*), the whole flower face just quarter the size of a pinkie nail and *Linaria tristis* which has a deep tap root to cope with the shifting screes but is very difficult to keep going in Britain where we just can't reproduce either the natural setting or the climate. There are a few species of alpines growing within spitting distance of the trig point on Toubkal; a draba (*D. Oreadum*) actually grew on the cairn.

Our GTAM ascent of the final ridge had an element of the farcical as the wind really caught us. Loose and 'scraggy' (terrain which is part crag, part scree) the climb needed care yet we were constantly buffeted off balance, feet falling wide of where we aimed. I'd about three litres of bottled water in a carrier bag over a shoulder and at one gust these were lifted by the wind and thrown onto my chest. The bag tore and everything went flying. My treasured straw hat flew up on a Cook's tour of the northeast flank of Toubkal and then dropped to the ground at my feet again. The plastic bag spiralled around a huge circuit with the speed and abandon of a crag martin before soaring up and away out of sight. One *Sidi Ali* bottle had cracked on the rocks at the neck, so I had to carry it in my hand which then froze with the cold, despite the sun still shining. There were plenty of lenticular clouds and the summit was too obviously thrusting up into a jet stream of wind.

Unsurprisingly, Charles and the Phuds party were not esconced at the summit. Ali was, however, and pitched inside the circle of stones near the big metal marker was a maroon Micro! A tent there seemed preposterous but made staying possible. Bivouac bags alone would have been beyond endurance, a hungry survival exercise at best, but with a tent—well, we could try. Ali was meant to have come up the Ikhibi Nord after us but instead went up with the two porters helping with our sacks and taking the *Vango* tent rather than bivvy bags. They also took a 5-litre container of water. The party met Charles and the others descending to the hut, all idea of a bivouac with their lightweight gear sensibly abandoned. Charles and I had once before carried up bivvy gear, on ski, to Toubkal's summit and had three hours on top until suddenly the clouds boiled up and snow began to fall. We decided not to bivvy after all, made some tea and skied down to the hut through the rising blizzard. The change from clear sky to driving snow took less than an hour.

We crowded into Ali's summit tent for a brew first then, with Lightning jacket, over-trousers and head wrapped in a *shen*, I had a look about—briefly. The dream of lolling in the sun to watch the world spin calmly into night was banished. The sunset colours were fierce reds and blacks and bruised blues, the beaten sun scuttling for cover. The cold was remarkable; my big toes began to freeze. Without gloves one could only bare hands for seconds. The most ludicrous pantomime was performed before finally bedding down when we had to dress in full armour just to go out for a pee. We could see the lights of Marrakech on one side and Ouarzazate on the other, as magical a moment as any on the trip. The clouds scudded across a three-quarter moon.

It says a lot for the tent that we felt completely confident about surviving. Any tent I'd owned previously would have rattled and banged all through the night, whereas the *Micro* was steady and quiet. It was a squash with three of us; Graeme was pushed to the back while I sat in the entrance with Ali in the middle. Ali and I made a good soup and then a simplified hoosh of meat, vegetables and *Smash*, with brews and biscuits to follow—exactly the meal we'd have had if we'd been lolling about on the balmy night one might have expected on 16th June. I was half out of the inner tent for sleeping, but far from cold on my *Therm-a-Rest*, inside the *Snugpak* bag and wearing thermals. A combination of excitement, being too warm and a slight headache made for a wakeful night but I wouldn't have been anywhere else in the world. Everyone should do something a bit special at least once in a lifetime, something needing both imagination and application.

In reality it was a wild night with about the worst wind I've camped in but even at the time the experience was sublimated into romance. Graeme's bladder led to a communal chaos at 0200, leaving three weary hours until dawn when I was glad to get busy. Brews, cornflakes, bread and jam and we were off; the biting-cold dawn being very much like the previous day's end, as if some economy of nature had simply put the movie into reverse. Yet, for Ali and me, there was a particular joy in gazing west. Practically all the GTAM still to accomplish lay in view, right to the ragged crest of the 'Ridge of a Hundred Peaks' leading to Jbel Tinergwet. Seeing the end on the skyline was a shock as what would come after had never intruded our thoughts during the weeks of wandering. I didn't want to think about such realities. East, the way led the eye along by Iferouane and Taska n' Zat to the Tizi n' Tichka peaks and beyond.

GTAM was a bit like a relay, for when one group had walked from an eastern horizon to wherever, the next group would go from there to the western horizon; horizon to horizon taking a month or so. Graeme, with Tony a few days later, would travel to Tinergwet and beyond and, when they left, we would have three days' tramping to Tamri and the sea. There can't be many years when I've not climbed my old friend Toubkal.

"All downhill now", I joked.

CHAPTER 12

Westward Ho!

The mythical hero Fionn once asked his sons what they considered the greatest music of all. One replied that it was the clash of swords in battle, the second that it was the baying of hounds on the chase, the third that it was the sound of the harp in the great hall. Their father shook his head and answered his own question, "No, my sons, the greatest music of all is what is happening".

Irish traditional

John Willison and Clare Wardle went through the Toubkal massif by the Ourika Valley, the Kissaria gorges, Lac d' Ifni, Jbel Toubkal by the OSO Arête (Clare's first rock climb!), and the lovely Agoundis Valley. They then hitched to the top of the Tizi n' Test and descended to the Nfis valley from the crest further west only to have a bit of an epic. In comparison, we took the wimp's way.

Toubkal's Ikhibi Sud is unhappily worn by passing feet so from the summit we chose to descend the Ikhibi Nord again; besides, I wanted Ali to see the wreckage on Tibherine. On the screes below Tibherine we met Hamish G plodding up so told him about the crash. He'd not noticed the bones! Our gang were all round the table in the hut, not setting off until noon. Graeme and I had a siesta and slept well that night despite the multi-lingual din. The whisky was flowing when we went to bed, which only partly explained Charles, Graeme and I being up long before the others despite their intentions of climbing Ras and Timesguida that day.

We ambled down for Mohammed's with a pause for tea at Sidi Chamarouch, then met the restless Hosain coming up the track on Taza. I led the others off along the *seguia* circling Aroumd to enjoy the flowers (orchids a metre high) and then, below the village, along to the flat-topped boulder perch where one can see a hidden *cascade* up a side valley.

Lying on that boulder alone, a fox once came right up to within a couple of metres of me before he caught my scent. He then did an instant back somersault and vanished among the walnut terraces. On another occasion, I'd once watched a dog and vixen nosing their way across the screes without noticing me at all. But I saw quite the strangest creature I've ever seen in Morocco off the Aroumd road. I had a favourite reading spot there, and was quietly doing that when a furry creature popped out of the rock near my feet. It looked like a big fat mouse but had a ridiculously elongated nose: for all the world like a miniature elephant's trunk. The creature approached my legs and raced back under the rock several times and then, as if deciding I was just a new part of the scenery rather than any threat, shot up my front and over a shoulder to disappear into a rock behind. I was probably sitting on its regular run. Nobody recognised my drawing of the 'mouse' and in the end I sent my drawings and descriptions to the Natural History Museum and they kindly sent back a description of the North African elephant shrew (*Elephantulus rozeti*). So there *is* a mouse with an elephant's trunk, but Mohammed doesn't believe it.

From the boulder perch, always a good pause heading home, we followed the *seguia* from the *cascade* stream all the way home to Targa Imoula. (*Targa* is Berber for a water channel, *seguia* is the Arabic word.) After a bit of repacking, we went down to the Café Soleil for an omelette lunch. Both Charles and I did a huge washing of clothes then scrubbed ourselves too, creating a semi-*hammam* in the tiled room. While we had a fairly easy attitude to the dust and dirt of the trail, any chance of being thoroughly clean was welcomed. The next hot shower would be nearing the coast, almost the finish. The 'end' kept intruding as we thought ahead and prepared for the trail once more. Ali, Hosain and Chris H appeared so we hurried on our efforts in case the rest arrived as well. We wanted both space and peace that day.

I'd made a *harrira* at dusk and, later, we were called up for a *tagine*, oranges and tea on the balcony and Graeme and I talked music until we were dopey with sleep. Graeme was the youngest involved in GTAM. He had already done a great deal in the Atlas (and all over the place), having quit working on the railways of Britain. Lean, fit and with many interests he reminded me of my own vanished youth when I too could take on the locals in running down from the Neltner. Dark and swarthy, Graeme was often taken for a local (useful sometimes) and he and Ali could have passed as brothers.

At Imlil we were being joined by a French woman whom I will call Monique. She had married an Englishman and lived in Rabat. I'd met her a few times and we shared an interest in the cultural and artistic world of Morocco. She had previously wandered in the Atlas so it felt reasonable to suggest she came along for a while, perhaps as far as the Tichka Plateau.

While we enjoyed the *Café Soleil* Graeme went off to Marrakech to link up with Tony, newly arrived. After a big shopping they would join us at Ijoukak, the last such addition of GTAM, a few days after we left Imlil. From Imlil to the sea was a major undertaking in itself and, once on the way, was absorbing enough that we lived entirely in it. '*La distance n'y fait rien; il n'y a que le premier pas qui coûte*' (The distance is immaterial, its only the first steps that matters) applied now as it had at Taza. One of the joys of such journeying is its enveloping demands that quite shut out other, exterior, matters. Hamish G blew in from the Neltner, having left the others just getting up. He and Graeme departed in a *camionette*. Later, trinket-seller Bari called me in to his stall for tea. He was doing quite well out of our gang.

A mule ran amok on the square, kicking out at cars and charging about wildly until someone was able to grab the flying rope halter. On the way up to Targa Imoula we looked in to inspect the new *gîte* Mohammed was building in the fields above the school; the view from the rooftop was a complete encompassing of the Imlil basin: all the circling peaks and radial valleys. The fields were all brown (planted with maize) compared to the previous week when they had been golden with grain. The cherry season, alas, was over. The Phuds were determinedly finishing off their remaining Duty Free booze and insisted on dancing on the terrace, a rather limp jollity. Mohammed took off the Marmite jar for the supper *cous cous* preparations. There was the porridgy-like soup first, a really good *cous cous*, the last cherries of the season and plenty of excellent mint tea, all consumed on the upper terrace under the stars. 'And so to bed.' (Did you know Samuel Pepys visited Morocco?) The sky was like black glass and the stars like Christmas lights down Oxford Street. A small cool breeze fluttered in the grilled window and I lay listening to the gentle noises of the night, relishing the thought of being on the way again.

Upstairs I could hear the less than happy complaints of Mustapha. He was Mohammed's firstborn and, as such, was the apple of his eye, as delightful and lively a lad as ever ran the slopes of Atlas. By the age of eight he was contributing quite effectively to the family finances, leading mules and generally the firm's 'gofor'. Tragically, he was struck down by some cerebral bug which had taken away his strength so he now sat in a crumpled heap in a corner, unable to walk or even talk properly. It was heart-rending and no less so because of the stony acceptance of misfortune.

At an early hour I was woken from my grateful sleep with the repeated phrase: "Pleased to meet you, Jimmy" coming in through the window grill. The voice was that of the local house bunting (*Emberiza striolata*) and during all the years we'd stayed at Mohammed's that refrain had been our reveille. It indicated that the song was passed down through successive generations for it was a version of the song unique to Targa Imoula. The local name of the bird is the onomatopoeic *teebeebit* which perhaps covers the three-noted callers. Many, if not most, give four notes and once the rasping "Pleased to meet you" is suggested it is hard to hear anything else. The bird is common and not harmed (not even in the grain *souks*) as, like the stork or swallow it is regarded as bringing good luck. A legend tells of the Prophet Mohammed waking to the bird repeating, over and over, the phrase "One month is enough, one month is enough" and this he took to be the answer to the matter he'd been considering: the duration of the fast now known as Ramadan.

Our tallest member was unusually silent over breakfast for he had charged into the guest room without allowing for the five foot eight lintel. You can tell the seasoned Atlas travellers: they are the ones who, at every village door, however high, give a sort of jerky bow on entering.

There was a general exodus after breakfast with Mohammed's mule taking the others' gear down to the car park for transporting to Marrakech. We met Monique and our cavalcade, still with the likeable muleteers Mohammed and young Omar and headed off for the Tizi Mzic, the western dominating pass. The ascent to the Tizi Mzic (2489 m) was hot work as usual and we buckled down to the slog: "One leg in front of the other, One leg in front of the other, As the little dog said".

From near the elbow in the Aroumd *piste* the current mule track traverses above the cultivation level and then thankfully reaches a shady walnut grove. It then heads up the streambed, leaving the stream to pass some *azibs* by a side stream, beyond which stunted juniper woods mark the final zigzags to the pass. Barbary partridge, great tit, redstart, green woodpecker and crimson-winged finch are birds seen from the path, bird-spotting being a useful excuse for stopping when in need of a rest. The air was snappy with the scent of the juniper. We met a solitary wanderer singing down the way and had a second breakfast on the col, a place made for lingering with balanced views. East, it was all gentle tones with Angour like a foresight beyond the gunbarrel Tizi n' Tamatert glen; west, we could see the forested foothills below the vast plateau of Tazaghart. The possible continuations from the *tizi* are like the introductory moves of a chess game, apparently few and simple but, before long, the options of the game are endless.

Below, on the west side, lay Tizi Oussem (a village not a pass) and from it the Azzadene valley runs down to the Oued Nfis at Ouirgane on the Tizi n' Test road. At Ouirgane was the Au Sanglier Qui Fume, an *auberge* of character long run by Madame Thevenin, a Flemish larger than life character who only left the hills when illness forced her. She dined with the guests, French style, and bullied everyone in loud tones. The staff remained the same for decades. Even when her husband died she stayed on. She loved flowers and the whole establishment was overgrown with scented wisteria. We knew she was not returning when the sunflower painting signed by a child '*pour mama*' vanished from the walls. The 1995 spate broke the bridge on the main road, filled rooms of the Au Sanglier with mud, wrecked part of the garden and swept away the stables (and stallions) where the national trick riding team practised across the river. I'm glad madame did not live to witness that heartbreaking scene. The smoking boar still adorns one wall and happily, now, madame's family run the hotel.

Turning up from Tizi Oussem (or Tizi Mzic direct) leads to the *azibs* of Tamsoult (2540 m) and a floral gorge with a spectacular track up to the isolated 3000 m Tazaghart (Lépiney) *refuge*. In winter, an ice axe may be needed just to reach the hut! Tazaghart is Ben Nevis writ large: miles of ridges and gullies topped by a huge stony plateau. The 600 m wall of the Clochetons overhangs the hut and facing the Tazaghart cliffs are gullies and ridges galore. The *Couloir de Neige* often survives, ice-filled, for years on end but all our attempts on it have ended with flight as the gully is a natural stone shoot. Some of the 4000-ers are accessible from the Tizi Melloul at the head of the glen, but that approach is defended by an icefall.

The hut guardian lives at Tizi Oussem. In the early years we sat out a couple of ferocious storms at the *refuge*, with the hut creaking and groaning like a wooden sailing ship and our minds dwelling on the nearby wreckage where an earlier hut had been swept away by an avalanche. We made several ascents of Tazaghart both for the climbing itself and for the atmosphere of the summit plateau, which can't be described any better than in the words of Dresch and de Lépiney in 1938: '*un désert de pierres, plat, nu, vide, si haut perché qu'on n'aperçoit rien sous le ciel; il constitue un des spectacles le plus saissants de l'Atlas*' (a desert of stones, flat, bare, vast, perched so high that one can see nothing but sky; it forms one of the most striking spectacles in the Atlas). From the Azib Tamsoult (a good camping area) you can also circle Adrar Adj (Haj), the nearest 3000 m summit to Imlil (3129 m), a worthy climb and with views of all the great peaks. Winter often covers the summit of the peak with snow. Returning pilgrims from Mecca often wear white turbans, hence the name.

None of these routes were ours on GTAM as we held resolutely westwards, quite against the grain of the land. We allowed three days to trek through to Ijoukak on the Tizi n'Test road, a route which had already become a great favourite of mine. We were able to 'float' up and down slopes now, distance meaningless, slipping into the restfulness of resumed routine, a friendly fitness. A path dropped brutally to Tizi Oussem but we preferred to skirt left and descend gentler slopes through the juniper forest, on a path which was not too easy to follow among the trees.

It zigzagged down towards an obvious graveyard *kouba* on a spur above Tizi Oussem, a very confusing village, built on top of itself as if thrown down the hillside.

We knew to double back on the fringe of Tizi Oussem and angled down to the river. After working our way up the Oued Azzadene, we turned off on a good track into Tizi Ouarhou (a village) where several terrace fields were growing irises, not just as a soil-holding margin but for dye and cosmetic use. There was a steep climb before we angled in to the riverside where we sat, feet in the cool water, for our picnic lunch. The stream was overlaid with the textured white of water crowfoot. There were several species of butterfly about and one innocently landed on a twig beside me only for a spider to rush out and grab it. The *arachnid* bit its victim whose wings soon stopped beating, presumably from a disabling poison. By then the spider had thoroughly parcelled up the butterfly in a shroud of spun threads. As a final gesture, the beast cut off the butterfly's wings which spiralled down into the stream and were carried away one by one. Monique was not happy about this performance.

We wended off and erroneously took a path *up* instead of crossing the stream (as we soon saw the mules doing) so had to traverse poor grazing tracks until we met the mule track again on our side. I stood on an apparently safe boulder only for it to turn under me, so I crashed down onto my right shoulder rather painfully. The shoulder seemed to be fine but over the months gave recurring trouble and a full year passed before it recovered completely. I was afraid I'd not be able to paddle a canoe, but several Highland trips passed uneventfully. Knees and thigh joints are also beginning to creak but most people our age, Charles pointed out, are using their free bus passes, not cavorting over trackless mountains. We have reached that certain age where we make comments about 'old' people only to discover they are younger than we are.

The mule track zigzagged up and ran on, dominated by the flank of Tazaghart, to reach a secret spring-fed green corner where the grass was starred by globe thistles. The track on was also rather furtive for it ran up bare strata in the rocks, easily overlooked, to wend through a knobbly area where the junipers gradually petered out. Ahead, we could see the cook tent and the mules grazing, tethered to our ice axes, banged in the length of their shafts. There was instant tea when we arrived. They were an efficient local team (the lads had been with us since Setti Fadma) and nothing was urgently calling for attention. We didn't even bother erecting our tents, but made scrapes on the gritty scree across the stream and used our bivvy bags. Hosain, hyperactive as ever, began supper early. Old Mohammed was being ribbed over the purchase of new canvas boots at Imlil: he'd been sold two left feet. As a result he'd crossed one pass and almost climbed another in flipflops. I worked on my book in bed and, as ever, found working out the next chapter a sure way of getting to sleep quickly.

In the night a wind blew up out of nowhere, a booming, gusty wind and, too late, I realised I'd left my mug perched on a stone. It had gone. This was annoying as the mug had sentimental value—I'd brought it up from the well at Asni youth hostel. There was a spell of seven years when there was no water on tap and so was drawn from the well by a bucket, and one day I brought up a red mug in the bucket. Now the wind had taken it—a bit Omar Khayyám-ish, coming by water and going by wind. Willy-nilly the wind went on blowing, so breakfast porridge had a sugaring of dark dust. Omar forgot all about snakes: the type of bushes on those slopes were supposed to be popular with a nasty species, hence our scrapes had all been on the open, bare screes. (Monique considered this spartan site a poor second to any house.) One of Charles's socks was found a good 100 metres down valley and other mugs and plates were well distributed. The slopes above led to a final gravelly tussle to reach the Tizi n' Ouarhou (Tizi n' Tougdal, 2672 m). The view back the previous night had been blue on blues, that day's colours were graceful greys, ridge on ridge.

Past experience helped to navigate the complex fields and we cut corners across to the main path up from Tisgui. Animals were streaming out of the village, highlighted against the crude variegated tones of strata. Girls rode mules with the metal 'panniers' used to collect wood and headed up a side valley towards stunted trees. We had a good long break in a shady nook before joining the grand highway, still traversing the sprawl of Tazaghart, an undulating track with plenty of indentations to cross streams descending from the high plateau snows. The Tizi n' Iguidi ahead was dominated by a strata-marked cone of hill, balanced on the left by a rocky peak which would bear a rock-climbing visitation. I let the others walk on to photograph them with that background, then just couldn't catch up again when I suddenly felt weak and queasy for no obvious reason.

Our destination was the last water before the zigzags up to the Tizi n' Iguidi, a pleasant corner except all the grassy bits had water seeping onto them and each of the many young walnut trees was being carefully fed by a trickle of directed water. Admiration for this horticultural application was rather lost on those wanting places for tents. I lay in the temporary shade of a boulder. Kind Mohammed brought me tea and Ali helped pitch my tent in the blustery wind. Rising from the ground my knees felt feeble and my right arm was useless. I felt about a hundred years old and I needed all my resolution to go and wash socks and feet and cream my spotty legs. I then slept in the shade of a walnut tree (one not standing in water) until supper was ready, not that I ate more than some bread and jam. After drinking plenty of liquid, I retreated to bed with a cocktail of pills—the thermometer in the tent read 100°F (40°C). In the morning I was fine. As earlier waters had drained to Tisgui these ran to the village of Ameslane, to which the Imlil pair descended for new shoes for the mules. Ali suggested Mohammed might buy new shoes too, a pair if possible, or two right ones.

The dawn sky went through the usual parade of opal to amber to turquoise to butterfly blue. Being off efficiently and regularly was a pleasant reversion. The slopes were still surfing with wind but our high camping meant an easy climb to the Tizi n' Iguidi about 2500 m. We descended a slope where the path sometimes barely marked the bulges of compacted shale and in others went skittering down loose chips that tinkled with metallic sounds underfoot. Humans and mules had a scree run. An old man with a donkey laden with wood asked me for a *bonbon*, Charles for a *stilo* (biro) and Ali for a *garro* (cigarette). We waited for the mules under some huge walnuts by a gushing stream, a site to camp at some day. We didn't have much useful shade thereafter and endured a throbbing day. Much of the country in the following few days was to have severe and damaging storms, but the Western Atlas escaped.

With such an abundance of water, the valley was well cultivated and we followed a *seguia* through the fields, crossed a jagged limestone area to reach the first village, Aït Zitoun. A path lead to the Tizi n' Test road, from where Ijoukak lies an hour's walk on. However, having gone that way several times and disliking tarred roads, we decided to cut over the hills to descend directly to Ijoukak. The route looked easy enough on the map.

We were directed and accompanied down to the river, but then took some tentative wanderings to find a way to Tazgalt. We chatted with a schools' attendance officer, home on holiday from Casablanca, who put us on the right road again. Once clear of the village we had oatcakes and *Kiri* cheese under a coppice of almonds. We could see the blue dots of our cavalcade wending down for the main road, and it was tempting to do likewise.

An orange and some drinks made the hot ascent bearable—just—and apart from the soil colours changing, the path just went on and on before steepening for a last red soil section. Suddenly, there was the Oued Nfis far below. In the aching heat it was too hazy even to pick out the historic site of Tinmal, but the Oued Nfis was our guide to the Tichka Plateau, the Ridge and the end.

Cutting in at Ijoukak was the Oued Agoundis (rising near Toubkal) with its zinc and lead mines. I wended over a strange plateau-like hollow to a gap in cliffs, from where a *piste* sphaghettied down to Ijoukak. A mule track, harsh and hard on the feet, descended more directly, criss-crossed by the *piste*. The day was desperately hot, I'd no water left but at least progression was downhill. When there isn't any alternative but to go on, it is surprising how one does just that. Ijoukak had a sea-green mosque tower with what looked like a rocket perched on top. I skipped a paddle in the river in favour of drinking three *cocas* in a row and then joined Graeme, Tony and Chris B for tea in the coolest room of our *auberge*. "*Mzien!*" the muleteers kept saying ("Excellent!") We agreed.

Graeme and Tony had met up at the Hotel Ali in Marrakech as planned, did most of the shopping at the handy grocery by the back door (there's a bakery by the front door) and brought everything to Ijoukak by taxi, negotiated at the Bab er Rob. The driver not only had to obtain the statutory police chit for the unscheduled journey, but he went home to obtain clearance from his wife! Chris Bond had brought out his cycle and stayed on after the Phuds left to make a cycle tour on his own. He'd cycled up from Asni that day, knowing we'd be at Ijoukak. Monique was off on her own. I'm afraid she had little in common with our trail-hardened party of individuals and, while we pulled together with common purpose, Monique seemed to live in a different world. We'd squabbled with her over her paying people to pose for photographs, as any doling out of dirhams soon leads to endemic begging. The remote Western Atlas was still free of this distraction and we wanted to keep it that way.

Utilitarian Ijoukak is only a row of *hanuts* and cafés and a closed-up colonial period *refuge* where the Oued Agoundis flows into the Oued Nfis. The buses crossing the Tizi n'Test stop there for breakfast *taghboula* (porridge), tea or *tagines*, scoffed at any time of the day. The westernmost café was our home for the night, as unpretentious as the rest but with attractive rooms and enclosed yards hidden behind. They did excellent *tagines* too. *Tagines* are invariably slow-cooked and not planned in advance so making one's needs known early is advisable. The cook will use what ingredients can be found readily which ensures no two *tagines* are ever the same. Likewise every household bakes its own bread, to its own recipe, which ensures a pleasing variety.

On a previous Flowers trip down the Nfis we stayed there too and, from the roof, watched the Aïd el Kebir *harma* (goat man) chasing the children up the street with a stick and much yelling. The figure looked like an anorexic gorilla. Once home from GTAM a friend showed me a brochure for holidaying in the Swiss Lötschental, which portrayed an ancient custom of figures dressing in skins. They looked extraordinarily like the Atlas goat men and I wondered if they had a common ancestry back in prehistory. Depending on the size of the village, chosen young adults dress up in the skins: the goat men. Like Ramadan, this is a moveable feast and if it occurs in high summer, one is advised to stand up-wind of the goat men after day one. Oddly, we had not seen any goat men at Tarbat where we'd celebrated the feast.

As the transport licensing laws are relaxed for the festive period, everything on wheels is on the road crowded with family and friends, webbing the country with chaos. We counted 27 minibuses at Ijoukak, all packed, many with a beast or two perched on top of the piles of baggage. It was good to be back although we were also aware that was the beginning of the final stage of GTAM. It was not one to be underestimated however, as several major 3000 m summits line the Western Atlas.

CHAPTER 13

Up the Nfis

I travel to see that with which I am already intimately acquainted, but to see it again in a
different light, to pronounce it seen more clearly or more profoundly, or just more.

J Crumley

Most of the GTAM party wandered up the north bank of the Oued Nfis but I kept up the main road to try and photograph various historical sites. Perched up on a symmetrical cone of hill is Agadir n' Gouj which, although not very old, catches the eye with its imperious setting. Down by the river below Talat n' Yacoub (a Wednesday *souk*) is the Kasbah Goundafa, the main base of the tribal lord who controlled the passage of the Tizi n' Test. The Goundafa were too powerful to be subjugated by the French so were used instead to control the Nfis and sometimes the southwest. As with the Glaoui, their strength was curtailed by the building of the road: the Corrieyairack of the Atlas.

Cunninghame Graham, *hidalgo*, traveller, writer and politician, made several visits to Morocco in Victorian times, the most interesting being an attempt to cross the Atlas to reach the fabled and then almost inaccessible city of Taroudant. The story is told in his rumbustious *Magreb el Acksa*. He travelled across the plains and followed the Oued Nfis from Amizmiz to modern Ouirgane and then rode up-river only to be stopped by the Goundafa, at the Kasbah Tagoundaf which lies further up the Nfis, perched high in an eyrie setting in a side-valley. His complaint that a few hours riding would gain the *tizi* and a view of the spires of Taroudant should not be taken too literally: the Test is not so easily climbed and Taroudant is still long, invisible, miles away after the 7000 foot descent. This book influenced Bernard Shaw who then wrote *Captain Brassbound's Conversion*, a play set in Essaouira and the Atlas.

In their heyday, the Goundafa were used by the sultan to reduce the rebellious Sous province to submission. The rebellious *sheiks* laid on a great banquet, including one dish known to be a favourite of the Goundafa *caïd*'s. He grew suspicious, however, when the delicacy was over-eagerly pressed upon him. He declared he would keep it for later and the meal passed harmlessly enough. As soon as the guests had departed he had the poisoned dish set before him and sent for the *sheiks* one at a time and pressed them to join him in this private treat as a mark of honour. Those who made to do so in all innocence were stopped from eating and sent out secretly but those who refused the honour were seized by the servants and made to eat. Their bodies were thrown to the dogs. At a stroke he had resolved the troubles in the Sous and returned to the thanks of the sultan.

Eventually I left the tarmac road and paddled across the river to gain shady walking up and along to Tinmal. Cycle tracks showed Chris had been through. He was heading for the Tizi n' Test and Taroudant. When Charles and Co. arrived we drank the small *hanut* dry before exploring the restored ancient monument which is, strictly speaking, a mosque and one of only two that non-Moslems are allowed to enter in Morocco. In a remote village in the Anti-Atlas, however, I was once taken in hand by a small boy who showed me everything of interest. He pulled me into a cool building and only as I stood in the middle and saw the *mihrab* (alcove) on the eastern wall did I realise I was in a small mosque. At Imoulas (Western Atlas) when two of us were trying to photograph a new mosque a local insisted on taking us in so we could admire, and photograph, a superbly painted ceiling. What delighted me was that such craftsmanship still exists, even in remote villages. In the towns and busier places if visitors look like accidentally straying into a mosque someone will always give a (polite) call to stop. In some cases there may be warning notices or a bar across, the latter as much to stop stray animals as errant humans.

Tinmal's fort-like mosque is all that remains of a twelfth century city, part of the expansion of the dynamic Almohad dynasty. This was founded by Ibn Tumert, a Berber from the Anti-Atlas, who returned from eastern travels and set up his *ribat*. He slowly converted the tribes, beating off Almoravid attacks, but died before he could capture Marrakech. His death was kept secret for three years to help establish his successor, the great Abd el Moumen, who took Marrakech in 1148 and eventually ruled from Spain to the Sahara. He created Tinmal as a great religious centre—but also quietly disposed of Ibn Tumert's children and relatives to ensure there were no rivals to his power. He was to be buried at Tinmal in a tomb next to Ibn Tumert's.

The roofless interior is filled with brick horseshoe arches, a bewildering, wonderful geometrical pattern. There is a courtyard and, unusually, a tower over the *mihrab* niche, where some decorative detail survives. The locals now use the mosque for Friday worship and visitors are not admitted on that day. Nothing remains of the city surrounding the holy spot, other than vestiges of the great wall barring any access from the Marrakech direction. As with the still impressive Almoravid walls on Jbel Zagora, these trace from river to high on the hillside.

Coming out from the *ribat* a hoopoe went looping off. "*Hudhud*" the *guardien* called it. Some of the names of birds were quite onomatopoeic (the cuckoo is *oukouk*, the chough *narrar*) while the names of others would fit well in Narnia (the golden eagle is *ogab*, the bulbul *bou laglag*, the pied wagtail *mizizi* and the greylag *wiz*). When it comes to different names for all the warblers and the like they are simply called 'little brown birds', with which many nascent bird-watchers would sympathise.

Paths known and new took us on up-valley from Tinmal. There was some childish chalked graffiti, but in what other country would I see chalked on a wall the English words: 'I am very happy'? A pleasant path took us angling up the fields to reach Mzouzit where we hoped the small roadside shops might sell drinks. Mzouzit guards the entrance of the Ougdamt valley which runs up to drain the peaks of Jbel Igdat (3616 m) and Jbel Erdouz (3579 m), the highest summits west of the Toubkal massif. This is a surprisingly neglected area with not only huge peaks and tough *tizis* but any number of criss-crossing mule tracks for high-class trekking. We once made a four-day traverse from Erdouz to Jbel Gourza, the 3000-er backing Tinmal.

Jbel Gourza was the peak bagged in 1871 by Hooker and Ball on the first real expedition into the Atlas with both scientific and exploratory ambitions. Sir Joseph Hooker was director of Kew Gardens, John Ball was also a botanist and the first president of the Alpine Club and George Maw (who had to go home earlier) was one of those versatile amateurs with many interests. He wrote the definitive monograph on the species *crocus*, for example. He was also a noted geologist and his studies of clay were linked to his family tile manufacturing business. He made a collection of Moroccan ceramics from 1869–71. All were experienced travellers and, despite every hindrance being put in their way, climbed to the Tizi Tagharat (3465 m) above Sidi Chamarouch. (Maw fought to the *tizi* in a blizzard, alone.) On a second sortie via Amizmiz they managed to elude their guides and climbed a hill they heard as Teza or Tezi (*tizi* probably, just meaning pass) but from their description is Jbel Gourza, a nine-hour slog for the first Atlas 3000-er by an outsider. Any speculation on this being the hill climbed was removed on our traverse, for the photograph in their classic book was recognised. The buildings on top which they described are still there, although propitiatory bull sacrifices may not be the order of today.

Joseph Thomson (famed for his travels in East Africa) visited Morocco; in 1888 he climbed from Amizmiz to the Tizi n' Imiri west of Jbel Gourza, thinking that was the watershed, and was appalled to find the Goundafa country lay, not south of the range, but in its midst (the Oued Nfis) with a further crest beyond. Despite an unfriendly welcome at the Kasbah Goundafa, a companion being stung by a scorpion lurking in his pyjamas and being threatened with a sword, he almost reached that southern crest from the Agoundis gorges. He returned to Amizmiz, travelled west to the Assif el Mel and from there doubled back, crossed the Tizi n' Tislit and climbed Jbel Igdat (the peak of the birds, 3616 m) the highest ascent of that period. He returned by a different pass, the whole being done in defiance of authority and considerable danger. His book is a neglected classic.

Our GTAM route kept to the Oued Nfis, and for one section we were forced to walk on its shingles as the banks were too jungly. We made the most of the band of shade under the Ougdemt road bridge during lunch. By the time we had demolished our runny cheddar and oatcakes, my soaking sandals and socks had dried out. A kingfisher flashed past and a pair of blue-bellied rollers perched awhile, an odd conjunction of brilliant blues. We walked along the road a bit but a loop had us crossing to the quieter mule track on the north bank which ran between attractive villages. The second of these was Ighil, backing a large hollow of intense cultivation, the valley smothered with fields, themselves nearly hidden by riverside poplars, oleanders, olive groves and almond and fruit trees. We undulated on and I was keen to see ahead in case the mules had sneaked past while we were out of sight. We'd just decided to wait when a smiling woman, a sprig of mint in her headscarf, asked us to stop for tea: what a good idea.

We were no sooner settled in a cool room with bright cream walls looking out to a sunny courtyard when I saw the mules come into view on the road over the river so I went out and made sure they saw us. Ali ran over to see what we planned and arrived not even out of breath. Fresh bread and new butter went with the tea, a bit of a female gathering in which we males were largely irrelevant. Monique had a great time and was shown round where we could not intrude. Cosmetics and clothing are a universal female talking point! The young girls of the house were as attractive as ever, in floral dresses over woolly tights, oval faces with such large eyes framed in unruly hair. One girl wore a charm against the evil eye, which proved to be the preserved eye of an owl.

A bit further on I yelled speculatively into the jungle below and Ali replied. We found a way down and along shingle banks to discover camp in a small clearing between walled fields and riverbed. After relaxing over drinks I did a major sorting-out of supplies for the foreseeable future.

I'd chosen a bivvy site below a briar covered bank but the wind steadily rose and eventually I had to pitch the tent in self-defence. Conditions had been building up for hours, a meteorological version of Ravel's *Bolero*, promising all the evil of that implacable piece; however we escaped the destructive drum beats of the storm that swept most of the country. We struggled to cook and crunched our way through the dust additives of supper.

Charles spent hours whittling a poplar stick, stripping off the bark and carving it to taste. He'd been using another stick but had left it at the ladies' teahouse. Young Omar stripped and carved a very ornate stick but the next day leant on it rather hard, snapping it. There was a large boulder holding back the river in a deep pool and most of us took the opportunity to bath and wash salt-stained garments. In those little tasks time soon curtains down on day. We had a night of deafening frog calls, glow-worms and lorries on the road passing like science fiction monsters. I found a chameleon and horrified some kids by picking the creature up and letting it perch on my arm. They regard these fascinating reptiles (*tatta* in Arabic) with superstitious horror. I discovered why: the chameleon once betrayed the Prophet Mohammed to his enemies. The Prophet was hiding in a cave when his pursuers came on an old woman gathering wood on the slope below and, at a promise of great wealth, she twisted her mouth and rolled her eyes towards the cave. She was immediately changed into the beast we know, with its grim mouth and erratic eyes, damned to all the faithful.

"So restful not to have dirty dust blowing for breakfast," I wrote. With rags of cloud on the peaks the night had been hot so I'd slept naked under my sleeping bag; was it only a week previously I'd been in the bag, wearing thermals? There was time to make porridge (always popular) and enjoy toast and marmalade before setting off on one of the best day's walking. Monique, however, had spent most of breakfast time cross-legged on a knoll meditating, and did nothing to help pack up and get away. She came trailing after.

A good path undulated on to Azal, and the route produced a variety of flowers we'd never seen before: a sweet-scented clematis and a shrub with a very similar flower. There was bright orange-red pimpernel too and a shrub like a small white-flowering oleander with bladders that looked like green gooseberries. A flycatcher was working overtime in the shrubbery. One village had a pond and a fancy mosque with a star carved over the doorway. Beyond, we went astray as the river had eroded away the path, so we ended up on the shingles again and crossed almost under a well-made suspension bridge leading to Assoul. Here we zigzagged up through the fields to gain the known up-valley *piste* which comes in from the main road below the steep climb to the Tizi n' Test. I'd once seen a mongoose there.

The *piste* made its way through the intensely-red *hamri* landscape, the soft layered sandstone symbolic of Africa which is always hot and hard on trekkers' feet. I knew of a small shop ahead where we might just find drinks—if open. I kept quiet so I wouldn't raise any hopes but the *hanut* was open and we all bought 1½ litre bottles of fizzy drinks to carry away, and consumed smaller bottles there and then. Men were bringing in sacks of grain and children came with coppers for individual sweets, a scene one sees the world over. A small girl, in tattered colours and untended hair, sat playing in the dust with a piece of rusty tin. We were at the top range for olives, a tree which may have had its origins in the Atlas foothills. Maize (sixteenth century) and potato (nineteenth century) are New World importations.

We soon came to our lunch spot at a bridge over the Nfis, Monique drifting in when everything was ready. She was not making herself very popular. The bridge was typically constructed: trunks across, branches and slabs of stones piled on top and belayed by a steel cable to the bank so even if damaged in a flood, the main trunks would be saved. We're always surprised this isn't seen more often but the attitude to bridges is quite casual and, if washed away—*mektoub*—they are easily rebuilt. The skills of construction, from generations of using local materials, are impressive. We lingered an hour on the hot rounded boulders by the water and paddled blissfully in common content. While novelty tastes, experience relishes, and all of us had had previous Moroccan visits, Charles a dozen or more, including previous treks up and down the Nfis. Black damselflies flickered over the tresses of water crowfoot.

Long poplar poles, stripped of bark, were being brought by mules and piled ready for building use. Large beams are laid across the house walls then thinner, shorter pieces are laid at right angles across them, with any amount of local variation. At Mohammed's house the cross pieces are what looked like long kindling, in others they use thin branches, in others strong reeds. Over this, layers of mud are pressed, with or without a lining of plastic sheeting. There is usually a slight rim and the accumulating rainwater is led out by a spout to pour clear of the walls. Often the first indication of rain when waking in the morning is the sound of spouting water "like an elephant urinating", as a disgruntled voice once suggested. Snow is shovelled off the flat roofs as soon as possible to stop them becoming waterlogged and eventually leaking. The four of us once spent a night at the end of a week of rain: great dollops of gritty mud splodged onto the floor all night and we cringed in the drier, safer areas, our sleeping bags covered by the mules' tarpaulins. Wealthier house owners will now concrete roofs or lay attractive tiling. Boundary walls too are always capped with overhanging stones, leaves, branches etc. as protection against the rain. One November, a gale from the east drove heavy rain against the houses of Mzic above Imlil and about

10 % suffered collapse. Mohammed's is set into an eastern hillside so survived unscathed. As one goes up a river like the Oued Nfis, the size of rooms diminishes in proportion to the size of trees i.e. the size of the main beams available.

If I mention rain rather frequently, its not because Morocco is a notably wet country (in fact, Morocco is a "cold country with a hot sun" in the words of the late king). It's because these occurrences are unusual enough to be News. Our mantra was: just another bloomin' sunny day. As we sat by the Oued Nfis on GTAM (and on every previous visit) we were being grilled by sun. For 80 % of the time sunshine is the norm, even in winter. What we recall and often gossip about, in the same way as the locals, are the escapades and sorrows where rain overdid its meteorological contribution. Sun is just sun.

One of the joys of the Oued Nfis is the constantly changing landscape. We entered a delightful section where pines (Aleppo pines, *Pinus halepensis*) dominated with a path clear. We passed the remote farm of Oukoun, the last height for growing almonds. We had stopped there for tea previously but as the campsite was not far ahead we went on while the muleteers stopped for cups of *leben* (buttermilk). A side stream had provided water (and a green water snake) previously but was quite dry and we had to fetch water from the main river. We carefully took water from places where there were braidings which acted as filter beds and, we hoped, removed most of the microbes and sediment. We never drank untreated water in doubtful circumstances and tended to boil water anyway, for tea or coffee.

The ground was shaly and mulched with pine needles and the spur by the stream was soon dotted with our tents or bivvy spots. The river came out of a gorge, silvery shining and edged with rosy oleanders in full flower: perfection. I went up the gorge and found a granite-held pool where it was possible to plunge into the glittering water. It was necessary to lie on my clothes as protection against the sun-heated rock. The last rays of the sun spotlighted my bivvy place on the spur and the dusk brought a breeze, warm and young.

Every site up the Nfis was marked as extra good and that was no exception, lying on the tent rather than inside with the stars glittering through the trees and the contented purr of the river below. Bivouacing under the stars we are wrapped in the warmth of wonder, we come nearest perhaps to perfect peace, inhabit awhile the still centre of pure happiness. This was why we journeyed—to pursue the persistent aspirations of our species.

From our spur camp we climbed up to traverse above the gorge where I'd had my swim. There's an invigorating feeling of spaciousness in traversing high above water level, especially when the view leads the eye through one craggy 'V' after another to distant peaks. Our first stop was to inspect an impressive new area of cultivation. A plastic pipe had been slung right across the valley (fixed to a support wire) to tap into a *source* on the other flank and the water made available from this had allowed the creation of a small farm on the slope below us: there was a holding tank and a score of terraced fields on what had recently been a steep slope of rubble. One constantly comes on such astonishing feats, for which a basic precondition is a country at peace and able to commit life and labour to creativity. (This is in contrast to what one man's misrule can do, say, to a country like Uganda under Idi Amin, or Zimbabwe under Mugabe.)

Coming round a bend we caused a scurrying and a waving of tails as several ground squirrels did their vanishing trick. *Sibsib* is the local name for this creature which looks a bit like a grey squirrel, but with a stripy tail. They don't climb trees but, when scared, go to ground. They are not uncommon, even along busy roadsides, but are wary of humans.

A few more wiggles and we came on the village of Idrarane, the first of a regular series that gives a day's walking through intensely irrigated and cultivated slopes with many villages of considerable architectural interest. Balconies, roofs with rustic railings and finely painted windows are a feature, with subtle differences in styles making the Nfis buildings an entity. It had some fine dry-stone walling, often several stories high, with the houses enclosing long, shady lanes. If I dropped my box of architectural slides I could sort them out again into their geographical areas. The same applies at home of course: you're not likely to mix architectural slides of the Yorkshire Dales with those of the East Neuk of Fife but you have to have explored a country fairly well to know this.

We shared the path with cows going to their fields and a colourfully dressed girl carrying a complaining chicken. The air was rich with the scent of lavender, and the path continued doggedly uphill to Lankayt. Leaving the village, a magnificent 200-year-old pine soared into a spreading canopy. There was a good view down onto Souk Sebt which occupies the spur where the Oued Oumsour joins the Oued Nfis (shown in the wrong place on the 100,000 map and not at all on the 50,000). Major paths radiate up every valley and over crests and a *piste* comes in down from the Tizi n' Test.

Sebt is seven, indicating a Saturday *souk* site. (*Souks* are very seldom held on Fridays.) The *piste* from the pass means that *camions* and *camionettes* can come down to the *souk* and over the last few years we have watched the steady progress of the building of a new *piste* up the south side of the Nfis. This ends opposite the last village Agadir, west of Ansiwi, despite what maps state. Very little mechanical aid is used in road building and the skill and speed with which long stretches of walling appear is impressive. Our descent to the *souk* was a bit of an obstacle course with *seguias* to cross, path and water for a while being the same. The *souk* was ghostly quiet and deserted. A shutter squeaking was almost eerie. Only a litter of cabbage leaves, squashed tomatoes and fresh mule droppings pointed to recent activity. Nothing was open on the north bank so we crossed the substantial bridge to the stalls on the south side, one of which had fed and housed us in the past and I hoped could provide refreshments. A quartet playing cards and an atmosphere of decay wasn't encouraging.

Here too, Monique's duck-nibbling annoyances finally broke my patience. I exploded, for the only time on GTAM. Many consider me pretty laid back but that is just the discipline from decades of having to be so, looking after hundreds of people, some who could be inefficient and irritating. Long-time friends knew of the volcano—and poor Monique received a high reading on the vocal Richter scale. Mine was the constant burden of ensuring this almost abstract yet so physical ploy kept on the rails and to schedule. In a hard-working team her languid style just did not fit in, and I said so. The muleteers looked a bit astonished. They, to me, are always such an example of happy cooperation. Their friendliness and kindness, among themselves as well as to strangers, are constantly both rebuke and encouragement. I had to live up to them—or try to. I just hope something of their graciousness has rubbed off on me. Anger is always regretted. I had a soft target.

We pushed on, once the muleteers were sure of our plans, to lunch down in the quiet shade of a tree with a view to Ouizammarn. We knew from experience the village would swarm with kids. Sure enough, they turned out in force to welcome us. The kids, far from fearing the camera, were all for posing—for a fee of course, which was denied them. Several older buildings were crumbling away and decorative chevron work and other details were being lost.

Some clouds battened down the heat and we had to toil up the sweep of path to Imlil, the biggest and most spectacular Nfis village. Buildings pile on top of each other with secretive dark alleys. There were several new buildings and the *marabout* had been rebuilt as a mosque. Imlil had associations with Ibn Toumert. A white flag hung limp from the gibbet on top of the shrine, indicating prayer was in progress. On a rooftop an old man was testing arthritic limbs with his devotions, each repeated bow and prostration quite audible. At least he had the direction correct. In Marrakech, I once observed someone bowing in quite the wrong direction. A passer-by took hold of the figure and rotated him ninety degrees before walking on, neither saying a word, neither interrupting the devotions.

CHAPTER 14

Guenfis Meadow on Tichka Plateau

Imagine... gazing on an entirely new scene; strange birds, unknown plants; and of beholding,
as it were, another nature, and a new world. There is a kind of supernatural beauty in these
mountainous prospects which charms both the senses and the mind into a forgetfulness of oneself and
of everything in the world.

J J Rousseau, 1761

Trying a new way through this other Imlil I became disorientated (mislaid rather than lost) but was rescued by a troop of pleasant kids who greatly enjoyed looking through my camera lens. Most were in decayed *djellabas,* with their heads shaved and pumpkin faces split by huge gap-toothed grins. While heads are still often shaved as a medical precaution, the religious-based habit of leaving patterns and tufts of hair has largely gone. There used to be regional variations (just as there were for tattoos on women's faces—also a dying tradition) and my informant was only half-joking when he said a tuft was left so Allah, if need be, could reach down and haul the child to safety. The kids said the mules had gone over a bridge and up the *piste* so I waited above the bridge for the others but out-voted, we kept on along the mule-track. As the mules were to stop as soon as possible beyond Imlil we went carefully, but after the first long straight the valley became craggier and we began to wonder if we'd missed the camp. Eventually the blue dome was spotted on the far side and a small path took us down to the river opposite the site.

We'd seen two snakes on the path and, from what I've read, the western end of the Atlas seems to have more snakes than many areas. We saw few scorpions on the other hand. Camp was in a walnut grove: there were both older trees heavily laden with green nuts and several younger frail-looking trees. The grove was backed by the new *piste* (two cars passed!) and caves could be seen in the crags. Hosain and Omar went off to Imlil for fodder, I worked at turning packets of tomato soup into something palatable and Ali made the regular pot-*tagine*. The site was another extra good one in our estimation.

I went to look at the cave above the *seguia* and, in doing so, spotted a treecreeper stuttering its way up a trunk, then flying down to work up another, and another: as busy as a mouse. On about the fourth tree, the bird disappeared round the back out of sight and I waited for it to reappear, only to receive a shock. The bird that came back into view was several times bigger, tail pressed to bark and bill questing for food—the treecreeper had metamorphosed into a woodpecker. Something similar had happened a few days earlier when a perky wren went scolding off round a bend in the river only to suddenly reappear as a dipper.

The Nfis valley is too good to rush and our days were intentionally short on walking to be long on enjoyment. A few more villages lined the rolling river before the next major landscape change. Agadir is the last village of the Ejanaten, as the locals call the villages ranging up from the *souk*, and knowing the village from several visits I was hoping a certain shop would be open. It was. Drinks and *Taggers* time, those chocolate biscuits Charles and I had been addicted to. (A newly constructed *piste* now links the villages, sad news for trekkers but undoubtedly appreciated by the locals.)

We weren't really surprised when Monique said she wasn't going any further. She'd stay in the village and work village to village back down the Nfis. Her gear was ahead on a mule, of course, and we said someone would bring it down to her. She found a mule in the village at an inflated price, an irony not lost on us as she'd been complaining at what we paid our muleteers (the official rate). We parted as graciously as we could.

We followed the path which was also a *seguia*, just keeping ahead of a minor spate created by someone opening a sluice to change the irrigation pattern. We crossed the boulder-strewn side valley leading to Oumzra and zigzagged up to the main valley track by a farm to begin some more determined uphill work. The rising sweep was through dry scrub, but ending on a prow with a view both up and down the valley. Adrar n' Oumzra (3451 m) looked dramatic from there and was scrutinised closely for another trip (*Insh'Allah*). We couldn't spare the time then.

That time came after GTAM when four of us met on the Tizi n' Test summit (Ali from Taroudant, the rest of us from Asni) and backpacked the crest to bivvy on Timesguida n' Ourkalt (2899 m). We had a spectacular view of the Flillis peaks, descended to the Nfis and went on up the Tiouyaline side valley, too steep and difficult for mules. We bivouacked about 300 m below the summit. The weather had been perfect for days so we were equipped with minimal gear. Ali had not even brought a bivvy bag. Rain seemed to be as likely as Tamri refusing food or Taza laying an egg. However, settled for the night on the platforms we'd levelled, it snowed: wet, slobbery, clinging snow. Ali wormed in under a rock, Peter snored all night and never knew of the conditions (he was in a decent *Gore-tex* bag) but Liz and I lay and shivered hour after hour in squalid misery, unable even to see the time. They were long hours that night and Oumzra escaped once more. We retreated for further days of perfect weather, camping the next night at the Imlil GTAM site and having a huge bonfire after dark.

We bagged Oumzra on a second attempt, reaching the peak by the side valley from Souk Sebt, walking up past Igg to camp beyond Zrit and, after a recce day of poor weather, carrying a high bivvy again. We abandoned prepared platforms to go for it there and then as conditions looked so threatening. Oumzra gave an excellent climb and Peter, Ali and I exchanged hugs of satisfaction on the summit. Aït Idir Mohammed and Stewart Logan (aiming for a Millennium tenth round of the Munros) were also in the party. The tents were blowing like spinnakers on return so we raced into Zrit in search of digs. Ten minutes later the street was a thigh-deep rush of water as the storm of storms arrived. We eventually escaped from Souk Sebt by *camionette* up to the Tizi n' Test and Ijoukak—fourteen of us, all the baggage, and three mules, on board the pick-up.

We exchanged greetings with a boy striding past with a sheep at his heels, looking just as if he were taking the beast for a walk as one might a pet dog. Flocks of sheep and goats in Morocco are of course still led and not driven: man, boy or girl, with bread in satchel and a can of water slung over a shoulder will be out on the hill with them all day long. They seldom set out before the sun reaches the *azib* or pen where the beasts are kept overnight. Their shepherds are their protectors and friends. The Bible is full of references to shepherding of this kind. One of the hidden stages of any society's progress is when men stop leading sheep and start driving them.

A wall was an unusual feature on the spur and enclosed what was probably the last farm in the valley. Workers were heading steadily up-valley, and when a gaffer on a mule passed with his brolly held aloft, I quickly followed suit with mine and enjoyed overtaking to see his expression. It was an extra hot area as the landscape was harsh granite, the path often composed of white sand which had weathered off the bulbous rocks. We lunched in the shade of massive walnut trees as we wanted to be sure Ali knew where to camp. He came on ahead, singing away, and we had no problem pinpointing the required stopping place: the spot where Tony had jumped into the river last time. He had done this fully clothed to show the qualities of the new Pertex-pile garments, a performance that had been mentioned frequently since then by the local lads who witnessed the strange event.

There was another steep pull, then the mules would have to make a long detour as the Nfis runs down through a deep-cut gorge, passable only for confident pedestrians. On one Flowers trip everyone came down that way including Mary, a lively septuagenarian who was only a fairly modest walker but she was happily taken by the hand by Aït Idir Mohammed and toddled along with great aplomb. When we traversed over the final rotten screes to regain the track she was tired enough to welcome the offer of a mule ride, but the casual effect was lost when she climbed onto the beast and ended up facing the wrong way.

We scrabbled across the rubbish slope to the gorge to pick our way on the angled granite slabs between the near-impenetrable verge of scrub and the sheer drop to the growling waters below, titillating and exposed but with the gritty granite giving a grip almost as sure as Skye gabbro. For the first time since Toubkal, I donned boots instead of my sandals. Just how a bit of knowledge eases progress can be seen in the fun John Willison and Clare Wardle had here. He wrote:

'We enter the Nfis Gorge which produces a beautiful river with perfectly formed pools every few metres. Not on the scale of the Tessaout Gorge but much narrower and the river undercuts both sides for long stretches and rather than climb out in the hot sun we first paddle, then wade and finally it is a case of actually swimming. I try to keep my sack dry so when Clare plunges into our fifth pool, I opt out and climb high. This turns out to be not much fun: loose rock, gritty holds and slippery wet boots do nothing to help. In fact it gets a little desperate and I find I can only go on up rather than rejoin the river; I shout to Clare my intentions and scramble for another quarter of an hour to the top of the gorge. To my annoyance I find a mule trail. I descend the next gully back into the gorge, shouting all the time; no sign of Clare, and as the going looks rather easier I carry on up the river. Half an hour more, I decide she must have stopped earlier, so I go right back to just above the pools; still no sign; time for lunch. Problem: I have the stove and the jam, she has the fuel and biscuits. It has to be sardines and jam—not my favourite meal—and I suddenly discover, having removed my boots, that my ill-chosen lunch spot is the home of a colony of large ugly spiders. I fight them off for an hour or so and then decide to go back along the river, leaving my pack under a rock. It starts to rain of all things, and the spiders are coming out in hordes.

'Four hundred metres down stream, I see a large bit of orange plastic that wasn't there last time; as I approach it becomes Clare's bivvy bag, and I surprise a very unhappy Clare underneath. She too has been up and down the sides of the gorge calling for me and had given up hope—I had presumably fallen off some climb and lay in unhelpful pieces at the bottom. She is rarely so pleased to see me; we walk back to my sack and try further on, but another series of pools sends us up the next gully. At last the mule track is gained and we walk on well into the evening, stopping in a sandy sparse copse with piles of dead wood. It's a lovely camp and we curl up in our bags beside the fire with an all-in-stew, playing the recorder to the distant animal yowlings.'

The slopes on the south of the river rise to extremely wild and rocky peaks. Looking to them Ali told us of a recent fatality when a bee-man, searching for wild colonies, spotted the nest of the rare, protected lammergeyer and, with old prejudices like a Highland keeper, tried to reach the nest to kill the young birds. One of the parent birds attacked the man and he lost his hold and fell, many hundreds of metres. Even with local guides the authorities took three days to reach the body—or what was left of it.

Once the main section of exposed gorge was passed we stopped for a swim in some of the granite pools (decorated with trailing white crowfoot) which reminded me of the golden granite waters in the streams of Ben Starav. The white mare's tail of a waterfall wavered in a dark slot. A path led us up a northern tributary, at one stage being simply a tree trunk wedged across the steep slope. Cairns ended the complex return to the path where we could see in the dust that Ali and the mules had already passed. A delightful wandering route through the dappled shade of the evergreen oaks of the Tiziatin forest led us to the camp.

This time it was my turn to jump fully clothed into the water. I was only wearing light trousers and a T-shirt let me add but we all (even Omar) had a swim and washed garments as that would be the last chance before the serious ending. When I found a large scorpion under a flat stone I wanted as a doorstep (to keep sand out of my tent) there was a general shift from bivouacking to tenting! Charles had some strange burrowing wasps on his doorstep. A dragonfly kept dipping its rear end into a pool in an exotic flying dance: egg-laying we supposed. A fire of juniper wood led on to a lingering supper under a large oak tree. We were aware of the Oued Nfis largely behind, the plateau ahead and the ridge beckoning beyond. We'd not have a fire like that again, nor indulgent swims or comfortable easy days. In my log, the previous three sites had been marked as especially meritorious—but then the next six would be as well. Ali alone seemed a bit subdued and I was also aware of the certain problems ahead. Had I been too hard on Monique because of this nagging problem? The others said not. Ali was our concern. We would finish a good piece of adventuring despite his fear and uncertainty—all together, tails up.

The Oued Nfis drains what the map indicates as the Plateau du Tichka which is really a saucer-like hollow within a mountain rim edging into the west. The outer rim is often steep or sheer so easy access is only possible in a few places. Fed by melting snows and springs, there are plenty of verdant meadows and these and the riverbank are a golden glory of jonquils in the spring. Later in the year there is a flush of orchids and a blaze of alpines. Herds are not allowed to graze its grasslands until high summer in order to preserve the richness. Many of these extensive green areas have *azibs* beside them. This remote upland, with its atmosphere of Conan Doyle's *Lost World*, would be our last Nfis romance. The plateau widens to drain into the Tiziatin forest where we camped. This huge oak fastness (with some juniper and ash) was once the lair of bandits and wild beasts with the rugged mountain slopes pressing in like a vice. Then follows the explosively rich valley we'd ascended with its succession of friendly villages and the lush pine forest before more ordinary riverine meanderings and habitations by the Tizi n' Test road. The river breaks out through a last gorge near Ourigane (now with a dam under construction to form a huge reservoir) to reach the Haouz plain southwest of Marrakech. Peyron describes the plateau as 'remote, lonely and somewhat mysterious—an unlikely place for the High Atlas'.

A steep path took us out of the forest before swinging north along a tributary that drains a huge area dominated by Amendach (3382 m). Although the highest peak of the plateau, it is often overlooked due to its remote location and the presence of the more obvious Imaradene (or Tassiwt, 3351 m). The whole northern rim is cliff-bound from which ragged peaks rise with climbs and near-inaccessible summits, some not even named. The major Tizi Asdim lies in this northeast corner, providing access to the Peyron-praised Seksawa, the country of the M'Tougga who lorded it over the Tizi Maachou pass linking Marrakech and Agadir. The modern road is only a few decades old, and before that one took the Tizi n' Test, or went via Essaouira. New *pistes* have now been driven in from the west but no road comes near the plateau so it remains inviolate, a very special place, pure and unpolluted.

When we came to a stream junction we had a view of the domed bulk of Amendach up its length and decided we would climb the peak straight away rather than wait until the following day as envisaged. Our only regret was Ali's absence; it was not often that we had the priority of exploration. We made our way along the steep glen to scattered *azibs* set on spacious meadows: a delectable spot. From there we followed a long ridge up the mountain, plodding steadily or scrambling up scraggy granite for two and a half hours. I drank something like four litres over the day. 'Ever-widening views and the summit one of the best here and of the GTAM. The whole plateau on display and away to Oumzra, Igdat, Erdouz, Angour, Sirwa, Aklim, the Tafraoute peaks, big Moulay Ali, Awlim and Tinergwet, Tabgourt, rocky Jbel Ikkis and others to the north on which even Peyron is brief yet must hold a major climbing area to equal any in the Atlas', I enthused in my log that night, adding 'Mountains make for poetry in our prosaic lives'.

The 100,000 misprints the height of Amendach as 3882 m and although a big, bulky hill, that extra 500m remains wishful thinking. We lunched on the summit among granite boulders, prickly scrub and bright flowers. We were determined to see over the northern rim, a fine-looking ridge to Oumzra and Igdat (what an alpine expedition that would be under snow). We headed down to reach a small stream whose banks were buttoned with blue carduncellus heads and—as we found when taking off footwear for a paddle—various other prickles. Amendach links with the northern rim, and from the *tizi* a trickle runs west, then south, to become the river we had ascended from the Nfis. We crossed further down and continued on a rising line beyond to the Tizi Agourzi (3007 m). We were astonished to see a clear path descending the other side, in a continuous series of zigzags with some built-up contortions to break through the upper crags. It probably allows the herds of Azrou Mellene and other villages north to gain grazing access to the plateau, a monster ascent on an astonishing pass, an inspired practicality which never ceased to amaze us in the Atlas.

We climbed Azrou Asdim which had brutal cliffs to the north with a jumble of some of the rockiest peaks in the Atlas crowding beyond. "Oh to be twenty years younger", I sighed to my older companion, '*Où sont les neiges d'antan?*' (Where are the snows of yesteryear?) We dropped down to add the nameless peak, a sort of southwest Top overlooking the Tizi Asdim, ascending by an ordinary easy slope only to find the ground cut off sheer beyond the perched summit. The Top appeared a fine prow from camp that night, which we reached at 1615 having set off at 0630. I think we were as mentally drained as we were physically.

A small diversion took us to a col but to reach the actual Tizi Asdim there was a Hobson's choice of going over an intervening bump or descending nasty ground to below *tizi* level and joining the trans-*tizi* path. Flanking across was not possible. Charles went the former way, the rest of us went down the screes and rubbish, hard on the knees and requiring constant concentration. The walk up the path to the Tizi Asdim was a weary toil in the heat, which always seems harder in a world of grim granite.

John Willison and Clare Wardle descended north from the Tizi Asdim to Aguersafene and then kept determinedly west to reach the main Agadir-Marrakech road. They then more or less hitched to Agadir as Clare was not at all well, barely able to eat or walk. They were just dumped on the coast somewhere south of Agadir and walked for three hours before a kind driver drove them right to the promenade itself.

'We park ourselves in cool white chairs outside a beach café, transfer most of what remains in our sacks to the nearest bin, then I stagger to the sea while Clare sleeps in the sun. What it is to be clean, to be totally immersed in the substance that has been our lifeline over the weeks; I thrash about in glee, to the horror of the other tourists, then rush back to Clare leaving most of my clothes in the sea. Clare can just manage a glass of milk. I order the entire selection of *coupes* on the menu, prawn salad, fruit, on and on for hours. We have fun in front of the restaurant mirror – neither of us ever believed that we looked as dishevelled as the other. Things come to an end after my sixth *coupe*, and we begin to think about going home.'

On the Tizi Asdim I hung myself out to dry like a cormorant until we saw Charles safely over the hill and descending to the *tizi*. We then continued on a good path for what we called Guenfis Meadow, after the *azib* of that name, where light and dark dots were surely our mules. Graeme and I talked our way 'home' with Tony and Charles coming along behind. In the light of evening the meadow was a dazzling viridian. As we arrived, a mule from the *azib* broke loose and chased our pair all round the meadow. "An amorous male", Ali grinned. Chased by its owner and our whooping assistants, the randy visitor fled over a softer patch and went head over heels. It was caught, chastised and ridden away. The flocks of sheep were led in to the *azib* and one of the shepherds opened his bag to present me with some bread, the gesture more appreciated than the bread itself which was well past its use-by date. Clouds billowed about to dramatic effect and the slope above was snowed with the dancing heads of thrift, always white in the Atlas (*Armeria alliacea*). The mules had a session rolling in the lushness followed by a noisy ear-flapping shake. They had their noses in their individual bags of grain while we ate.

We have long been impressed with the extraordinary provision the donkey has been given for its sex life: an organ of unusually large proportion for a creature of such modest size but whose amorous capabilities are flaunted and trumpeted with no inhibitions at all. That night's escapade brought the subject up—and the opposite case of the camel, a lumbering giant of a beast with the most pathetic equipment. As usual, there was an explanatory legend.

When Noah had built his ark and was taking in all the creatures of creation, two by two, male and female, his down-to-earth wife voiced her concern about what would happen if, as was likely, they all mated and produced offspring before the voyage ended. The weight and volume would sink the ark! The animals were told to wait outside while they discussed the problem and, not being in England, the beasts all milled about on the plain instead of queuing politely at the entrance. At last they decided what they'd do and Noah stood on the step, yelled for half an hour to get silence, and explained the problem to them. Would they agree? There was bedlam but eventually common sense won and they went along with Noah's suggestion. As each male animal entered the ark he unzipped his genitals and handed them over to be hung up in neat rows near the door so they could be reclaimed on leaving. They were strictly detailed to make their exit in reverse order and, after the long boring trip, they were only too glad to queue in docile fashion to reclaim their belongings—which most of them quickly put into use once ashore. After all, 'be fruitful and multiply' was the standing order.

The donkeys had been fooling about as is their wont and seeing only the ponderous camels left they barged past them so as not to be the last off the smelly ark. Noah handed out the next set from the near-empty store and the donkeys went off in glee for they'd been given the camel's huge genitals by mistake. Which is why they have behaved as they do ever since—and why the poor camel, coming last, despite all his pleadings, had to make do with what was left. He'd quite refused to begin with and had started to descend the gangplank, nose flaring in high dudgeon, prepared to do without, but Mrs Noah, horrified at what the Lord might say at the extinction of one of his creatures, rushed out and zipped on the pathetic remnant. That is why the little donkey has something so disproportionately big and the snooty camel only has a tiny bitty stuck on behind. Probably explains too why the camel is such a disagreeable beast.

CHAPTER 15

The 'Ridge of a Hundred Peaks'

So geographers, in Afric-maps,
With savage-pictures fill their gaps;
And o'er unhabitable downs
Place elephants for want of towns.
Jonathan Swift

Charles, Tony and Graeme were off first, a precedent of sorts, as I was taking a lazier day. This is something Charles is incapable of doing but I feel pacing is important and, besides, the stress of organising, planning and coping with the practicalities is as exhausting as any hill day and, just ahead, there were going to be the most complex arrangements of the whole GTAM. The others traversed two peaks on the south rim, Awlim (3043 m) and Askawn (3078 m), which have never been ascended via their impressive-looking granite crags. The views southwards from there look out over the big Sous plain to the many-tinted ranges of the Anti-Atlas. 'Wee' Moulay Ali, the mountain dominating the southern Tagmout valley, sticks up as an exaggerated Pap of Glencoe.

Our various parties over the years have made many ascents of wee Moulay Ali, perhaps the first foreign ascent and certainly the first in winter. We even beat Ali in reaching the summit, which towers over his natal village of Amghlou. Peyron is either brief or dismissive of what lies south of these peaks, perhaps because his natural way in was from the north (Seksawa) and perhaps also influenced by the granite bareness of Souk Tnine Tigouga. But the country is one of the finest we've found and return to annually with our approach from Taroudant. The journey always unreels bright variety: from date palms and prickly pear through argan forests and orange groves to almond and walnut spreads, to remnant oak forest and a barren mountain world of granite and marble—one of the favoured places of the earth. Wee Moulay Ali dominates views looking up the southern valleys and, not surprisingly, has gathered several stories and legends, including one concerning Portuguese treasure. Anything with foreign, old or mysterious connections is apt to be labelled Portuguese.

A girl herding her flock in the Medlawa came on a cave on the lower slopes of Moulay Ali and, summoning up courage, went in. There she discovered unaccountable treasure and laughingly began to fill every corner of her clothes with gold. In the end she even took the baby from her back and laid him on the ground so she could use the carrying cloth as a sack to bear off more treasure. She then ran down to the family home and poured out the treasure onto the kitchen floor. Unladen, she ran back for more and to rejoin her flock and her baby brother. However, she could not find the cave, and neither cave nor baby has ever been seen since. The girl went crazy with grief and wandered the hills, weeping and wailing for many weeks until she, too, vanished. They say if you go on the slopes of Moulay Ali at night you can still hear her cries echoing among the granite crags. Some locals quite believe there is a treasure on Moulay Ali and justify this by demanding to know how, otherwise, just one or two families in the Medlawa are so rich and prosperous. Treasure obviously occupies their thoughts for Ali told another legend of wishful thinking.

A lost traveller stumbled on a cave in the desert and crawled in to escape the killing heat. Following the passage, he came on a lost city where the streets were lined with gold and the gardens akin to paradise. Stumbling out again he continued on his journey but took care to drop white pebbles along his way and, miraculously, soon came to a well and was saved. He told nobody of his discovery but gathered together his best friends and relatives and they set out on the marked route for the cave and the prospect of a caliph's wealth. But the *djinnoun* of the desert were displeased and had moved the marking white pebbles and the party was led far into the sands of the Sahara where their bones no doubt lie until this day for no one ever saw them again.

Although I set off late from the Guenfis meadows, the grass crackled underfoot from a silvering of frost. I headed west, which was quite a pull up to escape our frost hollow, and undulated over a dip to reach a larger meadow marked by a French concrete building. This faces the Tizi n' Tifighelt pass up from Tigouga, with its scores of hairpin bends. There is no short or easy way onto the Tichka Plateau. The meadows by the ruins are often yellow with daffodils and the Nfis flows with chuckling humour. We'd once found it almost impossible to lay down sleeping bags without crushing the flowers. A spiralling of choughs speckled the blue, too high to be heard.

Beyond the French ruins I turned up a side valley and over the neck behind a hump of hill that fills the centre of the plateau then dropped again before the final run to the infant Oued Nfis below the Tizi n' Targa. The last bit of valley was lined with purple orchids. This switchback route along the northern slopes is less demanding and quicker than following the meandering *oued* with minor gorges and other hindrances. I arrived at 1000, and not long after my telephoto lens picked up figures on top of Awlim. This peak should not be mistaken for the finer peak of that name further west, one of the horns (Tinergwet the other) that are clearly seen from the rooftops of Taroudant. The mules arrived soon after and were turned loose on the lush strip of grass where we'd camp. They soon ate to repletion and lay sprawled for much of the day. We were advised not to sit downwind of the bloated beasts!

My rest day was spent sorting and parcelling food, going over the plan of what lay ahead and, when the others returned, ensuring that all was agreeable. As Ali baked bread I did much of the supper preparations, noting that we were tight on food—the planned Aziz supply team simply had to turn up. We made do with mushroom soup, curry and rice, apricots and custard, coffee and cake—it was probably not a good thing to be downwind of any of us that night.

A pack of yowling jackals traversed over to the *tizi* and down beyond. They had followed the line of an abandoned *seguia* from the stream where it tumbled down from higher feeders by some tiered *azibs*. Above us lay the remains of another French-built building, part of a *gîte* for visitors. Nothing much survived except the arched doorways. Ali's fragile old mother had danced before a colonel's party there when she was a girl. One of our Flowers gang once pitched in the ruins to break the strength of a gale. Another Hosain, who'd been chef to Yemeni princes, still managed to cook a classy supper and we had a great singsong round the fire with pots and pans, basins and water carriers used as instruments and everyone in *djellabas* or duvets and balaclavas. The dusty goat and sheep droppings blew everywhere in and out of the tents. The gardeners in the party rather wished they could have bagged and sold the product.

I slept well since the planning was done and it would only be tested in the doing. We had called up additional help from Ali's boss Aziz in order to get established at the Tizi Oumzra, the first saddle on the ridge west of the plateau, where we'd have two nights and a crack at the northern outlier of 'big' Moulay Ali. There would likely be three bivouacs while westing along the 'Ridge of a Hundred Peaks' before regrouping with Hosain at the village of Arg, he having taken Taza and Tamri round by a huge southern diversion. The hours poring over maps and gleaning every piece of information paid off as we kept to that final schedule. It was the highlight of the whole GTAM: a classic multi-day ridge, a Cuillin with sun.

We'd had several attempts over the years to try and ski on the Tichka Plateau. One sortie came to a halt below village level on the south as heavy snowfall meant the *camionette* could not even reach Tigouga. Another approaching up the Nfis found too little snow on the plateau and, a year after GTAM, Taza and Hosain between them scuppered another effort. With Ali, Hosain, Charles and Taza we were almost the complete GTAM team again. We came up the southern Medlawa to Tagmout and pushed on only to find the gorge below the Tizi n' Targa corrie was full of concrete-hard avalanche snow. Without a proper recce, Hosain drove Taza on and they ended on slabs. Taza scrabbled horribly and finally went over backwards to cartwheel down the slope, a horrible yet fascinating sight. She stopped on the rocks in a jumble of rucksacks, skis and panniers with loaves of bread and bottles of *Sidi Ali* rolling on below. Hosain had been stunned by a crack from Taza's head, but the mule miraculously only had one wound: a fist sized hole on a thigh. I squeezed most of a tube of *Savlon* onto this, used suture tapes and tried to bandage—but a mule's girth takes a lot of bandage! Taza carried on grazing as if nothing had happened, and Hosain was all for continuing. The skis were all in order and the only item of gear damaged was a kettle, which had been completely flattened. Maybe the site was jinxed. I've only seen three mule accidents in all my Alas years and it was almost on the same spot that a mule took a tumble while carrying camp for the BBC *Wilderness Walks* filming—right in front of the camera.

We had a rare static day at our GTAM site at the head of the Tichka Plateau. Tucked in below the Tizi n' Targa it would be more correct to say 'seeming head of' for the infant *oued* came down over some flowery crags from higher meadows to the north. It is an area with the huge restfulness of an unplanned garden filling a secretive basin. There is a rim of peaks over the 3000 m height, this circling array climaxing in Imaradene (Tassiwt). From checking on past visits I'd marked the start of our flanking way westwards, breaking out of that high world onto the start of the long ridge westwards. Graeme, being new to the area, went off for Imaradene (3351 m), the highest point at that end of the plateau. Ali took old Mohammed and young Omar down to the Medlawa to visit family and friends in his natal village. I sat in the shadow of a crag to add a chapter to my book, working until the shadow's chill drove me down for a coffee. Before I could drink the beverage the support squad arrived: two mules, four adults and two lively boys, an influx that set the camp buzzing.

With the numbers we had to eat in shifts: a *tagine* for the arrivals, one for us at dusk and a chicken (live on arrival) for a late feast. We gorged on melons and fresh vegetables. In Taroudant you don't just buy an orange: it is a Navel, or Valencia, a Maroc Late, or Washington Sangria. Our arrangement with Aziz had been for three porters and these had come—but so had he (on a mule) along with his boys simply for a bit of a jolly at our expense. Charles and I were not pleased, even less so when Aziz installed himself in Ali's tent (Ali still absent), and had the cheek to ask me if he could have it after GTAM. "Very nice tent. You give it me, eh Hamish?" Charles spluttered but we kept quiet somehow. This occasion was to be our final dealings with Aziz who had let us (and many others) down too often.

Thanks to several Europeans, myself included, Aziz had been set up in Taroudant as Tigouga Adventures, the only trekking company in the Western Atlas. He had every chance to create a good business but would not play straight and his crooked dealings saw very few groups employing him a second time. Ali had been taken on to help and did most of the fieldwork (at which he is brilliant). However, while walking across the Tichka Plateau about a year before GTAM, he had burst into tears explaining he was being treated like a slave as Aziz never paid him. Aziz had also taken all the clothing and equipment that had been given to Ali. The last straw was when Aziz double-booked us for a bigger, more profitable group, and denied all knowledge of our booking. *The Rough Guide*, which had listed his services, was receiving vitriolic mail, all very embarrassing as I'd been involved. However, with GTAM looming we hadn't much option but to use him to send up the support we needed for the ridge traverse.

At supper, Charles hissed: "Do you see he's wearing Ali's sandals?" He'd taken them while Ali was in Taroudant during our brief break in Spain. After GTAM, Ali was supposed to keep Tamri (and Hosain keep Taza) but Aziz somehow forced Ali to sell her. After GTAM, Ali didn't go back to Aziz but that meant he was only left with what he stood in—all his other possessions (ice axe, crampons, winter sleeping bag etc.) were lost. However, a decade later, Ali is a highly regarded leader, married with two delightful boys. Aziz is in gaol.

During supper a shepherd boy arrived with his hundred sheep and goats, shook hands all round and sat to share mint tea and oatcakes with us. After a look at the sun's position and a glance at his watch he ordered his flock (by voice alone) to begin making for the col. Ten minutes later he shook hands all round once more and strode off with effortless gait. Their *azib* lay 200 m down on the southern Medlawa side of the *tizi*. When we went up to look at the afterglow, a pillar of smoke wavered up from his lonely bivvy site and we bore the scent of it back with us to our draughty meadow strip. The Milky Way curdled across the sky and Polaris stood over the crags marking the start of the final effort, the crux of the whole GTAM: unknown ground with, no doubt, some interesting problems.

We had made a concentrated weight-cutting exercise to reduce our gear to basic necessities. There's nothing like a tough carry to discover how much one can do without. Perhaps we should be less lumbered anyway. I quoted Socrates, who, viewing the *souk* at Athens, commented, 'What a lot of things I don't need to have'. After a lifetime of backpacking I have this down to a fine art with a Basic List at the back of my diary from which I work. Equally important, of course, is not to forget essentials.

Our very first (winter) visit to the Tichka Plateau had given us a glimpse of what appeared to be a magnificent Alpine-like ridge running westwards from the upper end of the Tichka Plateau. I had thought of Alexander Pope's words then, but they had more relevance now!

> '...We tremble to survey
>
> The growing labours of the lengthening way;
>
> Th' increasing prospect tires our wond'ring eyes—
>
> Hills peep o'er hills, and Alps on Alps arise!'

Reading had produced little information. Peyron stated: 'To date only partial bits of this ridge have been followed', which was carrot enough. He only touched on the odd peak or pass. We found a photograph of Awlim's east face in a 1929 *La Montagne* mostly given over to Louis Neltner whose first ascents included Awlim and Tinergwet in 1927. There's a reasonable outline map though, oddly, the Tichka Plateau doesn't exist. The Plateau may not have had European visitors until the Polish 1934 visit, when they climbed Imaradene from the north and added Big Moulay Ali, Tinergwet and Awlim (Aoulime) again.

We dubbed the crest the 'Ridge of a Hundred Peaks' which was poetic licence, there only being about a dozen distinct peaks and as many tops to traverse. The ridge, however, with the allotted three bivouacs, would be quite enough for the old men. I'd done a careful graph-like diagram in the Route Book of all the ups and downs and was pleased that we did very much as expected. With minimum food in our packs there was no room for error.

Controlled chaos might be a good description of our breakfast. With 14 people and 6 mules packing and going, Hosain's *"Bonne chance"* in our ears, the humans set off up to the *azibs* and crags with one chosen mule doing a right flanker to keep on easy ground. When the mule appeared in the upper basin we filled all the water containers, loaded the mule and wended up to the crest where a cast or two soon pinpointed our way off. We (Charles, Tony, Graeme, Ali and I) carried our own packs with additional fresh food for two nights while the three locals had to hump rucksack-filling water containers, this supply allowing us two bivouacs on the first pass, the Tizi Oumzra, from which we were determined to have a crack at big Moulay Ali before starting westwards. Aziz and his boys simply saw us off, having contributed nothing.

We took a sad farewell of the Imlil pair of old Mohammed and young Omar, the latter a great favourite with everyone, his bubbling enthusiasm making him a sort of juvenile Hosain. Hosain alone had not come up to set us on our way, but stayed to strike camp and head off for the long circuit to Arg. He was walking down the Medlawa, all the way to Zawyat Tafilelt, home to Imoulas, then over the demanding Tizi Ifguig to descend past Jbel Tichka where he'd hopefully find a house for us all to stay in at Arg. Walking that route would have taken us four or five days: he took two! The Imlil mules reckoned to be home in five days. There were hugs all round and we went off on our different routes.

Our way led down steep loose ground with a couple of craggy gullies to scramble across, awkward with a hefty pack and a five litre container of water in one hand. Beyond that there was just a long traverse across steep slopes which largely consisted of prickly bushes of many kinds. The helpers beat us to the Tizi Oumzra and the local shepherds homed in on this event with understandable curiosity. Ali knew the senior shepherd, enough to arrange that he'd guard our gear on the following day so we could all go off for Moulay Ali, a relief to me at least, as nobody had volunteered the watchman's role. The water carriers soon left and, after a brew, Charles, Tony and Graeme went off to recce the ridge out to Moulay Ali, one of the last unclimbed problems in the Atlas.

Ali had a long talk with the oldest shepherd, the pair of them perched on the crest of the saddle like a pair of gnomes. The man had a face as weathered as a walnut but was lean and supple for all his years, with the presence of a monarch. In those hills, I reckon he was. The central peak on the ridge out to Moulay Ali had not been visited by shepherds, they knew no route along the crest so that was that as far as I was concerned (certainly for GTAM). We had to husband ourselves and not go to excess lengths at that stage even if we had approached Moulay Ali with the hopes of a terrier awaiting the postman.

I rigged a shelter against the sun and sprawled in the shade to think of my book instead of Moulay Ali. There was a tempering breeze on the south so cooking had to be done on the other more sheltered flank. I went over all the food logistics again and prepared the vegetables for supper. A beetle in a vivid orange and green away-strip tried to climb into the pot. Shepherds kept appearing and I'd hear, then see, flocks picking lines across the most unlikely places. When two flocks became mixed, one of the strays was lifted by its hind legs and wheelbarrow-ed back to its mates. Graeme was back first, traversing across the nasty slopes from the first col on the side ridge. Tony and Charles weren't back till 1700 and were somewhat weary as a result. They had gone down to the first col and then tried for the Central peak only to run up against the vertical wall of a gap which dropped hundreds of metres down the flank. In a sort of mockery of our efforts the sun set down that first dip on the ridge, a molten globe. It flared and died, then the sky repainted itself over and over in tones of red, mauve and gold.

Ali had been up Big (*Ras*) Moulay Ali quite a few times previously, but by an alternative route. From the top northwest corner of the upper Tichka plateau area, there is a gap below the peak of Tamguerd Lma'dene (3256 m) which gives a horrendous descent before the ascent of Moulay Ali. He'd had at least one epic when a companion became exhausted. Charles and I had dropped down from the Tizi Oumzra on a previous recce and had failed to find the Moulay Ali route from Ali's description though we tried one or two interesting lines. It was too late in the day for any more, but it had proved a useful recce and showed water sources and the easy zigzag of an old mining track from the Tizi Oumzra. The normal way to Moulay Ali is from the north, using a high valley to the northeast, then up the West Ridge. (Ali and an Imlil guide would ultimately make the first Moulay Ali climb from the south, traversing the ridge and Central peak which had defeated us on GTAM.)

Our day began with a considerable loss of height and we tried to minimise this with a shortcut but its technicalities lost us any time and effort saved. After the initial zigzags we took a traversing fork left which led to a gully and a one-time *adit*. We had to pick our way down the spur above the gully, a long, slow choice which simply added to our store of negative information. Once far enough down, we had to make a long, rising ascent over rubbishy slopes before arriving at a slightly greener area. We were pushed over loose, grit-covered slabs to a pinnacled ridge, a surface to keep the nerves tingling. The *arête* crossed, we angled up to a short chimney, where Graeme wondered how goats could deal with such a spot. I told him how I'd seen goats descend a much bigger chimney by simply bouncing off the opposing walls in turn, each time twisting so as to hit the wall with all feet together. A rising line followed where the shepherds had wedged stones to help access, an exposed spot with a gully dropping below us right to the bottom. We wove in and out, rising all the while, crossing necks of small walls or crests. We followed the easiest options to suddenly come on the *tizi* of the linking ridge, between the Central, unclimbed peak and Moulay Ali itself.

A clean buttress of yellow rock formed a shady nook where a platform had been built overlooking the *tizi*. The Central Summit was a long way beyond that as we could see on the profile photographs I'd brought with us. We had a good rest and studied the route of the main crest westwards for the following day, the huge valley beyond Moulay Ali dominated by Mtdadene. The lowest point on the crest had a comment from Peyron saying it was a bad mule crossing but Ali and I were instantly dreaming up possible circular treks that could include the valley. What a view there would be of Moulay Ali! Ali is quite unique among the Berber guides I know in maintaining a passion for new exploration. On any summit we automatically cast practical eyes on our surroundings and discuss other possible ploys. (Another active decade passed before those particular dreams became reality.)

As Moulay Ali's summit was savagely steep, the rocks many-hued or shiny with mica, it was a delight. There were plenty of climbing routes but it also yielded excellent rock for scrambling, rock which seemed to come in every colour and texture. When we reached the summit there was no Ali. But then his voice came from below my feet: he was hiding in a man-made cubby-hole. The whole hollow summit looked for all the world like a ruined broch with the tumbled remains of man-made structures—old shrines presumably. Tall mulleins and buttercup-bright wallflower grew on the ruins and Ali lit a skeletal bush to send a smoke signal to the shepherd on the Tizi Oumzra. 1st July seemed a suitable date. We had a lazy lunch but I kept wandering round that high rim just trying to absorb the wrap-around view. There was a lifetime of exploring in sight. We had a tube of cheese and chives with oatcakes and I recalled the amused astonishment that squeezing out cheese had once caused among the local women we met on the col behind the other 'wee' Moulay Ali. The girls tried the cheese and liked it fine, producing bread and walnuts in return.

We descended faster by some scree and followed ledges along and down to the *tizi* where we'd left surplus water. We drank plenty during the day so weren't dehydrated. Down in the valley we cut over to the sleepy stream where I washed my stockings: they were dry when we set off half an hour later. Charles insisted on carrying water up from there, a tedious task. I followed up the stream and filled my *Sigg* bottle later before enjoying plenty of scrambling onwards. I kept meeting a boy in a blue *gandoura* who was obviously fascinated by strangers. When I came in to camp he was sitting on the crest. He couldn't have been more than twelve, yet moved on the harsh landscape with the ease of drifting smoke. The older shepherds talked non-stop while we brewed and rested and I noted half a box of sugar had been used that day. Berbers have a sweet tooth. The old men look as if they, literally, only have a tooth each. Tinned turkey and fresh vegetables, after soups I'd bought in Gibraltar, made a good meal. The shepherds slowly drifted off as the sun's rays wrapped up Moulay Ali and posted the hills into dark. We had enjoyed what I call 'a day of glory given'.

Beauty, for me, is not just seen in inarticulate nature. Much as I love the pristine snows of the arctic north the fact that there is no human being within 200 miles makes me sad rather than glad. Humans, willy-nilly, are part of this terrestrial sphere. Ireland's hills are richer than the Scottish Highlands simply because they are still peopled: from a wild, high ridge one can catch a whiff of turf reek, hear children's laughter or see friendly white homes. It is the same in the Atlas.

The ancient shepherd on the Tizi Oumzra was a figure of majesty to me, the boy a prince of the peaks. They belonged there as naturally as the scrub or the rufous slices of rock. Their nobility and graciousness is as natural as the sun. In contrast, we were clumsy, overburdened intruders.

This is not some naïve view of Rousseau's noble savage, nor should they be so viewed. Years ago I sat on a rooftop at Aroumd with an unlovely group of Americans. The fresh spring air brightened the bursts of blossom and we could see the massive peak of Toubkal in the background. One of them turned to me said something like, "Say Hamish do you think they understand scenery? Do they appreciate views?" My reply was wasted sarcasm, "Oh I think so. They sang its praises a thousand years before America was discovered". I still gasp at the arrogance of the question. Our host, to them, was just a peasant, a sort of vacuous being—quite beyond their understanding. But for years after their visit I'd be asked, with a smile, "Any Americans this year, Hamish?" The 'ignorant' peasant had the sharper eye for the heart's character. The Americans pitied the Berber out of real ignorance, to the Berber the brash visitors were simply as transient as autumn wasps and as influential. "They go away. I can look at Toubkal tomorrow." We flabby westerners (flabby of flesh, spirit and mind) need to learn to walk humbly in the earth except it is probably too late. We have trampled too hard on too many and the cruel footwear of our west's walking tramples on the happier, barefoot world.

Besides the shepherds on the *tizi* there had been other human elements: an explosion from the mines to the north (on Jbel Tabgourt) and aircraft flying overhead (to and from Agadir one assumes) so even this 'remote' spot was only just that. Whereas so many wild areas of the world are simply abandoned these days, in the Atlas new cultivation and building is seen everywhere, *pistes* are replacing ancient mule tracks, electricity has arrived and mines obtrude - an impressive progress under difficult conditions.

We were up for another cruel, draughty dawn and packing up was a last-minute job. I needed to wear clothes for warmth, but also wanted them as padding in the rucksack against my back so had all the small but heavy items to pack, such as Gas *cartouches* and tins of meat. We left the two big water cans for the shepherd as a thank you, along with some food we felt we could do without as we were fighting every ounce of the way. We would eat simply but adequately to fuel our long days' efforts, would drink a lot, which is more important, and had *Therm-A-Rests* to ensure good sleep. We were confident of managing a Cuillin Ridge or three over the following few days. Water would be our main worry but we had Ali, with his inborn skill no outsider could ever match, to sniff out that essential. (Not literally, as Ali had lost his sense of smell as a youth).

I'll try and avoid a catalogue of largely unpronounceable names but at the same time I would like to provide a helpful and practical record for those who will repeat what was an excellent traverse, quite apart from being the climax of GTAM. We had the fun (which I now spoil) of setting off into the relatively unknown with a fair chance of technical difficulties (and lack of water) throwing our plans awry. We'd done all we could in the planning stage, however, and we had to dance to the puppet strings of expectation. We'd applied Thoreau's maxim: 'Simplify, simplify', to an extreme.

The first bump, Asziud, is where the untraversed ridge out to Big Moulay Ali breaks off and we outflanked this oft-visited top to tackle the first problem that had been a worry for years: Aqelmoun (3251 m). It has a shining white marble summit with the strata stood on end, an oddity that can be seen from far off down the northern Medlawa valley. The peak looked potentially difficult, and the north side was sheer cliffs. There was an intermediate peak first and the gap between is lost on the maps as 'Aqelmoun' is printed over it. We made a tortuous way down to the foot of the marble ribs and found all the difficulties could be outflanked on the south, which was immensely cheering not only for Aqelmoun but for anything else that might bar the way. At the highest flanking point we left our packs at a visible spot and enjoyed scrambling up the gleaming white rock, back along the crest to the highest point of Aqelmoun. We could see Charles still coming up so helpfully yelled down what we'd done only to receive a voluble response. He was not enjoying carrying a half-filled water carrier, sloshing about—as if any of us were!

We faced a long descending ridge, either followed on the crest or flanked but then found a deep gap running down to the south. This looked easy but was all jagged edges needing care. We would only drop below the 3000 m mark twice on the 'Ridge of a Hundred Peaks' and this long *tizi* of Imdlawn was 2971 m. Ali had raced on ahead and had a brew waiting for us in a nook out of the sun. 'Racing' is misleading; Ali doesn't need to race to leave us far behind, he is just super-fit and utterly at home in the hills, and drifts along with the ease of waves heading for the shore.

The Imdlawn pass is rarely used as there is no call to take mules over these days; traders travel in the lower valleys by *camionette*. The vast valley of Aderdour lay to the north, and heading south would take us to Fiyil and Tagmout. Fiyil and some other villages thereabouts still have some roofs that are pitched and thatched rather than flat: quite an oddity. Sadly, as older buildings fall down from neglect and families re-house themselves more comfortably, the pitched roofs are gradually disappearing.

The slope reared up to Adrar n' Fiyil (3114 m), which lay out on a spur slightly to the south covered in a foul, loose scree. We gladly left the rucksacks while claiming the summit, the second of two bumps naturally. Continuing, we crossed a rubbly bump and then a green-tinted one that had a strange flat area hidden in it. The map gave Tizi Igdal but we saw no indication of any pass, the north still being Moulay Ali's large basin, the south draining as the Agounsane valley which joins the main valley well below Tagmout. We travelled steadily southwest all day. Ali had a brew ready again and we lunched on the last of our bread and *Kiri*, the processed cheese, wrapped in squares rather than the wedges of *La Vache Qui Rit*.

Looming ahead was the huge bulk of Mtdadene (3366 m), or 'Tentaden' as a shepherd pronounced it. He confirmed we could outflank the peak and so avoid climbing up and down with packs on our backs. From Mtdadene a ridge curved northwards as the bounding wall of the great northern corrie of Aderdour, with a fine summit of jagged Aguer Skawn (3255 m) nicely balancing Moulay Ali. We duly crossed the high, complex east face to reach Mtdadene's southwest ridge which ran down to the major Tizi n' Tizzirt (2816 m) below which we hoped a small valley would have a stream for our overnight stop. As there were many grazing flocks we could not take the chance of leaving gear unattended so we sat down to relax while Ali nipped up Mtdadene and back in an annoyingly fast time.

The relaxing was very pleasant, although studying the route ahead was rather sobering. Our view from the top of Mtdadene was thrilling as always when completely new. North, we could see a sinuous new *piste* line following a long crest for Afensou and the mines. All the drainage went to the last major vehicular pass we'd cross, the Marrakech–Agadir highway. The warm palette of the landscape vanished to hazy horizons. Over the Tizi n' Tizzirt lay our next peak Wanourt off on a south spur, with a huge rock face on the flank and the crest beyond ending on graceful Azegza, which had long caught our eye as a desirable objective, dominating the foothills as it does. (Climbed on the final Christmas of the Millennium, Azegza proved a happy viewpoint to the 'Ridge of a Hundred Peaks'.)

Mtdadene had a shelter on the top, perhaps an old shrine and Ali had scratched our initials on a slab, laughing gently at our slowness. We straggled down again, following our own lines and, on reaching Ali, he shot off to try and find water in that small valley flanking the crest down to the col. He went a long way and we had to follow with an amount of uncertainty. Charles, who likes things to be clear, was not too happy. The water Ali found was a mere trickle, but by the cunning positioning of a leaf supported by a twig he managed to turn this into an effective spout. We had to do considerable digging in screes and levelling off to create bed spots and the stoves had to be set in stone-built nooks to protect them from a sneaky wind. Brews, soup, meat with pasta and dried veg, dried fruit, drinks and biscuits would become our standard lightweight menu. I forced myself to write my log of the day before sleeping, using the last vivid horizontal rays that lit up the flank opposite like fire: 'Dawn was ours, And sunset and all the colours of the earth'. Snuggling down under the cold growth of stars I slept well enough to be quite peeved at finding it was time to rise again. Good sleeping goes with good living; when one can no longer sleep then the living is in questionable disarray.

The Tizi n' Tizzirt (2816 m) was the lowest point of the whole ridge traverse and had a good if tortuous mule track crossing it, though now probably most used for grazing access to the higher slopes. We traversed along and up to the *tizi* then enjoyed the ascent beyond which was largely a white strata staircase, the geological agony that set such strata on end often being a contribution to our ease. I finally traversed across and left my rucksack before walking up to the highest point where the ridge curved out to Wanourt (3182 m). This peak lay on a contorted ridge to the south with a succession of false tops. On the left, there was a magnificent slabby rock face (still waiting climbers) while on the right there was a hollow with a brook treading through, akin to the meadows on the Tichka Plateau. We toyed with the exposure as we worked along to the summit, then just sat and gazed.

The whole Sous was covered in cloud, with tentative fingers of white creeping up the valleys to disperse like breath on a frosty morning. Out of this rose endless spurs of hill, in every shade of blue from duck egg to deepest ultramarine. One always associates blue hills with the Highlands where the dampness is assumed to be contributory yet there in the harsh, hot, dry south, the blues were the boldest of all. It was like the view from Jbel Rhat but biting deeper, morning clarity as against evening dissipation. Rhat now seemed a long way back. We could see Jbel Siroua on the margin of the visible—and it had been seen from Rhat. We were now on the last horizon assault, the ultimate momentum was driving us forward.

Continuing along the main spine we crossed a cleft bump at 3175 m, then the Tizi Igherm at 3166 m (with edge-up strata of charcoal-dark shaly rock). A hot pull up gained Tit Oulli (Willi) (3247 m) which sounded a bit Gilbert and Sullivan-ish, but soon became renamed Shit Willy. Redemption lay in a summit brew prepared by agile Ali but the way ahead was a crocodile-cruel mess of rock and scree with deep gashes and no alternatives. The easiest and safest way was to utilise all the exposed dark, shiny rock and scramble down to a deep-cut *tizi* with large cliffs that guarded the south for the rest of the day.

A surprisingly pleasant ascent took us up the double-headed Adrar Oulzguim (3235 m). All the southward drainage led to Hosain's home Imoulas valley so we felt we were progressing. Toubkal and the Siroua were becoming very small features. The valley down to Imoulas is big and fertile where irrigated; an unexpected verdure for a south-facing valley. There was a thrill, being perched alone on that rugged place. One can see why Christ was led high up into the mountains to be tempted. While part of me was sad at the prospect of finishing, that final flourish, inescapably there, fully occupied the mind. The thrill grew day by day and I looked on the views like a starved man outside a *pâtisserie*. Mallory certainly knew that greed for adventure, finding in it 'sheer joy'.

Jagged edges led us down off Oulzguim. I was startled first by a falling stone then by choughs exploding like shrapnel just a few metres away. We dropped to traverse lower, easier ground before cutting back onto crags and the corrie headwall of scree. We'd last seen Ali at about the lowest point (Tizi n' Tamjlocht, 3034 m) and were wondering where he'd gone when he came up from the north side with a replenished container of water. We promptly declared a lunch break. Ali is an enviable mix of gazelle and otter; while we were still coming along he'd descended and re-ascended 300 m to find water. He wasn't even puffed and gave us another folk saying, what we called Ali-isms, 'A camel is dear at a penny if you do not need a camel. A cup of water is cheap at a thousand gold pieces if dying of thirst'. We perched on rocks on the lip of the now huge northern cliffs—not the place to drop anything—and revelled in the eyrie-like exposure. From miles below us drifted up the piping voices of young shepherds. Choughs tumbled in the blue.

We then hid all the water we carried (as the containers would be treasure to any shepherd boy) and dropped down the northern Tamjlocht corrie to the water level. The village to the north named that part of the crest, but not those to the south where access was barred. The time was 1445 and looking ahead there seemed little chance of finding water higher so we had to make the most of what was available. We built a stone shelter for the stoves, soaked vegetables and Tony then used his forestry background to produce a brew on a scrub-fed fire. Gleaning burnable material was a useful occupation. The runnel was small but the line down the hill was marked by thistles. Ali had shown us to beware of thistle lines, usually they don't have water and one could lose hundreds of metres on fools' errands. My ability as a water-finder is not bad but Ali's is on a unattainable level, the craft of a man's affinity with this tough natural world. Later Graeme did a good job of fire-nursing so we had tea, stewed apples, and soup for the main course all prepared without using any of our gas supplies.

From a crag across our steep green slope, pixie-like figures watched us by the hour out of a halo of burning sun. None of us were very good at just doing nothing and we began supper earlier than necessary and set off afterwards, sooner than was best for digestion, a steady stomp up to the crest. Eating down at the water *source* allowed us to use as much of that diamond-precious commodity as we liked. What we carried up thereafter (or had left at the *tizi*) would see us through the next day with no concern over supplies. The following night's supper supply of water was assured assuming we kept to schedule; there were still several surmises and surprises to unwrap.

The white sun may have glissaded towards the horizon but we still had a hard, hot haul back up to the ridge. I went slow and steady, always the tortoise uphill, and arrived to find Ali had found all the water containers we'd so carefully hidden. My log records: 'Quite good up to the initial 3153 m top (we named it Birkwane East) and then became more jagged in character. Excellent fun but we were all tiring rapidly (just when accidents happen) and the sun, losing its bid to stay up any longer, had been packed-off to bed, not before setting the spires of Atlas on fire.' Just below the creamy-coloured rocks of the summit of Adrar n' Birkwane (3173 m) we called a halt upon finding a good area for clearing bivvy spots. I put on the tea and we had two mugs and a packet of *Golden* each (a plain but much-liked biscuit). Awlim was dramatic in the last flood of red light which also lit every top way back to the triangle of Ras Moulay Ali, small but still prominent. For an easy day as had been suggested at breakfast, we'd done not too badly. My notes continued: 'I set two bushes alight to dry off sweaty socks and, into bed, ate hoarded oakcakes and honey and now write up my log by torch light in the hour of stars wedged between dusk and moonwash. Shooting stars (one almost comet-like), a satellite and a UFO that blinks every ten seconds as it slowly travels from horizon to horizon. Wouldn't be anywhere else for all the worlds. Here is the deep magic one finds in the tidal stillness of high places.'

I woke with a start to find Ali had already put on water in a shelter he'd made of stone slabs, protecting the stove from a cold, seeping wind that had us dressed in all spare clothing. An efficient breakfast, I noted, just tea and muesli although plenty of each; it could hardly be otherwise. A ten minute scramble took us, by a variety of personal lines, to the knife-edge summit of Adrar n' Birkwane which, with serious scrambling approaches from any direction, must make it one of the rarer peaks to bag even if so overshadowed by Awlim, now near and awesome. We had to take turns to be on top as there wasn't room for more than one at a time on the pinnacle.

The route on to the waterless Tizi Oumassa before Awlim was hedgehog-like in quality. It gave a full hour's scrambling with our morning shadows dancing ahead of us. Originally we'd hoped to sleep on the col, maybe finding water close by so we were thankful how things had worked out: our water bottles were full and there was enough for a brew.

Most of the information I'd found on that east side of Awlim dated back to French or Polish expeditions of the late 20s and, Peyron apart, I doubt if many eyes since have seen what so impressed those early visitors. Awlim is all rock, the east face split by the *Couloir en Y*. Wrapped round to the south are cliffs, steep or sheer, of beautiful red tints—all untouched. Descriptions of the Y-gully made it sound tricky, but it was fairly obvious and technically easy. *Les Flammes de Pierre* and such names had been given to recognisable features. A series of jagged ledges led to *La serpent verte* and more wandering about led to the main ascent on the edge of (or briefly, in) the big Y Gully, which had a belly button of old snow. Both the *tizi* and the peak held a diverse and abundant alpine flora. We revelled in the ascent and tumbled out onto a crest by the north summit. As the south summit was marginally higher, we traversed and scrambled over to find a superlative viewpoint with the diminuendo of blues we'd had on Wanourt, the sort of view that makes one whisper. To the west, however, there was only Tinergwet bulking large. We were running out of Atlas.

Awlim was a third-time-lucky for me and a second for Charles. Charles, Keith and I had once succeeded with Tinergwet but then (wisely I think) left Awlim alone as we were very tired after a long ascent from the south. The following time, with an Over the Hill Club (OHC) group, we camped higher up the valley and were on the col between the peaks for dawn. However, there was a lot of snow about which we weren't equipped for, and the intensely cold wind was biting through all the clothes we piled on. We tried, but retreated. Only Ali, with one lad who'd done Tinergwet too, was able to add Awlim. Louis Neltner, the lucky geologist, made the first ascent of Awlim (Aoulime) in 1927 and was back a year later to ascend Awlim again, by the route from the east. He also made the first ascent of Ras Moulay Ali in 1928, and the actual summit of Jbel Siroua. The 20s was the Golden Age of Atlas exploration.

After some summit photographs (Awlim demanded the formalities) Ali shot off to make tea on the wide saddle of the Tizi n' Tajelt (3231 m) leading to Jbel Tinergwet. Ali had been up several times and, with his fast movement on rock, he'd disappeared by the time we'd even set off—and discovered the best scrambling ridge of the whole trip. There was even a Thearlaich–Dubh Gap! Lower, it was possible to outflank much of the crest on the north side. One by one we joined Ali's underground café.

He had discovered a cave below a large boulder, obviously used by shepherds, and made tea there out of the sun and the breeze. I peeled off sweaty stockings and dried them on the hot whaleback of rock where we sat. I was sad with the sweet sorrow of a completed challenge for Jbel Tinergwet ahead, fine though it was, would be our last major summit of GTAM. At 3551 m metres it rises as a curving wave above the broad *tizi* and Charles and I recalled our first time there when the peak flared in colours of sunrise flames. I'd compared its shape to the Sydney Opera House though the mountain is a bit more disciplined. With the OHC gang the dawn colours had remained muted but, like a paper lantern, the globe of a full moon hung over the summit. Now Tinergwet stood in stark day clarity, a cut-out shape stuck on blue wallpaper.

The slope swells up from the *tizi* and, looking back, the figures of the others appeared as tiny dots, like ants on a trail. Even on the ultimate ascent the scale still shook me but I smiled as before long I would reverse the process and gaze up some minor Scottish hill and see an Atlas giant and make crazy estimates of times and distances. There's a story of an alpine guide doing this in Edinburgh where he was shown a snowy Arthur's Seat (all of 251 m) and asked how long he thought it would take to climb. The guide considered and then voiced doubts if it could be done in a day.

The going on Tinergwet became rougher and, to use the lie of the dislocated strata, we bore well to the left, almost to the far ridge where Ali paused on a shelf of pink rock so we could lunch: tube cheese and oatcakes. There was no spare water for brewing and we rationed our own drinking supplies. (The bivvy planned for that night was 'anywhere past Tinergwet'.) A last steep tilt of rock and looseness and the angle eased and we stood by the tumbled remains of the trig point. We so far forgot ourselves as to shake hands on it. Ali hugged me with glittering eyes. GTAM had been his dream as much as ours and perhaps meant even more for he had made a mountain journey beyond the imaginings of even the best of the guides. That was Ali: the rare talent of being both cerebral as well as physical and if that meant moments of pain and suffering it also gave the visions and the wilder wings of glorious success which the average Toubkal plodder would never know.

For much of that day (and the day before) we had in sight the new *piste* which wove a line along the major but lower east–west crest from Jbel Tabgourt to the north of us. Often the dome-like swellings of a crest are easier for creating new roads than the deep-cut cliffs and gorges of the valley bottoms. That was a new way in to the Peyron-lauded Seksawa (his northern equivalent of our opposing Medlawa) and I'm sure a part of him is dismayed at the intrusion. Letting our eyes follow that wiggling line westwards, we were aware of the track vanishing into the maroon-hazed depths of the huge trench where the Marrakech–Agadir highway lay, the last great road over the Atlas, just a few days from the seaboard. Peyron's suggested GTAM description starts at the road, which always puzzled me as there was such good mountain landscape right to the ocean. Jbel Tabgourt, that northern outlier, is 3208 m and, on memorable visits has given us the finest panoramic views of that end of the Atlas.

The descent off Tinergwet I dismissed in my log as a 'foul flank'. We'd left our rucksacks where we'd eaten so had to traverse from there. We dropped down a gully to the south and wove a complex route along before a rake led us up to a 3394 m *tizi*. Beyond, the crest was a crumbly white marble intrusion leading to a contrasting black jagged summit and a complex continuation before we gained what we called the southwest top of Tinergwet. At 3434 m, it is quite a peak in its own right. I wondered if any European had been there since the Polish lads in their knickerbockers and pith helmets in 1934. We zigzagged down to continue the ridge westwards (still over the 3000 metre mark) with our tired minds beginning to think of some bivvy spot on the crest.

It suddenly struck me we could bale off to the north into a high valley with abundant grass patches and a thread of silver-glittering stream. These were the springs of the Assif Tichka, something of a mirror image of the infant Assif Nfis, though a deeper-cut plateau. The low crest (Jbel Tichka) deflects the Assif Tichka to the south further along, while the Nfis breaks out to the north. There was a delicious opposing symmetry to this layout, I thought. I also solved something that had puzzled me for years: the exact location of Jbel Tichka, since most general maps of Morocco seemed to place this name with complete randomness. Was it synonymous with Jbel Tabgourt? Was it Imaradene and/or the Tichka Plateau? This anomaly even existed in the 20s. Neltner, who explored there thoroughly, commented on everyone looking for this Jbel Tichka which was vaguely located around Awlim/Tinergwet. He discovered *tichka* was the local word for pastures so the present Jbel Tichka is apposite, looking to the Assif Tichka pastures while the Tichka Plateau is famously pastureland.

The demarcating Tizi Ifguig has an interesting derivation, the name referring to the zigzag stitching used to create matting for mosques. The marble banding along the south flank mimics this exactly. West of Tinergwet our crest fell, crest by crest to Tizi Ifguig beyond which nothing remained over 3000 m. There was nothing to call for the bold Jbel Tichka name which appeared on some maps as it was just a tree-spotted crest at 2300–2400 m that bound the Assif Tichka on the north—or so it appeared as we sat on one top.

Ali had shot off down to find a campsite. We scrabbled down a gully and loose flanks, sidestepped a red bluff and joined him by the blessed stream. We drank water, we brewed water, we sat in water, we washed smelly stockings and clothes in water. Had we been otters we could not have revelled in the stuff with greater pleasure. Sweat, dust and blisters were forgotten. The Assif Tichka appealed at once and I wrote 'If ever I head for Jbel Tinergwet again, it will be up this delectable valley and not the hard slog from the deep-set south'.

The upper valley of the Assif Tichka was filled with flocks of sheep and goats and our baths had to be taken quickly and discreetly. Blessed climate too when one can wash everything and know the clothes will dry in under an hour while spread on the warm rocks. The flocks slowly worked their way down past our site heading for their overnight *azibs*, a rhythm of life we were copying, free from the western mania for material things. An old shepherd in ragged *djellaba* and *selham* and rubber-tyre-soled sandals was last to leave the warm heights.

We scraped level platforms among the scrub and stones, drank several hot drinks and prepared a simple supper while eyeing the last two 3000-ers of our crest. One pointed, one rounded, they took on the fiery colours of sunset and lingered long as beacons in the afterglow.

CHAPTER 16

Slings and Arrows

And now that I have climbed and won this height,
I must tread downward through the sloping shade
And travel the bewildered tracks till night.
Yet for this hour I still may here be stayed
And see the gold air and the silver fade
And the last bird fly into last light.

Rossetti

Looking at our maps now I can only be thankful we had the 1:50,000 for the complicated detail of the ridge. The 50,000 is scant on names, however, and apart from sprawling Adrar n' Dern (Mountain of mountains) and Jbel Tichka along the north side of the river, there was no name between us and Arg where we planned to meet Hosain and the mules. The sharper peak on the crest was 3032 m and the more rounded was 3025 m; these were the most westerly 3000-ers in the country. The only 3000-er lying further south was Siroua. Although the crest had given us blessed breezes, from there on we had searingly hot conditions, a perpetual *moussem* of the sun.

I quite consciously savoured the intoxication of our last high mountain dawn. We made our own ways along and up onto the crest as we frequently did to suit our variable paces and choices of terrain. Graeme had the young man's casual speed while the rest of us plodded away: Charles both determined and cautious, Tony fit and myself aye ready for anything interesting. We regrouped on the shoulder of 3032 m where Ali had the coffee pot on a scrub fire. The ridge kept changing geologically from slate grey to white marble. The marble was an intrusion we kept running into since the first day on the ridge.

We had another bout of group photography on our last 3000-er and went our various ways again. Charles was determined to keep to the ridge over some lesser bumps to reach the Tizi Ifguig (2776 m) which the mules and Hosain would have crossed (*Insh 'Allah!*) but I was so enamoured with the Assif Tichka I wanted to see as much of it as possible before crossing Jbel Tichka. Ali, having run out of *Casa Sport* was going to fly to Arg to replenish. Poor Ali, he has tried several times to kick the weed, as set a sociable habit as mint tea almost. Interestingly, both Tony and Graeme accepted cigarettes at Arg too. Over several visits I'd never seen them smoking cigarettes (Tony was a pipe man) so the traverse had obviously taken it out of them, more so than Charles and me perhaps. Eventually Charles went off alone and we began our descent with a feeling of schoolboys heading for the train after the end-of-term prize giving.

Our descent was steep, into a corrie, and then along a central ridge where an ancient shepherd put us onto a path down to the Assif Tichka. We passed one big *azib*, reeking of the beasts. At the junction of our side valley and the main stream, we watched a seemingly endless number of sheep and goats come out of a small *azib* building. "They must have stacked them three deep", Graeme suggested. Grassy flats by the confluence would have made a pleasing campsite. "Next time!" I vowed, as I so often did. We cut the corner and crossed down the right bank of the Tichka. A first *seguia* ran to a patch with potatoes, tomatoes and mint under cultivation. We enjoyed delectable walking though our holiday mood may have given us somewhat tinted spectacles. We came on a big dam across the main river, so back-tracked a bit for flowing water and had a prolonged stop to brew, demolish the last of the oatcakes, paddle, photograph a gaudy caterpillar and a flightless locust and generally relax. A careful scrutiny of the map showed us the dam was feeding a large *seguia* which contoured above the descending river to be led over the Jbel Tichka crest and miles on to feed a far valley with vital water: one of the most impressive irrigation systems I've seen in the Atlas.

We might have been more impressed if we'd looked a bit more carefully at heights or contours. However, colour photocopying doesn't pick up the faint contour lines. Luckily, dotted blue lines marking river courses gave some idea of the layout, but not the verticalities. After our long stop, an ascending path led us up by some isolated old junipers and oaks to the modest crest of the Jbel Tichka. On the rim we discovered why it was called *jbel*, it was a mountain all right, but only to the northwest. We looked down immense depths and set off more soberly on what was possibly the longest slope *down* we'd faced on the whole trip. The 50,000 map didn't even show a zigzag. We traversed a grand balcony, with the sort of views one associates with hang-gliding then, after the path direct from the Tizi Ifguig joined ours, it was endless zigzags down. A *Brasher* set of prints in the dust indicated that Ali was ahead, Charles behind.

The hot, jarring descent was unrelentingly painful so we had a pause under trees on the last dome above Arg. Men were tamping soil between shuttering as they built a new house wall and the peculiar exhalation call accompanying each thump came up clearly to our ears. There may have been a wedding, as *youyous* (the strange ululations females make in greeting or celebration) set the hair tingling. Setting off, we met two boys who were too shy to speak but had obviously been sent up—like pilot cutters—to guide us in. With *djellabas* hitched up they skipped ahead on plastic-sandalled feet, turning every now and then to smile encouragingly.

We passed the wall-builders and, though just walking (desperately hot), we appeared to be sweating more than they were. A grinning fellow met us on the street and swept us into a house—but there were no Ali and Hosain so we had to excuse ourselves and go on with the embarrassed boys. We came on Hosain at the village shop and were given great hugs and kisses of welcome and litre bottles of *Sidi Ali* which we demolished in very quick order. The intended house was opposite the shop with a vine growing along the wall and Taza gazing out the doorway of the basement stable. A man with a *bendir*, the simple tambourine-like drum, grinned down at us from a rooftop as he fingered out a rhythm. We went round the back and were welcomed by the toothless granny of the house. Oranges and tea helped assuage our thirst then we went off, as Ali had done, to wash our clothes and ourselves in the river. Graeme talked and talked as the tension of the traverse drained away down the dappled stream of delight.

Children led us up to see the actual *source*, where water for drinking and cooking was collected, then we straggled back. We knew Charles had arrived; the familiar laugh floated out from the grilled window opening. The room was swarming with flies, but Hosain sprayed them until they tangled in our hair and the floor was crunchy with the dead and dying. Flies are as friendly as a wet puppy and I found life much more pleasant outside. However, it took some effort to rouse Tony and Graeme to view the sunset. I had all the kids round, having a hilarious time with the vanishing coin trick and then the plastic snake. The din overcame any social taboos and I was soon surrounded by all the women too. One borrowed the snake and I could tell her progress through the village by the yells and squeals as she went from house to house. They are a fun-loving people and the convivial gatherings were always a delight, though often we understood little of what was said. Even writing up my log was a spectator sport for the kids. With Tony and Graeme, we were taken along to a spur beyond the village to watch a molten sun tilt over the blue horizon, beyond ridges softly serrated with trees. We were done with barren summits. The sunset was dressed for a ball.

Tony spent an hour dealing with a toddler with a badly burned foot. The child never made a sound the whole time and the mother smiled and smiled whenever she met one of us thereafter. The flies—our only such encounter apart from the camp on the Oued Zat— subsided with the heat. Geckos scurried about, often up and down window panes as their feet have thousands of microscopic hairs that can grip even on glass. We hoped the poisoned flies were safe for them to eat. The only food we had left from our traverse was a little tea and milk, so the sugar eaters were glad to be onto unlimited supplies again. The rotund shopkeeper came in with our host for a tea and chat and later, we had chicken *tagine*: plain but satisfying.

An elderly uncle of Hosain had come with him to help with Taza and Tamri during their diversion. He planned to descend the next day and return by road to Imoulas via Agadir and Taroudant, an indication of how tough the mountain way had been. Inside was still hot and stuffy so I went off to sleep on the roof. A cat carried her kittens one by one across my corner of roof, surprisingly bright in the light of a half-moon. Neither mosquitoes nor barking dogs kept me awake.

Desperate for a pee, I was up before the sun drew a lipstick along the horizon and our early start was blessed for we had the hottest day so far. Cold conditions can be modified but heat just has to be borne. After a 'good, honest, wholesome, hungry breakfast' (Isaak Walton), Hosain watched us down and up the other side of the valley to see we launched correctly. From a col we looked down to Tafilalt in an avocado-green oasis with a conical red hill beyond, the first of many colour shocks of soil that day. Tafilalt was quite a large sprawl of village with several recycled doorways, the doors made of the printed tin sheets intended for sardine tins or engine oil cans. The Sidi Mohammed shrine had an attractive tower and, as ever, we felt the deep-rooted religiousness of the country; Christian missionaries had seldom made converts. In Tangier on one occasion a zealous young innocent missionary was determined to preach in the *Socco* (square), and even agreed to pay the interpreter considerable danger money. A large crowd listened attentively and dispersed peacefully to the preacher's relief but then he was not to know that the interpreter had simply given them, sentence by sentence, a story from *Arabian Nights* rather than the preacher's words.

Trying to work through Tafilalt we ended up in someone's yard. An old man rushed out then sped ahead on a devious field steeplechase to show us onto the main *piste*, demonstrating how enthusiastically helpful locals are to strangers. We went off the edge of our 50,000 map where it noted *Vers Argana*. If the map had been vague until then, the next sheet was so bald and bare of information we couldn't even pinpoint our location and were reduced to navigating by guess and gumption: if we kept going west we'd hit the tarmac after all.

We tramped on down the *piste* after the old man left us and, on the verge of the dusty red track, noticed a ragged argan tree, heavy with green fruits. More than anything this was a symbol of the approaching end of the traverse and the suddenness was a considerable shock. We paused to photograph this rude gesture of a tree but after that, of course, there were jagged argan trees almost continuously. We would pass our last night sleeping under one. Argan trees (*Argania spinosa*) only exist in this southwest corner of Morocco: roughly from Essaouira down to the Sous and eastwards along that valley to Taliouine. They dot the lower slopes as well as the plains and are a bit of a tourist attraction as goats climb them (a treeful of goats is quite a spectacle). Of course, the young boys herding the goats have latched onto this and lie in ambush for the cameras, ready to extort their toll: "*Un dirham, monsieur!*"

The goats are actually encouraged to climb the trees since they not only nibble the leaves as they tiptoe on the swaying branches, but they eat the berries. These look a bit like overgrown olives and, like olives, have a hard kernel inside the fleshy exterior. Argan oil tastes a bit like peanut butter and is used as a dip between courses or in cooking. The goats gobbling the berries is actually a help to the process as they remove the useless fleshy part and pass on the wanted kernels for collection, crushing and oil extraction. In season, the goatherd's brothers stand by the roadside waving honey-coloured jars at passing motorists and grandfathers squat behind stacked pyramids of golden-bright *Sidi Harazem* bottles. Something like 100 kg of nuts and 10 hours of work are involved in the production of a litre of oil. Argan oil, crushed almonds and honey combine to make a delicious dip called *Amlou*. Windo wrote that the origin of the argan tree can be explained by the following legend:

'Long ago, in the region of Souss, there was a holy man and magician called Sidi Ahmed ou Moussa. When Sidi Ahmed lay dying he called out to Allah to ask that He bless that region of terrible aridity with a fruitful tree. Then Sidi Ahmed took a jar of water, made a hole in the sand with his thumb and poured water into it. Just before he died, an argan tree grew up in front of his eyes and he said to a goatherd: 'Go and make your goats eat the argans and plant the seeds everywhere'.'

In that open country, landmarks were non-existent. At one spot, a mule track had worn so deeply into soft rock that we walked in a chest-deep canyon. We had a pause on a knoll and 'drank' the last of our chocolate. We may have seen a *zaouia* tower, but nothing on the ground and map agreed. The map was so old that the glint of traffic on the main road was meaningless. Bee-eaters twittered overhead. I cringed under my battered brolly as usual, though a *coup de soleil* at that stage was not likely. (Sunstroke has the charms of severe sea-sickness so is worth avoiding.) We could *hear* the distant traffic, the steady sort of buzz one hears standing under lime trees when the bees are busy.

Eventually we came on the main river, the Assif n'Aït Moussa, but it was dry. Only a few houses existed, but never any person to question. With nagging thirst we drank our last water on the assumption Argana was near. A flaking sign for Ifid (actually named on our map) gave a clue, but the new *piste* swung east of a hill so we toiled up and around and still Argana never appeared. An old *kasbah* on a dominant hill was suggestive, and when we came on some scattered houses we were told it was Argana. There were no shops, no café, no Ali, just intense, cruel heat so we retreated under a tree to try and survive until Ali showed up.

After being cooked for half an hour a boy playing on a bike explained to us that there was a café just ten minutes down the road. We were in two minds whether to say thanks for the information or lynch him for withholding the fact for so long. And no, we didn't want to buy a tortoise. Sure enough the road swung down below the dominating fort into Argana proper, a forgotten market town that would make an excellent location for a sphagetti western with empty streets of pillared arcades, doors creaking in the wind and the feeling of eyes watching in the silence. A dog barked but was too weary to rise to its feet. We walked down the tree-lined avenue like gunslingers coming into town.

At last we found some life round a pleasant small café and a few shops. We demolished welcome litres of *Sidi Ali* and then had coffees with big *Kiri baguettes*. Remote areas never stocked bottled water, just *Coca Cola*, *Sprite*, *Fanta*, etc. Sadly, over the years, every Moroccan soft drink company has been put out of business by this international giant and now they produce a Casablanca 'table water' *Ciel*, to try to eradicate the companies producing the natural spring water, such as *Oulmès*, *Sidi Ali*, *Sidi Harazen*, *Aïn Saïss*, etc. We were once shown around the *Sidi Ali/Oulmès* plant and were impressed at the endless bottles passing on the conveyor belt. As we left, our guide gave us each a bottle, showing us how the date and *time* were stamped on the lid! Hundreds of workers live in a village in that beautiful hill country; too precious to be destroyed simply to swell the profits of an international company.

Argana had been by-passed by the new highway and had largely died as a result, a story not altogether unknown in the UK, a sort of A9 Dalwhinnie. The old fort on the hill was a pointer to the days when this was an important spot on the westernmost of the great Atlas passes, at a modest 1770 m, called either the Bibouan Pass or the Tizi Maachou and controlled by the M'Tougga. Traffic pours through on the new road and the pass is seldom named unless as 'the road by Imi-n-Tanout', the only town of any size in the northern foothills. The Kasbah Bouaboud, the M'Tougga's base, lies further west, every bit as impressive as Telouet but seldom visited by anyone. The Argana *kasbah* was a French-built fort, straight out of *Beau Geste*.

We explained we were waiting for friends and mules as we sat on and on for a couple of hours, wondering where Ali and Hosain could have wandered to. Ali had the advantage of gaining clearer directions from the locals but we'd seen nobody all morning to ask anything. We were rather enjoying doing nothing in the shade, and the local company was cheerful. I recounted to the others how the great Scottish explorer Joseph Thomson had come through this long pass in 1888, planning to reach Taroudant, but was deflected a few miles south of Argana by inter-clan fighting and escaped to Agadir instead.

I went for a stroll as Ali had still not arrived, but the village nutter took exception to my photographing the scene. He became so aggressive we were hustled off to the *caïd's* office where he could hardly follow. "Would we like to lay a complaint?" The ramifications of that would be endless. "No, we have no complaint." Maybe they hoped for one as an excuse to take action with the local menace but we did not want to be tied up with officialdom. We were eventually given the escort of the *caïd's* assistant and a soldier and walked up to the highway with them. That was hardly how we'd seen ourselves reaching the last great pass over the Atlas, the GTAM equivalent of reaching the A9 on a TGO (The Great Outdoors) coast-to-coast across Scotland.

The crazed local followed, armed with a hulk of wood with a big nail stuck through the end. This was so cliché-ed as to be funny except we sat at a café table by the busy road keeping a very careful eye on the man who hovered around muttering imprecations in a selection of languages. No doubt we could have been enriching our vocabulary; such French as we understood was not complimentary.

We had a tense hour before the mules arrived. Our Argana escort had assumed we'd be catching a bus or *grand taxi*, not just sitting buying each other rounds of *cocas* and *madeleines*. I had my brolly on the table ready to hold it up as a defence. Once Ali explained everything (he'd also had to visit the *caïd*, delaying him even longer) the locals managed to entice the man inside and we fled down the road to get out of sight, an incongruous caravan straggling along the verge of a highway roaring with colossal lorries, buses and cars, the ditch waymarked with cans, the noise and buffeting fearsome. But that hell wouldn't be for long, I encouraged everyone. "When we come to a track off, that will do and, with so many villages, there must be water". But we had over an hour of fume-laden, juggernaut-shuddering air and sweaty tramping (my sweat soaked pants bringing on 'nappy rash'), before at last there was a *piste* in what looked like the correct place. Thankfully we turned off.

Tony and Graeme removed their rucksacks from the mules and we said casual goodbyes. We left them standing in the barbecued heat of the roadside waiting for the first Agadir-bound *grand taxi* or bus. An hour later I looked down to the road end, thinking to take them tea. They had gone. Although Graeme had been on a longer stravaig, Tony's two weeks' ration had made the parting necessary but, with hindsight, there was something almost symbolic in finishing with just the core team of Charles, Ali, Hosain, Hamish and long-suffering Taza and Tamri.

A good campsite lay over the first slopes which were dotted with failed eucalyptus plantings. The mules rolled in the dust with cumbersome exuberance but later Taza was loaded up with every possible container and Hosain rode off to find water. I worked in the scant shade of a stunted tree, the biro constantly sticking in the paper dampened by my sweaty wrist. The heat had a ferocious bite. A hoopoe, that hippie bird, fanned its crest at me and flew off. A frantic buzzing disturbed me and, just a metre away, I saw a bluebottle on its back, frantically trying to regain its feet but merely spinning. The noise brought a lizard out into the sun and it homed in on the insect as sharp and sure as if using radar. The lizard did a few press-ups then scuttled in ragged dashes from cover to cover to approach past my feet to near the fly. It paused, throat palpitating then, faster than the eye could follow, pounced. The buzz was cut off instantly. The lizard sat still again, throat still pulsing, as if nothing had happened. At dusk the bats came out. They will not fly by day because the sun, at creation, swore to blind them if they did. God granted Moses the honour of creating bats.

By that time we were thoroughly attuned to the heat. Only after experiencing it day in, day out, week after week, do bodies and minds accept the sun as the natural order. Our very marrow is so marked by half a lifetime of changeable, wet British weather. Memories of bivouacs at home normally conjure up pictures of storm and stress, of necessity, not pleasure, so to open eyes to a dawn of perfection, pale-lipped but warm-hearted, was almost tearfully delightful. Even if the night was cheeky enough to dust a frost on the camp, the jocular sun was soon there to laugh away the chill and bring us back to the sensuous present. Just to be warm, all the time, was something I quite consciously revelled in. I awoke, day after day on those last weeks, wishing for the ability to purr. That night I went for a walk in the moonlight and sat watching the loom of passing headlights, making me think of the distant displays of Northern Lights. The stars put on the most extravagant performance, in silence. Ali told me that a shooting star indicated the death of someone.

The next day gave the longest walk of the whole GTAM. This was not intentional (not in that heat) and is only amusing in retrospect. We planned about fifteen miles to reach the posh hotel at Imouzzer des Ida Outanane early enough to splash in the pool and enjoy a lazy, gourmet meal that others had prepared: a deserved celebratory luxury for the trip's ending. To ensure this, we rose at four and were off an hour later, tramping up our *piste* which ran straight for the western hills through which we would wend our way. Soon, however, I realised it was not the right *piste*.

We should have come to a large village set in a wide area of cultivation, but we hadn't. We turned to skirt along the foot of the hills hoping to reach where we should have been, presuming it was not very far. We presumed wrong, and hours went by as we strayed a complex route, the last straw being a deep-cut gorge that opened just when we were sure our village lay ahead.

We were at a known spot at least, as the map clearly showed the *piste* on from there. The village had Matisse-like floral paintings on the walls. We came to know these paintings well as we tried again and again to trace the *piste* out of the far side of the village, each sortie ending in a dead end and a return to base. There were no men about, only women and children who wouldn't or couldn't help. When we eventually hit the correct route a man did appear, and confirmed the facts. Being ahead of Ali at the day's start could give us interesting navigational challenges.

The *piste* led on and eventually swung up and up in linked bends: far too soon to be correct. We were nonplussed, again nothing fitted. We asked a rangy shepherd who wagged an admonishing finger at us and then pointed out a short cut. Rather than return to the school where the true *piste* kept on low for a few kilometres before starting its climb into the hills, we could go straight up from where we were, cut through a gap and hit the Imouzzer *piste* beyond Sinit, a name we actually found on the map. As the shepherd was watching us, we felt compelled to try his suggested route, a vicious assault up eroded gullies followed by a steeplechase to the gap where we collapsed in a dripping heap. The spot gave a bird's eye view down to the main road, the Abdelmoumen reservoir and all the world spread below. We traversed to the corrie with Sinit beyond and from there duly reached the Imouzzer *piste*, our diversions having taken some 3½ hours. So where were Ali and company?

The *piste* continued to corkscrew up and up, a strangely people-less landscape considering how well cultivated it was. When we collapsed by a rushing *seguia* to top up water bottles there weren't even kids about. We were climbing up the side of a valley to gain a linear balcony that ran west for a long way, but the endless uphill was enervating in the heat. Catching Charles in the shade of a thuya we declared lunch: over-spiced sardines, not being the best option. The French toast we put them on had the ominous brand name of *Grim*. There were no telltale *Brasher* treads in the dust, so we changed from wondering how far ahead the mules would be to speculating what they could be doing behind.

The long traverse was uphill enough to be taxing and the watershed never seemed to come. When it did, we looked ahead to a large hollow which didn't seem to fit the map. The road dipped to a village called Tikki then went on ascending wearily to the wide col beyond. We took a quite ridiculous time to come on an expected junction and we weren't walking slowly. The limestone threw back the heat at us. We collapsed in some shade for a break. A *camionette* stopped and a man clambered down with a bulging shopping bag. Seeing us, he came over and proffered a gift of some bananas and an orange each before stomping up the road. A sign back to Tikki indicated 4 km but this was just not right somehow. While Charles went off into the bushes I set off to wander steadily (3 miles per hour) up to the 1648 m high point which was, according to the map, exactly a mile off. The time taken confirmed what I'd thought sitting at the junction: we'd changed from 1:50,000 maps to 1:100,000 maps the previous day but not noticed!

In defence, the typographical style was oddly similar on both maps where normally the two versions look quite different. Our long walk down the highway now made sense, as did the reason why Argana took so long to appear as well as the fiascos of that day. There was a perverse pleasure in working out what had gone wrong but we'd had plenty of time to tease away at the puzzle. The discovery also brought home the realisation that Imouzzer was still ten miles ahead, the time was 1600, and we'd not been caught up by the mules. Could they actually make it to the hotel, walking 30 miles in one day? In the end we decided we had no option but to push on to the known destination where, even without the others, we'd be comfortable and fed. If we waited and the others had been forced to stop we'd have a hungry night with no food and no gear in the middle of nowhere. We rolled up the ten miles to Imouzzer in two hours, long miles with '*ce vieux pays immobilisé sous le soleil lourd*' (this old country unmoving under the weight of the sun).

My feet were hot and soles sore from the hard stony *piste*. Luckily, the heat created an afternoon breeze so I walked only in a *gandoura*. We had another long balcony route with a view over a frizzled tree-speckled red soil country that reminded me of Natal. The verges were covered in large thyme bushes, pungently scented. At one spot, we passed children playing a version of ring-a-roses until a *camionette* picked them up. They couldn't understand us *not* wanting a lift. "And where is your car?" came the familiar question. We were offered a consolation gift of cigarettes! Not smoking was even more incomprehensible.

We had an hour along this balcony road before peeling off downwards, the hard pebbly surface studded with fossil lampshells (*Brachiopods*). We cut a few corners and dropped off the scarp to gentler country. Only when a familiar mosque with an unusual red roof appeared did I know exactly where we were. (I'd walked up from the hotel on a previous visit.) A small shop sold *Coca*; bliss for we were as dry as Deuteronomy. The lads who gathered to talk to us would not believe we'd walked so far in the day. The dust lay so thick on our legs it looked as if they were covered in cement powder—I'm surprised the hotel took us in.

Having settled in, we were about to bathe when the others caught up. They looked like a patrol given a hard time by the Indians. Tamri was exhausted and Ali and Hosain had had an equally erratic navigational exercise. The hotel never batted an eye at this addition; they had stabling since they do mule rides for visitors. We were amused to hear illiterate Hosain being asked to fill in his hotel registration *fiche*, but he was not at all awed by the opulent surroundings. We all relished plenty of hot water; for Charles and me it was the first bath since the Hotel Ali resumption of GTAM. Dinner was very civilised and pleasant and, being a day ahead of schedule, we had no difficulty in deciding we'd stay the following night as well; after all, Tamri needed the rest!

CHAPTER 17

Down to the Sea

Yet the mountaineer who sidles on
And on to the very bending,
Discovers, if heart and brain be proof,
No necessary ending.

R Browning

The Hotel des Cascades name comes from an extraordinary feature on the cliffs below the eyrie-like setting: a petrified waterfall. Centuries of water falling had laid down deposits of limestone which had grown into the shape of a bridal-veil fall which had then largely dried up so a smooth rock torrent seemed to flow down the cliff, an 85 m 'frozen' cascade. A resurgence feeds the fall and a *seguia* angles along and down with a precarious footpath alongside to reach the valley below this spectacle. There are cafés below the falls and a motor road zigzags up from there to the actual village, a Thursday *souk*, which lies along an avenue from the hotel. The hotel has colourful gardens which fall, terrace on terrace, to a blue swimming pool and a view down rolling foothills: a delectable spot, the food delicious, the rooms pleasant. I've seen us jump on the daily bus from Agadir just to escape its Costa atmosphere and wend up the spectacular road to the mountain haven.

Odd though it felt not to be rising at the crack of dawn, we enjoyed being lazy tourists for a day. We sent off a huge bag of laundry and made the most of the breakfast spread of various cereals, fruit, juices, breads, hot doughnuts and *madeleines*, honeys and *amlou* and good coffee. I then had the last logistical session of GTAM and went up the almost-deserted street to buy a few fresh items of food. A signpost indicated Argana was 87 km from Imouzzer (waterfall) des Ida Outanane (the name of the local tribe). Lunch was a luxurious barbecue on the terrace with huge *kebab* sticks of everything imaginable, grilled chicken, fruit and coffee. No wonder the busloads of tourists who vied with flowers in colourfulness were the shape they were if they dined like that twice a day for their holiday visit. We were well trimmed by then of course, several holes taken in on our belts. Alas, most of the benefit would disappear before we left Morocco—the Essaouira ending saw to that.

We had our swim in the garden pool. Most of the day I worked steadily on my book (which was completed in Essaouira a few days later), when I wasn't just gazing westwards rather wistfully to the condescending last dip of the Atlas. A waiter stood watching awhile and smiled, "*C'est beau, n'est-ce pas?*" I whispered "*Bien sûr!*" We were all in bed long before the generator switched off the electric light supply, bloated from chicken in a honey sauce and a bottle of Meknes wine.

Tamri, our finishing point, lies at the end of an estuary where the coast road does a loop inland around crowded banana plantations, the streets lined with stalls with huge hands of bananas hanging for sale. We seldom passed without stopping to purchase a vast quantity. Many are small in size and taste superb, unlike the larger tasteless objects grown for export. Tamri had more or less chosen itself as the finish but there was a practicality in that as well. A huge river drained the hills and the Assif Tamri, or Assif Tannkert higher up, flowed below the hill setting of Imouzzer, the initial streams almost moating our high citadel. The road down to the petrified fall continued to the Assif Tannkert and we'd follow the river to the sea with one last camp on the way. Comments such as "Downhill all the way now!" were made very much tongue-in-cheek. The country remained grand, varied, and hot.

The hotel received brownie points by providing us with breakfast at 0600, although a simple one of gallons of coffee, fresh bread and famous local honey (Imouzzer has an annual honey festival in July). We relished the Africa of morning perfection, the brief cool freshness, swifts hawking in the sky, a continuo of doves among the colourful trees. Imouzzer was rather an unreal interlude in the continuity of hard grafting and we were soon returned to our reality, aided by loading the mules in a scruffy back yard.

We angled down the scarp for the zigzags of *piste* into the valley below. A family of uniformly tubby women were pushing a Renault 4 onto the *piste* to make a running start. How they all fitted in left us speculating. The zigzags just went on and on beyond the lower level which we could look down on from the hotel (marked by a dainty mosque tower) but we had not expected such a continuation of tortured *piste*. We suddenly looked down dizzy depths to the

Assif Tannkert which wended through a gorge of tiered verticality, far, far below. The capacity of the Atlas to surprise never fails. Any GTAM had to include an impressive ending; stopping at the Marrakech–Agadir road would not have made sense.

The map suggested the road looped down steadily, so a straighter pedestrian descent would cut out many miles but the links were more offset than indicated. My first sortie straight down ended in one of those nightmare limestone areas like a million Henry Moore sculptures heaped together then given a blast of *Semtex*. I tried to contour round but the way was barred by a cliff and I had to fight *maquis* and sun back up to the road. Even the dry-walling supporting the road was a VS (Very Severe). Charles had more sense than to try such variants; he followed the disappearing mules bend by bend. Eventually I found a path (there *had* to be one) and this direct line led me to a hamlet, Tichki, where there was a small *hanut* which had Sweet on sale, an apple juice we enjoyed rather than drank of necessity like the other fizzy drinks. When the other three arrived even Hosain had a *Sweet*.

Another series of big loops took us down into the Tannkert gorge, the bottom of which was well-irrigated with hedges of prickly pear and many villages. Maize grew to head height and there were graceful date palms. We enjoyed that atmospheric buzz that fills the air in summer places. I walked ahead to avoid the dust that was being stirred up by hooves and feet. Big bluffs and deflecting spurs (often the site of the villages—you don't build on ground that can grow food) led us steadily downwards. Eventually the cliffs eased but the *piste* headed off from the river for a huge diversion over higher levels so we had a break, stopping for an hour by a rushing concrete water channel where the mules could drink. They scoffed our stale bread and orange peel. Ali chatted-up a passing local and ascertained that mules could continue down the valley by the riverbed.

We rejoiced too soon as the initial shade vanished and progress was stumbling along the boulders of the riverbed in the sun. The going improved later but there was seldom a regularly used mule track so we constantly had to make speculative choices. We were forced up to join the *piste*, only to drop down into the valley again to follow its wending way. We'd become quite disorientated with both the landscape (sepia fold after sepia fold) and contradictory old and new *piste* lines but came on the compact, hidden, Souk Tlata n' Tankart, which lay separate from any of the valley villages (naturally, not on the map). The owner of a grain shop joined us for the last few miles. On arrival at the village he opened his cool cubicle, sent off for litre bottles of liquid and made mint tea for everyone. Taza and Tamri were unloaded. A second lunch was appreciated and the hour sitting in the shade was bliss.

Another old man brought in some local fossils, some ammonites and trilobites, but mostly various species of seashells; I bought a few. A sea urchin test was beautifully patterned with the marks of where the spines had been. I noted just how marvellous Morocco is for fossils on David Attenborough's *Life on Earth*. He travelled to Morocco to film a rare limestone location where thousands of feet of strata showed the unbroken succession of marine fossil life from the pre-Cambrian to the Cambrian. The site was Tiout, an oasis not far from Taroudant, over whose contorted strata Ali had often taken us.

The mules gave us a start and we left the large *souk* to sweat up a long *piste* ascent to a barren, stony limestone world. The stark stones of Taba village seemed to pulse in the heat. There was a fork and we swung westwards then sat under a black argan tree until Ali and Hosain caught up. We still had plenty of ups and downs and began to worry about water for the night, as any wells we had passed were on the outskirts of villages and noisy with women and kids. However, Ali found one that was more solitary, a concrete tank with a lockable lid. We camped under the nearest argan tree, quite a symbolic gesture in itself.

We only pitched the cook tent (because of a hot breeze) and just slept out, lying on our tents and groundsheets rather than inside them. We placed stones under the edge of the groundsheet so there was a raised rim all round, the theory being that any scorpion or other creepy-crawly would go under out of harm's way, rather than over to join us in the night. As we never had scorpions in our sleeping bags, either the ploy worked, or there hadn't been any nasties in the first place! The world has something like 750 species of scorpion and, of the few that are in fact lethal, several live in Morocco.

Ali went off with some visitors to purchase fodder for Taza and Tamri. We were adopted by a timid but hungry dog, and while willing to donate scraps the creature was kept at a distance due to his collar of revolting flies which had burrowed in under the matted coat to seethe secretively. When the same flies covered the sore on Tamri's back they were sprayed with *Baygon* (insecticide) and exploded from the mule with a roar. One of the more pleasant surprises of the GTAM had been how little we were bothered with insect or *arachnid* life. We made a satisfying last supper and watched the sun turn the sky red-gold as it dipped behind ragged tree slopes. Wishing can't stop the sun and day turned to darkness all too quickly. A camel plodded past in the dark, the restlessness of Taza and Tamri drawing our attention to its weird silhouette. They'd never seen one before yet had the mules' inborn dislike of camels. We were down to 600 m Charles reckoned. I didn't sleep for a long time as I lay under the last loneliness of stars, mulling over the journey. I hated the thought of stopping yet appreciated the completing of such a long chancy task. A dog howled in the night, sharing the bitter sweetness of being.

I was still half-dreaming reflectively at dawn. We watched tint on tint, tone on tone unveiling, merging into warmth. Then reality. I made porridge for a last morning treat. There seemed to be a general feeling of urgency and we were on 'the morning's amber road' by 0630. The mules were setting a pace which would have been uncomfortable to match if we hadn't been undulating steadily downhill, mostly through sparse argan forest. We were then looking down on the first banana fields, surprisingly far inland. The *piste* was inches deep in dust and the heat had our clothes saturated. Some of the soil was the rich red of Africa, as vivid at times as the sauce on a Chinese take-away. When we reached a wider plain we told Ali to wait for us at 1000, and off they went. The *piste* zigzagged down into a riverbed and on over the plain. A replacement *piste* had been made and crossed to the south bank without our noticing. Our older *piste* had been broken by spates and neglect which produced something of an obstacle course. However, the line swooped down to the Assif Tamri and up the next red bulge of hillside. As the river made a big loop to the south I argued us into going over to find the real *piste*, which we did after traversing barren country, interspersed with argan trees, euphorbias and tamarisk. We just made the *piste* at 1000 (another reason to have found it) when Charles declared, "Ali tracks!" almost as I said "Ali!"

They were under a shady tree, the mules' noses in their fancy fodder bags. We had a forty-minute lunch then pushed off in the sweltering heat, crossed a gulch, and walked doggedly on. "Just another bloomin' sunny day" I said grinning, but was inwardly sad, knowing it was the last. At the final descent a car stopped to offer us lifts (why on earth were we walking in that heat?) and we were given big handfuls of almonds by the driver. Moroccans are always very sympathetic towards the insane! We had another pause in the deep shade of a rubber tree, which has the delightful Latin name *Ficus elastica*.

A big place ahead suddenly became Tamri where we arrived at noon. Ali went into a mild panic at the thought of likely bureaucracy so we crept in by the back door and, while they unloaded Taza and Tamri, we consumed litres of liquid. It was 10th July. It seemed incredible that ten days had passed since we stood on Moulay Ali never mind 96 days of trekking (and the Spanish interlude) since Taza. The roadside café felt unreal, the TV an abomination, but to all who follow the road of the sun there comes the stabling sunset. I hated the ending. We should have started on the Mediterranean coast and made it a 'Sea to Ocean' trip, I suggested. Charles gave me a stony stare. He was a bit happier to be stopping, I suspect.

We had decided that Taza and Tamri should go by road to Imoulas rather than backtrack via Imouzzer, Arg and the Jbel Tichka. They might not make it over the Atlas, even lightly laden, for they had been pushed far beyond normal mule duty. Charles and I still planned to go to magical Essaouira for a few days (originally planned to occupy the days while Ali and Hosain took the mules back over the hills to Imoulas) then we'd all meet up again in Taroudant. Ali meanwhile had been to the *caïd*'s office and had to convince them he was not a wanted young Algerian terrorist and that his story of what he had done was actually true. He had to report back at 1500 so we had coffees and decided, as we were not particularly wanted, to head off and leave them to paperwork and finding transport for the mules. The latter was to prove the more difficult and they only got a *camion* to Taroudant late that night, or rather early morning (0330) and went on to Imoulas straight away.

Ali was back from his 1500 appointment before we left. I'd been snoozing on a straw bale that a lorry had dropped. I grabbed a local to take a picture of all of us together, the only one of GTAM, before we patted Taza and Tamri *B'slama* (goodbye). Hosain's Taza would journey with us again to the Tichka Plateau for *Wilderness Walks* filming a year later.

Taking our *au revoirs* of Ali and Hosain, we found places in a shared taxi heading up the coast. Charles had visions of throwing his stick into the sea, which he'd carried from the Oued Nfis. I joked we'd have to watch Tamri with his penchant for striking out over big waters, with an enthusiasm entirely lacking for small *seguias*. I'd even thought up a fine quotation to conclude GTAM. When Uqba, the first bearer of Islam to Morocco, swept across to be confronted by the western sea (*Maghreb* means 'land of the furthest west') he rode his mount into the tide and called Allah to witness that he had conquered as far as he could. Were there more lands to conquer, would he not have done so?

The taxi bore us off to Tamanar, linking along the coast to Cap Ghir, a wicked jaggedness of rocks, spraying the rollers into vapour. Weird, parasitic orobanche rose from the bushes by the verges: even the vegetation is cannibalistic! Past the lighthouse the road rears like a cobra to snake its way through the harsh, rolling, argan-dotted landscape, the roadside edged with millions of small, starry asphodel and friendly crested larks. After Tamanar the route stays inland on a rolling swooping road before sweeping down to Essaouira, the walled city of honey stonework and blue doors, which is where so many mountain ventures have ended over the years.

So, the trek was over. I felt, glancing at the sea, that we'd walked the tide out and all the journey lay exposed, fresh and glistening, wet with wonder but, all too soon, the tide would flow again and much would be washed away. How much would we recall a year or a decade later? There's always a slight sense of disappointment when an accomplishment is over, doubled when one attempts to write about it later, once more caught in the sedition of routine. But I am not a great one for the past, other than as a springboard for the future, and as the taxi sped us northwards I stirred the fire with the ringing words of the *Religio Medici*: 'We carry within us the wonders we seek without…There is all Africa, and her prodigies, in us.'

Appendix I
Summary

900 miles (1440 km) would be a more likely total distance (two hours of zigzag path could cover only a mile as the crow flies). The distance is for the basic route and side trips; peak-bagging, etc., is not included. The Spanish visit at the end of May was to comply with the 3 month tourist limit. The traverse could have been done within that time but that would have introduced an element of racing.

The first month (as the **R** symbols indicate) gave some miserable weather: rain on 19 out of 37 days. From 4 May to 10 July (end) there was no rain but occasional wicked winds. 31 nights were spent under roofs and 66 camping or bivouacking. The apparent discrepancy for the 96 nights is due to 16/6 when CK was in the Neltner Hut and HB and Ali (and GH) were being wind-blasted in a tent on top of Toubkal!

In the first half, the heavy snowfalls ruled out the planned Imilchil-Zaouia Ahancal route. Ayachi was magnificent but off-route and the upper Tessaout/Mgoun simply unreachable. The diversions proved just as entertaining, however. The high-level western traverse was a fitting climax. In all, about 25 people played an important part on the journey quite apart from our various hosts, our Hotel Ali base in Marrakech and Aït Idir Mohammed who managed affairs off the mountain.

The following statistical summary was produced after GTAM and rather brought home the scale of the traverse.
Symbols used:

⬔ nights camping   ↑ up

◭ the more outstanding overnight locations   ↓ down

☐ nights under a roof   R indicating rain (in the margin)

⋀ peaks climbed

Heights are in metres and distances in miles

DAY	DATE		OVERNIGHT	MILEAGE Day	Total	DAY'S DOINGS
		March				
1	T 28	△1	Dayat Chiker	11	11	Walk up from Taza start
2	W 29	△2	Bab bou Idir	8	19	Gouffre de Friouata
3 R	T 30	△3	Bab bou Idir	0	19	⋀ Tazekka 1980m
4 R	F 31	△4	Oued el Arba	14	33	Wild morning; on via Adman
		April				
5	S 1	△5	Oued Amezourou	13	46	Below Merhraoua. Windy
6	S 2	◭6	Souf Igrane	14	60	Slog to Guelta Tamda. Fine forest
7 R	M 3	△7	Bled Tiserouine	13	73	↑ Tamtroucht. Under Bou Iblane
8	T 4	△8	Taffert	10	83	⋀ CK Jbel Bou Iblane 3172m
						⋀ HB Jbel Achlem Alem 2462m
9	W 5	☐1	Arbal	10	93	Tizi Bou Zabel blocked; outflanking
10 R	T 6	△9	Oued Maasser	18	111	Tizi Ouiridene/Tafadjight/Tilmirat
11	F 7	△10	Jbel Tichchoukt Pass	11	122	Complex route - long valley to flank
12	S 8	△11	Boulemane	21	143	Foum Bessam pass
13	S 9	△12	Bou Beker	4	147	Rest day!
14 R	M 10	△13	Tatyiywelt	10	157	⋀ Jbel Habbid 2447m (mules frozen)
15 R	T 11	☐2	Aghbalou L'Arbi M.F.	14	171	⋀ Jbel Habbou 2488m (highest in area)
16 R	W 12	△14	Tizi Moudmam 2130m (Col du Zad)	17	188	Tizi Taddat 2256m/Aguelman n' Sidi Ali
17 R	T 13	☐3	Oued Serou 1640m	13	201	Forest. V wet descent below Timzought
18 R	F 14	△15	Below Kerrouchen 1300m	17	218	Cedar forest. Deluge ending
19 R	S 15	☐4	Arrougou 1380m	14	232	Mud! Stray to 1800m+ (souk stall)
20	S 16	△16	Oued Moulouya 1690m	17	249	Tizi Mouchentour/Pt. 1933m/Azerzou
21 R	M 17	☐5	Aghbala	18	267	Melwiya Plains. Thunderstorm
22 R	T 18	☐6	Aghbala	0	267	V Wet. Replenishing
23	W 19	△17	Assif n' Ikassene	15	282	Souk. 3 big river crossings. False ascent
24 R	T 20	☐7	Assif Tassent	11	293	Wet again
25 R	F 21	☐8	Imilchil. Hotel Atlas	15	308	Tislit Lake

Y	DATE	OVERNIGHT	MILEAGE		DAY'S DOINGS
			Day	Total	
	S 22	[9] Imilchil. Hotel Atlas	0	308	Souk day
	S 23	△18 Above Ayt Waghad 2210m	14	322	Messafragh crossing c. 2800m
	M 24	△19 Aqqa n' Tezgui	15	337	Assif n' Tafenda
	T 25	△20 Above Assif n' Oukhachane	16	353	↓ Anergi. Assif Melloul gorges
	W 26	△21 Tamga	8	361	Tizi Hammadin. Views of "Cathedral"
R	T 27	△22 Below Tifwina 1360m	12	373	Zaouia Ahancal piste contortions
	F 28	[10] Agoudim gîte	10	383	Zaouia Ahancal valley. Fine buildings
	S 29	[11] Agoudim gîte	0	383	Off day ride up to Taghia / gorges
R	S 30	△23 "Azurki View" 2435m	8	391	Tizi n' Illissi 2603m
May					
R	M 1	△24 "Azurki view"	0	391	◿ *Aroudane (Aioui) 3359m*
R	T 2	△25 Tizi Yllaz (near)	5	396	Tizi Yllaz 2805m
					◿ *Ifrilzene 3171m. CK*
R	W 3	△26 Lac Izoughar	6	402	◿ *Azurki, (E Top) 3640m. (Dust camp)*
	T 4	[12] Imelgas gîte	12	414	↓ Bou Goumez. (Chez Moh'd Achari)
	F 5	[13] Imelgas gîte	0	414	Rest day!
	S 6	[14] Imelgas gîte	0	414	'Flowers' gang join: Charles Aitchison, David Tattersfield, Francis Higgins, Lorraine Nicholson, Nicola Barr
	S 7	[15] Agouti gîte	6	420	Tabant souk. Bou Goumez valley
	M 8	△27 Targa (Bou Willi)	14	434	Bou Goumez - Bou Willi
	T 9	[16] Tarbat n' Tirsal	10	444	Tizi n' Tighist 2399m. Rock carvings.
	W 10	[17] Tarbat n' Tirsal	0	444	Feast of the sheep. CK, CA onto Rhat crest
	T 11	△28 Below Jbel Rhat 2490m	8	452	Tizi n' Kark 2850m
	F 12	△29 Tizi n' Iblouzane 3281m	6	458	◿ *Jbel Rhat 3797m;* HB, DT, CA, NB, FH
	S 13	△30 Tizi n' Iblouzane	0	458	◿ *Jbel Tignousti (traverse 3820m: ditto)* (Ali & CK do Tignousti / Rhat)
	S 14	△31 Ifoulou	13	471	Tissili gorges to the Tessaout
	M 15	△32 Aït Tamlil	10	481	Tessaout valley walking. Souk
	T 16	△33 Assif n' Terga 2040m	12	493	Long uphill day, via Terga. Snakes!
	W 17	△34 Tichkiwine Gorge (Assif n' Tamda)	10	503	Tizi n' Oumadghous 2800m ◿ *Jbel Tighaline 3326m*
	T 18	△35 Tamda n' Ounaghmar 2575m	7	510	Exit gorge. DT sick. Swims!
	F 19	△36 Tamda n' Ounaghmar	0	510	◿ *Jbel Anghomar (Ingehmar) 3609m and* ◿ *Zarzemt 3113m (various combinations by all*
	S 20	△37 Azib Anfergal	5	515	over the three days). Wind
	S 21	[18] Anmiter (Chez Eliyzar M'd)	6	521	Heatwave cont.
	M 22	[19] Anmiter (Chez Eliyzar M'd)	0	521	Local walks
	T 23	[20] Telouet (Auberge)	7	528	Tizi Tamraght/Tizi Tanbdout (Dar el Glaoui; Dancing)
	W 24	Marrakech, Hotel Ali			By Tizi n' Tichka
	T 25	Marrakech, Hotel Ali			Others fly home. Train strike. Ali / H home

247

DAY	DATE	OVERNIGHT	MILEAGE Day	MILEAGE Total	DAY'S DOINGS
	F 26	La Linea			HB, CK fly Casa - Gib - noisy pension
	S 27	Ronda			Algeciras and train up for Ronda
	S 28	Ronda			Pleasant pension / exploring
	M 29	La Linea			Gibraltar day. Cheap pension
	T 30	Marrakech, Hotel Ali			Fly Gib - Marrakech
	W 31	Marrakech, Hotel Ali			Ali / Hosain back
	June				
	T 1	Marrakech, Hotel Ali			Party joins: Max & Chris Huxham, Chris Bor John Barnard
58	F 2	[21] Telouet, Auberge	0	528	By Tizi n' Tichka, Dar el Glaoui. Dancing.
59	S 3	/38\ Titoula	7	535	Tizi n' Telouet 2567m
60	S 4	/39\ (Upper) Taddart	8	543	Tizi n' Telghist 2200m. Tichka road.
61	M 5	/40\ Imergen (Oued Zat)	15	558	Tizi n' Wakel 1836m. Epic!
62	T 6	/41\ Azib n' Tilst c. 2020m	11	569	Lower Oued Zat gorges. Wading!
63	W 7	/42\ Zat Gorges, upper	0	569	HB 2467m; others 3000m
64	T 8	/43\ Azib n' Tilst (HB); or high bivvy at 3000m, again (rest)	0	569	◭ *Traverse Taska n' Zat (via N Ridge) 3912m (C K/CB)* ◭ *Arjoût 3741m (M & CH/JB)*
65	F 9	/44\ Azib n' Tilst	0	569	◭ *Arjoût -* ◭ *Tougroudadane 3320m, (Tizi n' Tilst & down CK/CB) (Others back by gorges)*
66	S 10	[22] Setti Fadma (Hotel Bella)	10	579	Tizi n' Tilst 2800m. (Huge pass)
67	S 11	/45\ Timichi	9	588	Oued Ourika gorges, HB; rest track.
68	M 12	/46\ High Imanene (facing Tachddirt)	9	597	Tizi n' Tachddirt 3172m
69	T 13	/47\ High Imanene	0	597	◭ *Aksoual 3842m (via Tizi Likemt):* CK,CV,MH (HB/Ali to Marrakech: medical/dental aid)
70	W 14	/48\ Azib Tifni 2820m	9	606	CK, M&CH, CB, JB. HB/Ali, Hotel Ali, M'kech
71	T 15	/49\ Tizi Immouzer c. 3500m	6	612	Same party: Tizi n' Tagharat 3465m ◭ *Tichki 3753m* ◭ *Agoûjdad de Tichki 3607m* ◭ *Afekoï 3765m* (HB, Ali, Graeme Helliwell to Imlil - chez M'hd)
72	F 16	[23] Refuge du Toubkal (Neltner) 3207m /50\ Summit of Jbel Toubkal 4167m	4	616	◭ *Toubkal 4167m* (Morocco's highest, Ikhibi S↓ main party) ◭ *Toubkhal 4167m* HB, GH, Ali (HB/GH Ikhibi Nord). Jetstream camp on summit.
73	S 17	[24] Refuge du Toubkal	0	616	HB,GH,Ali ↓ Ikhibi Nord. Others fester. MH/JB wee climb
74	S 18	[25] Targa Imoula (Imlil/chez M'd)	8	624	HB,CK,GH ↓ Imlil early. CH later. ◭ *Ras 4080m* and ◭ *Timesguida Ouanoukrim 4088m* MW, JB, CE
75	M 19	[26] Targa Imoula (Imlil)			Preparing etc. Others ↓ from Neltner.

Note: rows 58–75 are bracketed under "HIGH LEVEL TRAVERSE" (vertical text).

AY	DATE	OVERNIGHT	MILEAGE Day	Total	
6	T 20	⌂51 Below Tizi n' Ouarhou 2530m	10	634	Tizi Mzic 2488. Others off to Marrakech &/or United Kingdom. Monique joins.
7	W 21	⌂52 Below Tizi n' Iguidi	11	645	Tizi n' Ouarhou 2672m. Heatwave/winds
8	T 22	27 Ijoukak café	11	656	Tizi n' Iguidi c. 2500m. Mules ↓, we over hills. Hot. Graeme Helliwell/Tony Meikle join. C Bond overnight (cycling).
9	F 23	⌂53 Ighil (O.Nfis)	11	667	Tinmal. Windy riverside site.
0	S 24	⌂54 Above Oukoun (O. Nfis)	9	676	Pine forest. Pool.
1	S 25	⌂55 Above Imlil (O. Nfis) 1751m	8	684	Souk Sebt - Imlil (villages)
2	M 26	⌂56 High Tiziatin forest (O. Nfis)	9	693	Gorge use/swims. Monique off.
3	T 27	⌂57 Guenfis Meadow (Tichka Plateau) 2510m.	10	703	△ Amendach 3382m / Tizi Agourzi 3007m / △ Azrou Asdim 3143m / △ Asdim Minor (Asdim SW) c. 3000m
4	W 28	⌂58 Tizi n' Targa (Tichka Plateau) c. 2800m	5	708	HB preparing: △ Awlim 3043m, (CK,TM,GH traverse) and △ Askawn 3078m
5	T 29	⌂59 Tizi n' Targa	0	708	△ Lma'dene 3256m (GH) / △ Imaradene 3352m (GH) / Support party arrive.
6	F 30	⌂60 Tizi Oumzra 3051m	3	711	Combination of mules, porters etc., get plenty of water to site for Moulay Ali & ridge traverse. CK, TM long reccy of Central Peak.
	July				
7	S 1	⌂61 Tizi Oumzra	4	715	△ Ras Moulay Ali 3349m
8	S 2	⌂62 Tizi n' Tizzirt 2816m	7	722	△ Aquelmoun 3251m / △ Adrar n' Fiyil 3114m / △ Mtdadene 3366m
9	M 3	⌂63 Adrar n' Birkwane c. 3150m	8	730	△ Wanourt 3182m / △ Tit Oulli 3247m / △ Adrar Oulzguim 3253m (re-water Assif Tamjlocht)
0	T 4	⌂64 High Assif Tichka c. 3010m	5	735	△ Adrar n' Birkwane 3173m / △ Jbel Awlim 3428m / △ Jbel Tinergwet 3551m / △ SW Peak 3434m
1	W 5	28 Arg	10	745	△ Adrar n' Dern 3032m/3025m (and over Jbel Tichka) CK ridge to Tizi Ifguig
2	T 6	⌂65 South of Argana, off Agadir road.	22	767	V. hot now for rest of trip. Exit big hills.
3	F 7	29 Imouzzer, Hotel des Cascades	30	797	Longest day (not intentional!) Hotel c.1350m
4	S 8	30 Imouzzer, Hotel des Cascades	0	797	Rest day celebration in advance!
5	S 9	⌂66 Above Assif Tannkert c. 600m	19	816	Downward and gorges day
6	M 10	31 Essaouira, Hotel des Remparts	17	833 (1353km)	Tamri finish / HB/CK taxi Tamanar, lift to Essaouira; Ali, H, mules, lorry to Taroudant for Imoulas

HIGH LEVEL WESTERN ATLAS TRAVERSE

Appendix II
Atlas Exploration

I can't resist beginning with a wandering Scot, although he only perhaps touched the Atlas well to the east. William Lithgow began his travels at the age of sixteen in 1598, being forced to leave Lanark when he had his ears cut off by zealous brothers protecting their sister. He wandered through France, Germany, the Low Countries and Switzerland before embarking on three major journeys which occupied nineteen years of the early seventeenth century. He covered most of Europe, Asia Minor, the Middle East and North Africa, usually afoot, driven on by his 'ambitious curiosity'. He visited Fes from Algiers, either crossing the rump of the Rif or by the Taza gap, and returned to Tunis by a southern mountain route along the Atlas. Three centuries would pass before other Europeans penetrated that region.

He suffered several shipwrecks, piratical encounters, imprisonments, violent robbery as well as being lost, starved and cheated. Determined to visit the Sahara, Lithgow was arrested in Spain as a spy and handed over to the Christian Inquisition. He was incarcerated in the dark, starved, beaten, subjected to water-tortures, racked and had his hands and knees smashed. He only escaped being burnt at the stake when visiting British ships at Malaga fortuitously discovered him. Lithgow was carried to England and slowly recovered although he did a spell in the Marshalsea for attacking the Spanish Ambassador at court. Returning to Scotland, he took to horseback, exploring Arran and the Western Isles. He wrote a book about his *Rare Adventures and Paineful Peregrinations* and was last heard of in 1645, hoping to set off for Russia.

The history of Morocco explains the late exploration of the Atlas by foreigners. Herodotus mentioned the Atlas and a Roman general must have seen Jbel Ayachi, as would Ibu Battatu. Several *renegado* (converted captives) under Moulay Ismaïl travelled, usually in military capacities, over the Atlas, from which came some topographic knowledge though maps from 1650 to 1850 would show little difference. I've a map (c1850) that hopefully sites Figuig, stating 'said to be a large town'.

One *renegado* who made it home was Thomas Pellow who wrote a book about his travels. This book, a record of how he was captured in 1716 at the age of 11, spent the following 23 years experiencing hardship and danger under despotic sultans and finally escaped, has been reprinted and much studied. He criss-crossed the Atlas in several places but, like all such crossings, the geographical details are scant—they were not important to him. A book by Giles Milton, *White Gold*, tells the story in vivid detail.

Pellow had sailed as cabin boy on a trading voyage for Genoa with his uncle Captain John Pellow on the *Francis* only to be captured, taken to Salé and marched to Meknes and the dreaded Sultan Moulay Ismaïl. The boy caught the eye of the sultan who presented him to a favourite son who set about torturing the boy to obtain his conversion. Eventually he succeeded but his continued ill treatment led to the sultan decapitating the upstart son with his own hand and taking Thomas into his royal service. He became guardian of the imperial harem and the sultan's personal attendant and eventually served as a soldier, based on various garrisons, or travelling extensively and fighting to order. He travelled as far as Senegal on a slave gathering expedition. He was wounded several times, twice tried to escape, was twice condemned to death and once reprieved seconds before having his throat cut. He married but lost his wife and much-loved daughter before finally an Irish captain smuggled him off to safety and home to Penryn. That Pellow came through all this is testimony to great character.

He almost certainly crossed the three great passes of the Atlas and probably once further east for the Tafilelt and perhaps other routes between Demnate and the Sous. They were simply another form of hardship while on duty and it is the objectives that are described rather than the journeys, where names would be few anyway and time short. Other slaves or *renegados* no doubt made similar journeys but we are lucky to have this record, however scant, about the Atlas.

The lack of detail in the early information is seen in the fairly haphazard way 'Mount Atlas' was positioned on maps. This was a general term rather than meaning any one mountain, the name being repeated along the whole range or used as a filler on the speculative early maps. The name does appear most often at the northeast and southwest extremities which I feel is a reflection of outsider contacts: mountains (with snow) were recorded by the early navigators off the southwest coast while any penetration from the northeast naturally funnelled down to run up against Jbel Ayachi. The route south to the desert gave Ayachi great prominence, besides which the mountain is a spectacular sweep of snow in season and was for long considered the highest mountain in the Atlas. Chenier, who lived and worked as French consul in Marrakech (his *Present State of the Empire of Morocco* was published in 1788), clearly describes 'Mount Atlas' as 'bounding the plains of Morocco' (i.e. Marrakech) and asserted this was 'the highest part of that mountain [range]'. Another century would pass before Europeans began to seek out that lure of the highest and show Chenier was correct. Joseph Thomson in 1888 first speculated correctly that Toubkal was the highest.

Great explorers like René Caillé (first to reach and return alive from Timbuktu, 1828) and Gerhard Rohlf (1861/2) simply crossed or rounded the Atlas; Lt Washington nibbled at the northern side (Oued Ourika) and a Spaniard, General Domingo Badia y Leblich, taking a disguise as Ali Bey, ventured as early as 1804.

The strong team of Hooker, Maw and Ball in 1871 made the first real scientific and mountaineering visit and, despite local harassment, reached the Tizi Tagharat above Sidi Chamharouch and climbed Jbel Gourza (3280 m). Charles de Foucauld in 1883–84 explored the Anti-Atlas (not revisited until 1917 by Bourguignon, then in 1926 by Dr Nain). Joseph Thomson (1888) climbed to the Tizi Likemt, ascended Igdat and, like Harris (1894) crossed the Tizi n' Telouet, and much more besides. Jacqueton and Brives repeated much of this ground in 1903 (reported in *La Montagne*, 1912). These were one-off ventures; most, like Cunninghame Graham's visit to the Nfis, were effectively stopped in their tracks. Success in the Atlas then was as unlikely as a man licking his elbow.

The real exploration by mountaineers, geographers, mappers and geologists only began early in the twentieth century. (Morocco only fell under European dominance slowly and the French protectorate lasted from pre-First World War to 1956, a very brief time in any country's history.) Louis Gentil, a geologist, was one of the surveyors of this old new world (Sirwa in 1908 to the summit plateau and also the Anti-Atlas in 1923). The Marquis de Segonzac climbed Ayachi in 1901 and, after other ascents, including Tifnout (Iferouane) in 1922, finally stood on top of Toubkal in 1923. He was the first president of the Morocco section of the Club Alpin Français (CAF), founded in 1922. Toubkal's height was carefully surveyed in 1924, measured as 4165 m (the height on modern maps is 4167 m). The instantly recognisable trig point was erected in 1931. Bentley Beetham made the first British ascent of Toubkal—solo—in 1926. He made about five visits to the Atlas, a unique British effort, about which there are scant details. Well-known climbers such as Heckmair (Eigerwand first ascent) visited, a shoestring effort, while 1932 saw a six-day traverse of all the major Toubkal *massif* summits by the Italians Pollitzer-Pollenghi, Botteri and Dougan. Dr Hauser made the first Swiss ascent of Toubkal in 1929.

In a very comprehensive survey of the Atlas Mountains (for its period) in the Alpine Journal in 1933 the writer Andrea de Pollitzer-Polenghi could only say of the country between the Tizi n' Tichka and Ayachi that knowledge was very vague and few reports existed. One comment of his that has not proved true was the unsuitability of the High Atlas for skiing; Lépiney and Neltner used skis on Aksouâl in 1927! In the 30s the Groupe de Haute Montagne (GHM) climbers like de Lépiney, Neltner, Stofer and de Prandières were active, mainly in the Toubkal massif. A Polish team visited not only Toubkal but the Western Atlas, M'Goun and Tessaout in 1934 and produced a good report. An incredible amount was done in that decade, climaxing in the 1938 Dresch and de Lépiney Toubkal guide, *Le Massif du Toubkal*. A recent reprint of this guide is still very useful. Climbing was interrupted until the 60s however, due the Second World War followed by the uncertainties leading up to Independence.

The Central Atlas region was long regarded as a Zone of Insecurity, with good cause. The French had left the mountain Berbers to the mercy of the Glaoui rulers and their tentacles spread along the south (as far west as Taliouine) and east into the Central Atlas, as far as the Bou Goumez. Zaouia Ahancal was the spiritual heartland of the Berber tribes east of there and their leader organised a common resistance that saw the Glaoui's forces beaten in the Bou Goumez in 1922. They then made their own peace with the French. In 1925 a group of French officers travelled from Azilal to the Dadès under the protection of the *marabout* himself. Another decade was to pass before pacification was completed so for years, as Peyron remarked, 'circumstances were hardly conducive to mountain exploration'. However one extraordinary character, René Euloge, wandered the area in the 20s, alone, disguised and speaking like a native. He visited the Tessaout *sources* and probably ascended M'Goun in 1928 and also Ouaougoulzat. Jacques Felze with an escort of local levies climbed M'Goun from the south about 1932.

In 1942 André Fougerolles, with Mailly and Lacaze, made a remarkable ski trip of only 10 days that took in Azurki, M'Goun, Rhat and the Tizi n' Aït Ouriat. In 1950 Colin Wyatt skied and climbed Azurki, Ouaougoulzat and M'Goun, exiting south by the M'Goun gorges. His trip is described in his book *The Call of the Mountains*. The first British traverse of M'Goun only came in 1972 by Donald Mill and Eric Roberts, from Tamda to the road out to Skoura, a winter epic entertainingly written-up in the 1973 Scottish Mountaineering Club Journal.

André Fougerolles has spent all his long life in Morocco as an engineer and surveyor, fought with the *goums* in the war, and has explored the mountains as few others have, to become a legend in his own lifetime. *Le Haut Atlas Central* (1981) is authoritative and more recently *Le Haut Atlas* (1991) covers many of the best areas. Roger Mailly was another Frenchman working in the country and his *Villes et Montagnes Marocaines* 1964 was the first guidebook to give some information on areas other than the Toubkal *massif*.

The French explored most of the rock-climbing post-war e.g. Charlet and Contamine opened up areas such as the Taghia gorges, Jbel Aioui and the Todra gorges. However, there has been relatively little done or publicised in the last decade or two. Long treks, of which GTAM is only the ultimate, appeal more than anything else in the Atlas. Colin Wyatt's north–south crossing via M'Goun in 1951 was the first notable post-war effort. Tom Weir was climbing in the Atlas in 1957 and Wilf Noyce romping over everything in sight from the Neltner Hut in 1961 but not really trekking. Wilfred Thesiger with a student, Colin Pennycuick, made a journey from Telouet to Zaouia Ahancal in 1955 and Louis Fougère went from Azilal to Kelaal de M'Gouna via the Tizi n' Aït Imi and the M'Goun Gorges—the sort of thing that is done regularly now. Current titles of guidebooks in English and French are given in the bibliography.

Peyron's article 'La Grande Traversée de l'Atlas Marocain' in *La Montagne* in 1977 must have come as a revelation and showed the immense advance in knowledge generally (and of one individual) concerning the whole length of the Atlas. The American journal *Appalachia* included a good survey in the December 1974 issue by Doug Teschner, a Peace Corps worker in Rabat. It was these enthusiasts on the spot who explored beyond the Toubkal Trail to discover just what marvellous country there is for trekking and climbing.

There have been several long sections of GTAM done by individuals and groups. In 1994 Michael Bradshaw set out on a solo attempt at the full GTAM, starting from Midelt with a long traverse of Ayachi, but ending at Abachkou where 'he decided to surrender to the sheer length of the walk'. I've not been able to find the details of one or two other known treks. While ambivalent about records as such, I am fascinated by others' experiences and how they took the magic hand of chance.

A good crossing of the still-neglected Western Atlas was made in a week over Easter 1964 by Guy Lecler. In the late 1970s Jacky de Cumont walked from Midelt to Imi n' Tanoute in just under two months and, in 1980 (the first GTAM effort), Patrick Rollier and three friends trekked Midelt to Ijoukak in over 33 days. To quote Peyron, to whom I owe much of this information,

> 'Between 8 May and 22 June 1989 a Portuguese, Pedro Cid, with a 6-kilo rucksack, soloed a GTAM from Timezgadiwin (the Tizi Maachou road) to Midelt, even finding time on the way to go down to Marrakech to renew his visa!'

These were admirable one-off ploys but for sheer ongoing commitment Peyron himself leads the way. Quite apart from endless weekend or short forays he made many extended treks. To quote:

> 'My principal long-distance efforts came during the spring and summer of 1976, when I covered the ground between Midelt and the Seksawa in three separate outings. Between 1972 and 1988 there were other multi-day forays at various periods for adding bits and pieces to the overall GTAM fabric. A Middle Atlas traverse came in July 1982 and I again reconnoitred fresh routes between Telouet and Tounfit over a 15-day period in the spring of 1988, not to mention an interesting 10-day crossing from Midelt to Tinghir in February 1992. Most of the time, I had three/four companions, but I also found myself soloing some stages.'

I've quoted periodically from the Willison/Wardle adventures of 1983; very much a leap in the dark and at times punished as a result—but they had a fine careless rapture our steady progress lacked. It has been a privilege to quote from John's journal.

One notable contemporary traveller is Jasper Winn, an equine enthusiast who has made a long study of transhumance in various countries. He rode a barb stallion from Marrakech to Fes in 1989, partly through the summer grazing grounds of the Beni M'Guild. In 1993 a Winston Churchill Travelling Fellowship allowed a year-round study of tribal wanderings from the Jbel Sahro to the Zaouia Ahancal pastures, staying in summer tents or winter caves and travelling 2000 km accompanied by a mule he named Mrs Bottom—that being his perpetual view of the animal.

Even as we were adding our GTAM to this long line of eccentrics the scene was changing (in an explosive fashion recently) as tourism is promoted in Morocco. A plethora of overpriced *riads* in Marrakech and visits by the affluent motor-borne to the Brides' Festival at Imilchil has killed its spontaneous originality and practical importance. *Pistes* are turning into *goudrons*, new *pistes* are reaching the remotest villages and pylons march on everywhere to detract from the splendidly isolated world we knew over the years. Our GTAM closed the Silver Age of Atlas wanderings. Now, there can't be many countries in Europe who do not have companies offering treks in the Atlas. Most, thankfully, keep to popular, well tried routes, which still leaves vast areas of the Atlas where one can wander as before. The magic remains.

Appendix III

Equipment

We are indebted to many people and firms for advice and contributions, which allied to our considerable experience, meant we had no practical problems on the journey.

Tents: Three individual *Vango Micro 2* tents and larger domed *Discovery* for multiple use.

Stoves: Reliable, common to Morocco for cartridges (*cartouches*) we simply used *Camping Gaz* stoves for minor needs, most cooking being done on large *Gaz* cylinders which also provided good lighting.

Clothing: Brasher shirts, trousers, jackets and lightweight fleece jacket were excellent. We also had heavier *Berghaus* fleeces.

Waterproofs: (Sometimes as important for windproofing.) *Berghaus Gore-tex Lightning* jackets and lightweight *Brasher* overtrousers.

Footwear: Brasher boots (which Charles used all the way and highly praised), *Reebok* sandals, suitable for rough walking which I used for much of the trekking. *Duofold* socks kept feet comfy.

Rucksacks: Berghaus Cyclops II Aztec: (which rode on the mules; we rarely backpacked) and *Berghaus Dart 30* day sacks.

Sleeping bags: We used our own, swapping to lightweight versions after leaving Imlil. (I went from *Black's Icelandic* to *Snugpak Merlin*.)

Other items: Brolly (for sun rather than rain); *Scottish Mountain Gear* provided *Arthur's Seats* which made for comfortable sitting; *Therm-a-rests* were used for sleeping on—and even carried on the final lightweight traverse; we all had *Petzel* headtorches and *Opinel* pocket knives. Other essential items included route book, maps, first aid kit, compass, whistle, suncream, sunglasses and emergency food.

First Aid: Small kits were always carried in a day bag but the mules also carried a comprehensive First Aid box. This included: items for upset stomachs, bites, sprains, antiseptics, dressings, *Potable Agua*, antibiotics, *Rennies*, assorted bandages, pain killers, sterile sutures, needles and syringes.

Food: This was more of a problem for the mules than for us. Plenty of fresh food could be carried and supplies were regularly renewed at *souks*. We had tins of meat, dried fruits, muesli and instant custard and those who joined us temporarily brought items such as Christmas pudding, rich cake, cheese and oatcakes.

Appendix IV
Glossary

Common, Arabic, Berber (B) and French (F) words

adfel snow

adrar (pl idraren) (B) mountain

agadir fortified granary

aghbalou (B) spring

Aïd el Kbir festival of sheep sacrifice

aïn spring

aït *lit* child of; used to form Berber tribal names, i.e. Aït Atta the Arabic equivalent is Ben(i) or ouled

amadir adze

aman water

amazigh (*pl* imazighen) Berber person

amlou a dip made from crushed almonds, argan oil and honey

andrair threshing floor

angour nose

anu well

anzar rain

aquelmane lake

aqqa (akka) gorge, box canyon

aroum bread

asserdoun (*pl.* iserdian) mule

assif (B) stream, mountain river

auberge (F) inn

azib goat/sheep shelter, huts

bab gateway

baraka the blessing lodged in a holy person or descendant of the Prophet

barakalafik thank you

bendir simple tambourine-like drum

Bismillah in the name of God

bled countryside

b'slama goodbye

burnous hooded cloak

CAF Club Alpin Français

caïd government administrator/magistrate

calèche (F) horse-drawn carriage

camion (F) lorry

camionette (F) pick-up, small lorry

charette (F) hand barrow

chergui strong, hot east wind (sirocco)

Chleuh Berber (southern)

chokrane (or barakalafik) thank you

cous cous milled cornflour and/or the everyday repast made from such

dar house

daya(t) lake, commonly in Middle Atlas; Tamda (B)

difa (diffa) luxury meal

djellaba long-hooded and long-sleeved garment, at one time everyday attire

djinn (*pl* jnoun) spirit, genie

douar hamlet, settlement (of buildings or tents)

erg area of sand dunes

eyewa (aye-wa) yes

fantasia mounted welcome charge with rifle firing

Fasi person from Fes

flous money

fibule brooch for pinning garments

gandoura sleeveless smock of cotton

gîte (F) official/semi-official hostelry

goudron (F) tarmac, tarred road

grand taxi (F) big taxis operating in and out of cities

Gnaoua negroid musical fraternity

Gueliz the new town in Marrakech, after the peaklet of that name

haik all-enveloping draped garment (now almost entirely female)

haj honorific title of a man who has made his pilgrimage to Mecca

halib milk

Hamadula 'praise be to God'

hammam public steam baths

hamri red-coloured soil

handira blanket worn like a cloak by women

hanut corner shop

harrira thick broth associated with breaking the fast during Ramadan

harka raiding/tax gathering expeditions

henna paste from plant leaves for staining patterns on hands and feet (females)

hobs bread

ifri cave

ighil (B) hill, arm

ighzer ravine

ikhibi valley

Illa 'Let's go'

imma mother

imi mouth, mouth of, defile

imlil white

imouzzer falls

Islam *lit.* submission—to the will of Allah/God—hence the religion founded by the Prophet Mohammed

jemaa gathering, assembly (mosque)

jbel (jebel, djebel, etc.) (*abbrev* J) mountain

kaftan decorative gown worn by women

kanoun brazier

kasbah castle

kebab (brochette, F) skewered meat, etc, grilled

kelim woven carpet

khaima low, brown nomad tent (Makhzen/caïdal tents are white, decorative pavillions)

kohl antimony, powdered, applied as eye shadow by women

kouba the domed structure often over a holy site

ksar (*pl* ksour) fortified hamlet

la no

lac (F) lake

lalla female saint, honorific title, 'lady'

leben buttermilk

litham veil

ma water

maquis (F) wild mountain scrub

marabout holy man and/or his tomb

mechoui roasted mutton

medersa residential theological college

medina the old (often walled) part of a city

merja marsh

Mektoub 'it is written'

mirhab alcove in mosque facing Mecca

moqqadam (mokadam) village head

Mouloud Prophet's birthday

moussem seasonal festival

mulet (F) mule

mzien good

Nazrani/Arrumi Christian, European

oued (*abbrev* O) river

oulad, ouled child of (as aït, ben)

petit taxi (F) 3-person taxis, within towns

piste (F) dirt track

piton (F) a pinnacle-shaped hill

place (F) square, often in town centre

pstilla (bastilla) rich, spicy, sweet pigeon pie

Ramadan the month of fasting

ras head, promontory, headland

ribat fortified monastery equivalent

sah-ha (B) thank you

sahra desert

seguia irrigation channel

selham cloak

sheik (cheikh) local headman, fraternity head

shereef descendant of the Prophet (used as honorific title)

shen fine muslin scarf (usually blue or black) wrapped round head and face as protection against weather

shooft (chouf) 'look'

shweeya a little

sidi sir (honorific title, often a saint)

smen rancid butter

souira small rampart

souk both the weekly rural market and town market quarter. Often shown by name of the day: Tnine (Monday), Tleta (Tuesday), Arba (Wednesday), Khemis (Thursday), very rarely on Friday; Sebt (Saturday), Had (Sunday)

source (F) spring

tabia/toub mud building material of many rural buildings: pisé (F)

tachelhayt/tamazight Berber languages

taddert (B) village/house

tagine a casserole-style stew and/or the conical dish it is served in

talat ravine

tamda (B) lake, pool. Daya(t) (Arabic)

targa (B) irrigation channel

tichka collective pasture

tighremt (B) fortified house or store (igherm)

timesguida (B) shoulder, mosque

tizgui (B) forest

tizi col, pass

touiza co-operative labour

trik, trek, traiq road, way (Trik es Soltan: *The Royal Way*)

wakka (wachha) OK, yes

Zaouia religious establishment, often attached to a marabout or mosque

zellij geometric tilework

Bibliography

The following is a selection of the most useful titles, although some are unfortunately out of print. Most of the English-language guides in print are obtainable from *Cordee* (3a De Montfort St, Leicester, LE1 7HD) while most of the current French guidebook titles are available in Marrakech bookshops or at the CAF *refuge* in Oukaïmeden. AMIS (26 Kirkcaldy Road, Burntisland, Fife KY3 9HQ) may also have some titles in stock, both new and secondhand. Dates given are first editions unless otherwise stated.

Abun-Nasr, J. M. (1971) *A History of the Maghrib*. CUP.

Aitchison, C. (1994) High Alpines of Morocco. *The Rock Garden*, vol 23. Scottish Rock Garden Club.

Arama, M. (1991) *Itinéraires Marocaînes Regards de Peintres*. Jaguar. (Illustrated artists' *Who's Who*)

Barbour, N. (1965) *Morocco*. Thames & Hudson. (The best history, sadly out of print)

Barton, T. (1980) *The Storyteller of Marrakech*. Evans Bros. (Folk tales)

Beetham, B. (1952) Haut Atlas. *Fell & Rock CC Journal*.

Bergier, P. and E. (1990) *A Birdwatcher's Guide to Morocco*. Prion. (The most useful work)

Bernezat, O. (1987) *Hommes et Vallées du Haut-Atlas*. Éditions Glénat. (Bou Guemez, good illustrations)

Bertrand, R. (1977) *Tribus Berbères du Haut Atlas*. Edita Vita. (Expert early photography)

Bidwell, M. and R. (1992) *Morocco, The Travellers' Companion*. Tauris. (Anthology of writing)

Blunt, W. (1951) *Black Sunrise*. Methuen. (Moulay Ismaïl)

Borgé, J. and Viasnoff, N. (1995) *Archives du Maroc*. Éditions Trinckvel. (Old photos/post cards)

Brown, H. M. (1966) The High Atlas in Winter. *Alpine Journal*, Vol LXXI, pg 43.

Brown, H. M. (1966) Return to the Atlas. *Alpine Journal*, Vol LXXI, pg 275.

Brown, H. M. (1967) A Hard Day's Night. *Scottish Mountaineering Club Journal*. (Winter ascent of Aksoual)

Brown, H. M. (1987) The Ridge of Dreams. *Alpine Journal*, pg 275 (Zat traverse)

Brown, H. M. (1990) Sirwa: Making Siccar. *Climber & Hillwalker*. September 1990. (Jbel Sirwa)

Brown, H. M. (1991) The Wonder Walk. *Climber & Hillwalker*. October 1991. (Tichka Plateau to Toubkal trek)

Brown, H. M. (2001) T to T in the Anti-Atlas. *TGO*. October 2001. (End-to-end trek)

Burckhardt, T. (1992) *Fez, City of Islam*. Islamic Texts Society. (See also *Moorish Culture in Spain*)

Burollet, T. (1990) *De l'Empire Romain aux Villes Impériales*. Musée de Petit Palais, Paris. (600 years of art)

Carrier, R. (1987) *Taste of Morocco*. Century. (Mouth-watering; now sadly out of print but 2 small
  booklets can usually be found locally: Bennani-Smirès: *Moroccan Cooking* and Benkirane: *Moroccan
  Cooking, The Best Recipes*)

Chenier, M. (1788) *The Present State of the Empire of Morocco*. London.

Chimenti, E. (1965) *Tales & Legends of Morocco*. Obdensky.

Clarke, B. (1959) *Berber Village*. Longman. (Village life)

Cliff, P. (1987) *Ski Mountaineering*. Unwin Hyman. (Moroccan *haute route*)

Collomb, R. G. (1980) *Atlas Mountains of Morocco*. West Col. (Toubkal massif)

Courtney-Clarke, M. (1996) *Imazighen*. Thames & Hudson. (Study/photos of Berber women's lives)

Davies, C. (2004) *Climbing in the Moroccan Anti-Atlas*. Cicerone Press. (Rock climbing guide)

De Amicis, E. (1882) *Morocco: Its People and Places*. Cassell, Petter and Galpin. (Early travels)

Dennis, L. and L. (1992) *Living in Morocco*. Thames & Hudson. (Interiors, etc)

Dickinson, M. (1991) *Long Distance Walks in North Africa*. Crowood. (Some Morocco)

Domenech, B. (1989) *Le Maroc*. Éditions Denoël. (Big format, pictures, maps, etc. for much of the Atlas)

Dresch, J. and de Lepinèy, J. (1938) *Le Massif du Toubkal*. Rabat Service du Tourisme. (A reproduction
  of the 1942 edition is now available)

Eitzen, D. and Khaji, M. (1991) *Agadir and Anti Atlas*. Éditions LIF. (Useful guide)

Ellingham, M., McVeigh, S. and Jacobs, D. (2004) *The Rough Guide to Morocco*. 7th Edition. Rough
  Guides. (The most practical general work, regularly updated)

Epton, N. (1958) *Saints & Sorcerers: A Moroccan Journey*. Cassell. (Travel/folk study)

Etchécopar, R. D. and Huie, F. (1967) *The Birds of North Africa*. Oliver & Boyd.

Everyman Guide: Morocco (1994) Dorling Kindersley. (Exhaustive, colourful work)

Fletcher, R. (1994) *Moorish Spain*. Phoenix. (Enjoyable history)

Fougerolles, A. (1981) *Le Haut Atlas Central*. CAF Casablanca. (Maps and illustrations)

Fougerolles, A. (1991) *Le Haut Atlas*. Éditions Glénat. (Large format, maps, pictures)

Freud, E. (1992) *Hideous Kinky*. Penguin. (Sixties setting, fiction; delightful film)

Galley, H. (2004) *Montagnes du Maroc*. Olizane (Good trekking/ski guide)

Gellner, E. (1969) *Saints of the Atlas*. Weidenfeld & Nicolson. (Z. Ahansal study)

Gilbert, R. (1979) *Young Explorers*. Smith, York. (Chapter on school Atlas expedition)

Goodwin, G. (1990) *Islamic Spain*. Viking. (Architectural guide)

Graham, R. B. Cunninghame (1898) *Magreb-el-Acksa*. Heinemann. (Visit to the Nfis)

Hargraves, O. (1995) *Culture Shock*. Kuperard. (Customs and etiquette)

Harris, W. B. (1921) *Morocco That Was*. Blackwood. (Reprinted by Eland Books)

Harris, W. B. (1895) *Tafilet*. Blackwood. (Early Atlas crossing)

Hedgecoe J. and Damluji S. S. (1992) *Zillij, the Art of Moroccan Ceramics*. Garnet Publishing.

Heinzel, H., Fitter, R. and Parslow, J. (1995) *Birds of Britain & Europe with North Africa & The Middle East*. Collins. (The best field guide; regularly updated)

Hooker, J. D. and Ball, J. (1878) *Journal of a Tour in Marocco and the Great Atlas*. Macmillan. (Early AC/botanists trip, still interesting)

Horne, J. (1925) *Many Days in Morocco*. McBride. (Fine B & W photographs)

Huet, K. and Lamazou T. (1988) *Sous Les Toits de Terre*. Belvisi. (Berber décor/architecture)

Huet, K. and Lamazou T. (1990) *Un Hiver Berbère*. Belvisi-Jeanne Laffitte. (Drawings of Bou Guemez)

Hughes, Richard (1979) *In the Lap of Atlas*. Chatto & Windus. (Hotchpotch of stories)

Ingram, J. (1952) *The Land of Mud Castles*. J. Long. (Wandering afoot, pre-war)

Jackson, J. (ed.) (2006) *Trekking Atlas of the World*. New Holland. (Includes Tichka Plateau to Toubkal trek)

Jereb, J. F. (2001) *Arts & Crafts of Morocco*. Thames & Hudson.

Kay, Shirley (1980) *Morocco*. Quartet. (Good pictures *and* text)

Keohan, A. (1991) *The Berbers of Morocco*. Hamilton. (A pictorial celebration)

Kininmonth, C. (1986) *Travellers' Guide to Morocco*. Cape. (Strong on history)

Knight, R. (2001) *Trekking in the Moroccan Atlas*. Trailblazer. (Toubkal, M'Goun, Sirwa, Sahro routes)

Landau, R (1969) *The Kasbahs of Southern Morocco*. Faber.

Légey, F. (1935) *The Folklore of Morocco*. Allen and Unwin.

Lewalle, J. and Montfort, N. (1997) *Fleurs Sauvage du Maroc*. Rossdorf.

Lithgow, W. (1640) *Rare Adventures and Paineful Peregrinations*.

Lovatt-Smith, L. (1995) *Moroccan Interiors*. Tachen.

Maalouf, A. (1988) *Leo the African*. Quartet. (Historical fiction)

Mailly, R. (1964) *Villes et Montagnes Marocaines*. Éditions la Porte.

Mardaga, P. (1999) *Le Grand Livre de La Forêt Marocaine*. Mardaga, Belgium.

Maxwell, G. (1966) *Lords of the Atlas*. Longmans. (A sumptuous illustrated edit from Cassell, 2000; also Eland paperback: a classic study of pre-independence history)

McGuinness, J. (2001) *Marrakech and the High Atlas Handbook*. Footprint Guides.

Meakin, Budgett (1899) *The Moorish Empire*. Swan, Sonnenschein and Co.

Meakin, Budgett (1901) *The Land of the Moors*. Swan, Sonnenschein and Co.

Meakin, Budgett (1902) *The Moors*. Swan, Sonnenschein and Co.

Meakin, Budgett (1905) *Life in Morocco*. Chatto & Windus. (Four athoritative, readable studies)

Melville, J. (1991) *James McBey's Morocco*. Harper Collins.

Mernissi, Fatima (1994) *The Harem Within, Tales of a Moroccan Childhood*. Bantam.

Michelin Guide de Tourisme: Maroc. (Always useful)

Miège, J.-L. (1952) *Morocco*. Arthaud. (English text, superb photos)

Milet, E. (2003) *Guide des Merveilles de la Nature, Maroc*. Arthaud.

Mill, D. (1973) The Crossing of Ighil M'Goun. *Scottish Mountaineering Club Journal*. (Winter traverse)

Miller, J. A. (1984) *Imlil: A Moroccan Mountain Community in Change*. West View Press.

Milton, G. (2004) *White Gold*. Hodder and Stoughton (Thomas Pellow story)

Morris, C. L. (1931) (translated from original text by Celarié, H.) *Behind Moroccan Walls*. Macmillan Press (Short stories)

Mririda n' Aït Attik (1986) *Les Chants de la Tassaout*. Éditions Belvisi. (Poems / photographs)

Noyce, W. (1962) *Climbing Solo in the High Atlas*. Alpine Journal.

Oussaïd, B. (1989) *Mountains Forgotten by God*. Three Continents Press. (Berber life)

Paccard, A. (1980) *Traditional Islamic Crafts in Moroccan Architecture*. 2 Volumes. Atelier.

Parker, R. (1981) *A Practical Guide to Islamic Monuments in Morocco*. Baraka. (The best guide / survey)

Pellow, T. (1740) *The Adventures of Thomas Pellow*. (see also Milton)

Pennell, C. R. (2000) *Morocco Since 1830*. Hurst & Co.

Peyron, M. (1989–90) *Great Atlas Traverse*. Vol 1: Moussa Gorges to Ayt Bou Wgemmaz; Vol 2: Ayt Bou Wgemmaz to Midelt. West Col Publications. (The most comprehensive and essential guide to the Atlas)

Pickens S., Richer X. and Renaudeau, M. (1993) *Le Sud Marocain*. ACR Éditions. (The best of the big general picture books.)

Ploquin P., Peuriot F. and Hassar-Benslimane J. (1992) *Maroc: Faune et Grands Espaces*. Daniel Briand. (Wildlife, pictures)

Porch, D. (1986) *The Conquest of Morocco*. Cape. (Turn-of-century history)

Randonnées Pédestres dans le Massif du M'Goun. (1989) Belvisi-Edisud. (Small guide, useful maps)

Rauzier, M.-P., Tréal, C. and Ruiz, J.-M. (1998) *Tableau du Haut Atlas Marocain*. Arthaud

Rogerson, B. (1989) *Morocco*. Cadogan Guides. (Comprehensive background)

Rogerson, B. (1998) *A Traveller's History of North Africa*. Interlink.

Rogerson, B. (ed.) (2001) *North Africa Travel*. Sickle Moon.

Rogerson, B. and Lavington S. (eds.) (2003) Marrakech: The Red City. Sickle Moon. (Anthology)

Salkeld, A. (ed.) (1998) *World Mountaineering*. Mitchell Beazley. (Includes Toubkal survey)

Searight, S. and Hourbette, D. (1992) *Gravures Rupestres du Haut Atlas*. Éditions Belvisi. (Excellent guide to prehistoric carvings)

Selous, R. (1956) *Appointment to Fez*. 1956. Richards Press. (Personal and historical)

Shepherd, M. (1990) *Let's Look at Southern Morocco*. Ornitholidays Guide.

Sijelmassi, M. (1986) *Les Arts Traditionnels au Maroc*. ACR: Vilo

Smith, K. (2004) *Trekking the Atlas Mountains*. Cicerone Press. (Toubkal, M'Goun, Sahro)

Spencer, W. (1980) *Historical Dictionary of Morocco*. Scarecrow Press.

Teuler, M. (1986) *Aït Imi, Morocco of the Heights*. Edition Soden. (Bou Guemez)

Thévenot, M., Vernon, R. and Bergier, P. (2002) *The Birds of Morocco*. BOU/BOC. (Definitive tome)

Thomson, J. (1889) *Travels in the Atlas and Southern Morocco*. Longmans. (Early explorations)

Triki, H., Hassar-Benslimane, J. and Touri, A. (1992) *Tinmal: L'Epopée Almohade*. Foundation Ona.

Watt, W. M. and Cachia, P. (1977) *A History of Islamic Spain*. EUP.

Weir, T. (1994) *Weir's World, An Autobiography of Sorts*. Canongate. (Chapter on the Atlas).

Weir, T. (1957) Spring Climbs in the High Atlas. *Scottish Mountaineering Club Journal*.

Westermark, E. (1926) *Ritual and belief in Morocco (2 volumes)*. Macmillan.

Westermark, E. (1930) *Wit and wisdom in Morocco: A study of native proverbs*. Routeledge.

Windo, P. (2005) *Zohra's Ladder*. Eye Books.

Wolfert, P. (1987) *Cous Cous and Other Good Food From Morocco*. Murray.

Wyatt, C. (1952) *The Call of the Mountains*. Thames & Hudson. (Chapter on Toubkal/ M'Goun).

Miscellaneous Information

Alpine Journal Early mountain doings by: Ball (vol 6, 1872–74), J de Lépiney 1928, Pollitzer-Polenghi 1933, Noyce 1962, Brown 1966.

Artists including Matisse, Majorelle, Delacroix, McBey, have books on their Moroccan work, else *see* Arama.

Carpets, textiles and costumes have several excellent volumes available.

Cookery books: see Carrier

Folklore stories: volumes in French are plentiful and there are several (French language) tapes.

Gardens have several illustrated works: *Maroc en Fleurs*, *Jardins du Maroc* among the best.

La Montagne (CAF) has many references; some of the more important are: July 1929; Dec 68; Feb 71; 1973 no. 2; 1977 no. 1; 1981 no. 2; 1985 no. 4; 1986 no. 4; 1989 no. 1.

M'Goun Massif, Central High Atlas (1994) 1:100 000 Map/Guide. West Col Productions.

Moroccan fiction is dominated by Paul Bowles translations of the rather grim writings of Mohammed Mrabet, Mohamed Choukri and Larbi Layachi. Other well-known authors are Driss Chraibi, Tahar Ben Jelloun and Fatima Mernissi. (Titles listed in *Rough Guide*)

Quotation Acknowledgements

numbers refer to pages

1 Mushariff-Ud-Din (1184–1291); 3 Harold Nicolson (1980) *The Harold Nicolson Diaries*. Collins; 5 Thomas De Quincey (1785–1859) (Title unknown); 6 Voltaire (1759) *Candide, ou l'Optimisme*; 6 T E Lawrence (1935) *Seven Pillars of Wisdom*. Cape; 9 John Muir (2001) *John Muir's Last Journey: South to the Amazon and East to Africa*. Shearwater; 15 Neil Munro. (1914) *The New Road*. Blackwood; 17 John Bunyan (1678) *Pilgrim's Progress*; 17 Charles de Foucauld (1888) *Reconnaissance au Maroc*. Challamel; 28 Robert M. Ballantyne (1858) *Coral Island*. W & R Chambers; 29 Hamish Brown (1983) *In the Rut* from *Time Gentlemen: Some Collected Poems*. Aberdeen University Press; 33 Frank Showell Styles (1950) *The Mountaineer's Weekend Book*. Seeley Service; 37 Edward Gibbon (1737–94) *Decline and Fall of the Roman Empire*; 47 Hamish Brown (1983) *Time Gentlemen: Some Collected Poems*. Aberdeen University Press; 54 Terry Pratchett (1987) *Equal Rites*. Gollancz; 68 Dervla Murphy (1965) *Full Tilt*. John Murray; 69 Louis Neltner (1938) *Le Massif du Toubkal*. Office Chérifien du Tourisme; 87 Author unknown, note in Marrakech branch of CAF newsletter; 101 Konrad Gesner, in a letter in 1541; 109 P. B. Shelley (1875) *Love's Philosophy*; 112 Norman MacCaig (2005) *Poems of Norman MacCaig*. Chatto Poetry; 121 Samuel Johnson (1775) *A Journey to the Western Islands of Scotland*. Strahan; 122 Eric Shipton (1943) *Upon that Mountain*. Hodder and Stoughton; 129 Charles de Foucauld (1888) *Reconnaissance au Maroc*. Paris; 137 Robert Browning (1855) *Bishop Blougram's Apology* from *Men and Women*. Royal Holloway, University of London; 139 Charles de Foucald (1888) *Reconnaissance au Maroc*. Challamel; 151 Emily Brontë (1818–48) *Often rebuked, yet always back returning*; 152 Nicholas Crane (1996) *Clear Waters Rising: A Mountain Walk Across Europe*. Viking; 159 Tom Weir (1957) *Scottish Mountaineering Club Journal*. Scottish Mountaineering Club; 160 Richard Gilbert (1979) *Young Explorers*. G. H. Smith; 165 Joseph Thomson (1889) *Travels in the Atlas and Southern Morocco*. Longman Green; 177 Irish traditional, source unknown; 179 Source unknown; 179 Samuel Pepys (1660–69) *The Diary of Samuel Pepys*; 181 J Dresch and J de Lépiney (1938) *Le Massif du Toubkal*. Office Chérifen du Tourisme; 187 Jim Crumley (1992) *Waters of the Wild Swan*. Cape; 197 J J Rousseau (1761) *Julie, or the New Heloise*; 203 François Villon (1431–c.74) *Ballade des Dames du Temps Jadis*; 207 Jonathon Swift (1733) *On Poetry: A Rhapsody*; 212 Alexander Pope (1711) *Essay on Criticism*; 225 D. G. Rossetti (1853) *The Hill Summit*; 228 Isaak Walton (1653) *The Compleat Angler*; 229 Pamela Windo (2005) *Zohra's Ladder*. Eye Books; 234 Pierre Loti (1890) *Au Maroc*; 237 R Browning (1883) *Donald* from *Jocoseria*; 241 Emily Dickinson (1862) #327 *Before I got my eye put out*; 243 Thomas Browne (1643) *Religio Medici*.

For Peyron quotes and extracts see Bibliography; Willison journal extracts quoted with kind permission of Graham Willison.